Shakespeare— The Theater and the Book

ROBERT S. KNAPP

Princeton University Press

PRINCETON, NEW JERSEY

Copyright © 1989 by Princeton University Press
Published by Princeton University Press,
41 William Street
Princeton, New Jersey 08540
In the United Kingdom: Princeton University Press,
Guildford, Surrey

Library of Congress Cataloging-in-Publication Data
Knapp, Robert S., 1940–
Shakespeare—The theater and the book /
Robert S. Knapp.
p. cm.
Includes index.
ISBN 0–691–06766–X (alk. paper)
1. Shakespeare, William, 1564–1616—Criticism and
interpretation. 2. Semiotics and literature.   I. Title.
PR2976.K57 1989
822.3'3—dc19   88–20917
                                                    CIP

This book has been composed in Linotron Bembo

Clothbound editions of Princeton University Press
books are printed on acid-free paper, and binding
materials are chosen for strength and durability.
Paperbacks, although satisfactory for personal
collections, are not usually suitable for library rebinding

Printed in the United States of America by Princeton
University Press, Princeton, New Jersey

For Christine

Contents

Preface   ix

Note on Texts and Abbreviations   xiii

ONE   The Literariness of Shakespeare   3

TWO   The Body of the Sign   45

THREE   The Idea of the Play   79

FOUR   The Moving Image   128

FIVE   Shakespearean Authority   182

Index   247

Preface

When I was a boy, my mother would sit in the car reading Shakespeare while my father and I walked the creeks, fishing. This book grows out of childish curiosity at such a choice, adult amazement at the semiotics of its staging, and a continuing wonder at the place of Shakespeare in the canon of English (and "world") literature, at his uncanny ability to be all things to all readers. Just his presence in that list ought to be surprising enough. Even in these days of pluralizing the canon, it is remarkable how few playwrights have made it out of the theater into the set of books used and taught as "literature." From this fact about exits and entrances, this question of drawing and crossing boundaries, there unfolded a problem about the difference between kinds of signs, ones that arrive by means of actors, and ones that come packaged exclusively as language. This difference between the theater and the book seemed congruent with a difference between modes of representation, to which Plato gave the names *mimesis* and *diegesis*. And the anaclitic relationship between these modes turns out to have profound implications for the way in which signs operate in and on the world, and especially for the production and reception of plays, and for their suitability to the sorts of purposes to which we put the literary. Unpacking these implications required eclectic recourse to what is sometimes called literary theory, and that in turn provoked conclusions that I suspect (and hope) will prove controversial. Among other things, taking for granted that "literariness" is an interested category, I have found myself arguing that mimesis sustains this interest in a way different from and perhaps more difficult than diegesis.

But Shakespeare's position in the canon is not just and not mainly a formal matter of representational mode. It is also a question of history. Or of several histories. There is an allegorical history that we keep retelling ourselves, wherein Shakespeare figures our coming of age, that moment when humanity supposedly turned away from childish things and accepted the burden of modernity. This history is bound up with the political, social, economic, and religious history of Britain, again often figured as in transition from delusions and comforts toward harsh realities, from an era of feudalism and belief to an era of possessive individuals, growing into psychosexual maturity within the mournful disruptions of a capitalist economy. Implicated in these histories is another, having to do with our relation to authority: the authority of kings, of fathers, of those literary heroes which the tradition has fetishized, and of a logocentric metaphysics within which such authority stages itself. My argument moves through all these histories, interweaving them in a way that I hope both plausibly revises our stories about the history of English drama—and of Shakespeare's place in that history—and also casts the larger fable about coming of age in an appropriately skeptical light.

Finally, in trying to comprehend the peculiar authority that Shakespeare has come to exercise in our civilization—an authority which many now wish to dispel, not least because of its overlap with the authority of class and empire—I found myself inquiring into the causes and effects of his unique generic range. To have one playwright flourish in both tragedy and comedy, and double these forms with others, which taken all together make his collected work seem to exhibit a whole world: this suggested that one way to understand the Shakespearean moment would be to see it as providing the historical conditions of possibility for making visible an essential logic of representation. Thus by a quasi-Hegelian route, I come to a partial account of the reasons both for Shakespeare's peculiar indeterminacy of meaning, and for the way he taunts us with the disappearing prospect of modernity.

I must thank a great many persons for inspiration, counsel, and support during the long making of this book. Footnotes can record only the smallest and most obvious of my debts. I owe much to my parents, who taught me more than they can have known about the margin between court and country, and who have unfailingly backed me, even when my choices led me very far from common ground. Ephim G. Fogel introduced me to the study of Elizabethan drama and directed a dissertation that I refused to try to publish; throughout the years of our friendship since, his capacious mind and heart have helped me sustain some optimism about the prospects for humanism. To David Bevington, to the National Endowment for the Humanities, and to my remarkable colleagues in a year-long seminar (Thomas Berger, Huston Diehl, Richard Kenneth Emmerson, Michael Hall, Ronald B. Herzman, Joan Marx, Pamela Sheingorn, and John Wyatt) I owe the extraordinary privilege of a learned, critical, and yet sympathetic audience for the seeds and weak beginnings of this project. To an equally remarkable group of secondary school teachers (Jane L. Bales, Judy Bower, Margaret Carlson, John P. Catalini, Frank E. Chew, Jackie Davis, Larry Deal, Toni B. Dorfman, Henry G. Kiernan, Robert E. Monson, Lora R. Owens, Robert G. Peck, George C. Pickering, Steven S. Schieffelin, and Charles West), and again to the National Endowment for the Humanities, I owe the privilege of a summer's collegial inquiry into the nature of Shakespearean genre. The late William T. Lankford III read an early draft of some chapters, giving me good advice and some hope for the general intelligibility of my as yet fragile ideas. Charles W. Crupi gave a close, expert, and very helpful reading to the first three chapters. Stephen W. Melville has helped me thread my way through the intricacies of literary theory; he and Barbara Jones Guetti have given me some confidence that I do not too much misrepresent the names and theories that I conjure with. Walter G. Englert kindly checked my translations from medieval Latin. David Harris Sacks read the manuscript in penultimate draft, gave me invaluable advice about the historiographical literature, and saved me from some naive mistakes. I have a special debt to Andrew C. Parker, who believed in this project from the start, who read more than one draft of the manuscript, and whose theoretical and practical advice has much to do with its finished state. David Scott Kastan and Bruce Ray Smith read the manuscript for the Press: I learned a great deal from their responses and their suggestions, perhaps most of all from those that I ended up not taking. I am grateful to Robert E. Brown, Literature Editor at the Press, for his careful stewardship of the manuscript's progress into public view and to Lise Rodgers for her exacting yet tactful editorial labors. Errors of fact, emphasis, and judgment should be laid entirely at my own door.

My one time colleagues at Princeton University helped me appreciate the strengths of the best sort of historicist literary scholarship. Reed College has provided an intellectual atmosphere in which my attempts at a more interdisciplinary kind of inquiry could come to fruition. My colleagues at Reed, especially in the humanities program—which throws together historians, literary critics, art historians, philosophers, and students of religion in an essentially contested enterprise—have helped immensely in the construction of a book that hardly anyone knew I was writing. To my students, who have heard, helped formulate, and criticized many different, usually less coherent, versions of these ideas, I owe much for their forbearance, their willingness to make connections, and their instruction. Two of them have played especially important parts in the completion of the manuscript: Willis Johnson and Kathryn Mary Pratt.

Above all, I want to thank Christine Knodt, to whom I dedicate this book. She has read and criticized the manuscript at several stages, has helped me talk through and make sense of many of its ideas, has taught me much of what I know about theater, and nearly all of what I know about love and friendship, and in her patience, courage, and dedication to her own difficult work, has set me the best of all examples.

NOTE ON TEXTS AND ABBREVIATIONS

Where I quote from English medieval plays, mostly in the second chapter, I cite the texts by page and line number throughout, using the following abbreviations for the various standard editions, full citations of which occur at first reference.

Richard Beadle, ed., *The York Plays*: Y
George England and A. W. Pollard, ed., *The Towneley Plays*: T
K. S. Bloch, ed., *Ludus Coventriae; or, The Plaie Called Corpus Christi*: LC
R. M. Lumiansky and David Mills, eds., *The Chester Cycle*: C
Norman Davis, ed., *The Non-Cycle Plays and Fragments*: NC
Marc Eccles, ed., *The Macro Plays (The Castle of Perseverance, Mankind, and Wisdom)*: MC, MM, and MW

Thus MC 19/530 refers to page 19, line 530 of *The Castle of Perseverance* in Eccles's edition of *The Macro Plays*. References to other editions of medieval plays, and to all editions of other plays, receive full citations at first reference and parenthetical citations thereafter. In some of these citations, SD stands for *stage direction*. Throughout the notes, PL stands for *Patrologiae Cursus Completus: Series Latina*, ed. J. P. Migne, with citations by volume and column number. Thus PL 113.535 refers to volume 113, column 535 of the *Patrologia Latina*.

Shakespeare—The Theater and the Book

ONE

The Literariness of Shakespeare

No one in 1623 would have said that Shakespeare's work marked and embodied some general change in European self-understanding. We often say so now. Portentous and wistful by turns, our talk about Shakespeare habitually sets him between times, last witness for the old, first prophet of the new, a genius of the divided vision and a symbol of our own life on the margins of tradition. Commonplaces can be false, of course, but the proof of this one is repetition, not only iteration of such judgments about Shakespeare's place in history, but our constant recurrence to his texts, which have thereby come to generate a body of commentary and wealth of allusion second only to that stemming from the Bible. If there were any doubt about the change that we imagine Shakespeare helped initiate and now stands for, this should dispel it: only on the near side of modernity could it happen that a group of plays would rival sacred narrative as a focus of interpretive energy.

Though this ultimate and perhaps not altogether happy result could not have been foreseen, it is remarkable that the process leading there—the persistent and even compulsive reading of texts that seem almost to rewrite themselves as we go—was urged and anticipated by the men who first presented Shakespeare to a reading public: "Reade him, therefore; and againe, and againe: And if then you doe not like him, surely you are in some manifest danger, not to vnderstand him. And so we leaue you to other of his Friends, whom if you need, can bee your guides: if you neede them not, you can leade your selues, and others. And such Readers we wish him." We need not make Heminge and Condell into prophets; they know that a sort of revolution really has occurred. In their call for a special kind of reader, they assert implicitly what Ben Jonson puts directly, and not without some envious sense of belatedness, that the playwright "to whom all Scenes of *Europe* homage owe" has entered the canon of literature, has become a "Starre of *Poets*," an event unprecedented since Rome.[1] Giving Shakespeare over to hermeneutics and all time, his actors thereby triumphantly announce that they have been unable to use him up.

Being used up, of course, is the normal fate of stage plays, even of those which at first seem to mirror universal concerns with extraordinary depth and brilliance. As Matthew Arnold was perhaps the first to observe, all literary history is discontinuous: some generations are luckier than others when it comes to writing texts that later readers will return to.[2] But the drama is a special case of this phenomenon. It has such an alarming way of reverting to pure and obviously bygone code that it is extremely rare for a playwright to convince more than one or two generations that the actor's hermeneutics—let alone a reader's—are worth the price of admission. For stage plays to become fully literary, participating in an enduring chain of influence, institutionally sustained reading, and recurrent commentary, is rarer still.[3] Moreover, the relation which the history of such

---

[1] See Richard S. Peterson's reading of the ode as a Horatian blend of praise and criticism in *Imitation and Praise in the Poems of Ben Jonson* (New Haven, Connecticut: Yale University Press, 1981), 160–88. For a fine discussion of the complexities in Jonson's view and use of Shakespeare, see Anne Barton, "Shakespeare and Jonson," in *Shakespeare, Man of the Theatre*, ed. K. Muir, J. Halio, and D. J. Palmer, (Newark: University of Delaware Press, 1983), 155–72. On the canonization of Shakespeare, see also John Freehafer, "Leonard Digges, Ben Jonson, and the Beginning of Shakespeare Idolatry," *Shakespeare Quarterly* 21 (1970): 63–75, Alfred Harbage, "Shakespeare and the Myth of Perfection," *Shakespeare Quarterly* 15 (1964): 1–20, E.A.J. Honigmann, *Shakespeare's Impact on His Contemporaries* (Totowa, New Jersey: Barnes and Noble, 1982), 25–52, Harry Levin, "The Primacy of Shakespeare," *Shakespeare Quarterly* 26 (1975): 99–112, and Kenneth Muir, "The Singularity of Shakespeare," in *The Singularity of Shakespeare and Other Essays* (Liverpool: Liverpool University Press, 1977), 124–37. On questions of canonicity in general, see especially Alvin B. Kernan, *The Imaginary Library: An Essay on Literature and Society* (Princeton: Princeton University Press, 1982), and the essays in *Canons*, ed. Robert von Hallberg (Chicago: University of Chicago Press, 1984).

[2] "The Function of Criticism at the Present Time."

[3] No definition of the "literary" could be uncontentious these days. Though essentialist views are out of favor, the history of theater makes it hard to doubt that literariness and canonicity have something to do with intrinsic features of the works that the community of readers continues to find useful, and that one needs some causal story about the conditions enabling these features. My own view of literariness eclectically derives from John M. Ellis's Wittgensteinian account, *The Theory of Literature: A Logical Analysis* (Berkeley: University of California Press, 1974), especially from his argument that one can attempt to discover those "general factors which relate to the ability of literary texts to function as literary texts" (231), from Paul de Man's arguments that literariness has to do with a text's knowing resistance to readability (especially in "Semiology and Rhetoric," *Allegories of Reading: Figural Language in Rousseau, Nietzsche, Rilke, and Proust* [New Haven, Connecticut: Yale University Press, 1979], 3–19), and from Hans-Georg Gadamer's notion of the classic text as one that retains its ability to challenge our particular and limited prejudices, *Truth and Method* (New York: Seabury Press, 1975), esp. 253–67. I have also profited from the various discussions in Paul Hernandi, ed., *What is Literature?* (Bloomington: Indiana University Press, 1978). James Kavanagh, "Shakespeare in Ideology," in *Alternative Shakespeares*, ed. John Drakakis (London: Methuen, 1985), 144–65, argues that the post-eighteenth-century assimilation of Shakespeare to the category of the literary amounts to the bourgeois appropriation and restaging of the dramatist's original ideological production. Though no one could deny

drama bears to other shapes of time is quite different from that of the epic from Homer to Milton, or of lyric since Petrarch, or of the novel since Richardson, to cite just three obvious lineages in other genres. Whatever may be said about their distinctive rhythms, about deliberate imitation and transformation, Oedipal struggle, or lonely attempts to begin some fictive community, none of these traditions manifests the peculiar clustering which has characterized important drama from the very beginning. Sudden efflorescence at crucial national moments—fifth-century Athens; seventeenth-century France; Russia, Ireland, and the Scandinavian countries in the late nineteenth and twentieth centuries; the less distinctly national but no less sporadic pattern since then—this is the arabesque which dramatic history occasionally performs beside the much more continuous history of theater, from which it is otherwise indistinguishable.

Such a seismic rhythm, general eruption followed by echoes and subsidence, creates an awkward but compelling problem for the literary historian. Some genres seem to lack origins altogether. Lyric must be as old as song, and to get to the roots of song would take us further back in evolution than literary traces can go. So far as these let us see, lyric is also more or less continuous: no times are so sullen that it is impossible to write honest and enduring verse which will compel a reckoning from future poets, even if not from other sorts of readers.[4] Epic comes round less often, though its origins are equally an abyss of difference in repetition, but its identity is distinct enough and its functions sufficiently clear that one feels fairly comfortable about its history: epic is foundation narrative for an epoch and people and at the same time a determinate form, alive in rehearsal and deliberate recollection from the West's beginning until its conscious departure from the ancients. Even its modernized and subjective stand-in, for all the notorious difficulties in defining the novel, nonetheless possesses a characteristic telos which marked it from the beginning as a genre of beginning, of a self-conscious struggle with narrative device that sets it apart from earlier literary kinds. Like lyric, the novel has a certain essence (albeit invented) that talent, once subjectivized, can always find out and adapt to new circumstances, no matter how unpropitious. Only the drama "develops," always suddenly, always in com-

---

that modern literary institutions differ from those available in the early seventeenth century, nor that these have a latently aristocratic cast, the publication of the Folio clearly makes a canonical gesture, shifting Shakespeare's texts into an authorized domain of reading.

[4] I think of three rather differently successful attempts at restoration of neglected figures to the canon: Eliot's of Donne (the story of which is told in Joseph E. Duncan, *The Revival of Metaphysical Poetry* [Minneapolis: University of Minnesota Press, 1959]), Yvor Winters's sponsorship of the sixteenth-century plain style, Robert Pinsky's (and before him, Ezra Pound's and Donald Davie's) promotion of Landor.

pany, and always from an obscure and inadequate theatrical past. And only the drama "declines," falling on worse days than lyric ever encounters, for the decline of drama takes a curiously schizophrenic form, splitting into the momentarily popular theater of an increasingly theatrical civilization, side by side with periodic eruptions of a self-consciously "literary" theater.[5]

In putting the case this starkly, I risk overstatement. Everyone can think of fallow periods where no genre in a given national literature excites much interest; and most professional readers will be able to supply a favorite play or dismal epic with which to threaten any claim for a systematic difference in "life cycle" between drama and the other genres. With due allowance for exceptions, however, the history of drama clearly presents special puzzles and temptations. This is not surprising, since the art is special too, in ways that structurally entail a problematic reception from the readers of a later age. As the most public of all literature, drama depends more obviously than other sorts of poetry upon a people's whole resources for self-articulation; no wonder, then, that most plays live only for their own age, or that yesterday's commonplaces seem an adequate map for the specialist who seeks to understand such plays. When drama does transcend ideology and social ritual, something needs explaining; evolutionary models tempt the historian's imagination. And the great author of genetic explanations, of course, also wrote our first poetics. Structure and genesis have never been inseparable, though it is hard to imagine from what position we could pretend to know their interaction.[6]

[5] These remarks derive in part from Northrop Frye, *Anatomy of Criticism* (Princeton: Princeton University Press, 1957), Edward W. Said, *Beginnings: Intention and Method* (New York: Basic Books, 1975), Claudio Guillén, *Literature as System: Essays toward the Theory of Literature* (Princeton: Princeton University Press, 1971), especially the title essay, and Earl Miner, "On the Genesis and Structure of Literary Systems," *Critical Inquiry* 5 (1979): 553–68. For the post-Shakespearean division between poetic and popular drama, see John Guillory's suggestion in *Poetic Authority: Spenser, Milton, and Literary History* (New York: Columbia University Press, 1983) that it was Milton's triumph over Shakespeare's influence which determined that subsequent poetic drama be "in the tradition of *Samson Agonistes* rather than Shakespeare" (189). Speaking to the exigencies of drama rather than the Oedipal struggles of strong poets, Coburn Freer supplies the other half of the story: "When dramatic characters become instruments more finely tuned to social adaptation, the verse they speak can naturally become smoother and more equable, if not less complex," ultimately tending, of course, toward prose. *The Poetics of Jacobean Drama* (Baltimore: Johns Hopkins University Press, 1981), 215.

[6] See Robert D'Amico "Text and Context: Derrida and Foucault on Descartes," in *The Structural Allegory: Reconstructive Encounters with the New French Thought*, ed. John Fekete (Minneapolis: University of Minneapolis, 1984), 164–82. D'Amico adjudicates and tries to go beyond the conflict between structuralism and historicism, in part by observing that Foucault and Derrida agree that "we cannot both represent and represent ourselves representing" (181). Marc Augé subjects the comparable issue in anthropology to an especially forceful analysis in *The Anthropological Circle: Symbol, Function, History*, trans. Martin Thom (Cambridge: Cambridge University Press, 1982), e.g., "if it is true that institutions

If anything, however, Shakespeare occasions more surprise than the phenomenon that Aristotle sought to understand. At least the Athenian drama kept continuity with a ritual past and was in part, we now believe, the consequence of a deliberate reworking of that past for fairly evident political and social goals.[7] For Shakespeare, there is no such excuse. Had he been the only significant playwright of the era, an isolated Homer of the stage, we might evade the question with bardolatry. Had his been merely the greatest in a chain of texts, however many the years between, we could speak with confidence about his appropriation of the ancestors (as we can, for instance, even in the warped lineage connecting Fielding, Milton, Spenser, and Chaucer).[8] But neither avenue will do. With at best an allusively surviving ritual context and with hardly any genuine predecessors, Shakespeare had fellows. None is so great, some are interesting mainly for the relation they bear to the "Soul of the Age," but all bear witness that the Elizabethan drama was new and general, a collective, intense, and short-lived revolution in genre somewhat before it was perceived as one more sign of revolution in the times.

Whatever else they do, great texts cannot explain their own originary force: they embody that resistance to theory, that unique and disruptive quality which for Derrida characterizes a real event.[9] In the effort to find out origins, and thus domesticate this force, there have been many subtle

---

serve a purpose *and* signify, it is also true that the secret of function does not lie in signification, nor vice versa" (8).

[7] See Gerald Else, *The Origin and Early Form of Greek Tragedy* (Cambridge, Massachusetts: Harvard University Press, 1965), and John J. Winkler, "The Ephoebe's Song," *Representations* 11 (Summer, 1985): 26–62.

[8] For quite different assessments of that lineage, see A. Kent Hieatt, *Chaucer, Spenser, Milton: Mythpoeic Continuities and Transformations* (Montreal: McGill-Queen's University Press, 1975), and Guillory, *Poetic Authority.* Harold Bloom, *The Anxiety of Influence* (Oxford: Oxford University Press, 1973), 11, excludes Shakespeare from his argument for three reasons: (1) his belonging to "the giant age before the flood, before the anxiety of influence became central to poetic consciousness"; (2) "the contrast between dramatic and lyric form"; (3) the relative insignificance of his "prime precursor," Marlowe. But as Thomas Greene has since demonstrated in *The Light in Troy: Imitation and Discovery in Renaissance Poetry* (New Haven, Connecticut: Yale University Press, 1982), there was before the flood an equally potent "anxiety of originality" (195) operative even in the relatively impoverished culture of pre-Shakespearean England. From this anxiety as from the other, Shakespeare seems to have been exempt.

[9] Jacques Derrida, "My Chances/*Mes Chances*: A Rendezvous with Some Epicurean Stereophonies," trans. Irene Harvey and Avital Ronell, in *Taking Chances: Derrida, Psychoanalysis, and Literature*, ed. William Kerrigan and Joseph Smith (Baltimore: Johns Hopkins University Press, 1984), 1–32. Certain great texts seem more resistant to theory than others, as Jonathan V. Crewe suggests in observing that whereas Milton has recently received satisfactory theoretical attention, Shakespeare's standing in theory and history is far more problematic: "despite Shakespeare's continuing nominal preeminence within the English tradition, the basis of that preeminence has defied adequate theoretical formulation in recent criticism." *Unredeemed Rhetoric: Thomas Nashe and the Scandal of Authorship* (Baltimore: Johns Hopkins University Press, 1982), 11.

strategies, some suggestive results, and much cudgeling of recalcitrant old plays. But the standard version remains much the same after very many books, and for that reason alone leaves one unsatisfied. The problem is not so much in accurately describing formal change, as in knowing what to make of it and how to understand the implications of any causal story that would cross the formidable gap from *Horestes* to *Hamlet*. On the side of playwriting, there is an evident process of learning and adaptation, together with some shift in the aims and tactics of representation. On the side of history, there is religious conflict and perhaps some skeptical disillusionment as well as an intensified, more inward piety; there is nationalism focused in the person of a royal actor; there is a general European shift in the ground of epistemology, a shift so basic that knowledge itself becomes constellated as a separate problem of unprecedented dimensions. The puzzle is how to connect one history with the other, how to describe a relation between the peculiar form of these plays and their historical moment without either falsifying our own sense of the drama or forgetting what else we know about cultural and literary history.[10]

Such a task engages us in more than a search for origins. As we try to see how Shakespeare relates to his own age and past, we must simultaneously devise some story about his relation to us, to what we think we have become since so-called traditional society gave way to our modernity.[11] Every dispute about the form and meaning of these plays thus rests upon a disagreement, often quite explicit, over the use to which we put them or which we find them having served, over moral imperatives and the different senses of identity that these entail. In one moment of the debate, universalizing (and often existentialist) humanists have celebrated Shakespeare's transcendence of his era and its metaphysical constraints,

[10] Of the vast literature on these matters, see especially David Bevington, *From Mankind to Marlowe: Growth of Structure in the Popular Drama of Tudor England* (Cambridge, Massachusetts: Harvard University Press, 1962), Horton Davies, *Worship and Theology in England: From Cranmer to Hooker, 1534–1603* (Princeton: Princeton University Press, 1970), Madeleine Doran, *Endeavors of Art: A Study of Form in Elizabethan Drama* (Madison: University of Wisconsin Press, 1964), Philip Edwards, *Threshold of a Nation: A Study in English and Irish Drama* (Cambridge: Cambridge University Press, 1979), Howard Felperin, *Shakespearean Representation: Mimesis and Modernity in Elizabethan Tragedy* (Princeton: Princeton University Press, 1977), Donald W. Hanson, *From Kingdom to Commonwealth: The Development of Civic Consciousness in English Political Thought* (Cambridge, Massachusetts: Harvard University Press, 1970), Richard Rorty, *Philosophy and the Mirror of Nature* (Princeton: Princeton University Press, 1979), Bernard Spivack, *Shakespeare and the Allegory of Evil: The History of a Metaphor in Relation to his Major Villains* (New York: Columbia University Press, 1958), and Glynne Wickham, *Early English Stages, 1300 to 1600*, vol. 2, pts. 1 and 2 (London: Routledge and Kegan Paul, 1963 and 1972).

[11] For a skeptical view of this transition, and an especially useful survey of its scholarly history, see Alan Macfarlane, *The Origins of English Individualism: The Family, Property, and Social Transition* (Cambridge: Cambridge University Press, 1978).

while a school of historicists (often "Christian humanists" themselves) emphasize Shakespeare's tie with the old plays and ways, finding in the frankly symbolic methods of that past a way of tying down what Shakespeare meant, of freeing him (and us) from the ethical and semantic relativism that defines and curses every "modern" era. In another and braver mood, so their demystifying rhetoric implies, a more recent controversy of critics sees quite different images in the glass. New historicists, Marxist as well as Foucauldian, examine Shakespeare's relations with power (often to debunk both these and the humanistic celebration of his authority). For an opposing party, both old and new historicists and the older generation of formalists have given way to a deplorable nostalgia: the corrective, sterner view discovers a Shakespeare not of an age but for all time textual, his universality consisting in a registration of hard truths, how provisional and fictive meaning is, how the nature of writing outruns our order, how a strong form can contain Nietzschean energies without controlling their ironic play.[12]

No doubt this puts it crudely and tendentiously. Pure formalists are as mythical as the historicists they always fight; and in recent years, there have been serious attempts to develop a theory of textual production that would transcend both the undialectical opposition between formalism and historicism, and the romantic epistemology underlying this opposition.[13] Nonetheless, nearly all histories of the drama turn on a small set

[12] As Stanley Cavell says, using the current debate in Shakespeare studies to warrant the general proposition, there is a perpetual "willingness" for crisis in the humanities. "Division of Talent," *Critical Inquiry* 11 (1985): 522. A more engaged formulation of the debate is Jonathan Goldberg's opening remark in *Voice, Terminal, Echo: Postmodernism and English Renaissance Texts* (New York and London: Methuen, 1986), upon "a post-post structuralism which some, these days, might even call formalism" and a "so-called humanistic criticism which has not failed to see itself threatened" as well as a "socially engaged criticism which has preferred to regard poststructuralism as a new formalism rather than confront its own sentimentality" (ix). For necessarily arbitrary instances of the debaters, see these: Harriet Hawkins, *Poetic Freedom and Poetic Truth: Chaucer, Shakespeare, Marlowe, Milton* (Oxford: Clarendon Press, 1976), and *The Devil's Party: Critical Counter-interpretations of Shakespearean Drama* (Oxford: Clarendon Press, 1985), and Jan Kott, *Shakespeare: Our Contemporary*, trans. Boleslaw Taborski (Garden City, New York: Doubleday, 1964); Roy Battenhouse, *Shakespearean Tragedy: Its Art and Christian Premises* (Bloomington: Indiana University Press, 1969), Edmund Creeth, *Mankynde in Shakespeare* (Athens: University of Georgia Press, 1976), and Alan C. Dessen, *Elizabethan Drama and the Viewer's Eye* (Chapel Hill: University of North Carolina Press, 1977), and in explicit opposition to the new formalism, A. D. Nuttall, *A New Mimesis: Shakespeare and the Representation of Reality* (London: Methuen, 1983); Francis Barker, *The Tremulous Private Body: Essays on Subjection* (London: Methuen, 1984), John Drakakis, ed., *Alternative Shakespeares* (London: Methuen, 1985), Jonathan Goldberg, *James I and the Politics of Literature: Jonson, Shakespeare, Donne, and Their Contemporaries* (Baltimore: Johns Hopkins University Press, 1983), and Stephen Greenblatt, *Renaissance Self-Fashioning: From More to Shakespeare* (Chicago: University of Chicago Press, 1980).

[13] Rodolphe Gasché, "Unscrambling Positions: On Gerald Graff's Critique of Deconstruction," *Modern Language Notes* 96 (1981): 1015–34, argues that the romantic notion of

of binary oppositions—the most basic being religious versus secular, and symbolic versus realistic—which only mythical beings could think were purely literary and atemporal in scope or uniquely characteristic of old against new. Yet argument that hinges on such labels makes easy prey for error: in each pair, metaphor insensibly overlaps some ostensibly recent change in our collective self-understanding, so that the more "modern" seems natural, new, and intrinsic to the formal essence of the genre. How commonly we say it, in effect: where Shakespeare's predecessors were medieval, he is modern; mimetic where they were didactic, verging on illusion where they were bound to emblems, riddling and complex where they were morally confident if not naive, insistently ironic where they were allegorical, iconoclastic where they were enthralled to images of truth.[14] In earlier works, the persons of the drama are signs, not characters; they figure forth idea rather than psychology; neither motivation nor consistency matters much, for inwardness is not a value in that theater. Instead of plot as classical and post–Elizabethan writers understood it, this drama gives us schemes, patterns of redemption and damnation rather than sequences of probable cause. But in Shakespeare, everything is transformed: we recognize ourselves in him; at least the selves we thought we were, before modernity began to turn against selves and plots, alerting us to other pressures and designs within Shakespeare's texts as well as in our own.[15]

Just this notorious capacity for changing shape and meaning as his readers change their habits of perception is evidence enough that form

---

self-reflexivity constitutes the "symmetrical and complementary" views of "both formalistic and historical or realist criticism" (1018). Among notable attempts to devise an integrated theory of textual production, one ought at least cite Fredric Jameson's several books, especially *The Political Unconscious: Narrative as a Socially Symbolic Act* (Ithaca, New York: Cornell University Press, 1981). Michael McCanles, *Dialectical Criticism and Renaissance Literature* (Berkeley: University of California Press, 1975), and James Turner, *The Politics of Landscape: Rural Scenery and Society in English Poetry, 1630–1660* (Cambridge, Massachusetts: Harvard University Press, 1979), have useful discussions of how one might "combine the insights of formalism and historicism without falling into either error" (Turner, 187).

[14] For recent versions of these contrasts, themselves combining useful surveys of the scholarly tradition with quite different views of its implications, see James Siemon, *Shakespearean Iconoclasm* (Berkeley: University of California Press, 1985), and Jonathan Dollimore, *Radical Tragedy: Religion, Ideology and Power in the Drama of Shakespeare and His Contemporaries* (Chicago: University of Chicago Press, 1984).

[15] Though reaction to realist, individualist, and characterological conceptions of Shakespeare dates at least from the work of G. Wilson Knight, several recent studies reread the matter of Renaissance individualism from a postmodern distrust of the centered subject. One should cite at least Anne Ferry's demonstration in *The Inward Language* (Chicago: University of Chicago Press, 1983), esp. 31–70, of the absence in the sixteenth century of modern concepts and terms for the self, Catherine Belsey, *The Subject of Tragedy: Identity and Difference in Renaissance Drama* (London: Methuen, 1985), and Joel Fineman, *Shakespeare's Perjur'd Eye: The Invention of Poetic Subjectivity* (Berkeley: University of California Press, 1986).

cannot by itself account for the plays. But their corollary ability to outrun determinate world pictures proves that certain kinds of history hinder as much as help responsible interpretation.[16] We can say that the texts are literary rather than instrumental; that they are radically ambiguous, refusing to allow sure resolution of the tensions which inform them; more radically, that they forestall any sort of closure, whether organic or dialectical. But all this begs the question: since such literariness, ambiguity, and openness appeal to recent rather than to older tastes, we cannot be sure that modern interpreters do not simply satisfy their own desires; and to say that tensions stay unresolved is no more than to say that for us the plays remain implacably dramatic. There may indeed be deep and perhaps intrinsically irresolvable contradictions in Shakespeare between different ways of apprehension and presentation. But the conundrum set us is that the poise he strikes is simultaneously diachronic and formal, part between eras and part between representational modes with only an imaginary link to temporal fashions or changing world pictures.

Yet just as a way of putting the difference between early plays and late, the simpler oppositions—suitably qualified—ring true to our experience. Compared to fully literary drama, medieval and early Tudor plays really are thin gruel. This is safe to say, despite those modern studies (and interesting shifts in modern sensibility) that have made it possible for us to see that the early plays, especially the mystery cycles, are neither the product of "Carpenters and Coblers," as Rymer thought (thereby maligning the Shakespeare derived from them) nor barely dramatized dogma, feebly enlivened by realistic comedy. Medieval and early Tudor drama has structural integrity; it is theologically alive, iconographically informed, and splendidly theatrical; it has moments both outrageously funny and genuinely moving.[17] But it does not, and as popular, occasional, and largely homiletic theater, cannot, arouse the interpretive instinct in the way that the later drama does. That it has required some explication is no contrary evidence; it is one thing to explain a forgotten semiotic and quite another to find in the text the kind of problematic interplay between code and noncode that characterizes works we continue to use for the purpose of cultural self-definition. Like the more academic debate plays, this drama is too transparent, too close both to oratory and to ritual (of court, col-

---

[16] This dilemma is best focused by E.M.W. Tillyard's reading of the history plays (*Shakespeare's History Plays* [1944; New York: Collier Books, 1962]) and subsequent reactions to that reading, among the most judicious of these being Herbert Howarth, "Put Away the World Picture," in *The Tiger's Heart* (New York: Oxford University Press, 1970), 165–91.

[17] On the intellectual and theatrical qualities of these plays see especially Joel B. Altman, *The Tudor Play of Mind: Rhetorical Inquiry and the Development of Elizabethan Drama* (Berkeley: University of California Press, 1978), and T. W. Craik, *The Tudor Interlude* (Leicester, England: Leicester University Press, 1958).

lege, parish, guild) to bear reading and rereading except for special purposes, whether of history or anthropology.

But it is very difficult to control the implications of binarism: if the
early drama is allegorical and homiletic where Shakespeare is not, must it
not therefore follow that his difficult mode of representation reflects a
world in which verities no longer hold? Plato and Oscar Wilde give both
theoretical and practical witness to the proposition that life imitates art
rather than the other way round, but the tedious and by now quite sterile
debate over the Christian premises of Shakespeare's art is ample proof
that the step from theater to world is very slick. We all know this, yet
even the most sophisticated and conscientious critic can let terms slip all
unawares from synchrony into diachrony. Treating Shakespeare's theatrical heritage as an incorporated foil against which his new mimesis tests
and proves its strength, one recent and rightly influential reader sees a
predictable supersession. On the one side is inherited structure, on the
other experience: "Christian vision" versus "Shakespearean revision." If
it were worth the labor, one could easily cite a hundred similar judgments.[18]

Unless we want to make Shakespeare a prophet as well as a revolutionary, such conclusions cannot hold. It is no more true in the history of
literature that the allegorical and the didactic cease to be viable, supple,
and engaging stances toward world and reader than it is that Christianity

[18] Felperin, *Shakespearean Representation*, 134. See also his typical suggestion that "Shakespeare's plays inhabit the gap between things and the preordained meaning of things, between experience and the inherited constructs of experience. Edgar's injunction at the end
of *King Lear* to 'speak what we feel, not what we ought to say,' formulates the difference
between our responses to the drama of naturalism and the drama of allegory, and might
serve as rubric to the history of Shakespeare criticism" (65). For a formulation which casts
such an argument in the terms of a Marxist poststructuralism, see Barker, *Tremulous Private
Body*, esp. 24, on the prebourgeois "early body" of Jacobean tragedy, which "lies athwart
that divide between subject and object, discourse and world, that characterizes the later
dispensation." A better nuanced statement of this view is Franco Moretti's, in *Signs Taken
for Wonders: Essays in the Sociology of Literary Forms*, trans. Susan Fischer, David Forgacs, and
David Miller (London: Verso Editions, 1983): "He [Shakespeare] may announce the dawn
of bourgeois civilization, but not by prefiguring it" (68). See also W. Thomas MacCary,
Friends and Lovers: The Phenomenology of Desire in Shakespearean Comedy (New York: Columbia University Press, 1985), 223: "While Shakespeare frees men from the bondage
which medieval deference to deduced patterns of perfection imposed on men in love and in
life generally, he also obliges them to shape their experience fantastically, to make of all
objects something rich and strange." For an especially sophisticated version of this story as
it concerns tragedy, see J. W. Lever, *The Tragedy of State* (London: Methuen, 1971): "the
serious playwrights of the age were aware of a wider transformation of society taking place
throughout Europe and undermining all traditional human relationships. It consisted in the
growth and concentration of state power, the destruction of the Italian city republics, the
conversion of English, French and Spanish noblemen into court parasites, the absorption of
petty despotisms by great monarchies, and the concomitant suppression of a wide range of
individual freedoms. The effect upon the victims was to promote a re-thinking of ancient
assumptions" (4).

ceased to articulate human experience during Elizabeth's reign.[19] Spenser and Bunyan in their different ways are more allegorical and surer of their vision than Chaucer and Langland; emblem books grow more popular in the early seventeenth century, not less; far from rendering Christianity obsolete or problematic, Protestantism arouses religious energies, personalizes them, and urges the converted to be certain of their fate.[20] Coherence did not flee the world with Copernicus, Donne's hyperbole notwithstanding.[21] Given these and a host of other truisms, it is plain that whatever the change in self-understanding which we persistently see mirrored in Shakespeare, it cannot be identical with any shift in representational methods from early drama to late. Even if that shift were more complete and consistent than the printed record shows it to be—and there are "neomoralities" to be coped with as well as the tendencies toward "reallegorization" that Howard Felperin nicely describes in younger Jacobean playwrights like Tourneur and Webster—we would still be faced with the problematic relation between the trope of any representation and that which it points to, incorporates, and constitutes.

Here the problem doubles back on itself in a rather disconcerting way. The relationship between a trope and the reality it institutes or captures, which is in one register the relationship between metaphoric and "normal" discourse, evidently correlates with the binarism of didactic and mimetic, emblematic and illusionistic standardly employed to characterize that part of the transformation from medieval to modern that Shakespeare seems to manifest. On the one side we can place all those texts in which it is both easy and important to read out a set of intentions and concepts; on the other side are texts which block communicative reading, serving to display something but not to configure and manipulate propositions about the world. One could easily assimilate other dichotomies

[19] L. B. Wright, for example, claims that the taste of "middle-class" readers grew more didactic rather than less during the century from 1576. *Middle-Class Culture in Elizabethan England* (1935; Ithaca, New York: Cornell University Press, 1958), 83–87. For accounts of the fortunes of allegory, particularly in its passage through the Enlightenment, see Michael Murrin, *The Veil of Allegory* (Chicago: University of Chicago Press, 1969), esp. 212 ("Like institutions, allegory never really dies"), Stephen Barney, *Allegories of History, Allegories of Love* (Hamden, Connecticut: Archon Books, 1976), and of course, Paul de Man, "The Rhetoric of Temporality," reprinted in *Blindness and Insight: Essays in the Rhetoric of Contemporary Criticism*, 2d ed. (Minneapolis: University of Minnesota Press, 1983), 187–228.

[20] As Lawrence Stone observes, one way to describe the effect of the reformers' "powerful drive for the christianization of society" is that the "Holy Spirit was partly domesticated." *The Family, Sex and Marriage in England, 1500–1800* (New York: Harper and Row, 1977), 134, 142.

[21] See Jacob Viner, *The Role of Providence in the Social Order* (1972; Princeton: Princeton University Press, 1976) and Clarence J. Glacken, *Traces on the Rhodian Shore: Nature and Culture in Western Thought from Ancient Times to the End of the Eighteenth Century* (Berkeley: University of California Press, 1967).

to this one, constructing a table of supposedly congruent oppositions: the instrumental as opposed to the aesthetic, the semantically transparent as opposed to the more or less opaque, argument as against analogy, "telling" as opposed to "showing," cognitives against performatives, the paradigmatic and metaphoric as opposed to the syntagmatic and metonymic. Whatever value such a table might have, however, it would not serve to convince anyone that the imaginary line dividing one column from the other was impermeable.

Quite the contrary. As the list gets longer, the polarities threaten reversal, as if written on a möbius strip, till it grows inescapably clear that the relation between terms is anaclitic and asymmetrical. On one hand is everyday reference, with its cunning but apparently easy construction and manipulation of the familiar world; on another is the seductive abyss of tropes and figures on which all discourse depends and into which any statement can be thrown by a clever deconstructor, who is stoppable only by silent deixis in a shared and immediate context. Neither rhetoric nor poetics can subsist without the other; neither science nor *sapientia* can achieve purity. The very act of reading supplies reference for even the most "writerly" of texts, the formal play with paradigms turning through temporal apprehension into a narrative of connectedness and concretion; yet no syntax can be strong enough to keep the tropes in check. Or put it the other way round. With great care in specifying conventions, one can construct a language of pure and unambiguous locution; yet to use that speech, as to set it up, requires those illocutionary gestures of stipulating and proposing that convert analytic snow-whiteness into synthetic and communal fiction. There is metaphor at the base of every statement, which can never contain but only model truth, which in turn is not a matter of saying but of seeing that snow, after all, *is* white. But to account for that whiteness is once again to engage the play of paradigms, keeping apodictic presence at bay. And for every account meant to tie down these statues of Daedalus, there is always an ironic Socrates ready to show that any version of the real is mere myth and allegory, useful as heuristic but sheer "wind eggs" by comparison with the unattained prize of certainty.

Texts we call "literary" operate in both these modes just as much as the most intentionally transparent speech act; the difference is simply that the literary text retains an ability to foreground what the others suppress. But when we see one of the three basic literary forms move suddenly from announcing its own "readability" to calling transparency in question, when we see this public art rearrange itself from stating and configuring apparent certainties to displaying what we take for ambiguity, we can hardly doubt that something basic is changing in the relation words and deeds are thought to bear to one another. Nonetheless, the fact remains that drama before the shift as well as after it can only serve as a trope and not as a faithful reflection of reality; indeed, the early drama insists with all its resources that the world it portrays is of the spirit rather than the flesh. We cannot use it directly as evidence of medieval vision or sophistication, or think that the Christianity it advocates is easier or more comfortable than later Protestant or even atheist existential stances toward the world and its potential meaning.

Nor can we think that its mode of representation is inherently defective by comparison with Shakespeare's. If it is true that all language depends upon both sides of our insistent binarism, that every poem and play rises out of and falls back into an unknowable morass of intentions and references, while every proposition rests upon a hidden fiction that will some day provide the only interest it retains, then it cannot also be true that the early plays are all transparent allegory and the late ones all dark and dramatic irony. This may seem unlikely. I certainly do not suggest we hunt either "ambivalence" or "naturalism" where none exists in the text, and I do not think the consensus of readers is mistaken as to what medieval and early Tudor plays say. But I do intend to argue the importance for the early drama of a fact that we have always known: its incompleteness without Christianity, without a willed engagement of the viewer's own moral and metaphysical self-apprehension. At least in the largely penitential drama of the mysteries and moralities, it is plain enough—though strange, perhaps, to say it this way—that the "natural" and the "ambivalent" reside on the side of the audience rather than that of the play. The problem these words present is not of how to read but of how to live, not of seeing enacted fiction as a mirror of the natural world but of seeing nature as a mirror of the reality to which the players gesture. In a certain sense, then, the riddle and the illusion is outside the text, which plays the part of reason to the watcher's sensuality, always in danger of being purely "aesthetic."

Yet nothing entailed by a text is really outside it; and certainly nothing in Christianity is outside what is fashionably called "textuality" and its attendant problems about the nature of reading. The rules of criticism would once have forbade our imagining the audience as part of the representation that we study, but those rules themselves—like the very possibility of "criticism"—depend upon a notion of art *as* representation which appears in European culture at about the same time as Shakespeare himself. Now that confidence in the exclusive truth of this version of the relation between word and things has begun to ebb, it is easier to see that the real newness in Shakespeare is not only his excellence or his literariness, but the negative definition of these qualities: that a play should pretend not to be implicated in the "nonliterary," that a playwright should be considered as more than the nearly anonymous servant of actors and of such authority, secular or religious, as their entertainment flatters and sustains. In short, what permits us to imagine that mysteries, moralities, and even interludes are all sign and statement is just our post-Shakespearean habit of separating a text from its "natural" context, its "ritual" occasion, and its social and ideological import. Considered in that frame, the early drama may turn out to present as many moral and epistemological puzzles as it purports to solve.

No amount of redescription, however, could make these plays capable of the effects which Chaucer, Langland, the Pearl poet, or even Henryson and Malory regularly achieve for modern readers. Medieval narrative so often and so cleverly takes its own status as fable and trope into account as part of a paradox in *being* as well as a paradox in *saying* that it can seem an uncannily avant-garde celebration of the delights and pitfalls of textuality. While knowing that doctrine mattered then in ways it does not now, we can cherish a Chaucer's tact in posing the connection between sentence and solace, and take that for a satisfactory problem in hermeneutics even as we take Dante's own allegorical method as itself the engaging subject of his poem. In such ways we bracket off our own implication in the text, ignore the existential trouble we would be caused by taking seriously all that responsibility for meaning that narrative inevitably—and this narrative explicitly—foists on its reader. As the Spaniard Juan Ruiz puts it, speaking not as author but as book, and exceptional only in making it so unmistakably hard to avoid substituting one's own intentions for "his":

> I, this book, am akin to all instruments of music: according as you point [play music] well or badly, so most assuredly, will I speak; in whatever way you choose to speak, make a point [stop] there and hold fast; if you know how to point me [pluck my strings] you will always hold me in mind.

> [De totos instrumentes yo, libro, só pariente;
> bíen o mal, quál puntares, tal diré, ciértamente;
> quál tú dezir, y faz punto e tente;
> si puntarme sopieres siempre me abrás en mente.][22]

[22] Juan Ruiz, *Libro de Buen Amor*, ed. and trans. Raymond S. Willis (Princeton: Princeton University Press, 1972), 28–29. See Marina Scordilis Brownlee, "Autobiography as Self-(Re)presentation: The Augustinian Paradigm and Juan Ruiz's Theory of Reading," in *Mimesis: From Mirror to Method, Augustine to Descartes*, ed. John D. Lyons and Stephen G. Nichols, Jr., (Hanover, New Hampshire: University Press of New England, 1982), 70–82, which argues that the "*Libro* is profoundly concerned with the problem of interpretation,

Chaucer on game and earnest, Langland on the relation between *visio* and *vita*, Jean de Meun (or even John Gower) with another version of the omnipresent Book of Good Love, all these are just self-conscious enough about the provisional character of any statement and just wary enough about the likely idolatry in settling on any "present" object for love or any temporal person for authority that their texts retain a delightful capacity for continued self-ironization. Thus riddling about the inherently Christian but no less inherently literary enterprise of relating spirit to letter, medieval narrative permits us to keep using it for (nothing but) literature.[23]

Medieval drama, on the other hand, no less predicated on a belief that meaning finally inheres in persons rather than in words, no less aware that an audience must complete the reference without which neither trope nor sentence can exist, nonetheless falls short of operating in this "literary" way: we can no more separate it from doctrine than we can make an individual text the bearer of so-called ambiguity. Where medieval narrative manifests genuine doubt about its ability to tell the truth—one thinks both of Chaucer's irony and penitential retraction and of Dante's recurrent deprecation of his own "infant" speech—medieval drama tells its tale with confident unconcern. Indeed, one simple way to distinguish Shakespeare from his early predecessors—even those who write for the court—is to say that they "tell" where he "shows."

This distinction retains considerable force even after one has admitted that neither mode escapes covert dependence on the other any more than propositions can avoid the awkward embrace of metaphor, or vice versa. No drama is pure show unless it be inexplicable mime, and no narrative in a single voice can so control itself that nothing shows besides intended meanings and effects. All this granted, and very well to say that the ambiguous letter of things reappears on the audience's side, whose part in the play is to some extent mimed by the world, flesh, and devil that the drama ultimately suppresses in favor of spiritual meaning; nothing can make us believe that the text as such manifests a sense of its inevitably maimed character as a bearer of truth. In fact, it is just when this unease arises, and playwrights begin to make semantic over-(and under-)determination part of their subject—as both Kyd and Lyly do in quite different ways—that the genre takes fire. And then one almost wants to speak of the reinvention of drama in structure as well as in literary effect. For as

---

that it in fact thematizes the problem of interpretation, functioning as a logical extension of Augustinian hermeneutics" (70).

[23] Peter Haidu, in "Repetition: Modern Reflections on Medieval Aesthetics," *Modern Language Notes* 92 (1977): 875–87, argues for the unwittingly deconstructive effects of this enterprise.

Madeleine Doran and many others have noticed, the reawakening of irony coincides with a reformation in dramatic method. Where drama before the 1580s is virtually narrative in technique, rather like Brechtian epic theater but with a less obviously complex mapping of the virtuous onto the real, later playcraft develops a properly "dramatic" method; it is focused, dialectical; its multiple actions unite in ways that seem less identifiably thematic and more figurative in import.

But this just puts our initial problem in a barely different guise: why should it happen that much medieval narrative and no medieval drama should achieve self-conscious textuality? If the foregoing discussion has accomplished anything at all, it should be plausible to say that the only likely solution must combine two answers, one a matter of form, the other a matter of history. First, drama alone of all the genres is an imitation by means of persons as well as words. And second, to put roughly and schematically what I shall shortly try to demonstrate with better tact and evidence, the early drama strikes us as naive about its representational sufficiency precisely because it relies upon a complex sense of the *world* as text which differs in important ways from later understandings of how the flesh bears spirit.

In other words, medieval drama can be transparent and unironic narrative only because the world it represents is itself a hardly unambiguous fabric of intertextuality in which every person is also a sign (a world in this respect quite like what ours is coming to be seen for, though without the theological authority). As this world changes character, so must the drama—which acts to sustain and create as well as to represent what serves an era for reality. And drama is not the only system of world construction to undergo a formal revolution in the sixteenth century. In religion, there is an incomplete movement from advocating the penitential imitation of an Image revealed in ever-present *analogiae entis* to a doctrine which makes the soul's inward reformation manifest only in acting out divine vocations: where the Catholic sees exemplars, the Protestant finds roles, to be enacted with a rectitude that makes the elect mirror glory back to God but not to men (unless with a scriptural warrant for the analogy of faith). In history and politics, we can detect a similar shift of paradigm, also incomplete. For one—call it "medieval"—the realm of fortune is discontinuous and unintelligible except with exemplaristic reference to custom, moral quality, and the symbolism of eternity, while for the other—hardly more "scientific"—there is what J.G.A. Pocock calls a politicization of grace, a resacralization of politics, and a renewed attention to the linear, shaping progress of second causes.[24] Archaeology

[24] J.G.A. Pocock, *The Machiavellian Moment* (Princeton: Princeton University Press,

of knowledge, one might say, as opposed to the technical manipulation of a public; more charitably, Herodotus versus Thucydides. Putting history and religion together, we could say that in one paradigm the book of the world is legible only insofar as it offers discrete occasions and suasive models for personal salvation (and advancement); in the other, history is more dramatistic and prophetic, the actors in it readier to practice the deceits of statecraft and more liable to the ironizing reversals of an imperfectly comprehended sequence of causes and intentions.

Such an exchange of paradigms, unfinished by the end of the sixteenth century and in fact unfinishable in principle, for the repressed mode always returns in disguised form, would obviously complement an idealized development from "narrative" Corpus Christi plays and moral interludes, the actors of which are legible signs, to linear, "dramatic" intrigues in which the actors are substantial presences with veiled motives and uncertain exemplary significance.[25] But to invoke these other systems of signification is not to "explain" what happens in the drama, save in such rare but important respects as Harold C. Gardiner's demonstration that the mysteries died a political rather than a natural death.[26] The value of reference to history and religion lies, rather, in its potential for demystifying such terms as the "natural" and the "allegorical." If such reference can also illuminate the logic of a general transformation in the relationship of words to deeds, helping suggest how that change could enable a literary drama without entailing the conclusion that Shakespeare really does embody the very moment of a momentous disjunction between traditional them and modern us, then so much the better.

In order to prepare for the somewhat different and yet parasitic version of dramatic history that I have adumbrated here, I want first to devote more practical and theoretical attention to the difference between the narrative and the dramatic. This most recent of my dichotomies repeats the basic binaries involved throughout this chapter at a higher and therefore more interesting order. Teasing out the implications of this difference

1975), 3–80. As just one indication of the incompleteness of this apparent exchange of paradigms, consider Robert Eccleshall's argument that custom, which for Pocock characterizes the medieval polity, receives its real sanctification in the seventeenth century, as an embodiment of the collective reason which in the eyes of many contemporary observers Parliament had ceased to exhibit. *Order and Reason in English Politics* (Oxford: Oxford University Press, 1978).

[25] As Mary Douglas observes, one may find nominally antithetical social and cognitive patterns coexisting in any era: strong group and strong grid arrangements (hierarchical and customary) may interact in the same economic and political space with weak group and weak grid arrangements (individualizing and highly competitive). *In the Active Voice* (London: Routledge and Kegan Paul, 1982), 183–234.

[26] Harold C. Gardiner, *Mysteries' End: An Investigation of the Last Days of the Medieval Religious Stage* (New Haven, Connecticut: Yale University Press, 1946).

will require some indirection, but the basic notion is as simple and elusive as the relationship, half symbiotic and half hostile, between the theater and a book.[27] The juncture between these, fluid and unstable as the line between signified and signifier, is the play. Without some change at each point in this imaginary figure, the oddity of Shakespeare's textuality could never have occurred.

✳

Those numinous metaphors, the book of life and the theater of the world, so pervade our literature and inform the work even of biologists and sociologists that it would be folly to argue that one or the other more typifies an era.[28] Yet with Dante and Bonaventure fascinated by the first trope and Neoplatonists, Protestants, and Shakespeare by the second, one sometimes finds temptation hard to resist. Surely there is truth to the hunch that a philosophical doctrine of exemplarism and a theological doctrine of real presence sort better with metaphors of readability, while notions of God's unsearchable grandeur, the spiritually defective reason of human beings, and the superiority of historical types to other kinds of allegory better suit the image of the Globe, that *theatrum mundi* in which divine intentions are not so visible as divine magnificence and vengeance. Rather than count *topoi*, however, I want to look at the way in which Shakespeare uses what is for him the less ubiquitous figure. The exercise has some interest in its own right and should begin both to establish terms and to lay a practical ground for the more abstract version of an interaction between theater and book that I will shortly advance.

At Act 3, Scene 1, of *2 Henry IV*, the insomniac king summons his aides. He greets their anxious entry with a rhetorical question about reading his letters: if they have read them, no need to ask why he is up at one a'clock and past. Then by association he moves both to lament his own

---

[27] For partly analogous ways of putting this relationship, see Bert O. States's discussion of the interchange between the semiotic and the phenomenological, the sign and the image, in *Great Reckonings in Little Rooms: On the Phenomenology of Theater* (Berkeley: University of California Press, 1985), and Robert Weimann's somewhat less analytic distinction between illusion and embodiment, representation and ritual in *Shakespeare and the Popular Tradition in the Theater: Studies in the Social Dimension of Dramatic Form and Function* (Baltimore: Johns Hopkins University Press, 1978), which he initially locates in the dialectic between *locus* and *platea* in medieval theater.

[28] For the ubiquity of the trope of the world theater, and the role of humanism in its transmission from ancient and medieval sources, see Jean Jacquot, "Le théâtre du monde de Shakespeare à Calderón," *Revue de littérature comparée* 31 (1957): 341–72. And of course both Francis Bacon and Robert Boyle employ the trope of the world as book. See David Bloor, *Wittgenstein: A Social Theory of Knowledge* (New York: Columbia University Press, 1983), 153–55, for an account of the social utility of Boyle's use of the trope of the book of nature after the Civil War.

inept construal of the letter of the world and to doubt that a better reading would be endurable.

> O God, that one might read the book of fate,
> And see the revolution of the times
> Make mountains level, and the continent,
> Weary of solid firmness, melt itself
> Into the sea, and other times to see
> The beachy girdle of the ocean
> Too wide for Neptune's hips; how chance's mocks
> And changes fill the cup of alteration
> With divers liquors! O, if this were seen,
> The happiest youth, viewing his progress through,
> What perils past, what crosses to ensue,
> Would shut the book, and sit him down and die.[29]
>   (45–56)

He goes on to rebuke himself for having failed to heed Richard's prophecy of Northumberland's betrayal, and then listens to what Warwick means as comfort:

> There is a history in all men's lives,
> Figuring the nature of the times deceas'd,
> The which observ'd, a man may prophesy,
> With a near aim, of the main chance of things
> As yet not come to life, who in their seeds
> And weak beginning lie intreasured.
> Such things become the hatch and brood of time,
> And by the necessary form of this
> King Richard might create a perfect guess
> That great Northumberland, then false to him,
> Would of that seed grow to a greater falseness,
> Which should not find a ground to root upon
> Unless on you.
> *King.* Are these things then necessities?
> Then let us meet them like necessities;
> And that same word even now cries out on us.
>   (80–94)

Coming on these lines after the more famous meditation on the cares of kingship, one nearly overlooks their curious intermingling of policy and theology. Indeed, so far as we can tell, theology has little part in the characters' intentions, yet what Henry and his minister avoid saying almost overrides what they evidently mean, for metaphor runs one way and proposition another. Turned though they are to psychological purposes, the terms of both complaint and consolation draw larger meanings in their train, for in the book, its figures, and such prophecy as gives

[29] All citations of Shakespeare are to *The Riverside Shakespeare*, ed. G. Blakemore Evans et al. (Boston: Houghton Mifflin, 1974).

figure an embodied form rest all those implications of authored and providential history that motivate Christian exegesis, whether practiced on
the Bible, the sixth age, or the Tudor myth in Shakespeare.[30]

Were these implications pursued in normal fashion, we would arrive at
the familiar conclusion that human events are the visible speech of God,
a sentence whose form is also its significance, for in conforming to the
hidden Word, each prophet ideally becomes both icon and predictive index of an unveiled showing forth, a final coming together of flesh and
spirit which will obviate the need for allegory. Those who read the promises well, and turn their own lives toward the Author's will, can be assured of some shadowy resurrection now and a better one to come; those
who remain blind to the spirit will suffer vengeance, even if left temporarily free to scourge the damnable and test the elect. Invoking such ideas
almost despite himself, Henry has warrant for unease: his competence as
reader and legitimacy as king are as much in doubt as the standing of his
soul or the intentions of his heir.

Providential history in its purest version is harder to find outside the
glossed Bible than we are sometimes led to believe. Of course there had
been no doubt since Augustine, at least, that history was the medium in
which the better city (and soul) turned away from the world, but the signs
of such conversion and reformation are generally conceived as personal
and spiritual, having to do with behavior toward the Christ in others
rather than with temporal success or its prediction.[31] Nonetheless, the
stronger and less orthodox thesis, chiliastic and by turns optimistic and
terrible, exerts a steady pressure from the Book of Revelations on, periodically surfacing as the assertion that divine purposes are coming to
fulfillment in some sort of agreement between the text of Scripture and
the signs of the present age. Sometimes this prophecy is bold and direct;
more usually it is oblique and retrospective, since few groups are so desperately alone or so stunningly dominant as to make tact unnecessary.
That the Tudor myth or the doctrine of the Elect Nation seldom receive
wholly unqualified endorsement should therefore surprise no one; the remarkable thing is how much the archetype informs sixteenth-century
thinking, whether in the relatively uncomplicated *Book of Martyrs*, the
more problematic *Mirror for Magistrates*, or the troubled histories, staged
and unstaged, of the late Elizabethan era. Whatever the excesses of commentary on the Henriad, the Queen's famously paranoid response to the

---

[30] See Tillyard's discussion, *Shakespeare's History Plays*, 330–31, which identifies this as
"the finest of all expositions" of the "general historical doctrine" expounded in his argument.

[31] Bernard McGinn, "The Significance of Bonaventure's Theology of History," *The Journal of Religion* 58 (1978): S74–75.

rebel Essex's revival of *Richard II* should be proof enough that providential history needed reckoning with.[32]

No such reading of time engages Henry and his minister, however. For Henry, the book of fate is simply a succession of pages, chance's mocks and changes overthrowing both nature and happiness. To read that book would be to despair; not to read it makes one impotent, overawed by the prescience of the king who did get at the figures (and whose speech and ceremony, we recall, kept insisting on a likeness to that Image which greater prophets imitated in their lives and deaths as well). For Warwick, still more skeptical, this last buried resonance—and the guilt it could imply—have no more force than the secular despair he sees his sick king yielding to. What Henry marvels at, he would thoroughly demystify: necessity is not in fate (much less in Providence) but in character, whose consistency stamps a man's acts so unambiguously that keen observation can seem and be prophetic. Though his words attribute animal and generative traits to history, Warwick intends to dispel even that aura of will and vitalism; the hatch and brood of time is sown neither by Nemesis nor by God, but by each man's unwillingness to mend his ways. Nestled in the rich metaphors of these lines is the mere banality this politician wants his king to hear: the leopard cannot change his spots.

To those of us who watch, however, this history is not so simple. Static individuality and random accident no more suffice to explain what happens than do the necessities of state or the cunning of statesmen: irony and pattern both forbid. The Wars of the Roses may not be that authored and meaningful history which would qualify as allegory; neither are events so manipulable as Warwick's politic optimism would suggest, or so opaque as they would seem were the only lens Henry's inability to get beyond the literal. For instance, we may not then know but we do sense that even in the midst of self-reflection, Henry misreads his own words, not only ignoring the implications of his tropes but also—as events confirm—misjudging their immediate reference, for in concluding the scene, Henry misses a microcosmic irony that undoes his intentions: "And were these inward wars once out of hand, / We would, dear lords, unto the Holy Land" (III.i.108–9).

Like the couplet into which it falls, this promise of penance is too effortless to be profound. Though the Jews had prophesied, they did not know fulfillment when it happened; and we soon discover that Henry, who had conveniently accepted the necessity that bowed the state, has

[32] See C. A. Patrides and Joseph Wittreich, eds., *The Apocalypse in English Renaissance Thought and Literature: Patterns, Antecedents and Repercussions* (Ithaca, New York: Cornell University Press, 1984), esp. Bernard Capp, "The Political Dimension of Apocalyptic Thought," 93–124.

neither remembered that Jerusalem is a room in his own home, nor fully realized that these inward wars are more than civil. His misreading lets us see that it is harder to find the necessary form than speak about it, that there is a gap between playing on the stage of the world and construing one's place in the book of life.

Urged by such implicit corrections of the player's understandings, an audience may still not apprehend the whole form of things, but it can hardly ignore the figures. We need not put on Fluellen's enthusiasm to think that Henry IV and his son operate in a world of meanings, of which each himself is one, a pilgrim with contrasting and complementary fellows in a dark wood of repeating prophecies, betrayals, and successes. As repetition accumulates, both of person and event, it assumes the character of regularity, of a hidden law with which the individual actor must strike some bargain. Yet the shape of this necessity is never clear: each of the iterations in which it manifests itself is partially counterfeit; veiled, misleading, flawed.

Part of what makes us notice such patterns is the inability of most characters to see a clear way to fit or control them. Led on by partial counsel and damaged example, seduced by apparent clarities that turn out to be the masks of some alien design, the actors of the Henriad both fail and succeed in ways that encourage our seeing them as victims or agents of intentions beyond their own. Several examples confirm this point. For Harry Percy, there is only his tergiversating father and the oracular Glendower to help him make his roan a throne, while to keep him from being true subject there is Worcester, holding back Henry's crucial offer of mercy. Percy may truly be Hal's factor, but it is not Hal who tempts or forces him to play precursor and yet fail to realize the glory that the Prince of Wales assumes. For the other rebels, when they go to kill a king, they can find only counterfeits, each—including Henry himself—as weak as Bullingbrook's title, but together as strong as the king's second body; royal policy victimizes them with a strategy that plays on metaphor in order to transcend it. For Henry himself, who initially relied on the necessity of his own will, there is now only age and dissension: a rebel most like his younger self and a son most like the depraved and giddy Richard he had dispossessed. Both inversions deprive him of autonomy, weave his intentions into a design that no single will has shaped. For the renewed rebels of Part 2, forced by the single-moving stream of time to decide which way true kingship lies, there is a dark inversion of another sort: lacking a mediating Worcester, they hear and believe Lancaster's offer of mercy, only to succumb to his unforgiving legalism. They are too shallow to sound talonic justice. Lastly, there is Hal, descending into the rev-

erend stews of that old man Falstaff, obscuring himself with all the world
so that he may renounce it, learning that prudence which Scripture associates with the world's children in order to become their wiser ruler, scan-
dalously comporting with shams and thieves in order to become, more
than ever his father could, the vicar of that King figured by the honeycomb in the corpse. " 'Tis seldom when the bee doth leave her comb / In
the dead carrion," says Henry, despairing of his prodigal (2.IV.iv.79–80).
He does not quite know what he is saying, nor do we quite know how to
take his words.[33]

Our hesitation on such a point—on any final naming of the form these
actors play—is often attributed to latent ambiguity in the text. Commonly understood as structured by dualisms, the plays appear susceptible
to incompatible explanations, as if each drama were one of those figures
that Gestalt psychologists love to tease us with, now a rabbit, now a
duck.[34] The analogy directs us to an important truth, that Shakespeare
will not easily submit to discursive translation. Yet like many other analogies, this one also sows confusion. Directing our attention mainly to the
cognitive dimension of the plays, the notion that Shakespearean reality
will accommodate contradictory descriptions is one which encourages us
to treat drama either as an object or as a statement. The results of both
new criticism and newer rhetoric may prove the usefulness of such a strategy, but the limitations are evident too, especially with Shakespeare,
whose texts do not simply present us with a describable object or a latently paradoxical assertion. It would be more accurate to say that the
tension these texts inspire in the interpreter's discourse is also one that
they embody: not a tension between cognitives, between versions of the

[33] This seems to allude to the story in Judges 14: 5–14 of Samson's killing a young lion in
whose mouth he subsequently found bees and a honeycomb. Expounding what Samson
himself calls a riddle, the *Glossa ordinaria* speaks of the kings of the world who roared before
Christ but afterwards proclaimed and defended the sweet words of the evangelists. "Ex ore
leonis occisi favus extrahitur, quia ut conspicimus reges terreni regni, qui contra Christum
ante fremuerunt, jam perempta feritate dulcedinem Evangelii praedicant, et munimenta
praebent." (A honeycomb was drawn out of the mouth of the dead lion, since as we see, the
kings of the earthly kingdom, who previously roared against Christ, now with their wildness extinguished proclaim the sweetness of the gospel and give it shelter.) *Patrologiae Cursus
Completus: Series Latina*, ed. J. P. Migne (Paris, 1844–64), Volume 113, column 531. Subsequent references to *Patrologia Latina* are abbreviated as PL, with volume and column number following.

[34] Norman Rabkin, *Shakespeare and the Problem of Meaning* (Chicago: University of Chicago Press, 1981), 34–35, which elaborates Rabkin's notion of Shakespearean complementarity, first advanced in *Shakespeare and the Common Understanding* (New York: Free Press,
1967). Sigurd Burckhardt independently offers the same scientific metaphor in his own
chapter dealing with the histories, *Shakespearean Meanings* (Princeton: Princeton University
Press, 1968), 183–84. Cf. Moretti, *Signs Taken for Wonders*: "In Shakespeare's intimately
paradoxical structure, two mutually exclusive positions appear equally real, and the same
world seems governed by two different systems of law." But Moretti conceives of the two
positions as "words impotent and actions mute" (69–70).

real, but between gnosis and praxis, between character or event as sign and as deed, between reading as a form of knowledge and as experiential (re)enactment.[35]

In other words, what forestalls our knowing how far to read the implications figured in Shakespeare's scripting of the Wars of the Roses is very like what keeps each actor in them from a perfect guess at necessity. Each sign we each encounter is also an intention, its reliability maimed not only by inherent incapacity to express the whole order of things, but by an asymmetrical duplicity as well. Though the regularity in events hints at a superordinate cause, so that individual deeds and persons acquire some characteristics of either natural signs or tokens set out by an extrapersonal will, any such order must stay latent, for it is refracted through the more evident purposes—however mistaken—of each player. The promise of readability keeps us fascinated with the action, but the grounding of that action in the motives and partial perspectives of the characters keeps the play from resolving into meaning. So rather than attribute our irresolution to some clever dividing of the audience's response, we might better argue that Shakespeare holds knowledge at bay by insisting on the equal rights of performance.

The best example to warrant this account is Hal himself. We withhold our full affection from him not so much because he fails to signify and manifest the pattern of all Christian kings, but because he does so willfully and knowingly. Insofar as his kingship fulfills a fiction of his own invention, we distrust it; it is Hal's design upon us and all the rest, an act rather than a self-effacing sign, a deliberate attempt to fuse an absent meaning with a present person. Only by forgetting Hal's self-conscious part in the plot can we take his meaning at face value; and what permits us to forget sometimes is just those parts of the pattern with which Hal has nothing to do. Yet this may include a great deal of Hal's own history, both inner and outer. Neither his consorting with Falstaff nor his subsequent reformation strikes us as adequately motivated or entirely "natural." Miracles are ceased, as Ely admits, but the means which whipt offending Adam out and put a courteous scholar in his place as much overgo mere policy and secret study as the veil of wildness outdoes the

[35] Maurice Blanchot, "Literature and the Right to Death," in *The Gaze of Orpheus and Other Literary Essays*, trans. Lydia Davis (Barrytown, New York: Station Hill Press, 1981), 59: "It is not just that each moment of language [language becoming literature] can become ambiguous and say something differing from what it is saying, but that the general meaning of language is unclear: we don't know if it is expressing or representing, if it is a thing or means that thing." As Tzvetan Todorov puts it in "Primitive Narrative," *Poetics of Prose*, trans. Richard Howard (Ithaca, New York: Cornell University Press, 1977), "Constative and performative continually interpenetrate, but this interpenetration does not do away with the opposition itself" (60).

needs and resources of princely hypocrisy. Hal defies prophecy, even his own, and can no more claim all the credit for his new life than for his daimonic success in France.

So in the end we are left with just the dilemma buried in Henry's complaint and Warwick's answer. Though we might wish either to yield ourselves to narrative pressure or else to elevate individual will to the status Harry Percy thinks it has, Shakespeare blocks both exits. Intrigue may inhibit allegory, but cannot contravene it altogether, for separate intentions coalesce in a larger design that grows to a disturbingly sharp focus in *Henry V*, where the final outcome is brief possession of the "world's best garden." Were there no subordinate plotting, no veiled intentions meant to catch up others in the actor's trope, and consequently no loss in either that mercy which even Jack Falstaff deserves or that autonomy which even a French princess ought to own, we might think ourselves coerced by some bare-faced concept, some solution to all riddles of which King Henry is the synecdochic embodiment. But we, and Shakespeare's reputation, are saved by irony, the irony of the actors' veiling and of their incomplete control both over events and over the French tongue. So the impersonal narrative which the actors draw upon and sometimes figure despite themselves founders both on their own duplicity and on that spontaneous and troublesome flesh which overflows the bounds of any script or meaning. As hypocrisy on the one hand and free play on the other, the theater triumphs over the book on which it nonetheless depends. And for that reason, the plays stay "literary," good to read because we cannot quite do so.

So far I have been talking as if theatricality always involved deceit and obscurity, as if the actor's intentions—which we cannot trust, knowing what we do about actors—regularly kept us from confidently reading Shakespeare's (or God's) will. This is only half the story, of course, for theatricality can also be a matter of seemingly unmediated vision, as is witnessed by the Renaissance habit of calling a play a mirror. John Taylor, for instance, in his prefatory verses to Thomas Heywood's *An Apology for Actors*, refuses to entertain any suggestion that theater deceives, or even works by indirection: "A Play's a true transparant Christall mirror, / To shew good minds their mirth, the bad their terror, / Where stabbing, drabbing, dicing, drinking, swearing / Are all proclaim'd unto the sight and hearing, / In ugly shapes of Heaven-abhorred sinne, / Where men may see the mire they wallow in."[36] We may wince at the old-fashioned sentiment of 1612 even more than at the doggerel; yet both could have

[36] Thomas Heywood, *An Apology for Actors*, ed. Richard H. Perkinson (New York: Scholars' Facsimiles and Reprints, 1941).

come a few years earlier from the pen of Hamlet, whose more famous definition of the purpose of playing has sometimes been taken as celebrating the new naturalism that Shakespeare helped invent. Whatever we think about Hamlet's talent for play-revising, however, his understanding of the final cause of theater differs from Heywood's only in a subjunctive, which lets us think he knows his metaphor for what it is: "to hold as 'twere the mirror up to nature: to show virtue her own feature, scorn her own image, and the very age and body of the time his form and pressure" (*Hamlet* III.ii.21–24).

Definition by ultimate purpose is in this case also definition by formal cause: one reflects nature by revealing both the feature of the atemporal and the archetypes imbedded in the present age; humanity must be imitated so that we know in both appearance and idea that man was better made than by "some of Nature's journeymen." Hamlet asks, in short, that playing be verisimilar, but in this he urges more than we usually understand by that word, or by its worn modern synonym, "realism." Of course the very notion of the mirror entails some reproduction of appearances, as we might infer from both Plato's use of the mirror as a figure for art, all phenomena and no true being, and from its long history as an attribute of Vanitas. But its equally long career as the instrument of contemplation, and the recurrent demand in Renaissance aesthetic theory that art be faithful to philosophical (and theological) realia as well as to the semblances of history, makes it certain that Hamlet's understanding of the verisimilar is best rendered by its etymology: "like to be true." Or in the phrase attributed to Cicero, theater should be both mirror of custom and image of truth (*speculum consuetudinis, imaginem veritatis*). And as we look *per speculum*, we may undergo reform ourselves, for the mirror's alignment of instant and constant has a corrective as well as a double focus. In a word, then, Hamlet's theater would be Realistic, neither a matter of crippled reading or deceitful play, but of true vision.

Shakespeare may be less sanguine than his character about the workings of drama, but *Hamlet* nonetheless swarms with action taken as revealed idea. The most famous instance is the fruit of its hero's instructions to the players, that mirror for the Danish court meant "tropically" to show Claudius his own image and practically to confirm for Hamlet that the ghost, enigmatic in status if not in counsel, had set the right historical particular beneath the universal of murderous envy. In both intentions, the theatrical mirror is a stratagem meant to unmask truth, to measure both these scheming elders by a standard which admits of no confusion between heaven and hell, and which should therefore burn away mere sophistry. Yet there is a certain contradiction here, caused just by the im-

possibility of ever shaping history to one idea, of ever representing anything except by indirect and tropic means. Thus Hamlet wants an unmixed revelation but can seek it only with a doubled instrument: in order
to expose Claudius's true feature, the play must show him someone else.
In fact, the very difficulty in making history transparent to ideas is what
enables it to be a mirror in the first place, for it is just by partial opacity
in the vehicle that reflection can occur at all: the sign of the self is always
something other, something which denies its own autonomy to give us
ours. *The Murder of Gonzago* makes a splendid touchstone for the truth of
this moral and epistemological commonplace; worthless in itself, perhaps, Hamlet's playlet lets us see, in one respect, how all plays work.
Above all else, *The Murder of Gonzago* mirrors by distorting. As history,
the play that Hamlet asks for is neither a repetition nor a passively accurate reflection of the life around it: it is a figure, something shadowing
common form in foreign substance. Though its story is factual, "extant,
and writ in choice Italian," it alludes (with unidentifiable revisions) to
present persons, while transposing their relations so as to hinder unambiguous reference. Thus even as allusion it goes on the bias: with the
Player King to be murdered by his nephew, the play looks back in victim
at Claudius's crime and forward in vision to Hamlet's threat. As representation, this "Mousetrap" is also distanced from the surrounding play,
as if its artificial couplets were meant to remind us of the gap between art
and life, to make us aware that the gestures suited to these words may be
no more like the "real" Gonzago's than they are like Claudius's. Yet the
idea may suit his flesh all the same, and that is the test. Claudius and
Gertrude are meant to see not their own faces but their true feature, to
see in *The Murder of Gonzago* what Hamlet sees in them: *exempla* of two
commonplace sins, murderous ambition and feminine inconstancy. If
Claudius also finds the dangerous figure of ambition in a nephew, so
much the better for the tormenting of his soul.

Hamlet makes no mistake about his play, however many errors he
makes in plotting out his own historical response to what the mirror has
shown. The best gauge of its true transparency, of course, is Claudius's
reaction, though only the audience sees it. The playwright within the play
sees only a strategic withdrawal, from which he infers what he will, while
we hear the first undoubted truth thus far from Claudius, who jumps
from the partial exemplum of murderous Lucianus to the false original of
them both: "O, my offense is rank, it smells to heaven, / It hath the primal eldest curse upon't, / A brother's murder" (III.iii.36–38). The modern reader may not expect "guilty creatures sitting at a play . . . to be
struck so to the soul." But Claudius, deft and hardened though he be,

knows the atemporal coordinate of his deeds: in this world, "Offense's gilded hand may shove by justice," but above, "the action lies / In his true nature" (III.iii.58–62). This is why he leaps to Cain, and why these moves and countermoves transcend the ordinary toiling of hunter and hunted: as Claudius thinks of the archcriminal, Hamlet seeks revenge for the archetypal crime. Yet in perceiving these true forms, Hamlet goes astray; nothing is perfect here below, not even villainy. Though it possess verisimilitude, *The Murder of Gonzago* is a mere play; Claudius, though unfree in soul, is consummately king.

Here is the other effect of history on ideas and the persons who seek and act them out. Though the imperfection of temporal performance is necessary to history's working as a mirror, and must be momentarily emphasized for the form to be noticed as form rather than particular, when one turns from contemplation to practice, it is easy to forget that neither actor nor action is in itself idea. One acts *upon* ideas, "plots" them out, giving temporal sequence to atemporal design; whereas one's own acts can only serve to others by abstraction as a form (except in empathy), nor can the performing self be truly known. If anyone could perfectly understand how much time is thus always out of joint, it should be Hamlet; no character in any literature outdoes his sensitivity to the distance between a role and the experience of living. Yet the world in which Hamlet finds himself so overwhelms him with mirrors that the temptation to confuse the two proves inescapable.

This excess of reflected presence is easy to show. We need only remind ourselves how many parts of *Hamlet* mirror one another besides the play within the play.[37] Laertes and Fortinbras are types of Hamlet that he himself acknowledges, Fortinbras as emblem of honor, Laertes as image of his own cause and grief. The imagined violence of Pyrrhus and the pitiable death of Priam, the feigned passion of the first player, Hamlet's own fustian soliloquy thereafter: all are glasses in which he seeks true form. In the process, circumstance and individuality go by the boards: Ophelia joins Gertrude as an icon of fickle womanhood, Yorick comes together with Alexander and Caesar as a memento of his own death, the type beneath the flesh. Always seeking the applicable universal, the unity behind proximate cause and effect, Hamlet even loses sight of the immediate issue. Laertes' having become his brother in sorrow and motive, Hamlet can finally be so moved to explanation and apology that he omits to think of those particular differences which make Laertes unforgiving, even

---

[37] For an analysis of this fact about the play which encompasses rhetoric as well, see Frank Kermode, "Cornelius and Voltemand: Doubles in *Hamlet*," in *Forms of Attention* (Chicago: University of Chicago Press, 1985), 34–63.

while he himself offers particular accident as his excuse. Yet earlier, Hamlet had seen in Laertes only his likeness in loving: a rival with whom to contend in piling Pelion on Ossa, again with utter disregard for the different circumstances of his own and Laertes' loves, and of the fact that he himself is hardly blameless in Ophelia's death. It is enough that both love Ophelia, and that forty thousand brothers cannot make up one Hamlet's sum. Painfully aware of his own individuality, Hamlet both ignores that of others and takes himself as the ideality they reflect.

Partly for this reason, we see more than Hamlet can in many of these mirrors. Seeing Fortinbras in a more general light, we finally know him for an ironically successful revenger of a father's death. But Hamlet forgets that Fortinbras like him has been deflected from revenge by Claudius. Seeing in the Polish wars only a spur to his own jaded honor, he misses the greater shared cause and thus overlooks the irony of that eggshell for which Fortinbras stakes his life, a prince even more than he the muddy-mettled John-a-dreams, self-distracted from the main issue. But there are mirrors that Hamlet cannot even see, the most important of which is the repeating series of advising elders and surrogate fathers: Claudius counseling sad Hamlet, the ghost teaching quite differently; these mirrors separated by Laertes lecturing Ophelia, and Polonius Laertes; Polonius then imparting flawed wisdom to Claudius, and finally Claudius ignorantly urging the ghost's morality upon Laertes. No character points to these correspondences, but we feel their force throughout, not however as the signs of some ordaining providence, but as the common form of error. These elders all are long in sentence but short in wisdom, their advice mortally warped by self-interest (the ghost's hatred and self-pity, Claudius's instinct for survival, Polonius's pride of knowledge) or dulled by complacency and banality. Directing all his energies to that place where action lies in its true nature, Hamlet finds no answer among these. But by looking only to the present time, his compeers fare much worse.

Finally there are in *Hamlet* mirrors of method as well as person, the archetype of which is the Polonian "assay of bias," the attempt to find by indirection where the truth is hid. It is a method familiar and exegetical, well suited to a world of semblances and repetitions. Polonius first sets Renaldo spying on Laertes by this means, then falls victim to it when he sets himself on Hamlet. Hamlet unwittingly imitates Polonius when he chooses the indirect probe of *The Murder of Gonzago* rather than some more immediate and Laertean challenge; Claudius warps even Laertes to his own devious ways as they both assault Hamlet on the bias rather than convert personal defense and revenge into the universal business of the

state. All these springes fail, only to issue in success for that uncomplicated Fortinbras who shifts open and unreasoned war from one enemy to
another, any cause for honor and ambition, and who stumbles through
no fault of his own into a claim he had abandoned. One looks into the
indirection of these mirrors to discover at last that indirection fails, while
direction works by accident. Hamlet's scrupulous and hermeneutic assays
of bias, unknowingly but very like a fool's, give way to his heir's blunt
assurance; the kingdom of the elder Hamlet accepts a new master of the
old stamp, alike perhaps in more than a habit of smiting "sledded Polacks
on the ice."

Enumerating these manifold reflections helps us see that there simply
are too many. No contemplator in the play (or out of it) can line them up,
work out one idea—however complex—on a successful narrative string:
there is too much spirit, and also too much flesh. One finally acts on
opinion rather than knowledge, not recognizing the mistake when it occurs, not understanding the trope in the mirror and of the self for what it
is. This is why Hamlet remains unable, despite so much activity, to plot
out a way to realize the form of his own canceled heritage, an idea which
is the highest mortal version of Sidney's "arkitektonikē," a thing both
inward and outward, ethical and political: kingship.[38] Perhaps the shape
in which this role presents itself is not wholly unplayable, though to be a
king by killing one is never easy, as Bullingbrook discovered, even with
his rival dying by a proxy's hand. But for Hamlet, so much more intent
on finding where truth lies and suiting action to it, the gap between ideal
heritage and temporal election proves too great to bridge. Instead of serving us as the mirror of royalty—that most social and representative of
roles—Hamlet becomes a splendidly unique particular, a mocker of all
exempla, an ironist who inhabits the undefinable space between the king's
two bodies, and who momentarily but regularly confuses realms.

This is why Hamlet's error about Claudius at prayer looms so large. It
is his first serious confusion of outer image with inner form, both his
opponent's and his own, and it is a confusion from which he never recovers the initiative. But the mistake itself is nearly inevitable: to kill
Claudius at prayer, Hamlet would have to combine the mercy of Christ

[38] Philip Sidney, *A Defence of Poetry*, in *Miscellaneous Prose of Sir Philip Sidney*, ed. Katherine Duncan-Jones and Jan Van Dorsten (Oxford: Clarendon Press, 1973), 82, defining
"the highest end of the mistress-knowledge, by the Greekes called *arkitektonikē*, which
stands, (as I think) in the knowledge of a man's self, in the ethic and politic consideration,
with the end of well-doing and not of well-knowing only." Cf. Moretti, *Signs Taken for
Wonders*: "As the one who, himself in equilibrium, provides the point of equilibrium for the
social body, the sovereign is the missing person, the impossible being in Shakespearean
tragedy" (68). For Shakespeare, he says, "the 'Christian prince,' wholly Christian and
wholly a prince, does not exist" (68).

with the vengeance of the Father, which would be to play at God rather than to be a king. And to know that Claudius only seems to pray, being therefore fair game by any count, would require a finer mousetrap than any man knows how to make. Weeding Cain's garden is simply more than history unaided by grace can undertake, and for signs of grace Hamlet never has anything better than his father's rising and his own doubtful election as scourge for Polonius's sins.

Compelled by his own vision *per speculum*—and by his sense of magistracy—to undertake this impossible task, Hamlet finds all his own devices overthrown. Each assay of bias, directed toward a timeless end, deflects him toward the gathering net of time into which he falls: his plotting ironically helps create the plot, that linked series of causes and occasions which finally kills him. His protective and investigative madness sets on Polonius and the king, who madden him in fact by making Ophelia their agent; his play forewarns his victim, and his equally fatal delay and haste, the one sparing Claudius and the other dooming Polonius, create the time and wrong which bring about his own death.

In short, every attempt to know and act that knowledge out leads to as much error as it does truth, so that even while seeing through time, Hamlet makes himself subject to its darkness. Perhaps the most poignant instance of this falling short is the late vignette with Osric. Hamlet penetrates him so easily, the puffy habit and corrupt letter of a doomed court; yet even while mocking this glass of fashion, he fails to observe the augury of his own spirit. Having spent a career in exegesis and deep plots, he gives them up when most he needs them, taking refuge in an improvident fatalism that brings on casual slaughter, making necessary a conclusion which taken on strict logic is simply the last thread in a "tangle of improbabilities, beautifully embellished and imperfectly rationalized."[39] This one time, Hamlet respects the veil too much, as before in murdering Polonius and sparing Claudius he had perhaps respected it too little.

Yet outside the errors and the plot, one somehow garners a better notion of true kingship than if Hamlet had actually been put on. In the usual manner of irony, this play offers some vision of the right way by showing up the wrong in every strategy really undertaken. All intentions are thwarted, their ultimate resolution achieved not because some deeper script exerts itself, but because the accumulation of torts and schemes can no longer be kept from bloody interaction. If the hand of God is here at all, it can only be in what the theologians call permissive rather than determinative will.[40] With so little latent providential narrative to sap our

39 Harry Levin, *The Question of Hamlet* (1959; New York: Viking Press, 1961), 8.
40 Richard Hooker, "The Dublin Fragments," in *The Folger Library Edition of the Works of*

energy in either reverence or distrust, and with the bare narrative of
events merely a recital of purposes mistook, we are still left not so much
with a sense of waste or disgust as with a perverse sense of possibility, as
if justice showed up all the more brightly in this general failure to attain
it in a just and proper way.

I have dwelt so long on *Hamlet* and the Henry plays not because I think
my readings new, but because I hope to have shown something of how
two rather different modes of presentation and apprehension are at work
in them. One is a matter of absent but effective control, real or pretended;
the other is a matter of presence, either the opaque mask of the actor or
the always invisible presence of an Idea. Both modes may be said to bifurcate, depending partly on our own interpretive focus, whether we take
the characters as persons or as signs, taking the sequence of events as the
product of the players' intentions—realized or mistaken—or as the temporal expansion of some deep design.

In the mode I have been calling "narrative," one senses some pressure
directed at players and audience alike to recognize and maybe conform to
or act upon a partly hidden will, a scripting agency which governs by and
maybe also in the persons of history. Take the represented action as a real
one, and we must call this agency by the name of providence, which sets
out opportunities for prophecy and fulfillment, which weaves a tapestry
of figures among which every man (and every woman) must seek the
form of a salvation and vocation. Take the represented action as an author's fiction; then we will incline to see it as at least some intentional
(and no doubt unwittingly ideological) account of how things are and as
at most an account verging on the allegory of the poets, where persons
move and speak with more fidelity to an author's concept than to a psyche's foreconceits and motives.

The mode I have been calling "dramatic" is commonly thought to root
itself in just those aspects of the person which poets' allegory overrides.
So it does, but in these plays at least, the expression of such motives is
duplicitous, the players' will to power setting out tropes in which other
selves may lose their way. When the act succeeds—which is to say when
no one sees the mask as mask—for a moment there may seem to be no
sign-play going on at all, just uninterpreted presence; but the illusion
soon partially recedes, for as one character falls in with another's device,

Richard Hooker, ed. W. Speed Hill (Cambridge, Massachusetts: Belknap Press of Harvard
University, 1982) 4: 129–33.

plot again begins its job of narratizing the successful lie, of making us imagine causal interconnection where in fact there is only metonymy and purposes mistook. Yet in these mistakes, in the aporetic demolition sometimes of every player's version of the difference between true and false, there can develop not only a vision of negative *exempla*, pure forms of sin and error, but also some notion of transcendent truth. One hesitates to call this vision allegorical, for there is strictly speaking no image at all, the available tropes having been ironized, each and every one. But the negative way of drama and dialogue, by directing the intellectual eye to something which conditions and enables even a failed harmony, manages occasionally to induce genuine *theoria* in a willing audience.

Perhaps the unregenerate Platonism of this last assertion will strike some readers as naive or misplaced. Though a strong case can be made for Renaissance theoreticians' having understood art in this quasi-mystical way, it may be thought too great a strain upon credulity to recommend it to moderns, especially when many have taken the Dionysiac inversion of Platonism as their special task. There is no proving anyone wrong in such skepticism, least of all when arguing from Platonic grounds, which seem to take it for granted that every attempt to justify will finally contradict itself, be shown up for *doxa* rather than *episteme*. Yet this very distinction offers perhaps the most basic way of putting the complex difference between book and theater with which this discussion has been concerned. After all, it is Plato who first makes the case against speeches, treatises, laws, and other fictions of the single voice which suppress the play of dialectic and difference, who proposes living dialogue as the better way while condemning theater above all other mimetic forms for its inability to get beyond phenomenal appearances. There is an instructive coincidence between these views—developed at the end of the only great theatrical era before the Renaissance—and those of the Reformers, Platonic not merely in their distrust of all attempts to represent what can only be known without images of any kind, but also in their faith in dialectic, in the promptings of spirit rather than in the rigor of law, which if divine can only condemn and if human can only err.

Subsequent discussion may show whether there is any use for this coincidence in devising a partial explanation of the rise of literary drama in the Elizabethan era. For the moment, it is enough to raise the question and seize on the difference between opinion and knowledge as one way of fixing the relation between theater and book. At least as they operate in *Hamlet* and the Henry plays, it seems that the book is either something lawlike to which the action conforms or some putative account of why things happen—the story which Hamlet hopes Horatio will tell, the signs of heavenly election on which and with which Henry V develops a history that justifies his claims. Like Platonic *doxa*, this mode of apprehension and rule for action is inherently provisional, based as it is on a trope or a self-presentation. The cognitive is fallible, and in actual statement, false; the performance founded on this guess may fail at any time of its effect. But not always. Episteme may be by nature inexpressible, but sometimes a hero seems to act upon it anyway; and even tragedy works to strangely luminous conclusions.

Here a glance at Aristotle may be helpful, for his attempt to pin down this last effect can serve as a springboard to the slightly different response I have in mind. For Aristotle, logical connectedness—that cross of probability and necessity upon which two centuries of criticism abused Shakespearean dramaturgy—has to do with how fate reveals its hand: the best tragedies are those in which "events replete with fear and pity" are "brought about . . . contrary to our expectation (yet) because of each other." As Gerald Else puts it, "the Tragic, the inrush of demonic powers upon a man's happiness, becomes merely the 'unexpected,' the unforeseen, and in this guise the Tragic is wedded to Causality (= probability or necessity)."[41] Fate impinges on humanity with such an overwhelming and unpredictable logic of its own that we could almost say that humanity is static and fate active. But for Shakespeare, at least, who took his education in plotting from the intrigues of Terence and Plautus and as a Christian would have understood by "happiness" something rather more ultimate than Aristotelian *eudaimonia*, plot seems to be what an individual attempts in time; and as the interaction of many such attempts, it is fortune (which may be the mask of Providence). The hero's task is to see through fortune so as to know and master a situation presented to us and to him in those dark reflections which interrupt his plotting to make the play almost a "series of separate effective actions."[42] The final end of the hero's plotting is thus to find mirrored in complementary actions something beyond them; at best, a shape of life which—given grace enough and time—seems both predictable and imitable. So the comic hero ultimately plays a perfect guess, as initially scattered images gather into one time-transcending chord; so the tragic hero falls, repeating a predicted fall, among his own shattered reflections. So on the one hand Endimion, Benedict, Theseus; on the other, Hieronimo, Tamburlaine, Hamlet,

[41] *Aristotle's Poetics: The Argument* (Cambridge, Massachusetts: Harvard University Press, 1957), 330–31.
[42] W. Creizenach, *English Drama in the Age of Shakspeare*, trans. Cecile Hugon (Philadelphia, 1916), 261, in an early formulation of what H. T. Price would later call "Mirror-Scenes in Shakespeare," in *J. Q. Adams Memorial Studies*, ed. James G. McManaway et al. (Washington, D.C.: Folger Library, 1948), 101–13.

Lear. And even in fall there is that upsurge of good feeling, more than purgative, perhaps inspired by a theatrical idea of the Good that fall makes clear by differentiation.

In sum, then, narrative is a fable of connectedness, of a seamless web which no synecdoche—itself included, if the author is mortal and honest—can properly master or represent. Drama, on the other hand, displays the face of things, or else those dark rules which provoke good metaphor, inform rich allegories, and inspire the merciless negation of all ironies that deconstruct our narrativity.[43] But if this is so, with plot on the side of metonymic narrative, and mirroring repetition on the side of drama, there seems to be something wrong with the proposal that medieval drama and medieval exemplarism are essentially "narrative" in character, for the most evident structural novelty of high Elizabethan drama is just its sure sense of interconnection, both causal and thematic, whereas the earlier drama—like the perpetual sacrifice of the Roman mass—takes timeless repetition for its founding principle. If my own tropes have not just gotten out of hand, there is still a puzzle to unfold before taking another look either at the early theater or at the literary drama which succeeds it.

It is time now to clear the air by briefly attending to an evident objection to my whole procedure thus far. Talk about "literary" or "dramatic" drama as almost generically differentiated from "narrative" stage plays may well seem to confuse categories for the sake of an obvious but naively humanistic point about Shakespeare's greatness. If not merely a synonym for writing, or *écriture*, "literariness" is a matter of canonicity; it describes the cultural use to which certain texts are put for those periods (often short, sometimes widely separated, rarely continuous) during

---

[43] Harry Berger, Jr., makes an analogous distinction in his "Text Against Performance in Shakespeare: The Example of *Macbeth*," in *The Power of Forms in the English Renaissance*, ed. Stephen Greenblatt (Norman, Oklahoma: Pilgrim Books, 1982), 49–79. Though Berger attends to the relation between the text that we read and the script that we see performed, his account of the relations between the two is like mine of the interaction between book and theater. As he says, performance "accentuates the positional status of the embodied speakers as individuals who produce and 'own' their speeches, while [textual] dislocation challenges both the private ownership of speeches and the individualism of speakers." Theatrical performance produces an effect of "ritualism and individuation," of the "collective and coercive," the "charismatic and ethical," dramatized "frequently in such a way as to create among spectators the vague uneasiness which the text intensifies and articulates." Performance asks us to submit to its spell, and the text asks us to examine the implications of that submission" (54). But as Tzvetan Todorov points out in his analysis of Artaud's theory of theater, the valencies of text and performance can be understood quite differently: he distinguishes two semantic networks, one dealing with repetition, psychology, and verbality, the other with difference, metaphysics, nonverbality. *Poetics of Prose*, 211–12.

which they satisfy hermeneutic needs. Beyond this rather circular account of how we use the word, there seems to be no good way of dividing the literary from other sorts of texts, of imagining a string of words intrinsically incapable of being treated in a "literary" fashion.

Drama, on the other hand, is probably the most distinct of all the genres, precisely because it is not entirely a matter of writing. Hard though it may be to sort out ritual embodiment from theatrical impersonation, Aristotle's definition with respect to method of imitation sets drama radically apart from every other kind of literature. "To have the persons who are imitated act out and perform everything" establishes drama as the art of doing—to drōmenon—rather than merely of saying, as mimetic rather than diegetic.[44] As Roman Ingarden observes, this methodological difference also introduces a disturbingly concrete factor into what would otherwise be pure textuality, calling the text's literary status into question by letting the player's substantiality fill the place of some of that cognitive overdetermination which is reading.[45] Concreteness, however, need not be identical with the "real," or at least not wholly so. For it is the presence of the actor that matters here. Ironist and liar by profession, but neither author of the text he or she speaks nor yet a "reliably" narrating stand-in, it is the actor first and foremost who keeps the text from being purely virtual, purely an abyss of absences and tropes, and who at the same time—as Samuel Johnson rightly insisted—keeps us from succumbing to illusion, from taking theatrical presence for the real thing.

Perhaps the fact of the actor is critical only to a reader sensitive as Lamb, or to a phenomenologist. Yet taken just as words to be read in silence like any others, the place which the actor would have filled still operates—as everyone knows—to make drama a distinctive mixture, part intentional structure and part something else, part the province of literature and part of theater, part fiction and part not. For the presence of the actor entails the absence of a narrator, or to be precise, the absence of any voice pretending to author this text, pretending to know the relation between these words and some referent, all the while covertly acknowledg-

[44] Though as Gérard Genette explains, "as far as representation is concerned, the only mode that literature knows is narrative, the verbal equivalent of nonverbal events and . . . of non-verbal events. . . . a perfect imitation is no longer an imitation; it is the thing itself." "Boundaries of Narrative," *New Literary History* 8 (1976): 4–5. See also the discussion in Keir Elam, *The Semiotics of Theatre and Drama* (London: Methuen, 1980), 110–17. Derealizing the actors (as in certain moments of Shakespearean romance, or in Brechtean theater) calls our attention to latent diegesis, to the mediating manipulation of codes which keeps us from taking the stage-action not as "a pretended *representation* of a state of affairs but the pretended state of affairs itself." For this last phrase, see John Searle, "The Logical Status of Fictional Discourse," *New Literary History* 6 (1975): 328.

[45] Roman Ingarden, *The Literary Work of Art*, trans. George Grabowicz (Evanston, Illinois: Northwestern University Press, 1973), 317–23, 377–96.

ing that its epistemological command is fictive and erroneous. If the constituting pretense of narrative is just this perpetually ironized claim to own a voice and a story which will "place" it, give it history, context, meaning, self, then the pretense of drama is the reverse: that there is no author, no governance, no dominant intentionality in the text which is played. In other words, the fundamental illusion is not so much that of being like "life," but of being *theater* in the root sense of the word, something seen (and heard) but not something "told." Describe narrative as pretended history, a point of view with some claim to privilege that permits at least the illusion of control; then drama sets up the mirror image, that all is freedom and play.[46]

This is probably why devices which emphasize theatricality are so common, invading even those plays which demand the least presentational performance possible. The curtain, the arch, the darkened house, these do as much as the celebrated *Verfremdungseffekt,* or the thrust stage, or the mocking aside, to foster the impression that "the persons who are imitated act out and perform everything," that the author and his privileges—which are the privileges of all authority outside the theater—have given way to the actor's freedom, which in essence if not in image seems to be the movement of life itself, irreverent, heady, autonomous, bound neither to concept nor to law. Actor and character, the actual and the virtual intertwined in one being: whether the conventions of the day emphasize one or the other of these inseparable natures, the pretense is just the same. It is that each actor/character speaks for him- or herself, for a reality—whether of working player or of represented character—for whom no better linguistic mediation exists, no superior point of view from which the meaning of things is clear.

Yet such a point of view seems nonetheless available, despite the pretense, or better yet, because of it: the uniquely vantaged perspective of those who watch. We are not the narrator, not even an implied one, and we are certainly no "narratee" conjured by the text. Deprived of the need to speak, we occupy the supremely privileged moment of pure cognition, leaving all performance—in the theater, even the metaphoric performance of reading—to those whose job it is. If they do it well, we gods of the gallery remain in the most flattering of all epistemological delusions, that it is others who do and we who know. Even when the actors surprise us, or amuse us, or move us to tears, we are freed from the obligation of putting our knowledge into some statement, some inadequate story of

---

[46] For quite different explorations of this fact about drama, see Jacques Derrida, "The Theater of Cruelty and the Closure of Representation," in *Writing and Difference*, trans. Alan Bass (Chicago: University of Chicago Press, 1978), 232–50, and Michael Goldman, *The Actor's Freedom: Toward a Theory of Drama* (New York: Viking Press, 1975).

the night. With neither pains nor responsibility—and here is the heart of Augustine's complaint against the stage (and probably of most antitheatricalism since then)—we have the impression of intimate knowledge without the need to exercise it and of real emotion without the obligation of a fellow to lavish care or joy upon.[47] All that courtesy demands of us by way of performance is applause, a hand and not a tongue.

Both these founding illusions can falter, of course. In fact, the first one must for the second to hold at all. One way of putting what theater is about, is to say that dramatic action shows up the actor's pretensions to freedom, proves him slavish to an unseen book, or exposes fraud in his illusion of the first time.[48] As events unfold, bringing together the partial and contrary understandings of the several players in them, each act and viewpoint ironizes every other, forcing readjustment to an authority behind the scenes which in the best instances seems more than a mere playwright could claim. The autonomy of play is always hollow; an alien will and an unperceived significance keep pressing the action into shape, leading one event into and out of another, drawing free or motivated impulse into figures and repetitions of an almost spatial sort, improvisation yielding to the ghostly paradigm of things.

If its splices and patterns are both devious and resonant enough, this spurious providence can also undermine the audience's claim to know better than the actors do. Let authority's mask slip just enough to prove it there but not enough to make the book of this invented cosmos readable, and the audience will be left with a puzzle. Aware of design, and convinced by dramatic irony that this design escapes the actor's grasp, an audience may still be unable to penetrate the deeper fiction of an authority thus confirmed as "real" in the by no means trivial sense that it preserves a hidden center. Unlike the point of origin in self-conscious narrative, however, this center seems empty but potent, rather than masked and displaced. Where the voice from which narrative springs always turns out to be an artifact of language, a hapless universal covering itself with particulars that on examination prove equally far from actuality, equally mere words, the hidden author in the script which actors play can sometimes stay outside the vertiginous orbit of textuality.

Here, perhaps, is a quasi-structuralist approach to the Platonizing con-

---

[47] Augustine, *Confessions*, trans. R. S. Pine-Coffin (New York: Penguin Books, 1961), 55–56. Jonas A. Barish, *The Antitheatrical Prejudice* (Berkeley: University of California Press, 1981), suggests that the "true meaning of the prejudice is elusive, but it would seem to have to do with the lifelike immediacy of the theater, which puts it in unwelcome competition with the everyday realm and with the doctrines espoused in schools and churches" (79).

[48] The phrase is William Hooker Gillette's, "The Illusion of the First Time," in *Actors on Acting*, ed. Toby Cole and Helen Krich Chinoy (New York: Crown Publishers, 1949), 564–67.

clusions of the previous section. The author's absence even as a persona within the work leaves a void at its center, a structuring empty space bounded by the action whose dynamic it defines and inspires. When that space stays empty, silent and unnarratized, when the conflict of interpretations inhabiting and surrounding the text stays unresolved, we imagine that we are in the presence of something *other* than text, something beyond metaphor, beyond lies sufferable only because ironized by other lies. This something other need not, however, be something higher or more spiritual; it can equally well be something more material, not demonic but chthonic: what matters is that the text perform so as to convince its audience that something has transcended the insistent but partly invisible semiotic upon which normal, pretended authority rests, outside literature as well as in it. Beneath and beyond them both, past the ken of any ego and outside the grasp of any net of meanings lies this deepest, most secretive, and perhaps most genuine of all authorities. It subsists precisely because it has no story; yet in the unfathomable book it writes, somehow it causes others to play the parts and act in their very differences as the shadows of its face.[49]

If not Platonic, then Trinitarian figures of speech beckon, even though the subject at hand is just the negative capability which Shakespeare, like Sophocles and Beckett, manifests to such an extent that his own identity seems fully dispersed among the persons of his plays, yet so distinct that it seems unmistakably his own. "Shakespeare": the metonym is not the man, but one has the odd sense of being familiar with him, despite our knowing none of his opinions, despite his being as fully hidden in his work as the Plato of the Seventh Letter claims (perhaps disingenuously) to be in his. Because these absent authorities are so strong, and yet so invulnerable to discourse, unmasterable by any teacher's program, whether Aristotle's or a Christian theologian's, or even a modern deconstructionist's, they also tend to be subversive, dangerous in the way that theater has always been, but over a vastly larger span of time. Centered in the text yet somehow circumscribing it as well, a nameless transpersonality threatens all orders and all codes; whence the nearly irresistible impulse on our part—bound to *doctrina* as teachers by profession are—to name it and claim that its allegiances are our own.[50]

[49] In what some would consider less mystified terms, one might associate this authority with the Lacanian "Symbolic," which Stephen W. Melville characterizes in these succinct and latently theatrical terms: "This Symbolic is not something one can come to have or master or be—it is the logic behind the veil, the real machine that moves the characters who claim intention and agency only through an inevitable misunderstanding of themselves and of their real position in the world." *Philosophy beside Itself: On Deconstruction and Modernism* (Minneapolis: University of Minnesota Press, 1986), 90–91.

[50] Richard Levin, *New Readings vs. Old Plays: Recent Trends in the Reinterpretation of Re-*

Fortunately for Theseus and his kind, however, such negative capability seldom displays itself. Especially at some remove of time, an author's mask usually strikes us as all too transparent: we see something of great constancy indeed, but nothing strange and admirable. Characters who might once have seemed energized by forces other than those of fiction now seem puppets of an obvious, hardly personal, but not at all subversive intentionality. Settling into patterns abandoned by those received ideas of "nature" which had once made them potent, the personages of used-up plays strike us as both amiable and forlorn. With our newer understanding of how nature is, the best we can do is play "against" such texts, intrude the actor's mystery in the place authority has fled. If this procedure will not work, there is no recourse but to forget the play, or else to "camp" it, as has recently been faddish for nineteenth-century melodrama, giving up mystery altogether as actors and audience join in self-congratulation.

The texts we can play with in this fashion, asserting the freedom of modernity, are plays which have degenerated into full readability. Because what we so easily read is an action and a set of stereotypes, nothing so articulated or complex as a string of words that has to mime the world without benefit of actors, the resulting "mere" discourse is deprived and unsubtle. Using persons for signs and counters, and naked plot for its syntax, the "sentence" such plays form seems not only unnatural, it also dehumanizes the world, cobbling it into rant and allegory.

But the allegory which thus always threatens drama is usually blind to its own character as fiction, possibly because the writer's main attention—especially in the highly plotted drama since the Renaissance—has been on exposing the characters' delusions or making their success seem probable. With the emphasis on necessities of plot, perhaps it is harder to see how even the most efficient Scribean machinery merely disguises a trope. Whatever the explanation, drama unmasked as allegory by changes in our own self-understanding is quite different from the great narrative allegories of the Middle Ages and Renaissance, and also from those modern allegories of unreadability which Paul de Man defines and describes.[51] Such plays behave in textbook fashion: persons and ideational postures so evidently correlate with one another, plot is so clearly program, that to

naissance Drama (Chicago: University of Chicago Press, 1979), and Rabkin, *Shakespeare and the Problem of Meaning*, supply all the evidence of this impulse that one could wish.

[51] De Man, *Allegories of Reading*. See Hayden White, "The Value of Narrativity in the Representation of Reality," *Critical Inquiry* 7 (Autumn, 1980): 5–27: "every fully realized story, however we define that familiar but conceptually elusive category, is a kind of allegory, points to a moral, or endows events, whether real or imaginary, with a significance that they do not possess as a mere sequence" (17–18).

take the action seriously is to feel coerced by ideology and overwhelmed by someone else's self-mystification. Perhaps this is why new comedy—Plautus, Etherege, Sheridan, Wilde—travels rather better in time than drama intended for serious: no comic playwright can succeed and be wholly mystified by the social construction of reality, those cultural habits so often undermined by the deeper ones of lust and greed. Lending sense and significance to action rather than exposing it as the expression of a hidden code (or an uncodifiable nature) is quite another matter. One generation's meaning is another's inherited and vulnerable structure, an acknowledged semiotic shedding no light on new human nature.

Revival, however, is always possible; sometimes old codes, like old fashions, stop seeming quaint and disembodied. Something of this sort may have been happening lately with medieval drama. If so, I would argue that part of the reason lies not only in the cyclic character of literary fashion, but also in the different and more explicit narrativity of medieval plays. Theirs is not the weak narrative bared by the decay of dramatic energies, but the strong narrative of a myth which is in essence not merely tropic but also tropological. Whether recounting sacred history or rehearsing fall and resurrection in the microcosm of Prudentian allegory, popular medieval drama manages to be both wholly transparent to any competent (or catechized) audience and entirely candid about its own status as provisional fiction.

By this I do not mean, of course, that medieval plays cast doubt upon the truths of Christianity. The Christian story, however, though simply and unironically told in both mysteries and moralities—as well as in gospel and homily—is in principle a story the words of which are also persons and deeds. Since the referent of these signs is by definition transcendent and incomprehensible, the medium can only be defective. Not that on any orthodox view Christ himself fails perfectly to embody the Father, but Christ is not "literally" present in the plays; he can only be recognized there or anywhere with the illuminated eye of faith. Yet in this respect, the paradox in moral epistemology that the Corpus Christi play or even *Mankind* forces upon both its audience and its actors differs in no way from the problem which the historical Jesus set his Palestinian hearers. The difficulty is not in grasping the letter but in comprehending the spirit. And the only way to comprehend the spirit is to take St. James's advice by being doers of the Word and not hearers only, for to those who only hear, Christ is a dead letter. But to perform the Word is to be "Christ-like," which is on the one hand to assume the burden of obedient self-sacrifice and on the other to confess one's own imperfection and unworthiness as a likeness of the only begotten Image, that one signifier ever perfectly adequated to its signified. In either respect, to be Christ-like is to perform penance; ideally, that perpetual penance which is very like irony in its continual acknowledgment that one's every gesture is inherently defective, whether taken as a sign or as a performance.[52]

As penitential narratives of faith and self-denial, then, mystery and morality plays are also exemplary; they invite fulfillment by the audience's seeing and doing the Word in their own lives, by their becoming to one another that mirror which Christ first provided humankind for its amendment. If these plays have also acquired some "literary" value in recent years, it cannot be on account of our ability to ignore their existential implications; we can do that only by treating them with the nonliterary detachment of the anthropologist or antiquarian. It seems more likely that their aesthetic interest derives from modern revisions of the whole notion of the aesthetic, its sublime disinterestedness having coincided with a sublimely autonomous ego, now supposedly exposed in both empirical and transcendental manifestations as a phantom in the mirror of language. Perhaps these plays work on us as a foreshadowing, but with happier moral implications, of the perpetually ironic play of signs and signals whose dissolution of an idea of humanity has come to be the humanist's last penance.

Still, this is not the literariness of a Shakespeare. For that to occur, the disjunction between the mimetic and the diegetic had to become more visible, an effect deriving in part from doubts about the ability of selves to signify the Word and in part from a new confidence in their ability to enact it, thus complicating the created world's capacity to be both book and mirror at once, as it is in Alain de Lille's famous lines: "Omnis mundi creatura / quasi liber et pictura / nobis est in speculum; / nostrae vitae, nostrae mortis, / nostri status, nostrae sortis / fidele signaculum."[53]

[52] See my "Penance, Irony, and Chaucer's Retraction," in *Assays: Critical Approaches to Medieval and Renaissance Texts*, ed. Peggy A. Knapp (Pittsburgh: University of Pittsburgh Press, 1983) 2: 45–67.

[53] "Like a book and picture, all worldly creation is a mirror to us, a faithful sign of our life, our death, our situation, and our destiny." For the complete text of the poem, see F.J.E. Raby, ed., *The Oxford Book of Medieval Latin Verse* (Oxford: Oxford University Press, 1959), 369–79.

The Body of the Sign

✻

All shifts in modern sympathies notwithstanding, the perplexing thing about late medieval theater is still its radical union of drama with doctrine. I do not mean that there is trouble believing in the orthodoxy of the nonliturgical religious stage: despite a resurgence of Marxist criticism, and our increasing awareness of the dialogic character of all texts, I would not want to claim that the plays embody a dialectical tension between official teaching and popular expression or entertainment.[1] The difficulty, rather, is the absence of such a contradiction, and of any other obvious opposition in these texts between earnest and game, high and low, or sentence and integument. In this drama, what is said and what is shown are one and the same for all who have ears to hear and eyes to see; and with no energizing differential between an outside and an inside, between a doing and a knowing, there can be no riddle, enigma, or genuine intrigue. In fact, without some gradient of interpretation—even if only a suppressed one—it is not easy to see how there can be any proper text at all. In this respect, the plays are not unlike the original kerygma, less a message to be interpreted than a disclosure that is either ludicrous and blasphemous or one that requires immediate existential assent.

An unambiguous and fully coded world, cheerfully unresistant to Christian exegesis, might seem to offer even more interpretive comfort and relief than the "classic" texts of later European realism.[2] Such relief as there is, however, should soon turn to puzzlement, for to see before one's eyes a glass with no darkness in it is by no means an orthodox or

---

[1] This is part of the claim, however, in Walter Cohen, *Drama of a Nation: Public Theater in Renaissance England and Spain* (Ithaca, New York: Cornell University Press, 1985), esp. 73–81, and in Weimann, *Shakespeare and the Popular Tradition*, esp. 49–97. For an authoritative statement on the union of drama and doctrine in the cycles, see Jerome Taylor, "The Dramatic Structure of the Middle English Corpus Christi, or Cycle, Plays," in *Medieval English Drama*, ed. Alan H. Nelson and Jerome Taylor (Chicago: University of Chicago Press, 1972), 148–56.

[2] That such comforts are delusory is one subtext of Roland Barthes, *S/Z*, trans. Richard Miller (New York: Hill and Wang, 1974).

even ordinarily didactic state of affairs. Doctrinally understood, such a
transparency should imply the restoration of that unity between flesh and
spirit which was the initial state of creation, is the revealed double nature
of Christ, and will be again unveiled at doomsday. There is nothing surprising about the proclamation of this vision, or in the fact that medieval
theater should take the figuration, disfiguring, and renewal of the original
deiformity of humankind as both its sentence and its principal dramatic
method. What is surprising is that this message should be advanced in a
way that admits so little obstacle, making fall seem perfectly avoidable
(though common) and restoration quite unproblematic, therefore making it something of a problem for us to see how such plays might have
worked upon an audience which had to know that present realities were
quite different. For in contrast to the world of these plays—as we know
from many sources both literary and otherwise—a late medieval audience's own region of unlikeness offered much chaff, little fruit, and considerable anxiety about both the temporal condition of the flesh and the
future status of the soul.

If these plays had nothing secular about them, if they engaged their
audience in liturgical rites of passage and union, there would appear to be
less difficulty, for such ceremonies plausibly claim to effect the restoration that they signify: in theological terms, they readequate the soul to its
Maker and rejoin Christ's members to his mystical body. We need not
endorse the Roman doctrine of the sacraments in order to agree that participation in the ritual process can momentarily cause the unity it represents, healing divisions, purifying the social order, recreating the *communitas* that the codes and structures of the everyday dissever.[3] But medieval
drama—although far closer to a condition of ritual than Shakespeare—
makes different claims for itself and upon an audience. Despite some distant formal analogies, the cycles and the moralities are not the Mass or
any other sacrament, nor do they pretend to substitute for these.[4] The
players imitate the Sacrifice rather than embody and repeat it; they exhort
to penance rather than perform it in any strict sense.[5] Their audience

[3] These terms derive, of course, from Victor W. Turner, *The Ritual Process: Structure and
Anti-Structure* (Chicago: Aldine, 1969). See the useful discussion of Turner in relation to
Bakhtin in Michael D. Bristol, *Carnival and Theater* (London: Methuen, 1985), 36–39.

[4] On the relationship between the ritual drama of the Mass and the representational drama
of the cycles, see O. B. Hardison, Jr., *Christian Rite and Christian Drama in the Middle Ages:
Essays in the Origin and Early History of Modern Drama* (Baltimore: Johns Hopkins University
Press, 1965).

[5] See Eleanor Prosser, *Drama and Religion in the English Mystery Plays: A Re-evaluation*
(Stanford: Stanford University Press, 1961); the discussion of the bearing on the plays of
the Pseudo-Bonaventuran *Mediationes vitae Christi* in Rosemary Woolf, *The English Mystery
Plays* (Berkeley: University of California Press, 1972), 105–302; and Robert Potter, *The*

watches rather than participates, and what it watches has little in it of that
magic which medieval sacred ritual generally traded upon.[6] Perhaps these
works could nevertheless have acted as efficacious signs of union. But
without the situational cues of the church and its ceremonies—and we
remember that the aura even of sanctuary was not always strong enough
to stop a good brawl during Mass—one would suppose that any such
union would have to derive from some interpretive process in the audience and from their shared willingness to suspend everyday tensions between cultural ideals and social practice.[7]

Interpretation cannot occur where there is no puzzle as to meaning and
application, yet these plays seem so insistent about their disclosure and its
use as to deprive an audience not only of enigma but even of the freedom
to misread, thus nearly forestalling reading (as opposed to mere decod-
ing) altogether. This is a situation that would normally be alienating
rather than engaging, and though we know that the reverse was (and increasingly is) the case, it is hard to explain why without just rehearsing
the givens of Christian doctrine that the plays themselves rehearse: to say,
in effect, that it must have been good to glorify God and teach the people
because everyone agreed that it was.[8] Without at all doubting the sincerity
of such statements—their performative aptness at official moments—one
would feel more comfortable with a less question-begging explanation.
We can *see* some of the interest and enjoyment that a medieval audience
must have felt just by looking at summer parades, Masonic pageants, and
grade-school plays, but the comparison with modern didactic fairs still
leaves explanation to one side. And to suspend the weight of medieval
didacticism by appealing to the playful and "openly unreal" character of
this drama rather violates one's sense of its genuine devotional intensity,
while to marshal the resources of patristic exegesis in an effort to complicate matters would be to draw up siege equipment against already open
gates.[9] In short, beyond requiring us to get our Christian commonplaces
in order, medieval drama has an uncanny ability to tease interpretation
with its own obtuseness and irrelevance. Thus it sets a problem oddly like

English Morality Play: Origins, History and Influence of a Dramatic Tradition (London: Routledge and Kegan Paul, 1975), esp. 30–57.

[6] For the magic of the medieval church, see Keith Thomas, *Religion and the Decline of
Magic* (New York: Charles Scribner's Sons, 1971), 25–50.

[7] Martin Stevens and Margaret Dorrell, "The *Ordo Paginarum* Gathering of the A/Y Mem-
orandum Book," *Modern Philology* 74 (1974): 50–51.

[8] Alexandra F. Johnston, "The Plays of the Religious Guilds of York: The Creed Play and
the Pater Noster Play," *Speculum* 50 (1975): 57; "The Guild of Corpus Christi and the
Procession of Corpus Christi in York," *Medieval Studies* 38 (1976): 382.

[9] For an emphasis on this drama's serious playfulness, see V. A. Kolve, *The Play Called
Corpus Christi* (Stanford: Stanford University Press, 1966); so far as I am aware, no one has
seriously attempted a patristic exegesis.

the one that certain modernist plays present: a plenitude but repeated singleness of sense baffles understanding almost as much as that relentless undercutting of code and content with which Beckett and Pinter torment their viewers (and their characters).

✳

By this point in my attempt to expose a perplexity about these plays that our own pleasure in rediscovering the intricacies of medieval Christian doctrine often causes us to overlook, several quick solutions must be clamoring for the reader's attention. The most obvious theological strategy for coping with this transparency is to deny that it is more than an illusion. Revelation these plays may be, opening the community to a true sight of its soul, to its eschatological participation in or denial of that mystical Corpus Christi which is the Church, head and members. Yet there is no revelation without attendant darkness. After all, the original of every *figura* was Christ himself, an accommodation in our mortal likeness and to our imitative capacity both of the transcendent Father and of that perfect Image which the Son has been from before all times and flesh. Thus even the Savior, though wholly true, was also wholly trope, a paradoxically revealing and concealing turn by which the Word assumed our flesh. And if Christ himself is tropical, we must perforce be more so; our best mimesis merely joins us to his Body, restoring the Image of nature, accepting the Likeness of grace, but never achieving more than a created and adoptive sonship.[10] Strictly speaking, then, the plays cannot be transparent, not if transparency implies an absence of the figurative.

Certainly it is the case that the plays continually present themselves as both tropical and tropological. They understand Christ as the creating *figura* of divinity, the saving mirror of man-(and woman-)kind, and the restorative light of the soul.[11] In Lucifer's misprision of an initially faithful yet unequal image of the Father they portray that moral and epistemological error which leads to the repeating Fall. Its effects are manifest in Satan's minions and associates, in Pharaoh, Herod, Pilate, Caiphas, and those others of Cain's city ("Som of you ar his men," says the Wakefield Garcio).[12] In one way or another from Creation on, the cycles (like the

---

[10] On the theology of image and likeness, see Robert Javelet, *Image et ressemblance au douzième siécle de St. Anselme à Alain de Lille* (Paris: Letouzey et Ané, 1967).

[11] R. E. Kaske, "The Character 'Figura' in *Le Mystère D'Adam*," in *Medieval Studies in Honor of Urban T. Holmes*, ed. John Mahoney and John E. Keller (Chapel Hill: University of North Carolina Press, 1965), 103–10.

[12] *The Towneley Plays*, ed. George England, E.E.T.S., E.S. 71 (London: Oxford University Press, 1897), 10, line 20. I abbreviate subsequent citations to this edition of the Towneley Plays as T.

moralities) forcefully elaborate the ontological pun and inherently necessary moral choice entailed by God's having first made man and woman
in his image and then having redeemed us by adopting "that selfe kynd
that thou hasse / take—[as] here nowe in this place / appeareth appert-
lye."[13] Thus when Cain's "semblant" shakes or the Tortores strain at their
work, the playwrights make it clear that "manunkind" disrupts more
than a legal "redde quod debes" by failing to return kindness for the double grace of creation and redemption: to be unkind is to deform the Corpus Christi. And when rendering the sacrifice of Abel or Abraham, or
performing works of mercy even though unaware that Christ's "poor
hyne" are his naked and hungry likenesses, man*kind* (male and female)
does more than demonstrate the fruits of election or verify God's providential scheme of history. As unkindness is forgetfulness and disfiguration, so kindness is discovery and revelation, the realization through one's
works of an ontological cause and destiny, the response to a Christ who
has his "doyng in ther mynde."[14] For this reason, we are metaphor and
potential metanoia all at once: the plays do nothing but show humankind
at this double and profoundly figurative process of fulfilling (or denying)
God's original and constant intention through the trope of works and
praise.

But in conceding and even emphasizing the explicitly figurative character of this drama, we rather aggravate than solve the problem of transparency. All we have done is elaborate a bit upon the proposition that
drama and doctrine radically unite in both mysteries and moralities, for
what the church teaches, the plays act out: Christ is, humankind was and
some of us someday will be, the faithful image and likeness of God. Difference there is and must be between one image and another, but this
difference is embodied in the action: no one urges us to mistake one of
thirty-odd actors for the really incarnate Christ. And aside from that difference, things still really are what they seem to be in these plays: all the
tropes unfold on notice into inescapably orthodox and uniform truth.

[13] *The Chester Mystery Cycle*, ed. R. M. Lumiansky and David Mills, vol. 1, E.E.T.S., S.S.
3 (London: Oxford University Press, 1974), 451, lines 378–80. I abbreviate subsequent citations to this edition of the Chester plays as C.

[14] *The York Plays*, ed. Richard Beadle (London: Edward Arnold, 1982), 184, line 94. I
abbreviate subsequent citations to this edition of the York plays as Y. The manuscript,
which Lucy Toulmin Smith in her now superseded edition follows exactly at this point,
makes clear that it is Christ who works in the human mind which mirrors him, thus preserving a point of Augustinian exemplaristic theology ("And sithen my selffe haue taken
mankynde/ For men schall me þer myrroure make, / I haue my doyng in ther mynde, / and
also I do þe baptyme take"). *York Mystery Plays* (1885; New York: Russell and Russell,
1963), 175, lines 92–95. On Augustine's conception of the Interior Teacher and the indwell-
ing Word which enables human beings to read the world, see R. A. Markus, "St. Augustine
on Signs," *Phronesis* 2 (1957): 60–83.

Since even the most ingenuous Christian would have found a fifteenth-century world much harder to read than this, one still experiences some difficulty in trying to describe how such a theater worked, to say nothing of how it might relate to the far less pellucid drama that followed and eventually replaced it.

We can meet a larger part of the difficulty by saying that the purpose of this playing is penitential and perhaps preparatory to contemplation, that it satisfies the viewer by showing up reality for the faithless and obscure trope it has become, individuals and their community alike defiled by sin, blind to the figuration that devotion patiently reveals. This account puts the line—and the crucial difference—between signifier and signified in a more suggestive place: the audience constitutes the material and active sign of which the plays are the spiritual and eternal sense. The play, in other words, becomes a reading of the world: we are the dark conceit; it is the gloss, the allegorical interpretation drawn from our literalness, literalness thereby to be purged through, in effect, an act of literary criticism.[15] Insofar as there is anything in need of exegesis and illumination, then, it stands on our side of the stage, for we are the world, gross and fashionable, to which Mankind's vices always lead, and we are the doubles of doubting Thomas, believing only in the convictions of our eyes and hands.

Thus to reverse the normal polarity of actors and audience has the advantage of giving proper weight to the prophetic aspect of this theater. Far from encouraging us to see our own reality mirrored on stage, both mysteries and moralities plainly urge us to take them as the reality for which we are the imperfect and distracted sign. When Death visits Everyman, or the bleeding Christ reappears to judge the world, God's forethought is accomplished: those who failed to observe that life inherently foretells both death and judgment are also those who have failed to notice the Christ in others. But those who believed the Sibyl's words (which are one in substance with the prophets', and which distill the essential message of all this theater) know that "he shall be sene in flesh and bone, / that kyng that is to com," and keep themselves "ffro syn and fro mysdede" (T 61–63/185–213). Like Noah, Moses, Mary, like Jesus himself, they trust the Word and make themselves its vehicles, denying various sorts of custom in so doing. We are to follow their example: with the

---

[15] For this formulation of the point, I am indebted to Charles W. Crupi. See also the subtle (but eventually too limited) account of the identity between allegory and criticism in Joel Fineman, "The Structure of Allegorical Desire," *October* 12 (1980): 47–66, and the ultimately more useful essay by Stephen W. Melville, "Notes on the Reemergence of Allegory, the Forgetting of Modernism, the Necessity of Rhetoric, and the Conditions of Publicity in Art and Criticism," *October* 19 (1981): 55–92.

Centurion, to take the truth of signs despite what Pilates say; with Mankind, to recognize Mercy in our priests.[16]

Yet to include an audience within the larger festival boundaries of the plays, though a necessary strategy for understanding them, still falls short of investing the overall situation with sufficient complexity and differential energy. A modern reader outside those boundaries still has no very precise way to get at what goes on inside them, being reduced to gestures toward the unexplained attractions of a devotion that we do not share. But this is not only the old problem about poetry and belief; it reflects the fact that on our account so far, the relation between drama and doctrine is still too effortless. After all, it is good Augustinian teaching that the world is full of signs that custom blinds us to, and that contemplation should unveil. And it is common Bernardine advice to begin such contemplation by accusing oneself of pride and sloth so as better to let the humanity of Christ draw our affections from their carnal haunts.[17] But these sayings stay dead letters if what the plays do is stage an Augustinian essence without also dramatizing something of Augustine's or Bernard's or Bonaventure's difficult and nearly erotic struggle with themselves and with the ambiguous text of things. To omit staging and inspiring that interpretive labor would be to perpetrate an idealistic fraud that could never hold a popular audience, no matter what its devotional norms. And whatever else we think about these plays, we know that they were not unpopular.

To propose an exit from this continuing impasse (which I trust is real and not just the artifact of a modern ideology that finds *différance* and contradiction in all things), I want to examine a work in which doctrine and drama are identified to such a point that the play at first seems baldly discursive, everything one always feared moralities would be, a sermon whose only claim to drama lies in being staged and whose staging only devotion could sit still for. The work in question is the one that Furnivall entitled *A Morality of Wisdom, Who Is Christ*. Since it gives us a short course in the theology and theatrics of image and likeness, it also provides an opportunity to see where the doctrine itself insists on a tension between substance and show that will help explain the undoubted attractions of these plays in performance.

The meditational design of *Wisdom* could hardly be more lucid. First,

---

[16] *Mankind, The Macro Plays*, ed. Mark Eccles, e.e.t.s., o.æ.s. 262 (London: Oxford University Press, 1969), 179, line 764. I abbreviate subsequent citations to this edition of the Macro plays as MC, MW, or MM (for *The Castle of Perseverance, Wisdom*, or *Mankind*).

[17] E.g., Bernard of Clairvaux, *On the Song of Songs, I*, trans. Kilian Walsh (Kalamazoo: Cistercian Publications, 1977), Sermon 20.6 and 8, 152–53; see also the Bernardine *Meditations on the Life of Christ*, trans. Isa Ragusa (Princeton: Princeton University Press, 1961), 260–65.

the soul receives instruction in her initial imaging of the Trinity; then
Anima deviates from Wisdom's likeness through both the suggestions of
a "galonte," Lucifer, and her inward Mights' own inclination, delectation, and consent thereto; finally, she reforms, being reminded of her
original deiformity and exhorted to perform deeds of love.[18] In the course
of Anima's progress, we learn an impressive lot of precisely articulated
theology, especially about the relation between knowing Wisdom and
doing what he wills, but we may well wonder where the drama is supposed to be. The only intrigue is Lucifer's, which succeeds too quickly.
Though the theme of the play is anagnorisis and peripety, the action leading to that Aristotelian moment focuses not on the heroine, but on her
faculties, on their gradual deformation of the pattern and telos they began
in. There is in fact no central focus even to reform, which takes place off
stage, and which is part of a process of continual displacement and transformation in which no single presence can be isolated. Like the rest of the
plot, the "crisis" is more a demonstrated incompatibility of images than
the product of human activity as we normally conceive it. As for conflict,
all there is amounts to the surrogate competition of these two images,
both veiled: the "dyrke schadow" of humanity hiding the semblance of
God within, and the gay exterior of Lucifer, who hides "wnder colors all
thynge perverse" (MW 119/166, 126/379).

Whether dramatic or not, the play of these contraries makes indisputably good spectacle.[19] Visibly elaborated, Wisdom's exemplarist theology
results not only in processions, dances, and the songs and fisticuffs of the
Three Mights, but also in the splendidly costumed transfigurations of
contemplative beauty into active vanity, ultimate foulness, and eventual
restoration as the Spouse of The Song of Songs. These tropes away from
Wisdom and back make up a richly intelligible show, miming inward
reform by setting one embodiment against and beside another. To do
this, of course, perfectly harmonizes with doctrine: the divine wisdom
took on flesh precisely in order to reform an already embodied creation
in its image. Yet this inescapable embodiment, these schemes embroi-
dered in full view upon the public face of things, finally mount up to a
first-rate moral and epistemological conundrum, a difficulty not in meaning, but in the vehicle conveying that meaning. In production, we could
see this difficulty. For these living signs of heavenly things—like all signs
of any sort—are irreducibly material. As the mere presence of the actor
implicitly acknowledges, the sentence of Wisdom may well be the soul's

---

[18] For an account of the theology behind the sequence of inclination, delectation, and
consent, see D. W. Robertson, Jr., A Preface to Chaucer: Studies in Medieval Perspectives
(Princeton: Princeton University Press, 1962), 65–113.

[19] See the discussion in Eccles xxxv–xxxvi.

exemplaristic Referent, but the soul's integument is nothing other than the body, that most riddling and ambiguous outside of all.

What drives home this point most forcefully is the costume change that signals "reform":

> Haue mynde, Soule, wat Gode hath do,
> Reformyde yow in feyth veryly.
> Nolite conformari huic seculo
> Sed reformamini in nouitate spiritus sensus vestri:
> Conforme yow not to þis pompyus glory
> But reforme in gostly felynge.
> Ye þat were dammyde by synn endelesly,
> Mercy hathe reformyde yow ande crownyde as a kynge.
>   (MW 150/1117–1124).

Our redeemed Anima does not now stand before us naked, for she is not the plain truth. Instead, she has been renewed "as a mayde, in a wyght clothe of golde gysely purfyled wyth menyver, a mantyll of blake þerwppeon, a cheueler lyke to Wysdom, wyth a ryche chappelet lasyde behynde hangynge down wyth to knottys of golde and syde tasselys" (MW 114/SD). Imagining the sheer cost of this garment, the visual impact of its "pompyus glory," then recollecting how much time, money, and corporate ego went into the undoubted splendor of the civic pageants, one suddenly understands that the text may be transparent and the image thoroughly spiritual, while the likeness remains spectacularly flesh. Indeed, the likeness in which Wisdom manifests himself is indistinguishable in glory from the "world" of which the audience is a part, and for which these plays attempt to unveil the hidden sentence. The real problem about the relation between drama and doctrine, then, is a very old one, that the means of revelation is the very flesh which constitutes our greatest obstacle to seeing and doing the will that is revealed.

In other words, the doctrine itself contains the seeds of a familiar dilemma about the relation between texts and intentions. There is no guarantee that God's image will stay stable and true in the world's performance of the text which it intrinsically is. Even when he begins by hearing God's intentions rightly, Mankind is too "flexybull" to be a faithful hieroglyphic; even when his name is strapped to his chest, this living trope "forgets" himself, warps away into something that was never meant (MM 178/741). And once deformed, only love and mercy can turn him "back"; but even then, his conformity is a "new" life, not the old and "literal" sense, but something spiritual and still unseen. Precisely this difference and problematic relation between knowing and doing makes up a crucial part of *Wisdom*'s lore. As it demonstrates, the performing part of the soul utterly disfigures the likeness of God by participating in the dance of the world and can be reformed only through penance. Knowledge (confession by and to the image) cannot cleanse the soul without the re-unifying work of the heart (restoring the likeness through contrition and satisfaction): there must be sorrow for sin and Christ's passion, and love deeds to one's neighbor and to God. Like the other moralities, *Wisdom* merely tells us what these deeds should be; it does not show them in the performance, but only through their result, the new-clad soul. In this sense, it gives us no more than a negative example by which to recognize deviation. Yet the very possibility of this recognition and confession depends upon a kind of certainty about the original image—and our analogous embodiment of it—that modern theorists of the text could find naive only if they mistook this "original" for something nonfigurative. For in this play's account of the faculties of Anima, the strictly cognitive part always remains that accurate (albeit implicitly troped) image conferred in baptism, even though darkened and masked by subsequent sin. Thus Mind can always mirror Wisdom when he calls, and turn from the sin of "Mayntennance" back to his own nature. But since the restored likeness (as well as Wisdom's appearance throughout) is so extravagantly physical, a skeptic (or Protestant) might think neither one truer than any other errant trope. After all, plain truths and gilded lies, or love and vanity, can no more be distinguished by appearances than a good disguise from a bad one, or a philosopher from a sophist. What can tell you the difference—so Wisdom says—is "gostly felynge," but that, however easy to be glib about, seems impossible to show on stage; like the precise moment of conversion, it is a mystery known only to the spirit (MW 150/1122). No true Platonist would ever try to stage "gostly felynge": he believes that gross incarnation merely swamps the uninstructed soul while giving no pleasure to anyone who understands. Yet this clerical medieval Christianity insists on theater, on likeness in addition to image, works as well as faith, action as well as contemplation, trusting to the spirit to guide humankind toward perfectible disguising rather than damnable.

We moderns, on the other hand, have no trouble with a continually tropic likeness; what dismays us is the notion of perfectibility. If we are to read these plays attentively, then, we must grapple with their theology on our own terms, denied the abstract refuge of historicism. To do so, we must suspend for a moment our certainty that everyone in medieval England "knew" (or should "learn" from this drama) what was true doctrine and what was false, what was of God and what from the world, flesh, and devil. For sorting these out was (and is) just the problem at hand. It is no good getting round the problem of staging "gostly felynge" by pointing to the preachy parts of both mysteries and moralities. I have already argued that the homiletic holds universal sway in this theater. But even if one could segregate drama from doctrine, the real problem is how one goes about acting out what everyone knows. After all, this is the dramaturgical problem faced by these anonymous playwrights, and it is also the moral problem at the center of every play, how to fulfill what we know, when what we know is a paradox, that reality is all figurative, and that the flesh has been redeemed. To put it most concisely, the problem is just how to make theater out of the Book.[20]

In enacting the Book or seeing God in his creation, one wants to avoid either idolatry or an undiscriminating natural theology. What this means in practice is that some way must be found to hold two incompatibles in constant view: that the regenerative *figura* is everywhere available and that the creating Word is continually veiled, betrayed, and crucified. Like the active Christian (and for the benefit of any who care to be contemplative), the medieval playwright had to find techniques that could ironize visible reality, not in a way that would yield intellectual abstractions—the gnostic and ultimately specious transcendence that retreats from a doomed creation—but in a way that would vivify the incarnate Christ. Putting these constraints in slightly different and perhaps more suggestive terms, we might say that the playwright had to focus attention on the body of the sign, for it is the body which is redeemed and resurrected in Christ; yet that body had also to be presented in a way that would prevent its becoming an idol.

To speak about the body of the sign seems by an easy and I hope not simply perverse association to draw the analysis toward modern teaching about the nature of poetic as distinct from other sorts of language. Since Jakobson (if not really since Kant and Coleridge) it has become conventional to understand the aesthetic as a kind of semiotic process which focuses interest at least as much upon the vehicle as upon the "content" it conveys.[21] One describes the specifically "poetic" as a kind of overcoding, a surplus and redundancy of discriminating features which in a sense "redeems" the medium by articulating it beyond communicative needs, thus unexpectedly refining both our model and the "reality" it gives us. Once the process of overdetermination reaches a sort of critical mass, it can

---

[20] By putting the case in these terms, I do not mean to deny the catechizing function of these plays. No doubt—as demonstrated by the famous anecdote about the old man in Chester who knew nothing more about Christ than something vaguely recollected from the plays—many rural English men and women needed these plays for religious instruction, especially given the absence of catechetical programs for children. See W. A. Pantin, *The English Church in the Fourteenth Century* (Cambridge: Cambridge University Press, 1955), 242–43 for an account of the plays' connection with a larger educational program.

[21] For an eclectic but reliable account of this understanding, see Umberto Eco, *A Theory of Semiotics* (Bloomington: Indiana University Press, 1976), 261–76.

acquire momentum of its own, so that the vehicle becomes a continually unfolding veil, structured in its possibilities, but unendingly reconstituted by an ongoing (and historical) dialectic of iconoclasm and iconophilia. On this account, differentiation—the embodied play of semiosis—is the ultimate subject matter of everything aesthetic, and the residual subject matter of everything else, all "texts" being in the last analysis about "textuality." Similarly, by the medieval account of human figuration, every body can be said to be "about" embodiment, the old man dying and the new reborn in a process which unfolds from "glory to glory" with the divine *figura* as its ultimate and infinite limit.[22]

The usefulness of this comparison lies not in its inspiring us to hunt aestheticism where none exists, but in bringing out a self-referentiality crucial to the workings of this theology and of the theater which expresses it. The "self" referred to, of course, is one of the two hidden images manifested by the likeness of one's deeds. The oppositional binarism here is absolute: since everything reduces to one or the other, all variety in the likeness is strictly gratuitous, an overcoding which makes no difference to the "message," though it does—at least in the case of the just—make for marvelous and engaging variety. But this message itself is really a choice between two conceptions of the vehicle or text: Satan's is self-referential in a way that permits no escape from the given; the self referred to (his "own") claims in Augustinian terms to be not *res et signum*, but *res tantum*, a nonfigurative reality.[23] Thus for Lucifer, the chain of reference closes, locking him (and his likenesses) in narcissistic rant that tries to guarantee distinctness, independence, and preeminence. But the image which is Christ's is by definition open and figurative, not literal; it is an image of union (as opposed to the fragmentation of fallen human beings and fallen angels) in which his members, being each both *res et signum*, refer (like the *Corpus Verum* itself) not to given things, but to the giving, to the mystic Corpus Christi and to the unencompassable Trinity which is the cause and object of all this figuration.[24]

To sharpen this distinction, two points. First, Satan's "colors" hide the

---

[22] For an account of this dialectical askesis at work in the letters of St. Paul, see Norbert Hugedé, *La metaphore du miroir dans les épitres de saint Paul aux Corinthiens* (Neuchatel: Delachaux et Niestle, 1957).

[23] Markus, "St. Augustine on Signs." See also Johan Chydenius, *The Theory of Medieval Symbolism*, Commentationes Humanarum Litterarum (Helsinki: Centraltryckeriet, 1960) 27: 5–42.

[24] See the discussion in St. Bonaventure on the referent of the Eucharist. *Opera omnia*, ed. A. C. Peltier (Paris: Ludovicus Vives, 1864–1871), *Sent.* 4, Dist. 8, P.2, A.2, Q.1. Given the Franciscan origins of so much medieval drama, it seems appropriate to cite Bonaventure here rather than St. Thomas. See David L. Jeffrey, "Franciscan Spirituality and the Rise of Early English Drama," *Mosaic* 8 (1975): 17–46, and Robert D. Marshall, "The Development of Medieval Drama: A New Theology," *Studies in Medieval Culture* 4 (1974): 407–17.

figurative process; but to "put on" Christ is to revel in *figura*. Thus one disguise lies about its tropism while the other admits it; this admission is the essence of "gostly felynge." Second, Satanic colors are necessary, but Wisdom's are gratuitous and free. Satan, in other words, has a "plot"— and so do Cain, Herod, Caiphas, New-Guise, Nowadays, and Nought— which is to advance themselves, to get ahead in the world by putting one over on somebody. Christ, on the other hand, has no need to put on flesh: the likeness of his humanity simply overcodes the Image so that we can read it, and what we read is an attitude toward the textuality of things. Similarly, those who conform themselves to Christ have no earthly reason to do so. Abel's sacrifice, like Abraham's, is gratuitous and unreasonable; so is Joseph's loyalty to Mary, the Virgin's purification in the temple, John's baptism of his Lord, and the Magdalene's anointment of the One who suspended the law for her and our sake. Christ's response (to Judas) on this last occasion emphasizes the extravagant character of all supererogatory works: they celebrate the grace of embodiment through an act which is equivalently free and needless, an act which participates in the foolishness of God that is stronger than the wisdom of men, "Pore men xul abyde / A-geyn þe woman þou spekyst wronge / And I passe forth in A tyde / Off mercy is here mornyng songe."[25]

Such a gesture, and Jesus' response to it, underscores a certain doubleness in all embodied love-deeds. Anointing the Christ can signify both Godhead and mortality, but the Magdalene's archetypal work of mercy is not ambiguous.[26] Instead, it points beyond either "referent" to the paradox of their union, the conjunction of opposed values which is the body of the sign, a global whole that transcends discriminating features. Demonstrating both her sorrow as sinner and her gratitude as one saved, Mary's gift (and this theater) equally memorializes the presence and the absence (both impending but both accomplished in prophecy and figure) of the flesh that manifests God. But to signify contradictories is to go beyond codes and meanings altogether: with everything pointing at last to the sign of signs, to the difference between eternal *figura* and dead literality, all other differentiation is suppressed. Before God's face, "All shal be les and more, / Of oone eld ichon" (T 62/188–89). To suppress distinctions by rendering them ultimately meaningless is not, however, to create dull uniformity. Released from normal duties of signification, ordinary

---

[25] *Ludus Coventriae; or, The Plaie called Corpus Christi*, ed. K. S. Block, E.E.T.S., E.S. 120 (London: Oxford University Press, 1922), 249, lines 522–25. I abbreviate subsequent citations to this edition of the *Ludus Coventriae* as LC.

[26] *Glossa ordinaria*, PL 114.167: "Haec devotio Mariae fidem significat Ecclesiae, quae dum deitatem Christi praedicat, caput ungit: dum humanitatem, pedes" (Mary's devotion signifies the faith of the Church, which while proclaiming the divinity of Christ, anoints his head, and anoints the feet while proclaiming his humanity).

tokens of rank, sex, place, and purpose do not disappear but instead become material for that regenerative delight which characterizes religious—as well as aesthetic—contemplation.[27] Rendered wholly figurative, radically compromised in its ability to say anything definite or enduring, customary semiosis ceases to matter *except* as spectacle, as praise of the only being who needs nothing at all. By comparison, normal reality is exposed for the sham and game it has always been secretly known to be. What remains real is charity, the open *figura* at the center, the tropic body that all this spectacle glorifies. And to let that spectacle be, without wanting to possess it or trying to make it redound to one's own significance, is to approach the perfected likeness which is Christ's.

In opposition to the charity that overcomes division and ownership, *cupiditas* thinks that it knows what everything means; it has a single-valued logic of exchange, a law which would parcel out the ointment or the garment according to its use and value. Such literal-mindedness, however, receives its just rebuke: Judas kills himself, Humanum Genus ends up willing his goods to "I Wot Neuere Who," Pilate exercises droit du seigneur over the dicers' undivided prize. Cupidity is always a threat, even to the just: Christ must chastise the disciples for disputing over precedence, and to the Peter who takes foot washing at face value ("Wasshe on my lorde to all be wete" [Y 229/55]), he must explain that it is not this specific deed but the embodied repetition of his mercy that matters, "Euer for to ȝeme in ȝouþe and elde," on the pattern of a lordship manifested in humility (Y 230/66). Customary semiosis works against such lordship; what counts *toward* it is a moving figuration that transcends the boundaries normally distinguishing high from low, innocence from trespass, pure from impure. This does not mean that good and evil are confused or that justice is abolished, but it does mean that merely human conceptions of guilt and innocence can only figure the everlasting Judgment, when it shall be clear "which bodyes, lord, that benne thyne" (C 456/506). Mercy thus prepares us for justice as death prepares us for life, by breaking idols, all those "barres and bandys" in which the devils keep Adam's kin (T 299/190): it is, we might say, a dehabituation of reality that comes from God and which must be returned to him through our own "mornyng songe." Yet Mercy itself is not boundless. "To truste ouermoche in a prince yt ys not expedient" (MM 182/846), even when this prince is one who "had neuer harbor, house, ne hall" (T 297/139): "In þis present lyfe mercy ys plente, tyll deth makyth hys dywysion; / But whan

---

[27] Cf. Augustine on the material being of the body in heaven: "Caetera ergo membra nostra erunt ad speciem, non ad usum; ad commendationem pulchritudinis, non ad indigentiam necessitatis" (As for the rest, therefore, our members will exist for form, not use, for the praise of beauty, not for the requirements of necessity). PL 38.1145.

ȝe be go, vsque ad minimum quadrantem ȝe schall rekyn ȝour ryght"
(MM 182/861–62).

Pursuing the implications of exemplarist theology, then, leads one to
think that doctrine and drama—or image and likeness—must stand in a
relation both of tension and coincidence. To properly describe that relation, we might say that what the plays teach their audience is the faith,
while what they do is direct that audience's gaze continually upon the
body as body, before and in a sense beyond the final separation into sheep
and goats. This would suit one's sense of these plays in performance,
where the dramatic union of spirit and flesh seems to engage us not first
with what it *signifies*, but with its variety, its irrelevant excess, its mortal
haplessness and beauty, its awkward but unending capacity for figuration, its participation in a unity that mocks the limits of merely cultural
convention. Yet this oneness beyond all differentiation is also *what* the
body signifies, mystically understood. The Corpus Christi is Mankind,
the integument of the Word, the Bride who is *negra sed formosa*. And the
interpretive labor which effects this union and this vision—the labor
which fulfills what we know by making the Word visible in *figura*—has
to be nothing other than that self-and-world-displacing work of love
which manifests the Christ within and which rectifies all tropes. As I will
try to show in the next section, the doctrine of good works is not merely
a matter for exhortation: understood as an activity of displacement, it
governs the setting, the incidents, and the dramaturgy of the surviving
English medieval theater.[28]

On the subject of making oneself capable and worthy of seeing God,
Gregory the Great observes that it is necessary to follow the example of
the *peregrini*, who recognized their Lord not while speaking with him,
but while giving him food. Gregory then draws the moral to an almost
epigrammatic refinement: "ad mensas vestras Christum suscipite, ut vos
ab eo suscipi ad convivia aeterna valeatis."[29] Though the immediate audience of this homily was monastic, the precept of hospitality extends to
Christians generally, for the religion rests upon an exhibit of revealing
charity recollected in a feast. The social scientific explanation for such

---

[28] At least for the London plays, even the performance was conceived as an act of charity,
if one accepts E. K. Chambers's inference from the 1442 charter of the Guild of St. Nicholas
of Parish Clerks, referring to "diversis charitatis et pietatis operibus per ipsos annuatim
exhibitis et inventis." *The Medieval Stage*, 2 vols. (London: Oxford University Press, 1903)
2: 381.

[29] "Invite Christ to your tables, so that you may be worthy to be invited by him to an
eternal banquet." PL 76.1183.

behavior is rather more drab, but wholly consonant with all but the supernatural aspect of Gregory's teaching: in order to re-create a people's sense of moral and spiritual unity, it is necessary to set aside prudence and self-interest, to restore society to itself through communal exercises of sacrifice and praise. Such occasions can come about only through some process of self-denial, not only because they cost money that might otherwise be spent on oneself, but because an individual must suspend his "own" pursuits in order to partake in the collective feast. Yet the festivities themselves are anything but ascetic. In fact, a certain extravagance usually characterizes them, as if to suggest not only that everyday limits will yield only to spectacular energies, but that those energies themselves are more fertile, more polysemous, and less susceptible to rationalized expression than normal life and symbolism admit.[30] And set in the context of the communal year, the mystery plays (and probably the moralities as well, if we knew more about the circumstances of their production) constitute just one extravagance among many.

In Coventry, at least, the Corpus Christi processions and pageants were the overture to an eight-day fair that might come as late as midsummer, and these festivities were themselves the climax of an intensive half year of ritual and celebration begun with Christmas and its ceremonies of inversion and exchange. Thus the high point of the city's economic activity coincided with a festival that concluded a long period of purifying and reintegrative measures. Charles Phythian-Adams's study of the town whose name became synonymous with the "genre" of the Corpus Christi play can serve as a reasonably sure guide to what happened elsewhere, for it is not likely that a community recognized by contemporaries as so typical in this one respect would be utterly divergent in others.[31]

---

[30] See, for instance, Emile Durkheim, *The Elementary Forms of the Religious Life*, trans. Joseph Ward Swain (1915; New York: Free Press, 1965), 337–92, and Lewis Hyde, *The Gift: Imagination and the Erotic Life of Property* (New York: Vintage Books, 1983). John Bossy suggests that much "eucharistic feeling" had been transferred, "especially in towns, where parochial feeling was often rather weak, away from the annual communion at Easter on to the brand-new feast of Corpus Christi." *Christianity in the West, 1400–1700* (Oxford: Oxford University Press, 1985), 71.

[31] Charles Phythian-Adams, "Ceremony and the Citizen: The Communal Year at Coventry," in *Crisis and Order in English towns, 1500–1700*, ed. Peter Clark and Paul Slack (Toronto: University of Toronto Press, 1972), 57–85; *Desolation of a City: Coventry and the Urban Crisis of the Late Middle Ages* (Cambridge: Cambridge University Press, 1979). See also Mervyn James, "Ritual, Drama and Social Body in the Late Medieval English Town," *Past and Present* 98 (1983): 3–29, and David Harris Sacks, "The Demise of the Martyrs: The Feasts of St. Clement and St. Katherine in Bristol, 1400–1600," *Social History* 11 (1986): 140–69. In some respects, of course, the cycles and their settings did differ from one another, in ways that my discussion necessarily elides. Martin Stevens distinguishes between the "city drama" of York and the "town or provincial drama" of Wakefield, N-Town, and Chester, arguing that this distinction helps account for the more compact, derivative, and in some senses more controlled and unified structure of the latter cycles. *Four Middle English Cycles:*

What that study demonstrates is that the medieval urban year divided roughly in two, a "secular" half extending from late June to the preparations for Christmas, and a "religious" half extending from Christmas to the set of moveable feasts which culminate in Corpus Christi and Midsummer. This differentiation should not be seen as absolute: its chief importance lies in indicating that the cycle of the whole year repeats and embodies a fundamental distinction that the ceremonies of the religious moiety depend upon and at the same time undermine. This distinction is the one that Victor W. Turner calls the "liminal" as opposed to the "juridical"; since liminality has to do with rites of passage and inversion, it seems essentially the result of the process I have called displacement.[32] Throughout the season of "extraordinary" time, the city engaged in periodic activity which reestablished its social and political norms, abstracting them from everyday application in order to purge the inequities and obvious falsification produced by any code, whether of behavior or cognition.

Well-known folk games made up an important part of this activity: especially the Hock-Tuesday combats and the May Day rounds, one using "the anonymity of a *generalized* division of the sexes to reverse temporarily the *in*equalities existing between married men and women," the other emphasizing unmarried equality and generalized sexual attraction as the prelude to a ritual pairing of "Maides and their Makes."[33] The Christmas Lord of Misrule, the Shrovetide King of Christmas, the Maundy Thursday washing of pauper's feet, the extensive feasting at the expense of those in positions of age and authority, the several public ceremonies that formally interrelated separate groupings of the social structure: all these occasions suspended the norms of medieval urban life, offering symbolic redress to the separate or inferior, assuaging the guilt of those with wealth and power, and generally demonstrating the provisionality of all types of rule. Even the rigors of "clean" Lent would have pro-

---

Textual, Contextual, and Critical Interpretations (Princeton: Princeton University Press, 1987), 28–29. It is no doubt significant for the history of English drama that London was the most important exception to the practices otherwise typical of county towns, its cycle plays having been performed by professional actors and their occasion of playing having no connection with the feast of Corpus Christi or the craft guilds. The tensions that the Corpus Christi plays normally express and symbolically transform had in London been suppressed when the urban oligarchy solidified its rule in the late fourteenth century. James, "Ritual, Drama, and Social Body," 23–25.

[32] See especially Turner, *The Ritual Process*, and with Edith Turner, *Image and Pilgrimage in Christian Culture: Anthropological Perspectives* (New York: Columbia University Press, 1978). For the process of displacement, a Freudian notion which Lacan associates with Jakobsonian metonymy, see Jean Laplanche, *Life and Death in Psychoanalysis*, trans. Jeffrey Mehlman (Baltimore: Johns Hopkins University Press, 1976).

[33] Phythian-Adams, "Ceremony and the Citizen," 66–67.

duced this leveling effect, not by suspending rules, but by enforcing a
class-transcendent purity. During the second half year, however, what
received emphasis was not the corporate body of the city, but those necessities and structures which surrounded and divided it: town authorities
rode the common fields, sheriffs for the county were designated and
sworn, officers were elected within the craft and parish guilds, and the
productive labor of harvest and commerce went on with relatively little
ceremonial interruption.

The single most elaborate festivity of the first half year was probably
the Corpus Christi procession, pageants, and fair. One might even argue
that this extensive devotion to the Body of God would have offered medieval Christians a better opportunity to participate in *communitas* than the
Eucharistic rite itself, which by the later Middle Ages had become too
much the exclusive property of clerics and too much the occasion for a
rather alienated and subjective piety on the part of the laity. In these mid-
year celebrations, there was no rood screen, nor anything remotely
equivalent.[34] As Phythian-Adams notes, even the order of the Corpus
Christi procession worked to emphasize corporate unity, for the arrange-
ment was "based not on a system of precedence reflecting some *economic*
class division of society (which might, for example, have allotted an inferior position to the handicraftsmen), but on occupational groupings
whose order was determined apparently by the contribution of each to
[largely unremunerated] civic office-holding."[35] Since the order of the
pageants would not have been identical with this order of procession, especially when and where the two occurred on separate days, even the
civic structure would have suffered some diminution in importance. With
guild responsibilities for the pageants shifting and amalgamating from
year to year, with some pageants (and in some localities the whole sequence) produced by organizations less directly connected with economic
or political structures, and with most crafts being particularly suited to a
given play with a fixed position in the narrative (as the shipwrights to the
Ark-building or the taverners to the Wedding at Cana), several different
hierarchies would have been asserted, intermingled, transformed, and re-
confirmed during the course of events. No doubt there was competition
as to which groups could put on the Corpus Christi in the most obviously
supererogatory way, but even this display of wealth—though advancing
the company's and the city's worship by conspicuous expenditures made

[34] J. A. Jungman, *Pastoral Liturgy* (New York: Herder and Herder, 1962), 67–76; Clifford
Davidson, "Northern Spirituality and the Late Medieval Drama of York," in *The Spirituality
of Western Christendom*, ed. E. Rozanne Elder (Kalamazoo: Cistercian Publications, 1976),
125–51.
[35] Phythian-Adams, "Ceremony and the Citizen," 63.

possible by the burgeoning economy of the late fourteenth and fifteenth
centuries—would have also been ironized by the substance of the plays
themselves, as well as by the memory and threat of those plagues and
depopulations which had helped bring this wealth into being in the first
place. The Mercers, for instance, should have been among the richest
companies in York, but their staging of the Last Judgment inevitably emphasized the transience of wealth and the need to expend it in a nominally
disinterested way, for the greater glory of God and the corporate whole.[36]

To pursue this sort of argument much further would require closer
analysis of a larger body of evidence about the context and details of medieval productions. Subtler conclusions will no doubt be put forward as
more records are systematically published and made available for comparative study. Even this cursory and derivative account of urban conditions, however, makes it clear how much the medieval theater was part
of a larger social practice that strove to readjust and reconcile, an intention
aptly symbolized for all by Aberdeen's custom of having its Haliblude
play directed by an "Abbot of Bon Accord." Generalizing from surviving
records of performance, it seems unlikely that any of the noncycle plays
saw production outside some festive and social setting, whether under
corporation auspices (as when the York Creed Play was presented for
Richard III on the eve of his son's investiture as Prince of Wales) or
through the sponsorship of an individual guild or magnate (as with guild-
hall plays or the indoor drama that Cardinal Morton encouraged).[37]
Without in any way romanticizing such activity, we have to see it as more
than mere entertainment or abstract didacticism: like the guild system
itself, such festivals express an ideal of collective unity in a way that subsequent divisions between "a ruling class of merchants . . . and a dependent class of small master craftsmen" and wage-laborers would eventually make impossible.[38] Just as the parish guilds of the city operated to

[36] Alexandra F. Johnston, "The Procession and Play of Corpus Christi in York after
1426," *Leeds Studies in English* n.s. 7 (1973–1974): 55–62; Carolyn L. Wightman, "The Genesis and Function of the English Mystery Plays," *Studies in Medieval Culture* 11 (1977): 133–
36.

[37] Chambers, *Medieval Stage* 2: 333; Johnston, "The Plays of the Religious Guilds of
York," 61. Lawrence M. Clopper, " 'Mankind' and its Audience," *Comparative Drama* 8
(1974–1975): 347–55, suggests private and learned auspices even for this play, which has
usually been taken as typical of a commercial public repertoire.

[38] See George Unwin, *The Gilds and Companies of London*, 2d ed. (London: Methuen,
1925), 254. For a contrasting view, see Raymond Williams, *The Country and the City* (Oxford: Oxford University Press, 1973), 31: "A charity of production . . . was neglected, not
seen, and at times suppressed, by this habitual reference to a charity of consumption, an
eating and drinking communion, which when applied to ordinary working societies, was
inevitably a mystification." And as David Harris Sacks suggests, the guild organization and
its economic policies were in the later Middle Ages not so favorable to certain groups (es-

unite neighbors with bonds that transcended kinship ties, and the trade guilds with bonds that transcended age and economic status within the craft, so these celebratory plays helped manifest a still less bounded corporate identity. John Stowe's description of the summer bonfires of medieval London makes a nice figure for the spirit of medieval theater, which like the bonfires had by Stowe's time largely been suppressed or replaced, for all these activities constituted a similar obstacle to the new ways:

> In the months of June and July, on the vigils of festival days, and on the same festival days in the evenings after the sun setting, there were usually made bonfires in the streets, every man bestowing wood or labour toward them; the wealthier sort also, before their doors near to the said bonfires, would set out tables on the vigils, furnished with sweet bread and good drink, and on the festival days with meats and drinks plentifully, whereunto they would invite their neighbours and passengers also to sit and be merry with them in great familiarity, praising God for his benefits bestowed on them. These were called bonfires as well of good amity amongst neighbours that being before at controversy, were there, by the labour of others, reconciled, and made of bitter enemies loving friends; and also for the virtue that a great fire hath to purge the infection of the air.[39]

The redundant, repetitive, and from a certain point of view superfluous character of these pre-Reformation festivals had its counterpart everywhere in the narrative detail of the mysteries and moralities. Their image of union and their message of conversion and repentance permeate the action to such a degree that the cognitive effect is of a sameness relieved only by variety in the vehicle. This drama glorified the One by making an audience see Christ in the many (and the need for his mercy) beyond any need of teaching except the essence of that teaching, his excessive presence increasing with each reading or viewing of the plays. What enables that presence, however, is the figurative displacement that evacuates substance from nominally authoritative forms. To displace, in fact, is to perform the likeness and assert the need of mercy: on the one hand, to reembody Christ through a free motion of submissive love; on the other, to let the unbounded body disrupt that limit. The difficulty in illustrating this process, not surprisingly, is to set some limit to one's sample that will not tire the reader's patience. Where the message is redundant, so is the sample, yet some sampling is necessary even to show that snow is white.

The most crucial displacement and most fundamental redundancy, of course, is the resurrection itself. Like the moment of Anima's restoration,

pecially cloth workers), which might therefore have withdrawn their support from both civic ceremony and its religious underpinnings. "The Demise of the Martyrs," 165–69.

[39] John Stowe, *The Survey of London* (London: J. M. Dent and Sons, 1956), 92–93.

the "historical" event finds expression not in some masquelike twinkling of an eye, but in a lyric on the Corpus Christi and the works of love. The Wakefield play illustrates this best. After the angels sing "Christus resurgens," Jesus exhorts all sleepers to awake: "Sen I for luf, man, boght the dere, / As thou thi self the sothe sees here, / I pray the hartely, with good chere, / luf me agane; / That it lyked me that I for the / tholyd all this payn" (T 315/292–97). One gives witness to the empty tomb through one's own renewal, exhibited by recognizing and returning mercy to the risen lord; thus the Wakefield play appropriately concludes with the hortulanus episode, Christ calling upon Mary Magdalene to respond to his figure: "woman, woman, turn thi thoght! / wyt thou well I hyd hym noght, / Then bare hym nawre with me; / Go seke, loke if thou fynde hym oght" (T 323/577–80).

As the *Glossa ordinaria* suggests, Jesus here tries to force Mary past her own misconception: he asks whom she seeks not because of his ignorance, but because of hers who looks for one taken away rather than for Christ.[40] Metanoia must precede the recognition of Christ in the flesh, for the disguise he adopts is one that both accommodates itself to human vision and provokes our moral exegesis: "talem se exhiberet oculis corporis, sicut dicit Gregorius, qualis erat coram oculis mentis."[41] But when the heart refuses any possibility of embodiment, Christ in his "own" body has no greater impact: they may touch, even as Pilate who "that lad has all to-torne" (T 306/18), but never see; Mary finally sees, but this time may not touch. Bernard says that this discipline is to help elevate her thoughts to heaven.[42] On stage, however, not to touch the gardener lends mystery to a "body" that is particular and placeless all at once, making it an occasion of mingled joy and pain such as no lord can ever be who thinks, like Pilate, "to abyde, and not to flytt" (T 306/5). Rather than try to hold fast to this person and this moment, Mary must communicate its bliss: "Mary thou shall weynde me fro, / Myn erand shall thou grathly go, / In no fowndyng thou fall; / To my dyscypyls say thou so, / That wilsom ar and lappyd in wo, / That I thaym socoure shall" (T 324/600–605).

So in the wonderful lyric that follows, Mary becomes yet another

---

[40] PL 114.425: "*Quem quaeris?* . . . Non quod dubitet quem requireret, sed quia illa quem quaerit ignoret, non enim quaerit Christum, sed quem putat raptum" (*Whom do you seek?* . . . Not because he was in doubt as to whom she sought, but because she did not know whom she asked for, for she did not seek Christ, but him whom she thought had been taken away).

[41] Bonaventure, *Opera Omnia*, Sent. 4, Dist. 12, P.1, Dub.1. "As he presented himself to the eyes of the body, as Gregory says, so he was present to the eyes of the mind." Compare the distinction which Gregory makes between the eye of the body and the eye of the heart, PL 76.1182.

[42] In Pseudo-Bonaventure Bernard, *Meditations on the Life of Christ*, 363.

prophet—to the disciples and to us—of that renewed body whose freedom is celebrated throughout time, contained in no one figure but ani-
mating them all, from Isaac and Moses to the last Te Deum of the just: "I
am as light as leyfe on tre, / ffor ioyfull sight that I can se, / ffor well I
wote that it was he / My lord ihesu; / he that betrayde that fre / sore may
he rew" (T 325/623–28). Those who betray and try to imprison that
"fre"—the word means "noble" as well as "free one"—suffer the insults
of burlesque rather than the immediate pains of hell. "Low" comedy itself
is a technique of displacement, helping in its own way to reunite the
members of the Body. Like all rituals of inversion, the portrayal of
knights, prelates, and princes as liars, cheats, and gross buffoons works
to restore the *communitas* that disappears wherever rank and decorum
keep people in their place. Worldly distinctions lose some numen when
the high estates announce a readiness to buy and sell the truth (Y 355/449),
when fat Caro presents himself as a great king (MC 10/235–74), or when
the prince of this world first sees hell, "Ffor fere of fyre a fart I crake" (LC
19/81). To comically undermine those who profess the "law" or insist
upon their rights and status is to restore an unruly wholeness that juridical
constraints and commercial fictions try to measure and control; it is also
to act out the implications of that commonplace of medieval political theory which describes an unjust ruler not as God's vicar, but as Satan's. To
laugh at Herod or Satan, however, neither renders them harmless in the
short run nor exhausts the range of our response to evil. Their attempts
to perpetuate an unjust lordship and foreclose the possibility of new life—
their conceited effort to bring about that stasis and final closure which is
the essence of moral death even more than of physical—must also
frighten an attentive audience, so that the comedy of our release from
their bands, however frequently predicted, comes also as some relief.
There is high comedy as well as low when everyday, Satanic logic fails.
Thus Pilate sets his seal on the four corners of the tomb; Pharaoh means
to keep the Jews in bondage; Balak thinks to buy some first-rate curses:
but none of these designs can work for long upon the Lord or his own—
the ass balks, the king drowns, Jesus' "fals quantyse" (T 259/32) renders
Pilate's "lawes forlorne / ffor euer more" (T 322/524–25).[43]

Even the character and virtue of "Mercy" has to take his licks, for the
most sacred figure will lose efficacy unless periodically cleansed with
irony. Mankind's "father gostly" is himself the consequence and the target of figurative displacement: priest, virtue, and earthly representative
of Christ, he is nonetheless a body so "full of Englysch Laten" that New
Gyse has reason to be "aferde yt wyll brest" (MM 158/122–25). For Mercy

[43] Cf. Kolve, *Play Called Corpus Christi*, 206–36.

to be able to "procede forth and do my propyrte" (MM 179/765), Myscheff, that "wynter corn-threscher," must both rid the father's "talkyng delectable" of its chaff (MM 155/53–65) and make Mankind see how much his own attempts to sow and reap need Mercy. This process has two aspects. First, "doctrine monytorye" (MM 183/879) must be brought to earth: after Mankind wins his first skirmish, buffeting his tormentors with a shovel, he makes the point that his action should be taken figuratively, not literally: "By þe subsyde of hys grace þat he hath sente me / Thre of myn enmys I haue putt to flyght. / Ʒyt þis instrument, souerens, ys not made to defende. / Dauide seyth, 'Nec in hasta nec in gladio saluat Dominus.'" But Nought knows better: "No, mary, I beschrew yow, yt ys in spadibus" (MM 166–67/394–98). The quick displacements here of meaning—not a spade but a weapon, not a weapon but grace, not grace but a spade—give us in low essence that union of contraries which is the body of the sign. As Prudentius observes of one of his own allegories, by which Judith becomes a figure of Chastity beheading Lust, in "our times" the "real power has passed into earthly bodies to sever the great head by means of feeble agents."[44] And this is the second aspect of the trials of truth (MM 163/286–88; 182/838): the feebleness of those bodies, that provisionality which comedy thrives upon, must be revealed in order for them to serve as vehicles of power. Lest figuration turn dead and tyrannical, the spade must be "merely" a spade, and Mercy "merely" a vulnerable man. To redeem the body, grace must put on all the body's frailty, till we love Mercy not only for its "propyrte" but for what it shares with us, a likeness that must be buffeted before its true kindness can appear.

With suitable modulations of tone, this analysis of *Mankind* can be extended to the "playful" reenactment of the Crucifixion: one restores the reality of signs by subjecting them to torment; man can signify God only if God's body is crossed, put *sous rature*. Without death, no resurrection; which is not to say that the Passion, however much it leads to joy, in any way inspires our laughter. Far from it. The evidence from popular meditations on Christ's sorrows and even from the hostile witness of Lollard critics of these plays suggests that spectators were not infrequently "moved to compassion and devociun, wepynge bitere teris."[45] The cause of this suffering lies with forgetful and spiritually illiterate humankind much more than with the devil. The trope of Christ must be broken for

[44] Prudentius, *Prudentius*, ed. and trans. H. J. Thomson, Loeb Classical Library (Cambridge, Massachusetts: Harvard University Press, 1949), 68–69. See Macklin Smith, *Prudentius' Psychomachia: A Reexamination* (Princeton: Princeton University Press, 1976), who argues for the integration of the historical and the abstract in Prudentius as in Christian figuralism more generally.

[45] Davidson, "Northern Spirituality and the Late Medieval Drama of York," 130.

our sake and because of our blindness; the fault is not in him, but in our seeing the incarnation as an affront to reason and good order which must be corrected, fitted to the law and to the cross. And the ultimate source of that affront is our own tendency to make an idol out of any revelation, to hold the body carnally rather than in spirit, and then to break it out of sheer revulsion. Rationalization and reification must both be overcome if the mystical body is to live: such comedy as arises from overturning the constraints of terrestrial reason finds its balance in sorrow at the numbering out of Christ's bones, sorrow which is no less pitiable for being both freely endured and absolutely necessary to salvation. Yet both such actions violate boundaries, humankind's ability to put God to death no less than God's ability to raise the body from the grave.[46] Fragmented humankind is reunified by that fracturing which the Mass commemorates in the breaking of the bread, by that transgression of all categories which the *Ludus Coventriae* so well captures in the rather giddying moment when Christ takes his own communion from the hands of an angel: "þis chalys ys þi blood þis bred is þi body / Ffor mannys synne evyr offeryd xal be / To þe fadyr of heffne þat is al-mythty / þi dyscipulis and all presthood xal offere fore the" (LC 264/953–56).

Thus we free the truth by breaking the body and the laws that claim to restrain it *or* reveal it, but only in order to enable reembodiment. "Deconstruction" finds its complement always in the body's restoration, especially through such small yieldings to convention as the boy Jesus' free obedience to Mary and Joseph. He who has just confuted the doctors of the law, and who justifies himself to worried parents by the higher need to serve his Father's will, goes on to answer Mary's bafflement—"There sawes . . . Can I noȝt vndirstande" (Y 181/261)—with yet another human figuration of charity: "My frendis thoughtis I wol fulfille / And to þer bidding baynely bowe" (Y 181/283–84). Leaving the befurred doctors for his poor and bashful parents, Jesus both ironizes and accomplishes the law, setting an example that neither respects nor omits loving submission. The N-Towne play points the immediate but hardly exclusive application: "Of ȝow clerkys my leve I take / Euery childe xulde with good dyligens / his modyr to plese his owyn wyl forsake" (LC 187/278–80).

Another way of noticing the glorification of Brother Ass in these plays is to observe that the response to Christ's kindness is generally homely rather than passionate or noble love. The resurrection signifies justification, and though that justification requires an obedient movement of free

---

[46] For a discussion from quite a different perspective of the ways in which medieval drama dissolves boundaries, see Robert Edwards, "Techniques of Transcendence in Medieval Drama," *Comparative Drama* 8 (1974): 157–71.

will—for as Bonaventure puts it, "he who made us will not justify without us"—God asks only that we do what lies in us to do; his mercy will make up the rest. The notion that small and hardly impressive gestures can accomplish a saving Christ-likeness would not always be uncontroversial: *facere quod in se est* was a doctrine that Luther vigorously objected to.[47] But in these plays, it is one of the chief means by which human unity is restored. Wisdom does not demand athletic self-denial: "Lett not thy tonge thy evyn-Crysten dyspyse, / Ande þan plesyst þou more myn excellens / Than yff þou laberyde wyth grett dylygens / Wpon thy nakyde feet and bare / Tyll þe blode folwude for peyn and vyolens / Ande aftyr eche stepe yt sene were" (MW 148/1039–44).

Not literal torment, but a handing on of God's mercy in modest deeds of love: one example that any "evyn-Crysten" might follow is provided by the York Flight into Egypt. This play begins with Joseph praising the Lord "that made me man, to thy liknes," but lamenting a feebleness that soon turns to sleep. After the angel's revelation of Herod's designs ("Wakyn Joseph, and take entente," [Y 162/37]), both Mary and Joseph grumble a good deal, cursing the king and mutually admitting that they have no idea where Egypt might be. But Joseph trusts God and finally takes up the burden not only of all their gear but of the child as well. Become a kind of theatrical St. Christopher, and thanked at that moment by Mary for his "grete goode dede," the old man suddenly recovers his strength: "Such forse methynke I fele, / I may go where I schall. / Are was I wayke, nowe am I wight. . . . / Nowe schall no hatyll do vs harme, / I haue oure helpe here in myn arme" (Y 166/217–24). Again, this action both disrupts the everyday and ornaments the body: Joseph and Mary must bid "gud day" to "oure kyth where we are knowyn" (Y 163/91), yet it is the simplest of domestic gestures that leads to and proclaims the renewal of corrupt nature which this play figures.[48]

Though he is an old man made new, Joseph is no "type" of Christ. Too querulous and generally too comic for that exegete's honor, he nonetheless participates in general restoration through the same yielding obedience which transforms the familiar figures of the old dispensation. In order for Joseph's obedience to receive proper notice, the playwrights

[47] St. Bonaventure, *Opera Omnia, Sent.* 4, Dist. 14, P.1, A.2, Q.2., "qui creavit nos sine nobis, non justificat nos sine nobis" ([He] who created us without us does not justify us without us); see Heiko A. Oberman, "Facientibus quod in se est Deus non denegat gratiam: Robert Holcot, O.P. and the Beginnings of Luther's Theology," *Harvard Theological Review* 55 (1962): 317–42, and " 'Iustitia Christi' and 'Iustitia Dei': Luther and the Scholastic Doctrines of Justification," *Harvard Theological Review* 59 (1966): 1–26.

[48] See the somewhat different discussion of this play in Woolf, *English Mystery Plays*, 200–201. Cf. PL 114.76: "Fugit in Aegyptum sicut natus est, ut corruptam reparet naturam" (Just as soon as he was born, he flies into Egypt in order to repair the corruption of nature).

comically emphasize the barriers in the way of his acceding to the will of
God. Much attention has been paid to the plays on his jealous suspicions
of Mary, wherein virtue eventually defeats backbiting and scandal, but an
equally interesting play of renewal is the *Ludus Coventriae* Betrothal,
where the theme of resurrection extends to the unexpected level of sexual burlesque.[49] Here the authorities profess themselves scandalized by
Mary's refusal to be married at fourteen for "þe Encrese of more plente"
(LC 83/11) but are convinced by the angel to conduct a test of David's
living kinsmen: each is to bear a white rod into the temple, and he whose
rod flowers will wed the Virgin. Joseph sees no sense to the test, is cold
without his gown (LC 88/185), and so feeble that he cannot stand without
a staff. When finally arrived at this barely disguised trial of potency, he
expresses his mortification to the audience: "now wolde god I were at
hom in my cote / I am aschamyd to be seyn veryly" (LC 88/201–2).[50]
Compelled at last to come forward, Joseph makes the cause of his embar-
rassment still more clear: "Sere I kan not my rodde ffynde / to come þer
in trowth me thynkyht shame" (LC 89/235–36). Yet when he finally tries
to offer it up, Joseph discovers that he cannot, for it has grown too heavy:
"I may not lyfte myn handys heye / Lo · Lo · Lo · What se ʒe now" (LC
90/255–56). And with this proof that a "ded stok beryth flourys ffre,"
Joseph has to overcome his conventional scruples about an old man's
marrying a young wife.

Joseph's sexual discomfiture takes nothing from the freedom or the
figurative character of his eventual submission, but it does help demonstrate once more how inevitably corporeal—and therefore paradoxical—
all signs of spiritual renewal must be. Breaking from the tomb or from
the bonds of ego and misconception, abusing the proud, dying in itself in
order to manifest new life, this restored and restoring Body both de-
means and sanctifies the very least of vehicles, even the literal body itself,
confessedly impotent but for just that reason able to signify and yield to
something greater. Because self-effacement—at whatever level of dignity—is the essential signifying gesture, displacing power and meaning
toward the metonymic whole from which it comes, heroism has little
place in this drama. For this reason, even the most insistently typological
plays render their characters more approachable and less abstractly admirable than they might be were strict prefiguration the sole emphasis.
Only Chester (and that only in the Doctor's gloss) tries to constrain our

[49] See Stanley J. Kahrl's fine discussion of comic realism in the cycles, *Traditions of Medieval English Drama* (London: Hutchinson University Library, 1974), 77–83.
[50] For medieval trials of potency, see R. H. Helmholz, *Marriage Litigation in Medieval England* (Cambridge: Cambridge University Press, 1974), 89.

understanding: "This deede . . . in example of Jesus done yt was" (C 78/ 464–65). But the Chester play as a whole, like the others on this subject, puts considerable stress upon the pathos of what Abraham is asked to do. It would violate the moral center of the Corpus Christi drama if we were to reason that Abraham and Isaac obey God because they are Christ's chosen types. The more appropriate response is to say that they, like Abel, Moses, and especially Noah, become types of the just because they obey, despite a cost that the flesh feels and sometimes expresses with much indignity. This, too, is an effect of displacement, perhaps the one most necessary to the homiletic enterprise, for it brings saving obedience within the reach of mortal feeling and capacities.

The playwrights make a connection between tropology and type in various ways. In York, Isaac (here thirty years of age and more)[51] asks to be bound, not because he himself is unwilling, but because his flesh might shrink at the last moment. In the *Ludus Coventriae*, Abraham weeps almost continually and must be urged on by a son whose bright innocence is perhaps less typological than inexperienced. In Wakefield, Isaac is querulous, insists on his own guiltlessness, reproaches his sorrowful but obdurate father, and staves off the uplifted sword by a last-minute appeal to his absent mother's love. Abraham's ensuing lament is anything but serene and God-like, though it does incorporate Pilate's judgment on the faultless Christ:

> let be, let be!
> It will not help that thou wold meyn;
> Bot ly still till I com to the,
> I mys a lytyll thing, I weyn.
> he spekis so rufully to me
> That water shotis in both myn eeyn,
> I were leuer than all wardly wyn,
> That I had fon hym onys vnkynde,
> Bot no defawt I faund hym in:
> I wold be dede for hym, or pynde;
> To slo hym thus, I thynk grete syn,
> So rufull wordis I with hym fynd;
> I am full wo that we shuld twyn,
> ffor he will neuer oute of my mynd.
>   (T 47/211–24)

Then this nearly tragic passion is undercut, not by Abraham's resuming a typological mask, but by fear of what his wife will say, and a resolution to run up swiftly and kill the boy while he lies quiet. The scene

---

[51] Rosemary Woolf notes that the York playwright here follows a tradition set by Peter Comestor. *English Mystery Plays*, 151.

lacks dignity, certainly, but it demonstrates that resolvable tension between kind and kind which is central to this theater, and it makes the
sacrifice possible, just because this Abraham is no hero, however exemplary his attempt to obey.[52]

The Northampton playwright carries the theme still further, expanding the claims of natural love into a whole episode. Unable to face his
wife's certain objections, Habraham lies to her about the purpose of his
journey to the land of Vision. When Isaac later asks if his mother knows
that he is to "be martyred in this mysse," saying that if she had known "I
had not riden out from her this day, / But she had riden also," Habraham
replies that he would rather displease Sara than God: "Ye, son, God most
be serued ay, / þi modre may not haue hir wille all way. / I loue þe as wele
as she doþe, in fay, / And ʒit this dede most be do."[53] To Sara's outraged
demand on subsequently learning his intentions, "Alas, where was your
mynde?" Habraham makes the same sort of answer: "My mynde? Vpon
þe goode Lord on hy! / Nay, and he bid me, trust it verayly, / þou it
had be þiself and I, / It shuld not haue ben left behynde" (NC 41/346–49).
As one Patristic commentator remarks on Abraham's preference for
God's will over the claims of his own flesh, whether wife or son, "If
Abraham could show himself obedient in such a serious and bitter thing,
by how much more should we obey, commanded to do things that can
be borne."[54]

And in the spirit of this comment, it is time to cease from illustration.
To do things that can be borne: unheroic, corporeal in both spectacle and
lack of dignity, exemplaristic in theology but content to celebrate the natural body of the sign, medieval urban drama reconciles humankind to a
figurative, limited, and transient condition by insisting only on a modest
likeness to Christ. Acting out the Book means in this theater to act out
the essential seamlessness of narrative metonymy by means of mirroring
episodes each of which exemplifies the fallibility of the flesh and of all
tropes whatsoever. Eschewing histrionics, showing up every plot for
fraud except God's forethought of revelation in *figura*, this drama expands
the only trope that can be true, one which gratuitously conjoins mortality

[52] John R. Elliott, Jr., "The Sacrifice of Isaac as Comedy and Tragedy," in *Medieval English Drama*, ed. Jerome Taylor and Alan H. Nelson (Chicago: University of Chicago Press,
1972), 157–76.

[53] "The Northampton Play of *Abraham and Isaac*," in *The Non-Cycle Plays and Fragments*,
ed. Norman Davis, E.E.T.S., S.S. 1 (London: Oxford University Press, 1970), lines 196–99.
I abbreviate subsequent citations to this edition of the play as NC.

[54] Pseudo-Augustine, *Quaestiones veteris et novi testamenti*, ed. Alexander Souter, vol. 127
of *Corpus scriptorum ecclesiasticorum latinorum* (Leipzig: G. Freytag, 1908), 354: "Si enim fi-
delissimus Abraham in re tam graui et aspera oboediens inuenitur, quanto magis nos, quibus
illa praecipiuntur quae possunt portari!"

and resurrection, displacing every given boundary in order to point again and again at that mysterious whole which is either the semiotic field in its contradictory entirety or the body of God.

One insistent theme of my discussion so far has been that the theology of image and likeness implies a specific kind of dramaturgy, one which is "narrative" in a double but not merely equivocal sense. On the one hand, because the theology holds that human action is inevitably tropological and figurative, the persons of medieval drama lack the clear definition and distinctive presence we would normally expect from characters in effective plays. Abraham and Humanum Genus are both tropes, and very fallible ones at that, of a persevering charity manifested only once in history: their theatrical interest derives not from their particularity and charisma, but from their imperfect figuration. The reality—*res et non signum*—which they gesture toward is never "present"; thus there is in each character a constant implication of representational insufficiency. Like the personages in modern "story theater," their unimposing, makeshift air suits them to amateur performance, and their frankness about both being in a story and being like the members of the audience allows the players to join modesty about their craft with modesty about their personal capacity for moral heroism. Representational candor and a lack of theatrical "presence" thus go hand in hand: where everything is in *figura*, neither the mystery of the actor nor that of individual psychology can arise.

The paratactic structure which develops these tropes is also "narrative" in effect. Where a less candidly figurative drama permits close focus upon the mysteries of self, here the boundaries of the historical moment and the individual person continually give way. Horizontal connections from one prophecy and Christ-likeness to another disperse the saving image throughout time, but not in a manner that either puts undue emphasis upon God's predestinating script or allows us to believe in a separation between historical reality and spiritual significance. Augustinian exemplarism and the doctrine of good works operate from both the form-giving and the form-seeking sides of creation to guarantee against either of these later versions of the relation between nature and grace.[55] In the epi-

---

[55] This is well-charted, yet contended territory. I rely especially on Javalet, *Image et ressemblance*; Henri de Lubac, *The Mystery of the Supernatural*, trans. Rosemary Sheed (London: Geoffrey Chapman, 1967) and *Augustinianism and Modern Theology*, trans. Lancelot Sheppard (New York: Herder and Herder, 1969); Heiko A. Oberman, *The Harvest of Medieval Theology: Gabriel Biel and Late Medieval Nominalism* (Grand Rapids: William B. Eerdmans, 1967); James Samuel Preus, *From Shadow to Promise: Old Testament Interpretation from Augustine to the Young Luther* (Cambridge, Massachusetts: Harvard University Press, 1969); and

sodic and expansive cycles, one play does not lead to the next as if setting
up a causal dynamic in the action, motivated either by individual knowledge and desire or by God's secret pattern-weaving in history. Instead,
Providence repeatedly offers saving opportunities and examples, con-
firming the omnipresence of mercy by turning all to good even when
humankind fails, breaking up every plot and worldly expectation that
works against humanity's liberation from sin and bondage.

In the moralities, this boundary-breaking tropism moves more "verti-
cally" than horizontally, destroying distinctions between psychological
"insides" and public "outsides": the Virtues fight in human form with
Christ as their example and roses for their weapons; Penance lances Humanum Genus's heart so that he may call upon the well of mercy that
Longinus opened; Mercy is as much priest as quality; Wisdom is Christ,
emperor, and doctrine all in one. There was a time when it was fashionable to deplore the abstractness of the moralities and praise the realism of
the cycles; by now, it should be clear that both genres exhibit an almost
postmodernist awareness of the difficulty in neatly dividing the concrete
from the ideal, the private from the public, the literal from the figurative.[56] Neither genre has a nineteenth- or even a seventeenth-century notion of the difference between matter and spirit; neither displays any interest in being illusionistic. Instead, like the Digby *Mary Magdalene* which
moves so easily and openly from history to allegory and back, both mysteries and moralities dramatize a textual world: they play a "sentens" in
their audience's sight.[57] That playing would connect realms that humankind has always risked severing. So in this theater, appearance displaces
difference: thus Jesus appears to Mary as the gardener because he works
inside the heart to sow and cultivate the virtues.[58]

Something remains to be said about medieval drama's part in Shakespeare's origins and practice. There is every likelihood that Elizabethan
players and playwrights had some immediate contact with the "medieval" stage.[59] There are many instances to be adduced—some more convincing than others—of the survival in later works of figures and patterns

Robert P. Scharlemann, *Thomas Aquinas and John Gerhard* (New Haven, Connecticut: Yale
University Press, 1964).

[56] One symptom of this affinity, despite the radically different onto-theological assumptions, is Rabanus Maurus's characterization of scripture as an abyss, PL 112.852.

[57] *Mary Magdalene*, in *The Late Medieval Religious Plays of Bodleian Mss Digby 133 and E
Museo 160*, ed. Donald C. Baker, John L. Murphy, and Louis B. Hall, Jr., E.E.T.S., O.Æ.S. 283
(Oxford: Oxford University Press, 1982), 94, lines 2131–32.

[58] "Mannys hartt is my gardyn here. / þerin I sow sedys of vertu all þe ȝere. / þe fowle
wedys and wycys, I reynd vp be þe rote! / Whan þat gardyn is watteryd with terys clere, /
Than spryng vertuus, and smelle full sote." Ibid., lines 1081–85.

[59] Emrys Jones, *The Origins of Shakespeare* (Oxford: Clarendon Press, 1977), 31–84.

from the religious drama. The problem, always, is what to make of contacts and survivals. If my discussion of the relation between drama and doctrine has shed any additional light upon the working of medieval theater, I hope that it has also made it plausible to suggest that mysteries and moralities are more than a problematic influence or a theatrical manifestation of the world that Shakespeare had lost. They are both these things, to be sure, and in the next chapter I shall try to say more about why the influence is hard to interpret even when its signs are unmistakable, and what the loss of old ways might have meant for the English community and its theater even if those old ways were in most respects reborn in strong, no less paradoxical, and often barely distinguishable forms.

For us, however, medieval drama can stand after all as something more than history. It gives us access not to a world view—exemplarist premises prevent anyone's taking that unengaged, perspectival stance—but to a sense of things (whether "premodern" and "traditional" is another question) as potentially figurative and substantive all at once.[60] One way to characterize this understanding of reality is to say that it tries to make every sign and thing simultaneously operate in and as both metonymy and metaphor: truly seen, every individual is "associat" to Mercy who has "partycypacyon" in "þe very wysdam" (MM 18/827; 160/210), yet every soul is also an image, both an extrinsic and an intrinsic analogy to God.[61] Thus insisting equally and at the same moment on contiguity and comparison, medieval drama makes us aware that everything is both more and less than it seems to be, unbounded and limited at the same time. This is a view of language, of course, one with affinities to modern theories of textuality that I have tried to make apparent. But it is also an understanding of life, a notion of humanity in which everything is "writing," and in which the only way to step outside of textuality would be to become the God who is pure spirit. That step is impossible for humanity, but the postulate of One who knows without a body and who needs no body if he wishes to say something to Mankind—for embodiment is gift and grace, not need—guarantees a way to bring tropism to judgment, even if only by making it confess to being wholly and defectively figurative. Thus a vision of the world as book can be one that implies both a transcendental critique of history and an ethics, a theory of how to act

[60] Martin Heidegger, "The Age of the World Picture," in *The Question Concerning Technology and Other Essays*, trans. William Lovitt (New York: Harper and Row, 1977), 115–54; Michel Foucault, *The Order of Things* (New York: Vintage Books, 1973), 17–77. But as Jacques Derrida argues, especially in "Sending: On Representation," trans. Peter and Mary Ann Caws, *Social Research* 49 (1982): 294–326, stories that single out one or more epochs as essentially "representational" ought to be viewed with a great deal of skepticism.

[61] Battista Mondin, *The Principle of Analogy in Protestant and Catholic Theology* (The Hague: Martin Nijhoff, 1968).

upon one's reading by confessing one's fault—one's cognitive overdetermination, perhaps, or one's need to own an idolatrous meaning and a
self—and by expiating that fault through self-abnegating, tropical behavior, through love of a truth beyond figuration.

Medieval drama does not constitute our only or even our best entrance
into this sense of things. It is explicit in Catholic theology, especially before Cajetan, Suarez, and Trent; it is implicit in medieval art, lyric, and
narrative; and it may be inferred from the rituals, both ironic and celebratory, of medieval life, rituals in which the highly "dividual" person of
Everyman, bound in his own estate but connected to the whole of things
through his different places in several overlapping associations and hierarchies, could finally become a natural symbol of the corporate body.
Such rituals depend upon a social structure which facilitates the recognition and expression of what Juri Lotman calls "high semioticity." One
suspects that gemeinschaft arrangements, which value status, custom,
mutual obligation, and a high degree of formal interaction among persons, do rather better than the more legalistic and utilitarian gesellschaft
systems at inspiring a richly articulated public code of classification and
behavior.[62] Precisely because such a code is both public and well articulated, practices must be developed to cope with the contradictions and
dissonances that inevitably accrue, and which if unattended to would finally cause the system to collapse. Medieval drama is one such practice
among many. We might well understand them all by saying that what the
modern academic does with little ironies or some form of therapy for a
private system of meaning—a system nonetheless given some publicity
in the embodied codes of dress, speech, and gesture by which academics
can almost always be picked out in any crowd—medieval urban Catholics
could try to do for an explicitly public system with penance and the Corpus Christi celebrations.[63]

[62] Part of the difference here is the one that Mary Douglas analyzes in *Natural Symbols:
Explorations in Cosmology* (1970; New York: Vintage Books, 1973), and in *Cultural Bias*
(London: Royal Anthropological Institute, 1978), reprinted in *In the Active Voice*, 183–234,
deriving her notions of strong grid and group in part from Basil Bernstein's work on the
difference between restricted and elaborated codes of speech, *Class, Codes, and Control*, vol.
1 (London: Routledge and Kegan Paul, 1971). For Juri Lotman's idea of "high semioticity,"
see "Problems in the Typology of Culture," *Soviet Semiotics*, ed. and trans. Daniel P. Lucid
(Baltimore: Johns Hopkins University Press, 1977), 213–21. However conceptualized, the
difference seems to be between the more or less embodied codes appropriate to a well-
bounded group, and those necessarily more elaborate and legalistic codes which serve to
connect one group with another and to regulate the entrances and exits from group to
group. No doubt groups can live well without the elaborated codes that schooling perhaps
most regularly supplies. That any group could function without restricted codes, even
though never raised to the level of civic ceremony, seems unlikely.

[63] Of course there is a difference in discursive articulation between a specialized body of

No more than we, then, did Shakespeare need to look at mysteries and moralities to think that persons could be signs and the world a book: the idea and its practice were his heritage and very much a living part of his surroundings, though threatened with further disturbance and transformation than had already occurred by the late sixteenth century. But the only slightly frivolous analogy to therapy suggests a deeper reason why he had no need to be an antiquarian in order to see this possibility. Even with the most modernized, rationalist, and syntagmatic view of things imaginable, there coexists a complementary though sometimes hidden awareness of pervasive and punful semiosis, so that the forest of symbols and the book of the world are always "there" to be rediscovered and reconstituted, even when suppressed by the dominant ideology or fenced away from reason in the tame preserves of poetry, politics, religion, and other modes of self-expression and self-help.

What mysteries and moralities show us, however, is that an ideal of transcategorical wholeness had been quite recently subject to public enactment, neither being kept safely distant as "art" nor rendered dangerously private as the energizing confidence of God's secretly elect. This older allegorical drama figures forth an idea of humankind in which reason and love—and image and likeness, knowing and doing, book and theater—tend toward an embodied unity in a Word that goes beyond words altogether. Here is the reason why these plays can be transparent and tropical at the same time: what they "say" is that every sort of speech and action will be judged for its conformity to that merciful and self-denying trope which is Christ. But this is to displace all saying whatsoever—and the world as well—from a posture of significance and importance. For a compelling "literary" theater to develop, such a radically deconstructive understanding of existence had to lose some of its potency (and the corresponding theology and social structure had to be transformed). Without the genuine possibility of heroism, of being able to know the secret levers of history and work them with one's immanent deeds, truly great drama is unimaginable. Yet without the real likelihood not only of a hero's being wrong in his guess at a vocation as well as in the acting of it, but also wrong in his initial decision to try for mastery rather than for surrender, such drama runs a considerable risk of being merely dishonest and sensational.

In other words, medieval drama helps us see and describe the theatrical implications—the theatrical necessity, I am tempted to say—of the mingle-mangle compromise that Elizabethan England managed between

---

talk and practice and the ritually embodied and encoded practices of medieval theater. This difference will inform much of the next chapter.

"old" and "new." Medieval drama matters not just because it is earlier and allegorical, but because it is allegory of a highly embodied and ultimately nonconceptual kind: its vision of penitential union through self-displacing works of love constitutes an obstacle and a challenge to both the drama and the world that followed it. There is no need to say that the union of spirit and flesh which mysteries and moralities propose continues to inspire Christian thought; in fact, the ideal of transparency grows much more compelling with the Reformation and its uneasy compromises with fleshly mediation and allegorizing glosses. It is rather the means of attaining that union which the new practice finds "old" in the devastating Pauline sense of the word. Yet in rending the veil a second time, the reformers (and the less deliberately intellectual forces of modernization) do more than rationalize the relations between God and humanity. Calling strictly false and useless a set of practices which had always—in the better understandings, at least—been known to be tropes of truth rather than its naked statement, the "new men" propose something beyond fiction, either an ideological conjunction of gnosis and praxis or an irreconcilable disjunction between idol and fact. Both moves help create the energies and differences that great drama thrives upon.

According to this line of argument, however, the old allegorical drama (and all that it implies and that sustained it, and that continued its impulses, though in other forms) constitutes just one side of a sixteenth-century dialectic. The other side, reform in its several shapes, has as its theatrical representative the new—and also largely allegorical—drama of humanist interlude, Protestant polemic, and courtly fantasy of power. Most of us, I think, find this drama less congenial than the plays whose origins are "medieval," but whose appeal extended far enough beyond the Elizabethan settlement that we can at least console ourselves by imagining that popular taste had not suddenly grown corrupt. Whether popular or not, the interludes and morals of the sixteenth century have considerable importance for literary history. This is not because Shakespeare and his fellows drew upon these plays in any very striking way, but because they let us see in a fairly clear and direct manner the theatrical consequences and construction of fundamental change in the social order and in religious and political self-understanding. Insistent on its own good doctrine in quite another way from mysteries and moralities, the drama of Tudor England is not part of an undifferentiated "tradition." Instead, it manifests in the theater just those forces of differentiation which set the tradition against itself in a largely unprecedented fashion, indeed in the very fashion that works both to constitute tradition and to make it into a problem.

THREE

The Idea of the Play

✳

Two related myths of closure inscribe themselves within most modern attempts to understand the literary past. Both are myths of community. The first evokes an unfallen, preindustrial age without moral uncertainty, personal anomie, or economic alienation: this is the era inhabited by Benjamin's storyteller or D. W. Robertson's Chaucer, an era in which everyone's experience was more or less public and shareable, as were the norms by which to judge it. Though hardly a world without sin and error, it at least permitted sin to be identified and at best was a world in which poetry mattered, not as unacknowledged legislation, perhaps, but as one among many recognized ways of enlightenment, correction, and vision. Such conditions obtain until after the "Middle Ages"—a period which occasionally lasts until Rousseau, or 1789, or the end of some favorite "traditional" society—by which time structural differentiation has completed its so far irreversible work, putting up class barriers where there once were orderly ranks, separating productive labor from the home and poetry from its public, driving fact and value into irreconcilable divorce. Then, partly as a consequence of this transformation, which is hard to distinguish from our postindustrial and postrevolutionary rewriting of the tale of a Golden Age, there arises a more esoteric but no less fabulous myth of another sort of community. This is the community of art, with true poets breaking down time and the subject-object split, great painters being gathered into spiritual villages at the newly opened Louvre and the British Museum, and the various strains of art engaging in discourse only with and finally only about their own purified traditions. And from the *Biographia Literaria* to *The Anatomy of Criticism* (if not backward in time at least to Johnson's *Lives* and forward to *Blindness and Insight*), the universe of reading and writing comes to be described as though it were a bounded, integrated, homeostatic whole. Whether the canons are those universal ones of taste or the Freudian ones of repression and displacement, family closure seems restored, for only endogenous rules can govern a truly textual tradition. In this second myth, there is even a gain in communal depth, since in the extended family of letters, far more generations dwell together than ever in the best days of gemeinschaft.[1]

It is no easy task to sift out the truth from these fables of union, difference, and reintegration, or even to say just what such a sorting might demand of us. Stated as an ideal type, neither kind of community ever has existed: even in the most remote, bounded, and primitive societies we know about, there is more structural dysfunction, personal and social mobility, and disagreement over norms than the myth allows. As for the community of letters, it derives from holistic and universalizing fantasies of the bookish, and also from the accidents and politics by which one set of books rather than another survives and finds a readership. Since "literature" is neither a natural nor an innocent category, rather than describe the great tradition as the dominant pressure on writers, or as a system whose growth depends largely on internal forces, we might better think of it as a historically conditioned aspiration. Whatever else it may be, literary history fashions the collective self-narration of those who make a

---

[1] Walter Benjamin, "The Storyteller: Reflections on the Works of Nikolai Leskov," *Illuminations*, trans. Harry Zohn (New York: Schocken Books, 1969), 83–109; Robertson, *A Preface to Chaucer*. From the economic, social, and political side of things, different versions of this story may be found in Karl Polyani, *The Great Transformation* (New York: Farrar and Rinehart, 1944), Louis Dumont, *From Mandeville to Marx: The Genesis and Triumph of Economic Ideology* (Chicago: University of Chicago Press, 1977), Jürgen Habermas, *Theory and Practice*, trans. John Viertel (Boston: Beacon Press, 1973), Peter Laslett, *The World We Have Lost,* 2d ed. (New York: Charles Scribner's Sons, 1973), and in the contemporary theory of modernization, e.g., Marion J. Levy, *Modernization and the Structure of Societies* (Princeton: Princeton University Press, 1966), and Shmuel Noah Eisenstadt, *Tradition, Change, and Modernity* (New York: Wiley, 1973). The survey and assessment of the literature on modernization that I have found most useful is Anthony D. Smith, *The Concept of Social Change: A Critique of the Functionalist Theory of Social Change* (London: Routledge and Kegan Paul, 1973); the most suggestive application of modernization theory to a comparable problem is Sarah C. Humphreys, "Evolution and History: Approaches to the Study of Structural Differentiation," in *Anthropology and the Greeks* (London: Routledge and Kegan Paul, 1978), 242–75. In addition to Alan Macfarlane's empirically based critique of the myth of community (with Sara Harrison and Charles Jardine, *Reconstructing Historical Communities* [Cambridge: Cambridge University Press, 1977]) and Keith Wrightson's more temperate assessment in *English Society, 1580–1680* (New Brunswick, New Jersey: Rutgers University Press, 1982), esp. 39–65, see Marc Augé, *The Anthropological Circle: Symbol, Function, History*, trans. Martin Thom (Cambridge: Cambridge University Press, 1982). Jacques Derrida disrupts nostalgic myths of unity throughout his work, especially in "Différance," *Margins of Philosophy*, trans. Alan Bass (Chicago: University of Chicago Press, 1982), 1–27. For the constitution of the modern notion of artistic tradition, see especially Lawrence Lipking, *The Ordering of the Arts in Eighteenth-Century England* (Princeton: Princeton University Press, 1970), and Michael Fried, *Absorption and Theatricality: Painting and Beholder in the Age of Diderot* (Berkeley: University of California Press, 1980). Though directed to a slightly different immediate issue, the attempt to privilege literature as the last remaining sacred text, Geoffrey H. Hartman's remark on de Man is much to the point for every theory of the movement from tradition to modernity: "literature cannot be explained or illumined by prevalent concepts of secularization, which are merely versions of 'lost object' theorizing." *Criticism in the Wilderness* (New Haven, Connecticut: Yale University Press, 1980), 179.

profession out of reading and writing, and like all autobiographies, it suppresses randomness, deceit, and uncanny synchronicity in order to mold a respectable but illusory image of authorial control.[2]

Yet even if gemeinschaft is our nostalgic fiction, and even if the literary tradition constitutes just one extrinsic influence among many in the complex of factors that inspires and limits the improvisation of a particular text in a particular moment, the interaction of these myths still merits notice. For it is during the period when the forces rather tendentiously ascribed to "modernization" work through Europe, starting from the Italian cities of the thirteenth and fourteenth centuries and culminating in the industrialized empires of the nineteenth, that the lure of humane letters is at its strongest. And it is just when modernity starts to go sour, when the political effects of revolution and the social consequences of industrial dislocation have begun to be clear, that Tönnies formulates his dichotomy, that Mallarmé announces an end to authorial closure, and that Arnold begins to worry about the death of poetry.[3]

If indeed they can be addressed in any systematic or responsible way at all, such grand coincidences are the subject for another book. I introduce them here only to frame the much more restricted coincidence which this chapter will explore: that a "literary" drama arises in England just at the end of that social and religious transformation which Henry VIII and his children reluctantly presided over. Of course the Elizabethan settlement hardly put a period to our larger metamorphosis in the direction of modernity; for us, it more plausibly stands as one representation among several of a particularly unsettling *concordia discors*. Let me pause a moment to consider what might be required to define its elements.

Take the religious settlement by itself. Elizabethan Anglicanism is just one part of England's general rearrangement in all the orders of representation, but it is a sensitive index of the forces then at work, of the general interpenetration of old and new, and of the particular adjustments required of both Catholic oldness and Protestant newness in order to suit an evolving church to the evolving interests of a state and people. *Via media* may have been what Elizabeth sought, yet it is important to remember that both the Anglican and the Counter-Reformation churches distance themselves from the past, that both are centralizing, rationalizing, and yet hierarchical and ceremonial institutions. At the same time,

---

[2] For a brief, authoritative account of the illusions and limitations of literary history as practiced since the early nineteenth century, see René Wellek, "The Fall of Literary History," *Poetik und Hermeneutik* 5 (1973): 427–40.

[3] Jeffrey Mehlman, *Revolution and Repetition: Marx, Hugo, Balzac* (Berkeley: University of California Press, 1977), thinks about this latter conjunction in an especially suggestive way.

we must keep in mind the fact that most of the Elizabethan bench of bishops, and a majority of that well-educated Parliament, and of the rising gentry itself, are properly described as Calvinist in their theology, if not in their more complexly political ecclesiology. The point here is not to attempt the riddle of the interaction (or even of the separate sixteenth-century existence) of Anglican and Puritan parties, but to observe that Elizabethan and Jacobean disputes over church doctrine and church governance betray not only a conflict between tradition and reform, but also a heightened awareness of the connection between structures and meanings, and a disagreement as to the proper way of conceiving and correcting that representational relation. Failing a consensus, and with the Queen politically unable and perhaps personally unwilling to give a clear lead, the Elizabethan compromise suspends the question for a generation or more, trying to create one uniform and largely coextensive state and church on the basis of studied ambiguity and policed conformity rather than on a platform of the explicit ideology that a rapidly enlarging political nation already required and would eventually construct on its own.[4]

Yet that new national ideology was considerably altered from the one that moved Cranmer, Latimer, Ascham, or Whitaker, much less Perkins and Wentworth, or that supposedly inspired the co-opted revolution of the saints. Remembering what we all know about subsequent events, it is clear that the seventeenth century hardly dissolved an old, hierarchical order, extended humane learning and the franchise, demystified the relation between sacred and secular, or disestablished ceremonial religion. Instead, the rearrangements which the English political nation ultimately found for itself were ones which restricted entry to education and to its own number, which made the king more an officer of a mercantilist state than a lord surrounded in (and out) of Parliament by great magnates, and which put the staffing of the nation's church securely in the hands of

---

[4] I rely for these questions mainly on John Bossy, "The Character of Elizabethan Catholicism," *Past and Present* 21 (1962): 39–59, Davies, *Worship and Theology in England*, A. G. Dickens, *The English Reformation* (London: B. T. Batsford, 1964), Geoffrey R. Elton, *The Body of the Whole Realm: Parliament and Representation in Medieval and Tudor England* (Charlottesville: University of Virginia Press, 1969) and *Policy and Police: The Enforcement of the Reformation in the Age of Thomas Cromwell* (Cambridge: Cambridge University Press, 1972), Hanson, *From Kingdom to Commonwealth*, Mervyn James, *Family, Lineage, and Civil Society: A Study of Society, Politics, and Mentality in the Durham Region, 1500–1640* (Oxford: Oxford University Press, 1974), Henry R. McAdoo, *The Spirit of Anglicanism: A Survey of Anglican Theological Method in the Seventeenth Century* (New York: Charles Scribner's Sons, 1965), Wallace T. MacCaffrey, *The Shaping of the Elizabethan Regime* (Princeton: Princeton University Press, 1968) and *Queen Elizabeth and the Making of Policy, 1572–1588* (Princeton: Princeton University Press, 1981), Roger G. Manning, *Religion and Society in Elizabethan Sussex: A Study of the Religious Settlement, 1558–1603* (Leicester: Leicester University Press, 1969), and John H. New, *Anglican and Puritan: The Basis of their Opposition, 1558–1640* (Stanford: Stanford University Press, 1964).

those who also controlled Parliament, leaving a now safely tolerable range of religious dissent as some comfort for those who possessed neither political power nor the benefits once derived from traditional good lordship or the urban guilds.[5] This familiar story of the postinterregnum consolidation of an expanded upper class has little or nothing to do with a movement beyond Christianity or allegory, and it therefore cautions the study of Shakespeare in two ways, one rather trivial, the other of some importance, and both leading to a more useful way of formulating the central issues in a transition from medieval to modern and old to new.

First, by looking ahead of Shakespeare, we are reminded that the immediate outcome of England's early modernizing process was a social praxis which fits badly with our own ideals of modernity, despite the suspiciously familiar ring of the epistemology and political theory of possessive individualism.[6] Whether from medieval perspectives or from our own post-Marxist and post-Freudian ones, there is as evident an allegorical element in the relation between person and property as there is in any doctrine of infused grace or in the fiction that one's priest stands in the place of Christ. Indeed, one might argue that the medieval view of persons and institutions has an advantage over later fictions in that it at least permits some ethical criticism of the established order, for it requires the temporal to justify itself in the light of that transcendent which it figures: thus medieval prudence (to take a shopworn instance) retains moral force on account of its status as the earthly version of divine wisdom, a force subsequently attenuated by the full temporalization of children's being given that name and of merchants' adopting the virtue as their own.[7]

Second, and more to the point in trying to describe Shakespeare's place on the borders between old and new, such a glance at the political and religious future helps us avoid misdefinition of the polarities involved in the Elizabethan settlement and in the years thereafter. Just as Kepler's and Newton's theological ambitions help show the danger in representing the prior age as one in which naturalism and religion were in delicate and

[5] These later developments are conveniently summarized by Lawrence Stone, *The Causes of the English Revolution, 1529–1642* (New York: Harper and Row, 1972), 147; for the maintenance of traditional notions of hierarchy, but with an increasing emphasis on the importance of economic circumstances during the period from Thomas Smith to Geoffrey King, see David Cressey, "Describing the Social Order of Elizabethan and Stuart England," *Literature and History* 3 (1976): 29–44.

[6] C. B. MacPherson, *The Political Theory of Possessive Individualism: Hobbes to Locke* (Oxford: Clarendon Press, 1962). J. P. Sommerville's *Politics and Ideology in England, 1603–1640* (London: Longman, 1986), suggests that Hobbes and Locke are neither so novel, nor so typical, as is often thought, and argues that all parties to political debate throughout the seventeenth century lacked any notion of rights inhering in the individual as opposed to rights conferred by the community or by God.

[7] Glenn W. Hatfield, *Henry Fielding and the Language of Irony* (Chicago: University of Chicago Press, 1968), 179–96.

irrecoverable balance, so the political and social progeny of the Reformation alert us once again to an error in characterizing Shakespeare as the witness of a transformation from providentialist certainty to secularist anxiety about the interrelation between self, state, and cosmos. After all, it is subsequent to Shakespeare, not before him, that the very shape of the continents (to say nothing of the existence of the poor) comes to be described as Providence's design for commerce; and in the Middle Ages, it was Solomon, not Tom Jones, who consorted with Sophia, and even then as his spiritual rather than his carnal bride.[8]

All this is persiflage, not argument, but it helps situate and circumscribe a larger problem necessarily implicated in the smaller one about the Elizabethan revolution in drama. That problem has to do with the nature of representation, or perhaps more generally, with nature and representation, whatever these may be and however they may be connected. When talking about the drama, it is easy to pretend that the problem is mostly aesthetic, having to do with the techniques of realism, with the theatrical realization of individual psychology, or with a stagecraft that relies more and more upon illusion, marking off a world which is image from that which it images. Yet even to conceive the problem as an aesthetic one is, of course, to see the aesthetic already established as that which represents without being useful, without having a functional connection to something else, and this in turn is to raise other questions about the economic, political, and religious orders. The eventual invention and recognition of dramatic art as a consumable product, separate from communal and occasional contexts, clearly depends upon a free-floating and wage-earning audience, upon a city large enough to support the entrepreneurial ambitions of a Burbage or a Henslowe. This city itself could arise only as a result of a disproportionate participation in the sixteenth-century growth in population, the price revolution, and changes in the no less biological, economic, and representational relations of lords to tenants, and of the displaced poor to both the distributors of alms and to potential industrial or mercantile employers. These relations profoundly interact with transformations in the (also representational) relation between theory and practice, the theory and practice of charity, the expanding theory of agriculture and manufacture and its practical application in an arena relatively unregulated (and therefore unrepresented) by national authority. Such transformations depend in turn upon revisions in the theory of learning itself, and upon its translation into condensed and pragmatic methods. All these interactive changes had their impact

---

[8] Martin Battestin, "Fielding's Definition of Wisdom: Some Functions of Ambiguity and Emblem in *Tom Jones*," *ELH* 35 (1968): 188–217; Viner, *Role of Providence in the Social Order*.

upon the church, upon the audience for drama, and upon such laymen as Kyd, Greene, Marlowe, and Shakespeare, none of whom would have had such literacy, such learning, or such opportunities for playmaking had they been born at the end of the fifteenth century. And to account for these social and intellectual reforms would mean also to engage the question of the changed relation between clerics and laity, which is once again to encounter a problem of representation, whether one thinks of the Crown's assuming the headship, or of believers pretending to the universal priesthood, or of the civic and religious self-consciousness that urged lay burghers and gentry to assert the right to represent themselves before God and the monarch, or that compelled Henry, Elizabeth, and James (despite their considerable religious differences) commonly to deny the fullness of that right (had it ever been fully expressed) in the name of their own gathering divine one, a representational claim more baroque than medieval, and expressing a sense of statecraft that thoroughly appreciated the uses and the implications of a new kind of stagecraft.

Thus conceived, the topic is obviously overwhelming. It lacks a logical or causal starting place, even for expository purposes, and it terminates only at the arbitrary point where one chooses to leave the trace to its own devices. Only the Absolute Spirit could achieve dialectical purchase upon all that interconnects whenever one raises the innocent-seeming question of how the drama changes in its representational mode. Absent that fulfillment, we can at least be warned that commonplace formulae about secularization and naturalism barely begin to touch the complex of questions that would have to be answered before one could adequately discuss the Elizabethan world picture, or properly grasp the social, aesthetic, and epistemological implications of proposing that there really is a picture to be apprehended or to be represented on a stage.

Even so, there is a statable problem about representation which has an evident connection with the putative breakdown of traditional English community, religion, and theater. One convenient but not quite sufficient way to put that problem is to identify it with the discovery of representation as such, with the recognition of an order of signification that purports to be, not natural, perhaps, but adequate in at least a provisional, conventional, or fictive way. Unmediated and deeply embodied community, that mythical community founded on Durkheimian likeness, for which we have a suitable image in a semiritualistic medieval theater founded on the intrinsic ambiguities of kindness, seems quite alien, and very vulnerable to such a notion. Not that a strong distinction between sign and signified necessarily threatens ideas of hierarchy, or of sacred authorization for the powers that be; these can coexist with either understanding of the way signs work. Where the patterns crucially differ is with respect to permeability of boundaries—between rank and rank, manufacturer and consumer, ideas and things, heaven and earth—and here the participatory and the representational models of reality are obviously at odds, at least if we think of the latter as yielding a mediated world constructed by rationalized and bounded presences, presences which claim to stand in the place of something else as representatives and factors guaranteed by writ or compact, themselves uncontaminated (or not to be judged or undermined) by any inherent and perhaps countervailing "inward" writing that would continue the tropic process beyond the limits of the order at hand. Here is the shift toward epistemology, abstract space, and universal mathesis which so many scholars have discussed, and rightly, for it is easy enough to document the invention in the Renaissance of some such purified representational logic.[9] It is there, for instance, in Calvin's (or John, Bishop of Ely's) insistence that the Sacrifice occurred but once, or in Sidney's wish that the drama not conflate times and locales, or in the transformation of Parliament from council and court to a representative assembly helping the Crown enact omnicompetent statute law.[10] In each of these cases, one fixes and privileges a set of signifiers, gives it univocal and universal standing as the determinate and perhaps also determining figure of another reality.

Yet the establishment of a Cartesian or Lockean order of representation is not the business of the sixteenth century, however much that new order may have as its precondition a sixteenth-century process of drawing more explicit legal, social, and epistemological boundaries. Therefore it cannot quite be our business here. To conceive the problem along the idealizing (or empiricizing) lines that these proper names suggest—and the suggestions are necessarily correlative—would be to risk missing a deeper prob-

[9] An early, concise account of the shift from metaphysical, figurative wordplay to the Baconian/Hobbesian concern to have words represent things plainly and clearly is A. C. Howell, "*Res et Verba*: Words and Things," *ELH* 13 (1946): 131–42. Lawrence Manley sees the seventeenth century's concern with epistemology as deriving from theological and political controversies of the sixteenth century, particularly as these concerned the relationship between nature and convention. *Convention, 1500–1750* (Cambridge, Massachusetts: Harvard University Press, 1980).

[10] "For Christ cannot be offered truly and properly no more but once upon the cross, for He cannot be offered again no more than He can be dead again; and dying and shedding blood as He did upon the cross, and not dying and not shedding blood as in the Eucharist, cannot be one action of Christ offered on the cross, and of Christ offered in the Church at the altar by the priest by representation only, no more than Christ and the Priest are the same person. . . . For then the action of Christ's sacrifice, which is long since past, should continue as long as the Eucharist shall endure, even unto the world's end . . . ; and the representation of an action cannot be the action itself." "A Sermon Preached at the Funeral . . . of Lancelot Andrewes . . . by John, Late Lord Bishop of Ely," Lancelot Andrewes, *Ninety-Six Sermons* (Oxford: John Henry Parker, 1843) 5: 287.

lem with a more profound implication for the drama. For a precondition of inventing a new order of representation seems to have been a reassessment not only of the techniques by which to picture nature, but also of the way in which nature itself signifies. That is to say, the question at hand is less that of how to represent nature than the logically prior question of what and how it is that nature represents. And with this, we precisely touch that shifty line which marks off the theater from the book.

Even the earliest Tudor interludes seem to put this question in a different way, and give it an answer different in emphasis, from anything that remains of the civic drama or the moralities that come to mind whenever one thinks "medieval." Perhaps by reason of condensation, or for purposes of polemic, or in satisfaction of humanist desires to see life represented as a proposition, arguable or self-evident, human nature appears on the interludes' stage not as a figurative abyss, capable of kindness or unkindness, but as a determinate reality, given, or to be discovered. Medwall's pair of apparently unlike banquet-plays nicely illustrate this tendency. The one that is called *Nature* exploits a latent possibility of older moralities (one uses the adjective as a convention and the plural as a matter of faith) like the *Castle of Perseverance*, but in a way that suppresses tropological play.[11] Like *Mundus and Infans*, it subsumes the whole of humankind's biography to the prodigal pattern of fall and eventual redemption, yet unlike the *Castle* (or *Wisdom*, or *Mankind*) it imposes that pattern as a kind of template, almost as a law of human behavior: till old age comes (or the end of Part 1), sensuality will reign, and then reason and charity may have a chance. Where the earlier plays make their hero a figurative nexus, drawn back and forth—in person or in proxy—along the chain of signifiers that leads to Christ or away from him, *Nature* is really one long tavern scene, with Mankind the dupe and cohort of vices which are also social types: he acts out the almost preordained shape of his own mortal time, and they enact their natures, too.[12]

[11] Unless otherwise noted, all assertions about dates and classification of plays derive from Alfred Harbage, ed., *Annals of English Drama, 975–1700*, rev. ed. by Samuel Schoenbaum (London: Methuen, 1964). Tudor interludes referred to in this section may be found in the standard collections indexed in Harbage and Schoenbaum, or in the Garland series of critical editions of Renaissance drama.

[12] As M. E. Moeslin argues, Medwall structures his play according to the "course and law of nature" (*Nature*, pt. 2, line 1032), perhaps with a humanistic emphasis deriving from Pico della Mirandola upon the microcosmic order. *The Plays of Henry Medwall: A Critical Edition* (New York: Garland Press, 1981), 247–73. But as Charles W. Crupi reminds us, whatever its newness, *Nature* remains firmly within the scope of orthodox Christian doctrine. "Christian Doctrine in Henry Medwall's *Nature*," *Renascence* 34 (1982): 100–112.

Even though *Fulgens and Lucres* adopts a different moral tone, and is much the more fetching play to modern tastes, it also puts the nature of nature in question, and similarly concludes that it has a fixed *virtù*, an essence separable from the rituals and fictions of culture, though here attached to differentiated persons rather than to the whole of humankind. We need not wonder how attractive this doctrine might be to "new men" who rose through learning and favor rather than through inherited position, or see in it a foreshadowing or psychological simulacrum of Reformation beliefs about election and reprobation. Plausible inferences, both, but the point I am after is the simpler one that in Gaius Flaminius and Publius Cornelius the signifier has been naturalized and historicized. Considered according to intrinsic "nature," these are not tropological potentials, but a pair of accomplished and incorrigible facts, whether by accident of birth or pedagogical success, and these two embodied facts—since they correlate with the opposed values of position and virtue (themselves fixed positional values in this fiction)—present Medwall and his audience with a nice topic for debate. No matter that the topos is an old one or that the outcome of argument is never really in question.[13] The implicit assertion, both predestinarian and Pelagian in its assumptions, is that some are born with a mark that differentiates them from the rest, and with this privileging of virtuous birth, the stage is set for the play of that idea, and for the sort of play that sets out to discriminate—whether by ironic reversal or by narrative demonstration—between the true and the false embodiment of that difference.

In other registers of discourse, and with far less tactful management of the proposition, such plays as *Jacob and Esau*, *The Disobedient Child*, *Nice Wanton*, *Enough is as Good as a Feast*, and *The Longer Thou Livest the More Fool Thou Art* portray nature as similarly significant of an embedded and unalterable order. In some instances the playwright aims to encourage early and disciplined education, in others to reinforce the doctrine of election, or rebuke those who fail to rouse the sleeping seeds of grace (or intellect) until such time as time for conversion is past (as in effect it never was, even past death, for the Humanum Genus of the *Castle*). The issues change and develop, the dramatic treatment is sometimes more extensive, sometimes the difference between the historicized heavenly man and worldly man is more crudely and univalently established. But the differences in dramaturgy are middling, mostly to the advantage of Medwall's

[13] As Ernst Robert Curtius says, "Every period of enlightenment reaches the conclusion that noble descent in itself is no guarantee of noble thought." *European Literature and the Latin Middle Ages*, trans. Willard R. Trask (1953; New York: Harper and Row, 1963), 179. See the discussion of Medwall's treatment of his Italian humanist source in Moeslin, *Plays of Henry Medwall*, 77–89.

talent, and not of the sort that obscures a shared appraisal of human nature not as a malleable figure of humankind's origins and eschatological outcome, but as differentiated in the life of some design, as separated into counters for the conceptual representation of a historicized reality. Even a "folk" play like *Youth*, or the satirical *Hickscorner*, or that *Lusty Juventus* which turns the prodigal plot against papistical elders, or the rather offensive *Impatient Poverty*, which like *Magnificence* abstracts a medieval figure from its larger context, all give the impression that their characters express an inherent shape of nature that is to be recognized as lawlike, as a formula that describes a particular section of the real without itself also participating in some metaphoric regression toward a transcendent "original" figure. At best, we may be expected to recall the fallen Adam in us all; but we are not urged to think toward a further *figura* which might be imitated.

It is usually argued that a new and more modern understanding of representation, or of what nature really is, must run contrary to the tradition of allegory. We are often told that the universals of the allegorical mode coexist uneasily, if at all, with the particulars of realism, and that increasing particularity eventually overwhelms allegory with a complexity that it is not equipped to handle. In the history and theory that have dominated the discussion of Tudor drama, this supposed contradiction between the abstract and the real serves as the motor of evolution. It is said to be partly responsible for the tendency of these plays to bifurcate into a set of human characters and an ultimately discardable set of personifications, it seemingly creates increasing difficulties in bridging the gap between historical action and moral application, and it is commonly held to express an underlying and irresolvable tension between alternative ways of analyzing reality, between the Christian and the secular, the exemplaristic and the historical, the ideal and the actual.[14] Plausible and inevitable though such theses seem when one's own understanding of reality makes a hard and fast distinction between that which is sacred and ideal and that which is secular and natural, there are two difficulties in accepting it. One has to do with the historical record itself. The other has to do with the nature of representation, at least if conceived as implying the existence of a fixed or self-motivated nature that can be encompassed in some image, model, or fiction.

On the side of history, one has to select quite carefully from the fractured remains of Tudor drama in order to show much tendency (and I

---

[14] The seminal version of this argument is Spivack, *Shakespeare and the Allegory of Evil*. Joyce E. Peterson sees the conflict between allegorical universals and realistic particulars beginning still earlier, "The Paradox of Disintegrating Form in *Mundus et Infans*," *English Literary Renaissance* 7 (1977): 3–16.

doubt that it is one that a statistician would trust) for printers and keepers of public records to prefer an increasingly larger dose of realism mixed up with—or separated from—their morals. In fact, "historical," "allegorical," and "hybrid" plays peacefully coexist from the beginning of the printed record, as indeed we should expect, given the existence of a medieval work like the Digby *Mary Magdalene*, and the continual pressure in medieval drama of what Robert Weimann calls "disenchanting" mimetic realism.[15]

I have already made the point that Medwall can commit *I and II Nature* (1495) as well as *Fulgens and Lucres* (1497); this balance of modes persists throughout the first three-quarters of the century. Changes in the personnel and ideology of the court do not seem to produce any consistent trend aesthetically. In 1516 the court can watch *Troilus and Pandar*, but it witnesses *Self Love* and *Genus Humanum* in 1552 and 1553, and *Truth, Faithfulness, and Mercy* in 1575. When we first encounter works for which there is independent evidence of their belonging to public players rather than having just been offered for acting, they have titles like *Samson* (1567) and *Ptoleme* (1578). Yet Tarlton was happy to crossbreed classical legends with a scheme of the Seven Deadly Sins in 1585 and Robert Wilson is writing moral plays as late as 1588. The unfortunate *Clyomon and Clamydes* (1570), assigned to unknown auspices, seems from the extant texts to mark a transition toward romance, yet the lost *Eglemour and Degrebelle* (1444) probably anticipates such a subject by 126 years.[16]

"Hybridization"—as in *Cambises* or *Appius and Virginia*—is supposed to be a late development, perhaps marking a transition to chronicle, yet both *Godly Queen Hester* (1527) and *King Johan* (1538) as freely mix the historical with the abstract as does the native dramaturgy of the earlier Digby plays or the classically inspired apocalyptics of Foxe's *Christus Triumphans* (1556).[17] *Godly Queen Hester* is not a play of the public repertoire, yet its "Vice" action is as wholly separable as any later one, its abstract qualities being entirely transferred to a worldly embodiment: Pride, Ambition, and Adulation cede their characteristics to the courtier who has robbed them of place, and then go off to the tavern, leaving the "his-

---

[15] Robert Weimann, *Shakespeare and the Popular Tradition in the Theater: Studies in the Social Dimension of Dramatic Form and Function* (Baltimore: Johns Hopkins University Press, 1978), 5.

[16] Bevington, *From Mankind to Marlowe*. See also Patricia Russell, "Romantic Narrative Plays: 1570–1590," in *Elizabethan Theatre*, Stratford-Upon-Avon Studies, 9, ed. John Russell Brown and Bernard Harris (New York: St. Martin's Press, 1967), 112, who argues that "the development of popular drama from *Cambises* to *Mucedorus* can perhaps be considered as an attempt to give romantic substance a proper dramatic form."

[17] *Hybridization* is Spivack's term.

torical" Aman to act their collective role, helped only by the mischievous Hardy Dardy.[18]

Bale's famous history expresses precisely the same relationship between moral idea and exemplary embodiment: Sedition disguises himself as Stephen Langton, and Usurped Power goes by the name of Innocent III; when King Johan dies, the actor playing him reappears as Imperial Majesty, who is in turn the figure for Henry VIII, fulfilling what Johan had begun. Even in the Terentian focus that John Foxe attempts, there is the same coexistence of person and idea, as well as of chronologically separate times: Eva and Mary come together in one scene, Ecclesia and Pornapolis in another; Antichrist is a series of historical popes, who participate in a psychomachian pattern with such other figures as Psyche, Populus, Nomologus, Europus, and a chorus of five virgins.[19]

Juli and Julian, Damon and Pithias, Jack Juggler (1570, 1565, 1555); *Cambises, Horestes, The Conflict of Conscience* (1561, 1567, 1572); *All for Money, The Trial of Treasure, Like Will to Like* (1577, 1568, 1567): it seems impossible to find a dominant tendency with respect to realism, abstractness, or ethical purpose in these plays. The record is sparse, probably representing printers' enterprise, evangelical excitement, and government policy as much as the cherished repertory of public troupes, but it provides little evidence of any bias, or of mounting disdain for either allegory or homiletic example in the period before the founding of the theaters. Instead, there is a kind of stylistic stasis in which classical legend, religious instruction, and pedagogical fantasies are all served up in a dramaturgy that persistently relates a governing idea to the concrete (or personified) reality which displays it.

Yet this is in the very nature of a representational mode that takes nature itself as largely nonfigurative. There is no question that the Tudor interludes generally go about their business in an obtrusively didactic way, but this arises, I think, on account of the newness that they attempt rather than in consequence of the oldness that they have not yet cast off. What is new probably comes directly from the newly explicit pedagogical intent of these plays; for unlike their medieval predecessors, *ideas* inform these actions. In our own post-Kantian era, it should need no proving that "nature" cannot be seen apart from the ideas with which "culture" apprehends it. This is not to deny that there is something "real"

---

[18] The argument distinguishing public from private repertoire, finding in the former a greater tendency toward separate Vice actions, is Bevington's, in *From Mankind to Marlowe*.

[19] John Bale, *King Johan*, ed. Barry B. Adams (San Marino: Huntington Library, 1969); John Foxe, *Two Latin Comedies by John Foxe the Martyrologist, Titus et Gesippus/Christus Triumphans*, ed. and trans. John Hazel Smith (Ithaca, New York: Cornell University Press, 1973).

apart from our constructions—though Lacan tempts one to agree that
reality is a cork which is always missing from the gaps in our own language, bodies, and desires—but it is to insist upon the inevitability of at
least tacit allegory in every one of our attempts to capture reality in some
representational net.[20] What nature represents, in other words, is our
model of it, our idea, and the main difference between so-called realistic
modes and others is that realism tries to make us overlook the shaping
pressure of ideas, or else—as in the naturalism of a Zola—urges us to take
such constructs as resulting from a supposedly natural law.

Certainly the Tudor interlude has not become realistic in this sense.
Quite the contrary. These plays make their ideological infrastructure part
of the dramatic action; they abstract the essence of the plot, display it in
the proverblike titles, in the staged debates about what principle the action illustrates, in the iconography, the dumb shows, and the names and
actions of the Vice. They are therefore didactic in more than the narrowly
moral sense. Such plays teach a way of seeing as well as a set of mores;
they urge an audience to conceive of their own lives according to some
transformation of the structure of causes, motives, values, and ideas
which governs these fables. Not the figurative displacement of structure,
but the historical and intellectual establishment of structure: this is the
basic difference between interludes and the tradition of mysteries and earlier moralities. That is to say, the Tudor interlude educates its viewers in
the ideological apprehension of human nature, thereby vastly enlarging
the representational capital upon which an English populace might readily draw in the effort to organize its own rapidly changing and differentiating experience.[21]

Concentrating our attention on the interludes as drawers of boundaries
and shapers of ideology releases us from the debilitating chore of trying
to talk about them in purely aesthetic terms. This is an important gain, I
think, for if there is one term that no modern reader would be disposed

---

[20] Jacques Lacan, *The Four Fundamental Concepts of Psychoanalysis*, trans. Alan Sheridan
(New York: W. W. Norton, 1978), ix.

[21] Whether one takes a Marxist or a Mannheimian view, most would agree that the con-
cept of ideology—as distinguished from the production and effect of ideology—develops in
the late sixteenth or early seventeenth century. I rely especially upon J. G. Merquior, *The
Veil and the Mask: Essays on Culture and Ideology* (London: Routledge and Kegan Paul, 1979),
Jorge Larrain, *The Concept of Ideology* (Athens: University of Georgia Press, 1979), Niklas
Luhmann, "Positive Law and Ideology," in *The Differentiation of Society*, trans. Stephen
Holmes and Charles Larmore (New York: Columbia University Press, 1982), 90–121, and
Donald R. Kelley, *The Beginning of Ideology: Consciousness and Society in the French Reforma-
tion* (Cambridge: Cambridge University Press, 1981). Though not the only deliberate process of ideological formation, that which humanistic education and the cause of the gospel
provided for the new Elizabethan aristocracy was surely the most important. See Wallace
T. MacCaffrey, "England: The Crown and the New Aristocracy, 1540–1600," *Past and Present* 30 (1965): 52–64 and Fritz Caspari, *Humanism and the Social Order in Tudor England* (Chicago: University of Chicago Press, 1954).

to privilege in talking about the experience of these plays, "art" would surely be a prime candidate. But in introducing the notion of ideology, I do not want to risk the opposite error—which David Bevington has convincingly refuted—of taking any interlude, much less every one of them, as bound in an exclusive way to the particulars of an immediate historical context.[22]

Certainly some of the plays—*Gorboduc, King Johan*, or the vastly more sophisticated *Endimion*—refer directly to living persons and current problems, but such referential contexts hardly exhaust the didactic and rhetorical potential of these works. In fact, historical reality is just one instance of the universal truths which these plays purport to set before their audience. It is for that reason that they merit the adjective *ideological* in a strict sense: not only elaborating what Pierre Bourdieu calls *doxa*, that collectively improvised sense of reality which implicitly structures every group's practice and self-definition, they also bring a bounded part of that structure to conscious articulation, establishing the steps by which sixteenth-century persons and events may be connected with and understood in the light of a set of beliefs that are certified for true by virtue of being distinguished from those which the fable proves "false."[23]

Thus *Gorboduc* makes a general statement about the nature of political inheritance, proving its king wrong in a way that Elizabeth also risks being; *King Johan* argues the reality of providential forces in history, making Henry VIII an imperial monarch on the side of right; *Endimion* both compliments and exhorts its royal audience, summing up a courtier's renunciation of the queen's mortal person and celebrating the apotheosis of her sacred person, its stage figure (Cynthia) being assumed to the stature and the life-bestowing functions of the Godhead whom the living queen must mirror as the moon the sun. "Flattery" or "historical allegory" no more name all the use and meaning of *Endimion* than the term "political satire" can account for Skelton's *Magnificence*. Perhaps Wolsey is less surely one referent of the earlier play than Elizabeth (and Oxford, or Leicester, or some other courtier) is of the later one; but in either case, what enables allusion is the symbolic structure that defines the role which historical actors play. No "real" person is represented on the stage; rather, the stage gives us (and them and their contemporaries) a system of ideas by which they may be known for beings of a certain kind, the beings, that is, who instance these meanings.[24]

[22] David Bevington, *Tudor Drama and Politics: A Critical Approach to Topical Meaning* (Cambridge, Massachusetts: Harvard University Press, 1968).

[23] Pierre Bourdieu, *Outline of a Theory of Practice*, trans. Richard Nice (Cambridge: Cambridge University Press, 1977).

[24] William O. Harris, *Skelton's "Magnyfycence" and the Cardinal Virtue Tradition* (Chapel Hill: University of North Carolina Press, 1965).

Of course there is some special pleading in my taking historical allusion as the basic type with which to understand the interludes' redefinition of what nature represents. Despite the *aporia* that our own new philosophy has been inducing with respect to differences between fact and fiction, one is inclined to think that the theatrical representation of real persons necessarily involves ideology in a way that the staging of fictions should be able to avoid, or at least disguise. And even if there is more historical allusion in Tudor drama than in medieval, the practice is by no means new or unique; one thinks immediately of Aristophanes, where the references are far more direct, or of *Mankind*, which goes to the point of naming individual justices of the peace as agents of Titivillus. Yet the allusions in *Mankind*, like the satire on tyrannical prelates and princes which recurs throughout the Corpus Christi plays, never reach for any conceptual complexity. Staying at the level of a very individual tropology, medieval drama lets us think of real persons who stand with Satan rather than with Christ, but the plays do not force us to think further about the specific kind of evil or goodness which a given character might exemplify. Even the seven deadly sins serve as a way of elaborating the variants of a Fall which is always one and the same rather than as a way of distinguishing one kind of character from another. Indeed, it is an essential trait of exemplaristic theology that such distinctions are only provisional: one vice may take the lead, but "euery synne tyllyth in oþyr / And makyth Mankynde to ben a foole" (MCP 33/1033–34). Thus emphasizing tropological performance rather than cognitive discrimination, medieval drama brings everything back to questions of charity and concupiscence: being concerned with the way in which individuals enact the one figure that all of us inevitably are, these plays have little interest in constructing those more artificial figures that allow finer distinctions among persons and within which it is possible to build up the complicated meanings by which the world is governed rather than renounced.[25]

These latter figures are ones in which the Tudor interludes seem to have specialized. Sometimes their method is the rather obvious one of turning an old image against the beliefs and practices it had formerly sustained. As Richard Axton has shown, this is the strategy of *Calisto and Melibea*, which puts Mariological piety in the mouth of Celestina and of her victim, thereby turning the bawd (a conventional antitype of the Virgin) into the vehicle of a covert attack on good works, Mariolatry, relic worship, and other such delusions as lead to corrupt rather than to wholesome

---

[25] And as Wilfred Cantwell Smith suggests, the modern understanding of faith as a matter of assent to cognitive propositions derives from Reformation theology and differs from the essentially performative character of the earlier understanding of faith. *Faith and Belief* (Princeton: Princeton University Press, 1979).

charity.[26] Or again, an interlude may abstract a pattern from its earlier doctrinal context in order to make it serve differentiating purposes. Just as *Lusty Juventus* turns the prodigal-son plot against the older generation of Catholics, so Wager turns the life of Mary Magdalene against the penitential doctrines it had formerly justified; and in *God's Promises*, Bale not only brings the doctrine of the Seven Ages into a sharp focus it never attains in the civic drama, but does so precisely for the purpose of advancing a dogma of *sola fides* which the cycles could never have supported.[27]

Yet the habit of portraying reality as illustrative of ideological constructs is by no means limited to plays that take up cudgels against the old religion. Foraging on the great commons of classical and medieval exempla, newly available in print and in translation, Tudor playwrights provide townsmen and schoolboys with a more articulated range of social types, moral concepts, and positive or negative behavioral ideals than could ever have been garnered from the medieval stage or supplied by earlier educational practices to so large an audience. Confined to the narrow limit of an interlude, bound in these chapbook *libri laicorum*, the old examples no longer work for a select audience within the extended—and therefore complicating, if not also ironizing—narration of Chaucer, Gower, Lydgate, Boccaccio, Apuleius, Herodotus, Arthurian legend, or the Bible itself. Not set in a larger figurative or dialectical pattern (not even that of a sermon), but extracted as distinct and independent biographical moments, admirable or deplorable each in its own right, the lives of ancient noteworthies are served up as types for civic and vocational emulation or eschewal and as opportunities for self-defining, self-regarding, and self-escaping fantasy. The list of these concrete universals is as long as the audience's appetite was apparently insatiable, and can be added to almost at the reader's pleasure: Griselda, Palamon and Arcite, Troilus, Gismond of Salerne, Abraham, Susanna, Orestes, Cambises, Ajax, King Arthur, and a ghostly troupe of chivalric heroes whose names survive mainly in the titles of lost and probably unmemorable plays.[28]

Partly as a consequence of being reduced to the manner of an interlude,

[26] Richard Axton, "Folk Play in Tudor Interludes," in *English Drama, Forms and Development: Essays in Honor of M. C. Bradbrook* (Cambridge: Cambridge University Press, 1977), 12–21. For evidence of a deliberate program of turning the new stage against the old, see Sydney Anglo, "An Early Tudor Programme for Plays and Other Demonstrations against the Pope," *Journal of the Warburg and Courtauld Institutes* 20 (1957): 176–79.

[27] John N. King, *English Reformation Literature: The Tudor Origins of the Protestant Tradition* (Princeton: Princeton University Press, 1982), 271–318; Wickham, *Early English Stages* 2: 28.

[28] C. R. Baskerville, "Some Evidence for Early Romantic Plays in England," *Modern Philology* 14 (1916): 37–59.

and partly—one suspects—as a consequence of the strongly pragmatic cast of mind shared by the politicians, schoolmasters, reformers, and unknown intellectuals who wrote these plays, most such exempla have a notably formulaic character. In fact, it would not be far off the mark to call them formulas *for* character: King Cambises' "vein" is not only a manner of speaking, it is also a way of being, an *eidos* which bespeaks tyranny not in the manner of a Herod—for he is defined by a metaphysical contrast and terminus—but by virtue of a cruelty and blustering caprice that Preston insists upon to melodramatic excess, partly by juxtaposing Cambises' tyranny with the stoic righteousness of the good knight Praxiteles. Like Plautine stock characters, braggart, parasite, lecherous father, and so forth, the exemplary personages of the Tudor interlude offer an audience unflattering stereotypes with which to see its fellows, but unlike Plautus, they also supply glasses of virtue in which to see oneself, or with which to define the ideals an audience would like its wives, children, friends, and masters to exhibit in deference to a sense of proper order. One need not even have read *The Commodye of Pacient and Meeke Grissill* to know that it diminishes Chaucer's enigmatic fable about providence into a cartoon homily for goodwives, "Whearin is declared, the good example, of her pacience towards her husband: and lykewise, the due obedience of Children, toward their Parentes."[29] Nor is there any way of elevating *Appius and Virginia* into a moral complexity that would give Isabella much discomfort about the relative merits of virginity and death. *Damon and Pithias, Jacob and Esau, The Most Virtuous and Godly Susanna*: one need not belabor the point that such plays are all glasses of government in one way or another, that they define and display the sort of roles and the patterns of loyalty, deference, and private virtue which contribute to the creation and the maintenance of civic and domestic order.

Nor does the contrast with cycles and moralities need much emphasis. Where medieval plays ironize the juridical structure while simultaneously reconciling persons to the givens of temporal existence, here the stress is on that internalized sense of worth, place, and godly virtue that will allow one to play out a destined role to its conclusion, however heroic or bitter it may be. Even the moral vacuity of a *Clyomon and Clamydes* or a *Common Conditions* does not disable them from serving a similar function. Like the Accession-Day tilts, staged so that commoners could witness the formation and enactment of Elizabethan mythology, such romances—transposing a courtly ideal into the vulgar key of *Mucedorus*—certify a set of stock

---

[29] John Phillip, *The Play of Patient Grissell*, ed. Ronald B. McKerrow and W. W. Greg, Malone Society Reprints (London: Chiswick Press, 1909), title page.

responses for coping with the ultimate irrationalities of love and fortune, irrationalities shared by court and commons alike.[30] Plays like these offer paradigms of valor and sentiment which might not receive Quixotic imitation in real life, but which surely helped undergird a developing national identity in much the same way as the American western movie has ours, everyman his own knight in the chivalric combat with good and evil—and therefore common—conditions.[31]

"Common Conditions," of course, is the name of a Vice as well as of the play in which he figures. This fact, and the oddly amoral and erratic character of the little "hourchet" who facilitates the plot of this anonymous work, afford one more way of getting at the Tudor representation of nature as graspable by the ideas figured forth in art. The origins of the Vice-convention are famously complicated; part jester and fool, part Satanic subaltern, part comic vehicle for the leading actor, the Vice—like much else in the Tudor interlude—focuses and develops an aspect of the old "native" dramaturgy in a way that subtly estranges it from urban and medieval contexts and purposes. The name itself poses a suggestive problem. Though we are naturally disposed to derive it from moral theology, Prudentian programs of instruction, or the various tempters of the medieval stage, the theatrical use of the term first occurs in the early sixteenth century, in 1515 as a name for the mechanical angel in the Canterbury burghers' St. Thomas play and about 1528 as a designation for Heywood's "Mery-Reporte" in *The Play of the Weather*. Such usages make one suspect that the word connotes "device" as much as it denotes some specific tropological deviation.[32]

Rather than embodying a tropic disfiguration of humankind's potential, the Vice of Tudor drama seems often to be the trope which turns, motivates, or conceptualizes the particular action at hand. Not that ultimate self-referential negation which is Dante's (or *Wisdom*'s) Lucifer, nor that sum of all vices which is *Mankind*'s Titivillus, these specific figures—Infidelity, Ill-Report, Natural Inclination, Ambidexter, Haphazard, Covetousness, Politick Persuasion—each suit and help determine a bounded set of characters and a bounded problem to be explored and solved.

Of course particularity in Vices goes hand in hand with the necessary particularity of historical exempla; the further the remove from that uni-

---

[30] Frances A. Yates, "Elizabethan Chivalry: The Romance of the Accession Day Tilts," *Journal of the Warburg and Courtauld Institute* 20 (1957): 4–25.

[31] For an analogous argument about the function of a new form of drama in a changing national situation, see James L. Peacock, *Rites of Modernization: Symbolic and Social Aspects of Indonesian Proletarian Drama* (Chicago: University of Chicago Press, 1968).

[32] Giles E. Dawson, *Records of Plays and Players in Kent, 1450–1642*, Malone Society Collections, (Oxford: Malone Society, 1965) 7: 192–97. Spivack argues against the pertinency of Heywood's usage, *Shakespeare and the Allegory of Evil*, 136–37.

versal figuration in which the cycles and the moralities specialized, the
more need for particular rather than universal *radices malorum*.[33] Yet there
is more than a difference in specificity between Ambidexter and his medieval brethren. The scholarly tradition which saw in irreligious and
sportive Vices some foreshadowing of a spiritually indifferent realism no
doubt misconceived the function of religious instruction even in a "secu-
larizing" society, yet it is right, I think, to suggest that the mischief of a
Politick Persuasion (or a Hickscorner) somehow differs in function and
import even from that of the character named Mischief in *Mankind* and
certainly from the antics and temptations of medieval sins and devils.
One way of getting at this difference is to notice, with other commenta-
tors, that the Tudor Vice is often a companion or a separable analogue
rather than a tempter of human character.[34]

   To be sure, such figures as Hypocrisy (in *Lusty Juventus*) and Infidelity
(in *The Life and Repentence of Mary Magdalene*) tempt their worst and temporarily succeed in drawing hero or heroine off the path of righteousness,
but these Vices differ from old devils partly in the obvious ideological
implications of their names and motives, and partly in their designating a
state of life and mind that characterizes the specific delusion which overcomes their victims. A further mark of difference is the greater emphasis
which such plays give to the old business about the devil's disguise: when
Hypocrisy calls himself Friendship, or when Infidelity dilates upon the
implications of his pseudonyms (Legal Justice and Prudence), the playwright forces intellectual discriminations on his audience that require
their assent to an explicit dogma with immediate social and historical
consequences. Rather than being asked to choose the contemplative life
over the active one (at least for the moment of the play, as a way of seeing
into their own souls), an audience can respond to these Protestant *Lehr-
stücke* only if it is willing to conceive of itself as defined by ideological
roles, and to see the choice between these roles as governed by epistemological insight or mistake about the nature of the (divine or human)
Other rather than by a recollection or forgetting of one's "own" mirroring self.

   Like the exemplary "human" characters in these and other interludes,
such Vices clearly help establish a net of meanings which contemporary
events and persons can instantiate. But the manner of this instantiation
seems crucially different from the figurative conformity or deformity that
establishes a relation between the characters of medieval drama and the

   [33] This is Spivack's point, somewhat recast.
   [34] Bevington, *From Mankind to Marlowe*, esp. 80–85. See also the useful discussion in Alan
C. Dessen, *Shakespeare and the Late Moral Plays* (Lincoln: University of Nebraska Press,
1986), 17–37.

original *figura* of creation and mercy. Borrowing a theological term, one is tempted to say that the medieval relation depends upon intrinsic analogy while the later one relies upon external likeness only. One of the great differences between medieval and Protestant (or even sophisticated sixteenth-century Catholic) views of the formal exchange and spiritual intercourse between humanity and God is that Reformed theology rejects intrinsic natural analogy altogether (while Cajetan takes the less radical step of inventing a doctrine of proper proportionality which puts more distance between humanity and God than Thomas ever had envisaged, to say nothing of Bonaventure).[35] Thus the medieval playwright makes Cain and his men members and images of Satan, but one cannot sensibly say that Cambises is a member of Ambidexter, or Horestes a member of Revenge, or Mary Magdalene a member of Infidelity, however much these figures sum up the essential character, motive, or error of the historical persons in question. In the earlier case, the relation between the figurative character and the person seems ontological, depending as it does upon a shared concupiscent denial of the incarnating Word which must nonetheless be signified, if only by negation. In the latter cases, the relation seems to be rhetorical, even intellectual. Politick Persuasion does not share so much as a mystic body with the Marquis, nor is Revenge the image to which Horestes conforms himself. Instead, the one Vice names, advises, and helps rationalize the motives of Griselda's tormenting husband; the other is simultaneously an amoral force from the gods which fuels both Horestes' violence and the horrors of war and a logical contrary of the Amity which concludes the play, for which reason Revenge must be sent packing once the deed is done, his usefulness over, and Horestes about to be crowned by Truth and Duty.

This is why the Vice need not be a tempter in order still to function as an integral part of the play, why he fits so well with a structure of alternation and suppression.[36] No doubt that structure developed for many reasons, theatrical economics perhaps chief among them, but the habit of separating one's serious and "concrete" characters from one's mirthful "abstractions" also enabled both playwright and audience to establish a certain conceptual control over what might otherwise have been a purely sensational spectacle of history. Serving as the analogue or companionable *raissoneur* for those persons who are the titular heroes or villains of

[35] Battista Mondin, *The Principle of Analogy in Protestant and Catholic Theology* (The Hague: Martin Nijhoff, 1968); Joseph C. McLelland, *The Visible Words of God: An Exposition of the Sacramental Theology of Peter Martyr Vermigli, A.D. 1500–1562* (Grand Rapids: William B. Eerdmans, 1957), 76–85.

[36] These terms are Bevington's, employed to describe a scenic structure moving back and forth between sets of characters, some of which disappear altogether in order to enable the actor to pick up another part.

the action, the Tudor Vice gives us a merry report of what the action is about, abstracting a narrative context into a thematic statement, helping us to formulate the rhetorical point of the play and thereby to answer that pragmatic question which medieval drama never seems to pose: what is the playwright trying to say?

In short, the Tudor Vice is a description rather than a negative metaphysical potential. Instead of helping us assimilate all character to the basic binarism of tropic openness and atropic closure, instead of forcing us to see all reality as falling into two radically unlike kinds of Sameness, these figures are agents of differentiation. We might even go so far as to say that the Vice gives us the essential name of the Other, that inevitably ideological formula by which our own secular identities are forged and imaged: he is haphazard, ambidextrous, iniquitous, a carrier of ill report; his is the common condition of humanity, or the activity of revenge, or of the policy, the politic persuasion that rules great officials. And always, in thus identifying and articulating our public experience, the Vice displays that amoral, witty, and dangerous essence which marks him as a figure more of the social intellect than of the religious soul. Like Mery-Reporte, he is the distanced, tricky, and usually scurrilous inner voice of the plot, brought on stage first to puzzle us about his name, and then to make us see his name as the mainspring of the puzzle in order and identity which his play sets us—even if that puzzle is so slight a matter as converting the meteorological self-interestedness of different stations, sexes, and occupations into a merrily reported fable of the mutual yielding that must occur if the commonwealth is to prosper.[37] On this view of the convention's function, Ambidexter is no deviation, nor is Heywood's Vice a courtly anomaly: like their more obviously "vicious" brethren, these figures help shape a stage nature which is not more lifelike than that of medieval drama, but is more rationalized, having to do with the construction rather than the displacement of an inescapably symbolic order of the "real."

As with the Vices, so with the plays as a whole. Spread by the printing press to parish churches, and elsewhere throughout the countryside by a steadily growing number of actors who achieve a dominance of public entertainment by midcentury, the Tudor interludes offer a more intellectual and educative fare than the songs of minstrels and waits, or the festival games, devices, and dramas of townspeople and neighbors. In the long run, their effect is an audience grown self-conscious about the forms and fictions that organize existence—the sort of audience, courtly or pro-

[37] David Bevington, "Is Heywood's *Play of the Weather* Really about the Weather?" *Renaissance Drama* 7 (1964): 11–19.

vincial, which could appreciate the formal frolic of Peele's *Old Wives' Tale*, respond to the visual rhetoric of a *Tamburlaine*, or grasp the niceties of Faustus's extravagant case of conscience.[38] Such an audience is not traditional or "medieval," however medievalizing and insistently traditional the ideology of the Elizabethan court and gentry. It is an audience that has been trained to recognize the ideas that define and differentiate its values, ideas whose explicit formulation establishes tradition itself.[39] Needless to say, these are also the ideas which distinguish the new men and ways from the old, and which create those powerful conundrums about the difference between restorative and corruptive innovations, between legalistic preciseness and ceremonial laxity in one's definition of the forms that body forth supposedly aboriginal and essential truths about a human nature now become subject to dispute.

One subtext of my argument so far is the unsurprising assertion that new puzzles in cosmic order and personal identity grew out of the new drama and social reality which English men and women invented in the sixteenth century. Having tried to suggest some ways in which the Tudor interlude construes nature in a newly rationalistic manner, I want now to state more precisely one of the puzzles thereby engendered. As a more or less inevitable place to begin—just how much so, I hope the discussion will show—I want to take up the theology of penance. The immediate justification for this choice is that the civic drama and moralities depend in a fairly explicit way upon a set of penitential assumptions which the Reformation (here a code word for social change as well as for religious) put radically in question; part of the newness of the Tudor interlude is that it either simplifies, revises, or altogether avoids these assumptions. But the theology of penance should interest us for more than this immediate contextual relation or lack of relation. As the symbolic expression of an individual's relation to community and as the ritualized embodiment of a semiological relation between humanity and God, penance has essentially to do with just those questions about meaning and its performance which determine the nature and the understanding of drama, whether lived or played.[40]

---

[38] L. B. Campbell , "Doctor Faustus: A Case of Conscience," *PMLA* 67 (1952): 219–39.

[39] See John S. Weld, *Meaning in Comedy: Studies in Elizabethan Romantic Comedy* (Albany: SUNY Press, 1975), 21–97, for an especially sympathetic account of a late Elizabethan audience's "training in the theater of metaphor and ideas" (57).

[40] For the theory and practice of penance, Catholic and Reformed, I rely on John Bossy, "The Counter-Reformation and the People of Catholic Europe," *Past and Present* 47 (1970): 51–70, Ernest F. Kevan, *The Grace of Law: A Study in Puritan Theology* (London: Carey

It is easy enough to put the difference between old penance and new repentance. One can find it stated again and again in sermons of the period, and always it has to do with exactly apportioning the roles of God and humankind in the inspiration and enactment of a new life. What had been a partial, cooperative, and analogous cause of the sinner's justification becomes a sign and demonstration of antecedent faith, of a preordained conversion at the hands of an already accepting God. On this subject, here is John Bradford, one of the first Marian martyrs and one of the more influential of his generation of home-grown Protestants:

> We say, penance hath three parts: contrition, if you understand it for a hearty sorrowing for sin; confession, if you understand it for faith of free pardon in God's mercy by Jesus Christ; and satisfaction, if you understand it not to God-wards (for that only to Christ must be left alone), but to man-ward in restitution of goods wrongfully or fraudulently gotten, of name hindered by our slanders, and in newness of life: although, as I said before and anon will shew more plainly by God's grace, that this last is no part of penance indeed, but a plain effect or fruit of true penance.[41]

What saves Bradford from mere quibble and distinction without difference in this standard formulation of overlap and unlikeness between two ways of understanding that behavioral newness which all Christians seek, is the fact that the newness itself develops an essential paradox in the relation between grace and nature, one which Catholics and Protestants ground in fundamentally different ways.[42]

Kingsgate Press, 1964), Imogen Luxton, "The Reformation and Popular Culture," *Church and Society in England: Henry VIII to James I*, ed. Felicity Heal and Rosemary O'Day (Hamden: Shoestring Press, 1977), 57–77, McLelland, *Visible Words of God*, 126–66, Reinhard Schwartz, *Vorgeschichte der Reformatorischen Busstheologie* (Berlin: Walter de Gruyter, 1968), Thomas N. Tentler, *Sin and Confession on the Eve of the Reformation* (Princeton: Princeton University Press, 1977), Alfred Vacant and E. Mangenot, eds., *Dictionnaire de théologie catholique* (Paris, 1909–1950), vol. 12, pt. 1, cols. 948–1054, and Ronald S. Wallace, *Calvin's Doctrine of the Christian Life* (Grand Rapids: William B. Eerdmans, 1959). For other, rather different attempts to specify a relation between religious controversy and the drama, see Robert G. Hunter, *Shakespeare and the Mystery of God's Judgments* (Athens: University of Georgia Press, 1976), and Martha Tuck Rozett, *The Doctrine of Election and the Emergence of Elizabethan Tragedy* (Princeton: Princeton University Press, 1984).

[41] John Bradford, "Sermon on Repentance," *The Writings of John Bradford*, ed. Aubrey Townshend, Parker Society Publications, vol. 5 (Cambridge: Cambridge University Press, 1848), 51.

[42] There are other avenues to analyzing this paradox, since many other essentially contested dogmas are constellated in its field. Let me just allude to some of these other disputed questions, partly as a gesture toward the interconnectedness of all these issues, and partly for future reference. Some, like penance, are also sacramental (or merely ceremonial), having to do with the relation between men and women, priests and laity, spirit and matter; others are hermeneutical, having to do with how one reads the Book, or with the relation of history to revelation, how the text of that revelation relates to the text of a world which it either figures as an allegorical potency or governs and inspires as immanent law and beckoning promise; still others have to do with the composition and governance of the church, and with the relations between temporal and sacred powers and purpose. It seems intuitively

One usually names this paradox with the theological categories of grace and nature, but it is as true and considerably more suggestive to name it with another möbian pair, knowing and doing. Of course it is not the case that grace is the same thing as knowledge or that nature will serve as a synonym for the performing capacities of the soul, though even to put the possibility of these equations helps define the tension between old Catholic and new Protestant ways of conceiving the relationship between erected wit and infected will. Precisely the issue between them is how much by way of salvific knowledge and activity can be attributed to our own nature and how much to grace, and whether that saving grace works "in" us or only as imputing merit to us. But there is no difference as to the occasion or need for repentance (though Catholics allow a perfectibility, a freedom from all but venial sins, which Protestants think impossible). Aside from this different estimate of human capacities, however, both schools agree that the necessity of penance springs from a disparity between what we know and what we do, from our inability to do what we know we should, to follow the law of God rather than the law of our dissociated members: "For that which I do I allow not: for what I would, that do I not; but what I hate, that do I. . . . For the good that I would I do not: but the evil which I would not, that I do."

Furthermore, in both Catholic and Protestant views of the dividedness from which sin grows, humankind suffers a double contradiction, one between the two natures of the individual, old and new, outer and inner, corporal and spiritual; the other between the individual thus at war and that wholeness from which the race has fallen, whether the Eden of prehistory or the mystic body of anticipated union. Where the doctrines differ is with respect to the means of perceiving and healing these contradictions. For the Catholic, grace is inscribed within nature from at least the moment of baptism, so that recollection of the original image and restoration of the abandoned likeness are always possible, inspired by and inspiring additional increments of grace (which may nonetheless mysteriously be withheld or refused); but for the Protestant, grace must in a sense abolish that nature which the law convicts, must restore the spiritual image of God to an integrity which the Fall had destroyed, and then complete the work of sanctification by molding the life of an already justified sinner into a conformity to the image of Christ that glorifies the

---

clear that there are structural homologies which integrate these matters of contention into the characteristic gestalts that they assume when the construction begins from Lutheran, Calvinist, pre-Tridentine, Arminian, or Counter-Reformation premises. But to undertake the task of demonstrating such affinities would not only overburden my own analytic skills and lead us a weary way over the most thoroughly harrowed field of any in modern scholarship, it would also go very much beyond the needs of the present argument.

Lord without in any sense participating in an exchange of sacrifice and charity.

We can sum this well-known difference—which is ultimately the dispute as to the relative value of faith and works—with a precise comparison from Hooker's pen:

> Our doctrine is . . . that God doth justify the believing man, yet not for the worthiness of his belief, but for his worthiness [Christ's] which is believed; God rewardeth abundantly every one which worketh, yet not for any meritorious dignity which is, or can be, in the work, but through his mere mercy, by whose commandment he worketh. Contrariwise, their doctrine is, that as pure water of itself hath no savour, but if it pass through a sweet pipe, it taketh a pleasant smell of the pipe through which it passeth; so, although before grace received, our works do neither satisfy nor merit; yet after, they do both the one and the other.[43]

As this curious image suggests, it is all a question of vehicle; does the trope of conveyance alter that which is conveyed, does the mere "outside"—here a figure for nature restored by "inward" effects of grace—lend saving meaning to our works? or is the knowledge of our salvation completely independent of those works which we are nonetheless obliged to do? Here, as in all the tedious and vertiginous disputes about the nature (and number) of the sacraments, the basic issue is a semiotic one: what kind of a sign is a human being, how does that sign relate to the will of both speaker and hearer, and who is to be credited with the intention which any sign presumably expresses? Complicating the problem above all else is the fact that the sign which a human being is, is inevitably an act, and in some sense always an ornamental act, a temporal embroidery upon the eternal cognitive of God's purpose, and of that remnant of his image still lodged either in mind, will, and understanding, or in the intellectual faculty of the soul.[44]

For this reason, we can properly say that the argument between old Catholics and new Protestants turns not only on a different understanding of nature, but also on a different belief about the semantic potential of the figurative, and not just with respect to Biblical hermeneutics. Neither party would have said that human charity was more than an ornament to God's glory, but they differed on whether that ornament carried semantic value, whether in a sense it could "cause" God to recognize (and save) himself in penitent humankind; or whether God would instead choose not to "see" the deviation of those to whom He has imputed

---

[43] Richard Hooker, "A Learned Discourse of Justification, Works, and How the Foundation of Faith is Overthrown," *Works*, ed. John Keble, 7th ed. (Oxford: Clarendon Press, 1888) 3: 538–39.

[44] On the character and locus of the image of God in reformed theology see especially T. F. Torrance, *Calvin's Doctrine of Man* (Grand Rapids: William B. Eerdmans, 1957).

Christ's righteousness.[45] It is no accident, then, that radical Protestants should have trusted nothing but plain speech and plain living. Not only did they have Paul's warrant for great plainness of speech (a warrant somewhat undercut by its originating with the man who claimed to be all things to all men), but they also had a theology which viewed good works not as a redoubled kindness metaphorically and metaphysically offered for a complement and even supplement to Christ's, but as the required and yet utterly gratuitous obedience to the law, God's law and the nation's, a situational and metonymic duty to one's neighbor. Nor—as is well known—is it any coincidence that Peter Ramus was a Protestant, for his "natural" method of instruction and his relegation of rhetoric entirely to the purpose of expressing what dialectic has already invented, proved, or found in nature itself, correlate quite nicely with the general Reformation view of the relation between sign and signified.[46]

Germane though such connections in intellectual history must always be to our efforts at seeing the Reformation whole, I raise them here only to provide a context in which to approach the question about the signifying power of human acts, a question that I propose to discuss not with reference to sixteenth-century theories about the nature of language, but with reference to the dispute about free will. For at issue in every argument about the nature of textuality is a dispute as to whether or not the signifiers themselves are bound or free, whether they move so to speak of their own will, independent of the intentions of the speaker, or whether they are essentially dead marks, wholly controllable by a sufficiently provident intention. In theological terms, the issue is between kinds of grace; granted that humankind the signifier has fallen so far away from initial likeness that left to ourselves the sentence of our history would be sheer noise, semantic entropy on a cosmic scale, does enough of the Word still dwell within us that we can cooperate with grace? or are we spiritually dead in nature, left in reprobation or restored by irresistible grace so as in either case to play out the drama of God's purposes, that terrible display of the Editor's judgment? Everyone knows where the Reformers stand on this question, but I cannot forebear quoting from William Perkins, that most published and most influential of all the Cambridge divines:

> They say will hath a naturall cooperation: we denie it, and say it hath cooperation only by grace, beeing in itself not actiue but passiue; willing well only as it is mooued by grace, wherby it must first be acted and mooued, before it can act or will. And that we may the better conceiue the difference, I will vse this

[45] Torrance, *Calvin's Doctrine of Man*, 65–95; Kevan, *Grace of Law*, 100–101.
[46] See especially Peter Sharrat, "Peter Ramus and Imitation: Image, Sign, and Sacrament," *Yale French Studies* 47 (1972): 19–32.

comparison: The church of Rome sets forth the estate of a sinner by the condition of a prisoner, and so doe we: marke then the difference. It supposeth the
said prisoner to lie bound hand and foote with chaines and fetters, and withall
to be sicke and weake, yet not wholly dead but liuing in part: it supposeth also
that being in this case, he stirreth not himselfe for any helpe, and yet hath ability
and power to stirre. Hereupon if the keeper come and take away his bolts and
fetters, and hold him by the hand, & helpe him vp, he can and will of himselfe
stande & walke, and goe out of prison: euen so (say they) is a sinner bound
hand and foot with the chaine of his sinnes: and yet he is not dead but sicke,
like to the wounded man in the way betweene Ierico and Ierusalem. And therefore doth he not will and affect that which is good: but if the holy Ghost come
and doe but vntie his bands, and reach him his hand of grace, then can he stand
of himselfe and will his owne saluation, or any thing els that is good. We in like
manner graunt, that a prisoner fitly resembleth a naturall man, but yet such a
prisoner must he be, as is not onely sicke and weake, but euen starke dead:
which can not stirre though the keeper vntie his bolts and chaines, nor heare
though he sound a trumpet in his eare: and if the said keeper would haue him
to mooue and stirre, he must giue him not onely his hand to helpe him, but
euen soule and life also: and such a one is euery man by nature; not only chained
& fettered in his sinnes but stark dead therein: as one that lieth rotting in the
graue, not hauing any abilitie or power to mooue or stirre: and therefore he
cannot so much desire or do anything that is truly good of himself, but God
must first come and put a new soule into him, euen the spirit of grace to
quicken and reuiue him: and then beeing thus reuiued, the will beginneth to
will good things at the very same time, when God by his spirit first infuseth
grace. And this is the true difference betweene vs and the Church of Rome in
this point of freewill.[47]

Some might call this an unattractive, misanthropic doctrine, atypical
of English humanism (though Hooker also holds this Genevan view of
the will, even while parting company with Calvin on the precise nature
of the double decree and on our ability to resist offered grace).[48] If we
suspend distaste, however, this question of the freedom of the will turns
out to look very much like a modern problematic. In question here is the
status of the cognitive, the interdependency or separateness of intellection
and affection, truth and trope. In order for the image of God to be pure
and as perfect as can be—so perfect that God "may be able to behold

[47] William Perkins, *Works* (Cambridge, 1600), 911–12. On Perkins's place in late Tudor
theological controversy, see H. C. Porter, *Reformation and Reaction in Tudor Cambridge*
(Cambridge: Cambridge University Press, 1958), esp. 288–313; on the influence in Shakespeare and elsewhere of the casuistical techniques which Perkins and William Ames were
first among English protestants to develop, see Camille Wells Slights, *The Casuistical Tradition in Shakespeare, Donne, Herbert, and Milton* (Ithaca, New York: Cornell University
Press, 1981).
[48] Richard Hooker, "Dublin Fragments," in *The Folger Library Edition of the Works of Richard Hooker*, ed. W. Speed Hill (Cambridge, Massachusetts: Belknap Press of Harvard University, 1982) 4: 128–67. As Ian Breward puts it, both Hooker and Perkins were Calvinists,
the one "satisfied," the other "dissatisfied." *The Works of William Perkins* (Appleford: Sutton
Courtenay Press, 1970), 16.

Himself in man as in a mirror"—it is crucial that the signifier be passive in all "significant" respects, that the imprisoning letter/flesh not infect the spiritual signified with any of its "own" impulses or corrupt imaginings.[49] Of course it could only be a wholly transcendent, omniscient, and indeed hidden God who could exert such perfect control over his created signs: were there any active spark of divinity left in natural man, salvation and signification would have to be a cooperative affair. Yet the purifying impulse which attempts to set an impermeable bar between signifier and signified here as much as in the Eucharistic rite itself does not simply demystify the world and purge it of superstition and vanity; it also transforms the nature of the text which human beings are, making us not generative tropes but the expression of a script, so that figuration becomes a matter of variation and arousal rather than of essence. Thus Christ is to be followed, not imitated, and our business is to be *larvae Dei*, masks of God; rather than presume to make ourselves into metaphors and shadows, we should trust God's promises and providence, serving in our single vocations instead of overlaying the everyday with idle ceremonies, allowing our lives to exemplify what God wills while struggling not to let old Adam supplement that will with fantasies of his own.[50]

But this is to say, oddly enough, that the Christian's duty is to be literal, that we are to trust God to weave our personal and collective history into whatever fictions he pleases, fictions that while always true may be so in ways that remain inscrutable to us, however much they may stimulate others to believe or may glorify God by participating in the intricately ordered artifice of creation. For Calvin and Luther, mystical union is the point from which the Elect *begin* their pilgrimage, not where they end; we are to accept ingrafting to Christ rather than seek the *visio Dei*, and be content with certitude rather than perfectibility.[51] Our spirituality, then, consists in trying to see God's meaning, and in believing that he has chosen us to be his people (and his signs); but it does not consist in our attempting to fulfill his figuration with our own: that Sacrifice was once by One for some, and our subsequent charity is proof of election rather than the ascending response of loving kindness. In other words, the activity of our will has become a different sort of sign: the "natural" sign which expresses the activity of some antecedent or hidden force, or which predicts an inevitable consequence, but not the "nonnatural" sign which

[49] For the quoted phrase, see Torrance, *Calvin's Doctrine of Man*, 51.

[50] Gustaf Wingren, *The Christian's Calling: Luther on Vocation*, trans. Carl C. Rasmussen (London: Oliver and Boyd, 1958), esp. 138, referring among other instances to Luther's Sermons of 1525 on Exodus, "Man must plow, reap, sow; but he is God's mask."

[51] Otto Gründler, "John Calvin: Ingrafting in Christ," in *The Spirituality of Western Christendom*, ed. E. Rozanne Elder (Kalamazoo: Cistercian Publications, 1976), 169–87.

manifests intention, convention, and mutual communication.[52] Or to put it in terms of the previous discussion, our "nature" has come to represent a new idea; better yet, it has come to represent only part of what it formerly did: that which is capable of representing without thereby affecting and partially creating the nature of that which is represented.[53]

We are nonetheless left with the question of ornament, with the inevitable excess of the body. Everyone who uses words or does theology must admit that the vehicle has energies of its own to be mastered or redeemed, if not enjoyed. Thus Calvin, even while insisting that the "faithful act, if I may be allowed the expression, passively," acknowledges that "carnal indolence" is not to be allowed: "Wherefore, when Peter exhorts us to 'add to' our 'faith, virtue,' he does not allot us an underpart to be performed, as though we could do any thing separately, of ourselves; he only arouses the indolence of the flesh, by which faith is frequently extinguished."[54] Again, a curious image: it is usually the flesh against

---

[52] Cf. Bradford, "The Flesh and the Spirit," in *Writings*, 303–4:

If any man would alter the natural course of any water to run a contrary way, he shall never be able to do it with dams; for a time he may well stop it; but when the dam is full, it will either burst down the dam or overflow it, and so with more rage run than ever it did before. I will not speak of the often weesing out, mauger all the diligence that can be. Therefore the alteration must be from the head, by making other thoroughs and devices. Even so, if any man would have the streams of his nature and will altered, to run after the will and nature of God, the same shall never be able to do it, nor all the world for him, by making of dams; that is, by telling and teaching us by the creatures, works, and word of God, how that we should do, speak and think otherwise than we do naturally. For a time the streams of our affections may be stopped by telling and teaching, and other corporal exercise; howbeit so yet that they will weesel out now and then, and at length break down all our dams and devices, or else so overflow them that "the latter end will be worse than the beginning." Therefore the alteration hereof must be at the head-spring by making other throughs and rivers of incorruption for nature and will to run in. But who can do this? The spring itself? Nay, God himself, and that alonely and alone, which worketh this in whom, when, and however, it pleaseth him for his own good will's sake. And they in whom he worketh this are his elect children "before the beginning of the world;" who may and should feel their election by loving the good and hating that which is evil, although in great imperfection: whereas the hypocrites have a thousand parts more shew of holiness, but in deed less love to God and hatred to evil, yea, in deed none at all as it is in God's sight.

[53] One indication among many of this change is Calvin's denial of the earlier distinction between image and likeness, a denial repeated by later Reformed theologians in England, e.g., by Andrew Willet, *Hexapla in Genesin; That is, A Sixfold Commentarie upon Genesis* (London, 1608), 11–12: "there is no difference in the sense and meaning of these words, but that one is the explication of the other."

[54] John Calvin, *Institutes of the Christian Religion*, bk. 2, chap. 5, sec. 11, trans. John Allen, (Philadelphia: Presbyterian Board of Christian Education, 1930) 1: 296. The French text of the quoted passage is as follows: "C'est pourquoi S. Pierre, en nous exhortant d'ajouter vertu en foi (II Pierre 1:5), ne nous attribue point une portion de faire, comme à part de nous-mêmes, rien qui soit, mais seulement il réveille la paresse de notre chair, par laquelle souvent la foi est étouffée," *Institution de la religion chrétienne* (Genève: Labor et Fides, 1955) 2: 89–90.

which the restored spirit must combat, as if with Satan himself, yet here
we might think that the flesh is urged to stir itself, or at least to being
stirred. But that would be a Catholic misreading or an Arminian reem-
phasis.[55] Calvinistic evangelical passion—that passion for sermon-going
which Andrewes would later satirize ("The corps, the whole body of
some men's profession, all godliness with some, what is it but hearing a
sermon?")—works to awaken the spirit from fleshly torpor, making
Christians recognize both their salvation and God's purposes in their
lives, spurring them to direct the flesh into single-hearted agreement with
the significance(s) which God intends.[56] The individual's vocation thus
becomes God's trope, not a mimesis of the inner Christ (who cannot be
copied except in the sense that the Law is his representation), but the figurative expression of the Father's incompletely revealed will. At this
point, indirection reenters the picture with immense force, for our so-to-
speak passive action as God's letters creates a fiction (the world) which
must be related on a different basis—if at all—to that charity and humility
we must always inwardly feel and which we know to be foretastes of the
love and equality that will characterize the eventual community of the
Elect in heaven. Rather than the world's being an enigma which love
must unravel in order to see God at its center—so that we contemplate
God by in a sense undoing creation, taking it as the interactive puzzle of
his providence and our free will—the juridical structure of the everyday
acquires the sacredness of an ordained rite or revealed text in which even
the noise is foreknown, significant, and in one sense divinely intended.[57]

With this the argument comes round again to the question of governance, to the relation of microcosm to macrocosm, how the order of
things is marked with the justice that supposedly established and informs
it. The positions that we coarsely label "Anglican" and "Puritan" stake
out two polarities with which this question may be answered: both are
intellectual visions of the figurative intent of God's fiction, one allowing
it some metaphorical display of the eternal harmonies, the other permitting only the metonymic fulfillment of the one revealed law. But both,
by denying the possibility that human acts can of themselves acquire
merit and meaning, fix the text of the world into a new representational
conformity with that which it figures, and thereby produce a new cog-

[55] Cf. Porter, *Reformation and Reaction*, 282–85, and Carl Bangs, *Arminius: A Study in the
Dutch Reformation* (Nashville: Abingdon, 1971), 206–21.

[56] Lancelot Andrewes, in an Ash Wednesday sermon preached before King James on Feb-
ruary 26, 1623, *Ninety-Six Sermons* (Oxford: John Henry Parker, 1841) 1: 421.

[57] Edward A. Dowey, Jr., *The Knowledge of God in Calvin's Theology* (New York: Columbia University Press, 1954), is especially useful on these matters. See also B. A. Gerrish,
"To the Unknown God: Luther and Calvin on the Hiddenness of God," *Journal of Religion*
53 (1973): 263–92.

nitive anxiety. For in this scheme of things, there is no real possibility that
the juridical order can or should be suspended, except at the Last Judgment, when all temporal forms will disappear. Yet since everyone knows
that the world is fallen, divine right, elect nation, and visible sainthood
notwithstanding, there is a perpetual disparity between the outer form of
the world and its eventual significance, a dissonance between desire and
actuality which is intensely social—and dramatic—in character. One way
to express this disparity is to load the world with a quasi-erotic tension,
in the manner of Lyly, Davies, or Spenser, as if fulfillment were always
round the corner, or even already at hand could one see things rightly. In
this vision, universal harmony is an ever-luring potential, not a gift ob-
tained by contemplative withdrawal, but an epideictic mirage leading on
God's Englishmen. Or comforting and inspiring the members of his invisible church within, for the alternate way to express a Reformed disparity between earthly ornament and divine reality is more psychological
than theological; it is that absolute separation between the "regiment of
the world" and the "regiment of the gospel" which William Perkins
enunciated in his doctrine of the "double person." Both views are available possibilities rather than settled dogmas for the Elizabethan era: had
most people believed in the actuality of the harmonies which Davies celebrates, *Salmacida Spolia* could have been written forty years earlier, as a
popular piece; and had everyone been convinced by Perkins, there would
have been no theater at all. One temporal masquerade would have suf-
ficed, as indeed the player-scourging Puritans thought it should.

To clinch this point, Perkins is worth another moment's hearing. He
does not—as Davies would—make the world one "large volume" from
which to read the rules of dance that link "all men in sweet society."[58]
Instead, he makes the world all theater, restricting the Book to a guide
for secret sentiments and a set of ground rules for outward policy and
combat:

> Now every person is a double person and under two regiments. In the first
> regiment I am a person of mine own self, under Christ and his doctrine, and
> may neither hate nor be angry and much less fight or revenge, but must after
> the example of Christ humble myself, forsake and deny myself, and hate my-
> self and cast myself away, and be meek and patient and let every man go over
> me and tread me underfoot and do me wrong. And yet I am to love them and
> pray for them, as Christ did for his crucifiers, for love is all and whatsoever is
> not of love is damnable and cast forth of that kingdom.
>
> In the temporal regiment, thou art a person in respect of another. Thou art
> husband, father, mother, daughter, wife, lord, subject and there thou must do
> according to thine office. If thou be a father, thou must do the office of a father

---

58 John Davies, *Orchestra, or A Poem of Dancing*, ed. E.M.W. Tillyard (London: Chatto
and Windus, 1947), 25, 40.

and rule, or else thou damnedest thyself. Thou must bring all under obedience, whether by fair means or foul. Thou must have obedience of thy wife, of thy servants and of thy subjects. If they will not obey in love, thou must chide, fight and correct as far as the law of God and the law of the land will suffer thee.[59]

Setting Davies against Perkins does not show the "old" vision of a loving community of integrated selves at war with the "new" vision of a divided self in the kingdom of Leviathan; it does not frame the confrontation of a "readable" medieval world with a "dramatic" modernity. Poetic and perhaps sycophantic allegory on the one hand, realistic and perhaps offensive policy on the other: taken alone, neither can give a true picture of the Elizabethan polity and psychology. But taken together, *Orchestra* and *A Treatise Tending unto a Declaration Whether a Man be in the Estate of Damnation or the Estate of Grace* make a convenient and illuminating figure for the range of possibilities in the interaction between spirit and flesh which could coexist within one state and one continuum of knowledge, speech, and action. Yet they do not exhaust that range (as if any available set of illustrations could). At the very least, we would have to supply some remnant of that old Catholic sensibility, perhaps from the devotional intensities of Southwell, Campion, and those other new Catholics who give a baroque turn to the old faith, perhaps from those like William Barrett who turned against Calvin and back to Rome, or perhaps just from the never very latent possibility that any attempt to know and perform God's will in some way shapes and changes it, even as the individual speech act, the *parole*, works with others to create the governing and ever transcendent providence of *la langue*.

Having used theological controversy in this highly selective and speculative way, I want to round off the fable with a tentative argument about larger historical causes. The temptation, of course, is to leap to familiar conclusions about the sixteenth century's invention of a new, dramatic, and highly individualistic kind of self. Accounting for that supposed psychological and social transformation by means of an appeal to the synergistic interaction of the Reformation with market capitalism, we could effortlessly slip back into a reflection theory of the relation between art and life, retelling the story of lost community and newly alienated selves as the movement from a narratival to a theatrical view of the world. In place of old cognitive certainties about the individual's place and meaning, the sixteenth century would thus be seen generating new disjunc-

---

[59] Breward, *The Work of William Perkins*, 382.

tions between person and office and new anxieties occasioned by the attempt to perform roles and fashion selves without the comfort of
extended families, unquestioned beliefs, and a stable social order. Though
I want to resist much of this speciously attractive history, it should be
obvious that I do not base my reluctance upon any delusion that the
drama fails to change.

Indeed, the difference between Tudor interludes and the civic drama
and older moralities is almost as striking as the difference between high
Elizabethan drama and the interludes, romances, heroical morals, satirical
morals, moral allegories, tragedies, comedies, classical histories, didactic
histories, Biblical interludes, neomorals, neomiracles, neomysteries, and
polemical shows which fill the columns of Harbage and Schoenbaum's
Annals. One significant difference is just this copia of form: desperately
categorized, no doubt, and better evidence of generic uncertainty—or indifference—than of increasing definition in generic expectations during
the sixteenth century. Nonetheless, there is clearly more experiment with
subject matter and dramatic paradigm than the records let us imagine for
the fourteenth and fifteenth centuries. The taxonomic problem thus created may partly be the artifact of our own desire to assimilate unknowns
to familiar categories of the same and the other, yet this wealth of possibilities finally did inspire contemporaries to academic anxiety, as both
Polonius and Sir Philip Sidney amply witness. Nor should it be forgotten
that the folio makes three genres fit Shakespeare with relative ease.

This is a small point, but it indicates larger ones. The relatively undifferentiated plays and "gamys" of the medieval theater, which casually in-
termingle something not quite history, tragedy, or comedy with an embodied sort of allegory, needed no finer generic labels because the
experience they encourage fits within the figurative logic of urban and
corporate ceremony rather than within the representational logic of an
emerging civic consciousness: where everything is tropic and tropological, there is no more need to sort out actions by predominant tonality
than there is to separate the history of the nation from the history of humankind. This latter separation, of course, is one defining characteristic
of the Tudor Reformation, which constitutes the English nation, church,
literary language, and extraurban playhouse as sharply different from
what remained of the baronial alliances, corporate independence, universal *ecclesia*, restricted literacy, and occasional theatricals which had been
the approximate medieval norm. Among European states, only England
went through all this differentiation and reintegration at once, making
Crown, religion, language, and a great deal of its theater into ideologically congruent representations: the palimpsestic portrait of God's Eng-

lishman. Given the coincidental rise of the Tudor interlude, there must
be a more than coincidental connection between this multiple transformation in patterns of self-perception and the mongrel proliferation of
subjects, moods, and pseudo-genres which Sidney found so offensive and
which yielded to the stronger but hardly classical sense of genre that Kyd,
Greene, Marlowe, and Shakespeare manifest.

I think that the best way to name that connection is with Anne Righter's phrase, "the idea of the play."[60] Her well-known study is somewhat
marred by evolutionary premises, and by a rather condescending estimate
of medieval spirituality, the nonrepresentational aesthetic of its theater,
and that "tyranny of the audience" from which she says drama was lib-
erated in the latter part of the century. Nonetheless, her central thesis
remains strong and illuminating. The metaphor of the world theater, so
implicated in the moral and epistemological problems that the great plays
address and create, encourages and depends upon a different set of assumptions about the relation between stage and audience than those
which govern medieval drama. Dilemmas in the interaction of illusion
and reality cannot come into sharp focus when the dramatic emphasis is
more upon the problem of being charitable than that of knowing truth,
when the audience is the tropological subject of the drama and must
therefore be encouraged to think that God turns all to good, and when
the boundaries between figurative and "real" space are casually violated.
Whether or not direct address decreases or illusionistic closure grows
more confident during the first seventy-five years of the century is another question. Though there seems to be an increasing fascination with
playworld metaphors, most differences with respect to presentational or
representational stance appear to reflect the different occasions and assumptions of hall plays and Protestant teaching pieces as opposed to
works imitating continental or classical models. In any case, the decisive
change in the relation between actors and audience comes only with the
full transition to a commercial theater, freed from immediate social contexts, ritual occasions, and persuasive interests, a change whose impact
shows among other ways in the total disappearance of the term *interlude*
from the title pages of plays printed after 1576.[61]

Illusionistic closure, however, is not the most important development
of the sixteenth-century stage. Even if it were complete—but the meta-
theatrical implications of the motif of world as play always disrupt any
pretensions to total closure—illusionism is merely one symptom and

---

[60] Anne Righter, *Shakespeare and the Idea of the Play* (London: Chatto and Windus, 1962).
[61] Allardyce Nicoll, "Tragical-Comical-Historical-Pastoral: Elizabethan Dramatic Nomenclature," *Bulletin of the John Rylands Library* 43 (1960): 80–81.

mild tendency of this new idea of the play. It offers grounds for such mockery of old styles and attitudes as occurs at the end of *A Midsummer Night's Dream* and throughout *The Knight of the Burning Pestle*, and it contributes to the increasing tension between visual and verbal modes of knowledge and analysis that breaks out in the quarrel between Ben Jonson and Inigo Jones. But I do not think that the essence of illusionistic dramaturgy is its magic realism (hardly a new thing, as Lee Simonson long ago observed) or its tendency to inspire perspectival kinds of staging.[62] These effects, though they can masquerade as independent motives, spring from a more basic reassessment of the relations between the knower and the known that can perhaps best be designated with a term that has figured rather prominently in this part of my discussion, and which now needs further analysis: *rationalization*.[63]

In restricted literary usage, one tends to associate rationalization with the aesthetic and moral standards that Sidney would have brought to bear upon literature in general and the drama in particular.[64] Given Sidney's own standing as the flower of Christian knighthood, there can in his case at least be no question of these standards having been meant to undermine religion, even though they served as one warrant for what we properly call the secularization of dramatic subject matter. Yet there is a sense in which this effect seems odd, for it takes little imagination to see a certain congruence between Sidney's theory of the purposes of poetry and the practical religious purposes which Corpus Christi plays and moralities tried to serve. Certainly medieval plays seem designed "to lead us and draw us to as high a perfection as our degenerate souls . . . can be capable of"; moreover, they do so by a means that it seems right to call *eikastikē*, "figuring forth good things," and the good thing that they figure forth is better than Cyrus, for it is ultimately Christ himself, the divine archetype and model.[65]

---

[62] Lee Simonson, *The Stage is Set* (1932; New York: Theatre Arts Books, 1963), 172–93.

[63] The social-scientific discussion of rationalization derives mainly from Max Weber, though as Gordon Marshall points out, Weber himself was well aware of his own antecedents. *In Search of the Spirit of Capitalism: An Essay on Max Weber's Protestant Ethic Thesis* (New York: Columbia University Press, 1982), 19–40. For Weber's seminal distinction between *Zweckrationalität* and *Wertrationalität* see *Economy and Society*, trans. Ephraim Fischoff et al. (1968; Berkeley: University of California Press, 1978) 1: 24–26; for his late and relatively incautious remarks on the "specific and peculiar rationalism of Western culture," of which the "rational ethics of ascetic Protestantism" is the critically influential instance, see the "Author's Introduction" to *The Protestant Ethic and the Spirit of Capitalism*, trans. Talcott Parsons (1930; New York: Charles Scribner's Sons, 1958), 26–27. David Little offers much evidence in favor of Weber's thesis in his *Religion, Order, and Law: A Study in Pre-Revolutionary England* (New York: Harper and Row, 1969).

[64] The story of the Italian literary theorizing that devised these standards is told in Bernard Weinberg, *A History of Literary Criticism in the Italian Renaissance*, 2 vols. (Chicago: University of Chicago Press, 1961).

[65] Philip Sidney, *A Defence of Poetry*, in *Miscellaneous Prose of Sir Philip Sidney*, ed. Katherine Duncan-Jones and Jan Van Dorsten (Oxford: Oxford University Press, 1973), 104.

Nonetheless, we can be sure that Sidney would have disapproved on both aesthetic and doctrinal grounds of any attempt to describe mystery plays with his new terminology. As drama, the Corpus Christi play obscures that difference between reporting and representing which Sidney thought crucial to the genre: it shows salvation whole, and does not make even the Passion the principal point of its action, an action unified by being an eternal trope rather than by happening to a single hero in a single and explicit time and place. Taken as doctrine, the cycles not only fostered papist superstitions, they also fell under the Reformers' more general prohibition of idols, being so direct and immediate in their anthropomorphic expression of divinity that even the Counter-Reformers agreed that decorum was better served by their abolition.[66] Like the Mass itself, the cycles were not allegorical enough for advanced Elizabethan taste, not sufficiently feigned, or perhaps allegorical in the "wrong" way, being too embodied and insufficiently conceptual. Lacking the intricate veils of fiction, they seemed too subject to misinterpretation, or to none at all, too grossly incarnational, too unaware of the gap between the thing itself and its sign, and thus more apt to profane the sacred than to sanctify the everyday. Perhaps most offensive of all to more sophisticated and educated wits was the way in which the cycles refused to grant a temporal and spiritual distance to the Christian mystery: they made Christ uncomfortably present, in a veritable host of guildsmen, and thereby failed to preserve—as Sidney would—the purity "of that unspeakable and everlasting beauty to be seen by the eyes of the mind, only cleared by faith."[67]

There is an evident parallel between the critical reflex and the religious one: in both spheres, the newer taste deplores a confusion of realms. Where Protestant theology sets a categorical (though moveable) barrier between the divine and the human, between the Sacrifice then and the elect or reprobate now, the cycle plays demand actors—no matter how lewd and corporeal—whose outward gestures portray a Christ whom the actor also inwardly signifies with a perpetual analogy of being that is to be perfected by moral deeds in this life. Like the scene in which he plays, the actor is real and ideal at once: just as there is no distinction between English facts and Biblical ones, so there seems to be no impropriety in having the flesh enact that Image to which the spirit should conform. And if the soul is indeed the form of the body—rather than its prisoner—one

---

[66] Harold C. Gardiner, *Mysteries' End: An Investigation of the Last Days of the Medieval Religious Stage* (New Haven, Connecticut: Yale University Press, 1946), 100–107. As Grace Frank notes, however, the *mystères sacrés* continued to be played under the classicized designations of tragedy and tragicomedy. *The Medieval French Drama* (Oxford: Oxford University Press, 1954), 210.

[67] Sidney, *Defence* 77. Andrew D. Weiner demonstrates that the premises of the *Defence* derive from Sidney's Reformed convictions, in *Sir Philip Sidney and the Poetics of Protestantism: A Study of Contexts* (Minneapolis: University of Minnesota Press, 1978), 3–50.

can hardly be embarrassed by a decently anthropomorphic drama. One might say, then, that the medieval authorities (most of them, at any rate) saw no harm in representing what subsequent reformers believed could only be reported.[68] Such a quibble with terms is illegitimate, I think, only in that it fails to go far enough: in the world of the Corpus Christi play, the representation *is* a report. No action or thing is merely an image or a portrayal; it is also a vehicle of the Word, whether vestige or similitude, a phrase in that book which taken whole is index, symbol, and icon of its maker.

We can approach the same phenomena from a different angle by saying that medieval drama is unconcerned with those nice distinctions between showing and telling that compel Sidney to insist on the "difference betwixt reporting and representing."[69] Like Castelvetro, Sidney doubts the semantic flexibility of the stage: it can only represent a single, self-contained reality (whatever else it may figure forth), a reality tied to the laws of corporeal actions.[70] However universalizing it may be in moral intention, the drama has for Sidney a decidedly particularistic status in ontology: it is immediate and present, unlike narrative—and language generally—whose function is to mediate among several times and places. "Again, many things may be told which cannot be showed." The point here is not the jejune one of proving that Sidney's aesthetics fit medieval drama even more poorly than they do the Elizabethan; it is simply to recast the familiar observation that both Renaissance criticism and Reformation theology move away from ontological ambiguities toward rationalized clarity in defining the relationship between what a later epistemology might call code and content.

But rationalization can hardly be restricted to literary and religious effects. In the larger Weberian (or Marxist or Baconian) sense of a general demystification, functional reordering of ends to means, and deliberate attempt to govern practices according to order and rule, a widespread, reasonably explicit, and unprecedentedly rapid process of rationalization

---

[68] On the fears of idolatry informing sixteenth-century attacks on the religious stage, see Gardiner, esp. 89–90, and the more sweeping argument about a new reverence for the naked truth in Russell Fraser, *The War Against Poetry* (Princeton: Princeton University Press, 1970), esp. 3–51.

[69] Sidney, *Defence*, 114. As William Nelson observes, for Sidney, there is "no difference in didactic force between verity and the verisimilar." *Fact or Fiction: The Dilemma of the Renaissance Story Teller* (Cambridge, Massachusetts: Harvard University Press, 1973), 57. Instead, as Forrest Robinson argues, Sidney's effort to introduce logical rigor into the theory and practice of poetry required the utmost conceptual clarity, especially concerning the relations between an order of representation, of intellectually visible concepts, and an order of written or spoken words. *The Shape of Things Known: Sidney's "Apology" in its Philosophical Tradition* (Cambridge, Massachusetts: Harvard University Press, 1972).

[70] Weinberg, *A History of Literary Criticism* 2: 695.

seems to be an inescapable theme in whatever sixteenth-century history one chooses to write. Consider the following instances, all well-documented and reasonably secure parts of the historiographical landscape, and each some confirmation that the sociological theory of modernization—whatever its diminishing value for predicting the future of third-world countries—has its firmest empirical ground, its real intellectual origins, and its greatest heuristic utility in the study of the English Reformation and eventual revolution.[71] To begin with, not in fact but as a matter of expository convenience, there is the Tudor revolution in government—now thought to be more gradual than sudden—whose most salient feature was the substitution of a dependent bureaucracy for the older household system of administration. Though household titles were retained, the men who filled them were different in social origin and increasingly in function: with no status or base of power separate from the king, they served less as indispensable consultants than as shapers of what aspired to be coherent policy. Yet their expertise and the increasing political as well as administrative complexity of things made them more than mere personal agents of a monarch whose territory and conception of rule had coincidentally come to be defined more in imperial than in seigneurial terms; they were the officers of a relatively abstract Crown, whose power, though vested in the sacred body of the king (in person and in Parliament) derived from increasingly legalistic and deliberately ideological foundations.[72]

The development—or consolidation—of bureaucratic government coincides with other transformations. There is the larger-scale shift over four or five generations from a social order based in the higher ranks if not so certainly in the lower ones on lineage and kinship ties, or upon relatively independent urban centers, to a civil society and political nation increasingly governed by the interplay of personal and party interests, increasingly defined by contract and omnicompetent statute law, and dependent for its operation upon systematic and extensive record keeping, information gathering, and methods of police.[73] These same years see the creation of an educational system separate from noble households and the

---

[71] Hanson, *From Kingdom to Commonwealth*, 530.

[72] Geoffrey R. Elton, *The Tudor Revolution in Government* (Cambridge: Cambridge University Press, 1953). Recent critics of Elton's thesis have shed considerable doubt on the suddenness, deliberateness, and intentionality of the revolution. But even as a "readjustment" rather than a self-consciously modernizing achievement, there is little doubt that monarchs and their partially independent agents transformed the institutions of government into something more like a national bureaucracy administered by specialists than a magnate's household, with the king as chief administrator. See Christopher Coleman and David Starkey, eds., *Revolution Reassessed: Revisions in the History of Tudor Government and Administration* (Oxford: Oxford University Press, 1986).

[73] Elton, *Policy and Police*; James, *Family, Lineage, and Civil Society*.

church, and increasingly designed to fit people for the arts of governance
and other special callings in an economy where professional or technical
training had become indispensable to advancement (and to employment
in the seventeenth century).[74] At the other end of the scale there is a shift
in poor-relief from almsgiving relayed through the church or its foundations to a more or less systematized public obligation, evidenced both in
the government's promotion of charitable trusts and in a progressively
more humane and realistic series of acts for regulating and relieving poverty.[75] There is a rationalization of methods in industry and especially in
agriculture, stimulating and stimulated by an increasingly efficient set of
commercial institutions.[76] There is the recovery and reinvention of classical canons in architecture as well as in literature; and a general interest
in purity and decorum of which the whitewashing of church interiors and
a concern for authentic Latinity can serve as two commonplace examples.
And almost indistinguishable in origin and effects from these political,
intellectual, and economic revolutions there is, of course, the Reformation itself, moving from a theology that casts salvation in terms of the
ontological relation between nature and grace to one that establishes a
dialectical relation between God as speaker and humanity (enabled by the
Spirit) as hearer of a specific saving intention in the Word.

In order to make the notion of rationalization more useful, some distinctions are required. As a description of a social and intellectual process,
the term need imply no value judgment: to differentiate and organize
functions according to specific ends hardly guarantees more equity or
beauty and may indeed produce more mystification, especially about the
way in which social and intellectual purposes come to be defined and selected. As an operative principle of behavior, however, and not as an eth-
nocentric term of approbation, there are three specific senses in which a
growing rationality seems to be at work in the changing patterns of the
sixteenth century.

First, and in the strictest sense, there is an obvious exponential growth
in attempts to organize separate bodies of knowledge and methodically
apply them to the solution of particular problems. The scientific revolu-

---

[74] Joan Simon, *Education and Society in Tudor England* (Cambridge: Cambridge University
Press, 1966), Arthur B. Fergusson, *The Articulate Citizen and the English Renaissance* (Dur-
ham, North Carolina: Duke University Press, 1965), Ann Jennalie Cook, *The Privileged
Playgoers of Shakespeare's Globe* (Princeton: Princeton University Press, 1981), esp. 18–19,
David Cressey, "Educational Opportunity in Tudor and Stuart England," *History of Educa-
tion Quarterly* 16 (1976): 307–13.

[75] John Pound, *Poverty and Vagrancy in Tudor England* (London: Longman, 1971).

[76] John U. Nef, *Industry and Government in France and England, 1540–1640* (Philadelphia:
American Philosophical Society, 1940); Eric Kerridge, *The Agricultural Revolution* (London:
George Allen and Unwin, 1967); L. A. Clarkson, *The Pre-Industrial Economy in England,
1500–1750* (New York: Schocken Books, 1972), esp. 45–158.

tion is one long-term instance of this intellectual labor, but it begins in
England most notably with the early humanists, and their systematic textual criticism, pedagogical theorizing, educational reorganization, political programs, analysis of statecraft, and even scientific inquiries.[77] There
is an indisputable continuity between these efforts and the Reformers'
inspiration of widespread public discussion of intricate religious questions.[78] The publication of self-help manuals for the practice of catechism,
farming, child-rearing, astrology, arms-wielding, and gentility; the public interest in such exemplary histories as the *Mirror for Magistrates*,
North's Plutarch, Foxe's *Book of Martyrs*, and the Bible itself; the appearance of "methods" for logic, rhetoric, the reading of the Word, the discovery of witches, and the determination of one's own divine election: all
these manifest a similar impulse, to bring the lives of lay Englishmen into
conscious order, giving them at least the illusion of rational system and
control.[79]

Partly as effects of this deliberate intellectual labor and partly in consequence of economic and political processes that are harder to define,
much less to account for, two other sorts of rationalizing activity appear
to increase. One is described by a hoary term from the sociological theory
of modernization that I have already let slip in this discussion: *structural
differentiation*.[80] As an equally barbarous but nonetheless accurate name
for its corollary in more obviously representational systems such as religion, let me coin the term *conceptual disembodiment*.[81] Each effect is impli-

---

[77] Neal Ward Gilbert, *Renaissance Concepts of Method* (New York: Columbia University
Press, 1960); Marion Trousdale, *Shakespeare and the Rhetoricians* (Chapel Hill: University of
North Carolina Press, 1982), esp. 3–38.

[78] For evidence of such discussion, even in rural areas, see Margaret Spufford, *Contrasting
Communities: English Villages in the Sixteenth and Seventeenth Centuries* (Cambridge: Cambridge University Press, 1974), esp. 171–352.

[79] As J. P. Sommerville points out, perhaps the most popular category next to religion in
late sixteenth century publishing was political theory. *Politics and Ideology in England*, 39.

[80] I rely especially on the discussion in Niklas Luhmann, "The Differentiation of Society,"
in *The Differentiation of Society*, trans. Stephen Holmes and Charles Larmore (New York:
Columbia University Press, 1982), 229–54. Luhmann analyzes structural and functional differentiation as "system differentiation," "a *replication, within a system, of the difference between
a system and its environment. . . .* This conception implies that each subsystem reconstructs
and, in a sense, *is* the whole system in the special form of a difference between the subsystem
and its environment. Differentiation thus reproduces the system in itself, multiplying specialized versions of the original system's identity by splitting it into a number of internal
systems and affiliated environments. This is not simply a decomposition into smaller
chunks but rather a process of growth by internal disjunction" (230–31).

[81] I use this term in preference to Weber's "disenchantment of the world," both to bring
out its relation to iconoclasm as defined by James Siemon and others, and to connect it with
the reformers' insistence that sacramental signs refer to but do not exhibit the matter of the
sacrament. Cf. McLelland, *Visible Words of God*, 246. The process of disembodiment, of
differentiating signifier from signified, of acknowledging the temporal and epistemological
disruption of that imaginary unity, also has to do with the difference that Basil Bernstein
analyzes between restricted and elaborated codes of speech. *Class, Codes, and Control*, vol.

cated with the other, as social praxis with cultural hermeneutics, but artificially separating the functional and structural from the semiotic and symbolic makes analysis easier and its results somewhat more suggestive.

Like many accounts of literary history, the theory of modernization assumes that its object of study is a homeostatic system undergoing intrinsic and evolutionary change; it posits an immanent mechanism of dynamic self-regulation, which both governs future development and works to adapt a society to external stimuli while preserving the integrity of a bounded system. The mechanism in question—very like a process of misreading and rewriting—is the double motion of differentiation and reintegration. Sociologists sometimes speak of this process as if it were an impersonal, almost magical force, inexorably driving the world toward a western future: it disrupts closure, disentangling unanticipated functions and purposes from some imaginary, primordial state of structured integration, then reembodies them in new institutional arrangements, in some momentarily "natural" harmony of structure and function, which in turn yields to the same rationalizing forces. Under the impulse of this motor of modernity, persons lose their ascribed statuses and acquire new ones through individual achievement; they abandon particularist loyalties and local purposes in favor of national and universalistic ones; they cultivate special skills to be exercised in realms of activity interconnected through an ever more complex network of exchange. For the old coherence permitted by everyone's supposedly having an adequate set of categories with which to keep knight and miller in the same cosmos, the modernizing society must substitute some sort of formal political representation, and some new set of associations based on specific professional, economic, avocational, or even voluntary religious interests.[82] In England's case, Parliament eventually comes to fill some of the representational functions which guilds and fraternities, urban corporations, the universal church, and the reciprocal relations of lineage and good lordship once performed. What this formal political institution does not supply—that is to say, the bulk of what needs doing in any society—was made up by new integrative groupings which ranged from societies of antiquaries for the well educated and a much enlarged tavern culture for the poor, to small-scale factories for an increasing number of wage

1, esp. 170–89. The construction and proliferation of the elaborated codes of specialized discourses necessarily emphasize this disembodiment.

[82] Patrick Collinson, *The Religion of Protestants: The Church in English Society, 1559–1625* (Oxford: Oxford University Press, 1982), discusses, pages 242–83, the forms of voluntary religion in the Elizabethan and Jacobean period and suggests that within the boundaries of the godly, persons sought and found a kind of community missing in the late medieval parish (281–82).

earners and a more restricted and intensely patriarchal family structure for the gentry.[83]

Of course this picture of a modernizing England has to be viewed with extreme caution. Even used as a heuristic, it must be shorn of implications that cultures ever attain "modernity," if by modernity one means a real break with "tradition." The processes that modernization theory would describe must not be imagined to be linear; instead, these processes are dialectical and cyclical, with differentiation and reintegration continuously redefining the boundaries between communities and their imperfectly excluded others, and so also recasting the relationships of authority and deference, freedom and competitive self-interest, that are always in play along these boundaries. And even thus qualified, the theory risks doing considerable violence to the facts of English history, distorting them in ways that stem from more than my rather glib truncation of the model itself or from my condensation of the first industrial revolution, much political turmoil, and startling material improvement into one swift paragraph.[84] In the first place, medieval society was hardly so ascriptive as the theory might imply; in fact one suspects that the difference between ascription and achievement is always very much a matter of relative generational perspective and (mis)perception.[85] Certainly the traditional estates had been a way of defining persons by their functions—warfare, prayer, and labor—and these probably had no greater tendency

---

[83] As Reinhard Bendix says, in the course of a discussion seeking to " 'de-ideologize' the conventional contrast of tradition and modernity," there is a "contrapuntal interplay between differentiation and reintegration" which gradually relocates those sites where social actors feel the gains and losses of identity most keenly.

> Typically, traditional societies achieve intense solidarity in relatively small groups that tend to be isolated from one another by poor communication and a backward technology, and that also tend to create for their individual participants an intensity of emotional attachment and rejection which modern men find hard to appreciate and which they would probably find personally intolerable. Typically, modern societies achieve little solidarity in relatively small groups and by virtue of advanced communication and technology these groups tend to be highly interdependent at an impersonal level. In this setting individual participants experience an intensity of emotional attachment and rejection at two levels which hardly exist in the traditional society, namely in the nuclear family at its best and its worst, and at the national level where personal loyalties alternate between being taken for granted in ordinary times and moving up to fever pitch during national crises or other direct confrontations with alien ways of life. ("Tradition and Modernity Reconsidered," *Comparative Studies in Society and History* 9 [1967]: 320)

On this process in England, see especially Keith Wrightson, "Aspects of Social Differentiation in England, c. 1580–1660," *Journal of Peasant Studies* 5 (1977–1978): 33–47; on the more patriarchal family, see Lawrence Stone, *Family, Sex and Marriage in England*, 151–218.

[84] For somewhat less drastic summaries of the model, see E. A. Wrigley, "The Process of Modernization and Industrial Revolution in England," *Journal of Interdisciplinary History* 3 (1972): 225–59, and Humphreys, "Evolution and History."

[85] Anthony Esler, *The Aspiring Mind of the Elizabethan Younger Generation* (Durham, North Carolina: Duke University Press, 1966).

to harden into fixed statuses than the finer reticulation of duty in modern bureaucracies, *apparatchiki* being notoriously sensitive to status and resistant to genuine rationalization of what they do.[86] There was also much more individualism in patterns of ownership and kinship, and much more practice of politics, than the received picture of celestial and temporal hierarchies admits.[87] As for localization, though the villager's cosmos must have been restricted, a suburbanite's is not much broader or less mythological, and the dwellers in English cities had from early on far more interaction with the larger polity and economy than myths of localism would suggest. There also seems to have been a good deal of migration for economic betterment; and of course there was the omnipresent fact of the church, whose formal emphases could hardly have been more universalistic.[88]

On the other side of the so-called great divide, it is important not to exaggerate the dislocating effects of modernizing change. Though London tripled in size over the sixteenth century, with 95 percent of that growth from 1550 on and would more than double again during the seventeenth century, most people still lived in villages of less than five hundred souls.[89] Though Britain's industrial output grew at an even faster rate, such that many English traders could anticipate "a doubling of their business almost every decade" of the years when Shakespeare was alive, it is important to remember that the bulk of this production took place in enterprises no larger than a dozen workers, and that most trade and manufacture still occurred within the familial setting of a master with his wife, children, and apprentices.[90] Though the New Model Army would eventually put into formal practice the notion that talent matters more than rank, and though some of its soldiers would express the genuinely leveling views that still later found a more permanent place in revolutionary America, the social experiments of the Civil War were soon suppressed; and in the earlier period, *virtù*—except when aided by royalist

[86] Ellery Schalk, "Status and Vocation in Sixteenth-Century France: The Problem of Nobility as a Profession or Function," *Studies in Medieval Culture* 13 (1978): 22.

[87] Alan Macfarlane, *Origins of English Individualism*; Wrightson, *English Society*, esp. 44–51. But see the skeptical review essay by Stephen D. White and Richard T. Vann, "The Invention of English Individualism: Alan Macfarlane and the Modernization of Pre-Modern England," *Social History* 8 (1983): 345–63.

[88] David Harris Sacks, "Bristol's 'Little Businesses' 1625–1641," *Past and Present* 110 (1986): 69–105; Peter Clark, "The Migrant in Kentish Towns, 1580–1640," in *Crisis and Order in English Towns, 1500–1700,* ed. Peter Clark and Paul Slack (Toronto: University of Toronto Press, 1972), 149.

[89] Laslett, *World We Have Lost,* 53–58. See also Roger Finlay and Beatrice Shearer, "Population Growth and Suburban Expansion," in *The Making of the Metropolis, London, 1500–1700,* ed. A. L. Beier and Roger Finlay (London: Longman, 1986), 37–57.

[90] John U. Nef, *The Conquest of the Material World* (Chicago: University of Chicago Press, 1964), 209; Laslett, *World We Have Lost,* 1–21.

success—did not triumph over lineage so effortlessly as Medwall's tactful and quite conventional fantasy suggests.

These caveats notwithstanding—whatever the political and economic preconditions of the Reformation, however much the nation-building of late medieval kings or the persistent individualism of English social structures, and however successful the ideological controls of England's subsequent governors—there is no question that the social, political, and economic order underwent substantial change of a sort that disrupted and rearranged the ties that bound institutions, functions, and values together, nor that this change was accompanied by a general reconception of the individual's relation to community and cosmos.[91] The crucial word here is *accompanied*, for I think it is probably futile, and certainly beyond the scope of this argument, to search for some causal relation in either direction between what a vulgar Marxist would call the base and the superstructure. In any case, the energies that seem peculiarly dramatic could not have arisen from a correlative shift in representational systems and in those systems of economic, political, and marital exchange that can so easily be mistaken for the nonrepresentational stuff of which commonsense reality is made. Instead, they must have sprung from a different sort of interaction, one in which the activity of structural differentiation cooperates with what I crudely term conceptual disembodiment in order first to raise to visibility and then to complicate the problem of authorial and thespic control (and readability) in the theater of the world.

At issue here is a hermeneutical divide by no means unique to the young Luther's exegesis of the Psalms; it is that generally heightened awareness of the mental character of representation, and of the difference between its figures and the illustrative, law-abiding orders of history and physical reality.[92] We can all too easily evoke this moment of conceptual disembodiment with a few phrases and allusions. One thinks at once of that potent wave of iconoclasm which begins sometime before Henry broke up Beckett's tomb, and which did not end with Bacon's exposure of the several idols of imagination and the tribe, or with the forcible severance of the king's natural body from his attenuated body mystical. Of course the persistence through the next three hundred years of typological readings of Scripture and history amply refutes any fantasy that all allegory had been swept to merited oblivion, but not the fact that postmedieval allegory is importantly different in theory and operation. The Reformers themselves were anxious to demonstrate this difference, and

---

[91] For an especially comprehensive account of the way in which the interaction between integration and differentiation transformed the older order while preserving much of its essential structure, see Wrightson, *English Society*.

[92] Preus, *From Shadow to Promise*.

it is clear in literature as well, as every reader knows who has set about comparing Bunyan's tropes to Jean de Deguilleville's, or Spenser's to Chaucer's and Langland's.

Take typology as the clearest and best explored instance. As distinguished from conventional medieval exegesis, typology is a more abstract and yet more literal understanding of God's work in history. In Whitaker's well-known analysis (which sounds remarkably like Eric Auerbach on *figura*), there is a concerted attempt to suppress polysemy in either the words of Scripture or the events they represent; instead, the archbishop would have us see two events, each perfectly literal, connected by a mental comparison which the Holy Ghost intends and enables us to make, yet which in Protestant sermons can inspire an intricately wrought and highly conceited rhetoric.[93] With somewhat different effects, a similar dividing of an earlier ontological continuum into a charged historical reality on the one hand and a heightened spiritual apprehension on the other is evident in *The Faerie Queene*. While Spenser seems more insistent about matters of doctrine and politics than Chaucer or Langland ever are, he also elaborates the veils of fiction in ways that strongly dislocate the field in which morality and policy are to be practiced, making the connection between history and doctrine both more to be desired and more problematic. Chaucer the Pilgrim and Long Will are personae at once less and more oblique than Colin Clout; and Gloriana has an ideal significance and a historical counterpart whose Utopian implications (and implied epistemological paradoxes) go much beyond anything that medieval poets were concerned to figure forth. In both the interpretation of Scripture and the writing of at least this one poem, the line between language and reality has become less permeable, the allegory more obviously a matter of words, the historical actuality more that which the words attempt to describe than something which itself participates in figurative play (though it may still signify).

But this is to suggest that the movement of conceptual disembodiment is at heart an ironization which literalizes the world, while constructing an ever more elaborate and inward spirit which attempts to signify both that world and the larger structures of meaning with which it is to be understood. But at the same time, structural differentiation works in an allegorizing fashion to widen the gap between social institutions and those holistic meanings to which everything must eventually refer, even

[93] Barbara K. Lewalski, *Protestant Poetics and the Seventeenth-Century Religious Lyric* (Princeton: Princeton University Press, 1979), especially chapter 4; Charles Cannon, "William Whitaker's *Disputatio de Sacra Scriptura*: A Sixteenth-Century Theory of Allegory," *Huntington Library Quarterly* 25 (1962): 129–38; William Whitaker, *A Disputation Concerning Scripture*, ed. W. Fitzgerald (Cambridge: Cambridge University Press, 1849).

if only in a deluded and privatized fashion. Thus these artificially separate processes, both of them rationalizing activities, not only cooperate in undoing and reforming the tropes and customs of pre-Reformation England, they also work upon that common past in quite different ways.

Left to itself, conceptual disembodiment would tend toward political democracy (or anarchy), intellectual skepticism, and isolation—whether legalistic or ironic—in matters of morality and religion. No public fictions and unifying rituals could long survive intense analysis, sustained deconstruction, or such mockery as that tonsured cat, host in mouth, which some anonymous Protestant hanged upon Paul's Cross during Edward's reign. And when institutional tropes give way, there is no recourse but tense conformity within the sect of truth, or else that masquerade which keeps its barrier around the sect of one.[94] Structural differentiation, on the other hand, pulls a contrary way, toward the mysteries and the ascriptive statuses of class, profession, wealth, and government. Specialization, whether in techniques of material production, the arts of rulership, or the life of the mind, notoriously widens the conceptual distance—and often exaggerates the economic difference—between the ins and the outs. In the long run, specialization thus sets limits to most iconoclasm. With centuries of effort, it may be possible to reduce public metaphors to an atavistic and irreducible minimum, but in order to expose the fraud in a specialist's claim to mastery, you have to understand it; unless you recognize and grasp the allegory, you cannot subject it to irony.[95]

At the Shakespearean moment, however, these contraries stand in a remarkable balance. Specialization had not progressed far enough to embarrass Bacon's ambition to claim all knowledge, an ambition that method itself enabled, nor had iconoclasm—and education—done more than make many people intensely aware of the fictive, rhetorical, and political character of their symbols and institutions. But such a balance is fragile: the idea of a genuine commonalty, of the achievable prospect of a true church and an equitable nation, becomes available to public articulation just at the moment when the possibility of common understanding is being undermined by the very processes which inspired it in the first place. For it is the social, political, and intellectual activity of rationalization which had abstracted a notion of commonweal (and of representational accuracy in several senses and domains) from the rituals in which it was formerly embedded, and which had also offered the laity some vision

---

[94] Davies, *Worship and Theology in England*, 238.

[95] On the effects of sustained attempts to substitute elaborated codes for restricted ones, and the inevitable exchange of new embodied symbols for old ones, see Mary Douglas, *Natural Symbols*, esp. 189–201.

of Christian freedom and temporal improvement as well as the promise
of at least a truce in the wars between spirit and flesh. Yet what rationalization gives it also takes away. As the first Elizabethan generation discovered—the generation who came to maturity in the 1580s—Reformation
leads everywhere but toward ideological agreement; and as the second
and third generations proved, the interests of court and country grow
swiftly incompatible (and mutually unintelligible) when techniques of
political control are not elaborated in concert with the demands that
growing differentiation places upon those traditionally charged with preserving peace and upholding equity.[96] Rationalization does not stop at the
moment when symbols are recognized for mental constructs, but are still
sufficiently dense, ambiguous, and familiar that they can serve as public
currency. The analytic (and in one sense, repressive) work of disambigua-
tion continues, once begun: the dualist polity gives way to the unitary
state, and custom yields to policy; the Corpus Christi becomes, in George
Fox's challenge to a Jesuit priest, a subject for empirical investigation;
Christ keeps his place in heaven; and the drama seeks perspective, even
begins to trouble itself about the unities of time and locale.[97]

   The consequence we might infer from all this: not only greater inwardness and a greater attempt to secure obedience and decency within the
immediate community, but also a heightened awareness of difference and
strain within that community, a pervasive legalism (whether scriptural or
of the ecclesiastical and civil polities), and an acute sensitivity to the use
and abuse of signs and ceremonies. What various forms of communal
organization had provided by way of both structure and its ritual assertion
and adjustment now more often had to be supplied by some explicit intellectual construct, some revelation capable of close explication, or else
some convincing (and potentially Machiavellian) fiction, whether regal,
literary, parliamentary, or sacramental. In "beginning" an unfinishable
relocation of the mystery in things from metaphysics to epistemology,
from ontological embodiment to dialectical acknowledgment and enactment, from participatory analogies to representational figures and types,
Elizabethan culture thus constructs itself a richly dramatic set of tensions.
Not only is there the tension between "old" and "new," between the incompatibles of inherent grace and imputed merit, or between ritual and
fiction. There is also tension in the new orthodoxy itself, which rests
upon—and sharply restates—an irresolvable paradox of social as well as

---

[96] See especially Lawrence Stone, *The Crisis of the Aristocracy 1558–1641* (Oxford: Clarendon Press, 1965).
   [97] *The Journal of George Fox*, ed. Norman Penney (Cambridge: Cambridge University
Press, 1911) 1: 325–26. It is worth remembering that Fox's empiricism on this question went
hand in hand with a firm conviction of his own prophetic and visionary powers.

theological and intellectual origins. Arising from an inevitable disparity between the world as object of knowledge and as active process (or as the given in which we are known compared with the artifice which we will into being), this paradox partly manifests itself as the interaction between narrative and dramatic modes which I have already discussed, will return to in a later chapter, and can redefine here as a problem about how to understand the basic stuff of experience: those selves, institutions, actions, catastrophes, and the semiotic field itself—the light-bearing Word—in which and through which microcosmic and macrocosmic history lives and moves. Something told or something performed, perhaps this history is the direct illustration of knowable commonplaces, or the dark expression of designs still to be fathomed, or an ornament with no semantic value whatsoever, or the irreducibly figurative unfolding of an origin which is at the same time a teleological end.

And the role of Tudor interludes in preparing for a theater that would grapple with these contradictions? They help educate an audience in the dubious ways of representation, they whet an appetite which they themselves could never satisfy, and they open up a free space which sharp wits would find an unprecedented way of filling. In part, they open such a space by putting ideology in the place of ritual (or in a ritual place), thus eventually permitting the question of how well history fits ideas, of what to do about the unfillable gap that always subverts attempts at representational control. More importantly, the interludes participated in a national attempt at representational control which itself did more than literary evolution ever could to clear a space for the aesthetic. For as Harold C. Gardiner and Glynne Wickham have taught us, there is a sense in which the Elizabethan theater is the epiphenomenal effect of suppression and censorship.[98] A long tradition of amateur acting in occasional contexts and a young tradition of frequently controversialist plays performed under a hodgepodge of popular, genteel, and educational auspices are both overwhelmed by an urban oligopoly of licensed professionals whose idea of the play is necessarily literary in at least the sense of having no evident use, of being an empty space in the otherwise more or less rational order of days, an illusory presence whose relationship to the "real" is unfixed and oblique, except as the tactless and unwary may choose to apply it.

[98] Gardiner, *Mysteries' End*; Wickham, *Early English Stages* 2: 54–149.

The Moving Image

✳

I want now to sum my argument so far, develop a few of its implications, and show more precisely how the genealogy I have described sets the stage—in a quite literal sense—for the theatrical and dramatic innovations of the 1580s. Reduced to the limits of a precis, the story I have been trying to tell is this. There is, most of us would agree, a certain tension in Shakespeare—call it ambiguity, complementarity, dialectics, or indecidability—which keeps him readable. That tension, I have been claiming, does not grow out of some radical split in Shakespeare between two versions of reality, one medieval and the other modern, even though it appears to be the case that Shakespeare's peculiarly "literary" drama could not have been written at any moment other than the one we often think marks the boundary between these hypostasized eras. Moreover, though we often argue out differences between two accounts of what a given play "means," Shakespearean indecidability does not finally have to do with a contradiction between meanings, at least not in the strict, propositional sense of the word. Instead, it is the dramatic manifestation of a tension inherent in language—and perhaps in any modeling of reality—between two not quite complementary poles that have been variously conceived and named. Jakobson called them the metonymic and the metaphoric, locating poetry at their intersection. Operating in a psychoanalytic register, at the conjunction of the prelinguistic organism and the order of language in which the subject operates, Kristeva calls them the semiotic and the symbolic. Perhaps misappropriating Austin in order to attend to the rhetorical deflection of structured meaning, de Man calls them the performative and the cognitive. Transposing a Hebraic/Hellenic tension, Hartman sets the work of writing and reading against the iconic; Felman, ultimately finding in the performative and cognitive a new notion of the relations between energy and matter, speaks of the interaction between events and things, between scandal and structure.[1] Rhetoric as against on-

---

[1] Roman Jakobson, "Closing Statement: Linguistics and Poetics," in *Style in Language*,

tology; the procedures of irony as against those of allegory; setting (or unsettling) the terms of discourse as against trying to say something; (narrative) construction and deconstruction as against (theatrical) displays of appearance: all these partial (and anaclitic) antinomies appear to compass at different moments and for different analytic purposes a fundamentally indecidable relation, not in each case the same, yet always obeying an equivalent asymmetrical logic. At the one pole we attend to continuity, to a potentially endless—and endlessly troped—process of displacement. At the other, we attend to limit, to bounded—and substitutable—entities.[2] Or in my own eclectic terms, we have on the one side an independently figured, but finally unbounded reality (the body of the sign); on the other, representation (the idea of the play).

Insofar as this tension structures everything that we can say, no specifically critical insights can come just from pointing to its foregrounding or suppression in a play. We might as well—and with no less or greater interest—talk about the interaction in literature of time and eternity, or of particulars and universals. Indeed, Jakobson's account of the special character of poetry, its mapping the vertical axis of language onto the horizontal one, seems very like a linguist's version of large notions, Aristotelian or Coleridgean, about what poetry does, how it stands at some intersection of history and philosophy or pleasure and truth.[3] Such notions may get at general truths about art but cannot by themselves specify the particulars essential to any less mystified account of literary history.

In reworking the story we usually tell about English "modernization" and pre-Shakespearean drama, however, the tension between these poles has acquired a historical dimension that seems to give it further explanatory force. Again to put it simply, the process by which England grew

ed. Thomas A. Sebeok (Cambridge: MIT Press, 1960), 350–77. De Man poses the tension between performatives and cognitives throughout his work, but especially in the much reprinted "Semiology and Rhetoric." Stanley Cavell objects to his appropriation of Austin in "Division of Talent." Geoffrey H. Hartman throughout *Criticism in the Wilderness*, esp. 63–85, 161–88, 265–83; Shoshana Felman in *The Literary Speech Act*, trans. Catherine Porter (Ithaca, New York: Cornell University Press, 1983), esp. 146–50; Julia Kristeva, *Desire in Language: A Semiotic Approach to Literature and Art*, ed. Leon S. Roudiez (New York: Columbia University Press, 1980), and *Revolution in Poetic Language*, trans. Margaret Waller (New York: Columbia University Press, 1984). Bert O. States describes a similar tension between the semiotic and the phenomenological approaches to theater in *Great Reckonings in Little Rooms*.

   2 Though this formulation draws tacitly on the distinction between analog and digital processes (and implies that this distinction underlies that between metonym and metaphor), I do not wish to suggest that any of these anaclitic pairs can simply be reduced to a mere difference between kinds of codes. As Kristeva observes, *Revolution*, 64–67, the semiotic contains both and is part of a linguistic process that transcends codes and code-making by virtue of being doubled as signifier and signified, ego and object. See also Anthony Wilden, "Analog and Digital Communication," *Semiotica* 6 (1972): 50–82.

   3 Jakobson, "Closing Statement," 358.

progressively more differentiated amounts at one level to a pervasive assertion of the symbolic over the semiotic. During the late sixteenth century, when a whole new generation of intellectuals had received a humanistic and Protestant training in governing themselves and others by the elaborated code of the book (rather than by the restricted code of embodied custom); when new versions of old kinds of authority—patriarchal, political, theological, mercantile—were being put forward; when English actors found themselves in need of new authority (both political and literary) in order to occupy their newly cleared and commercialized space for drama: this was a moment when the two axes of language could display themselves in the structure and the subject matter of that most public of arts, the theater. For the issue so visibly in question at this moment—perhaps the most fundamental of all personal and social issues—was just the one that theater can best model: the question of whether an individual actor is a nonunitary sign in some larger writing, or himself (herself being interestingly problematic, as I shall soon argue) a writer of signs.

I choose this formulation of the issue for three reasons. First, and most obviously, it casts the dramatic relationship between free will and necessity in terms associated with the opposition between symbolic and semiotic, thereby posing a central question of authority in an especially suggestive way.[4] At the one pole (the symbolic), we actively write on a passive, neutral medium—a page, a set of minds and feelings, a pacified people; at the other (the semiotic), we are secretly written—by the rhythms and transferences of unconscious life, biological, psychological, and social, and by illicit cross talk within any medium whatever.[5] This is not just an issue affecting the king's two bodies, or those who experienced the continuing conflict of conscience between Catholicism and varieties of Calvinism, or those whose privileges (clerical, urban, customary, "feudal") were being revised by a centralizing, reinscribing authority. In the first decades of stabilized professional theater in England, just the same issue would have been keenly felt by both actors and playwrights: the actors unable to function—to signify—in their "own" free space without the protection afforded them by their part in another code (as servants of various lords) and without the added significance accorded them by

---

[4] In Martin Hollis's recent rephrasing, this is the choice between active and passive models of man: *Models of Man* (Cambridge: Cambridge University Press, 1977).

[5] See the discussion throughout Kristeva's translated work, especially in *Revolution in Poetic Language*, 21–106. At page 40, Kristeva acknowledges the connection between the semiotic and Derridean *écriture*; both have to do with that which escapes *Bedeutung*. André Green's remark on great tragedies seems generalizable to other dramatic genres: "It is the privilege of masterpieces to be embodiments both of the power of the signifier and of the power of the forces that work upon it." *The Tragic Effect: The Oedipus Complex in Tragedy*, trans. Alan Sheridan (Cambridge: Cambridge University Press, 1979), 17.

their participation in the newly elaborated code of a writer's script; the writers working as literary masters of these puppets, yet paid by the piece, subverted by clownish improvisation, and shut out by their very means of livelihood from a legitimate place in the social order which the actors served.

Unbeneficed scholars, declassed sons of tradesmen, unsuccessful courtiers, members of a profession that did not yet exist: the first plays in English which exercise any continuing authority in our literary tradition were written in the 1580s by men who lacked authority themselves. Dependent on gentry for official sufferance, and for more of their audience than we have often acknowledged, none of these early playwrights more than nominally attained that status themselves, except for Shakespeare—who midway in his career procured for his father a coat of arms, and for himself the second-best house in Stratford.[6] The rest, even those like Lodge, Greene, and Marlowe, who had gained ascriptive gentility through education, lived displaced lives of ungenteel poverty. Shakespeare, of course, bought his house and coat of arms not with his pen but with the proceeds from his share in the disreputable business of acting. By contrast, none of the other founding playwrights of the Elizabethan period were actors; instead, they worked for actors, not as sharers in the profits, but as hirelings. They may have given words for the puppets to speak, but it was the puppets who gave them pay, and a place—however socially ambiguous—for their words to find a hearing.[7]

My interest in this familiar story concerns the continuing obsession with authority that these early "literary" plays exhibit. No one wonders that the Wakefield master has no other name, or that even those Tudor interludes whose authorship we know come from persons with little independent claim to knowledge and power, no place in the chain of "auctors" that medieval writers acknowledged, even before the creation of what Foucault calls the "author function," and seldom any noteworthy social standing in their own right.[8] Medieval and early Tudor playwrights

[6] Samuel Schoenbaum, *Shakespeare: A Compact Documentary Life* (Oxford: Oxford University Press, 1977), 227–37.

[7] Lodge's father was a bankrupt grocer and Lord Mayor, while Lyly's father began as a yeoman but worked through wealth and self-cultivation into the ranks of landed gentry. The rest were all sons of tradesmen: glovers, scriveners, butchers. Edwin H. Miller, *The Professional Writer in Elizabethan England* (Cambridge, Massachusetts: Harvard University Press, 1952), 7–10. Miller's summary judgment on the lives of all Elizabethan writers, not just those who wrote for the stage, bears repetition: "With the notable exceptions of Shakespeare and Spenser, the lives of Elizabethan authors comprise case histories of poverty" (12).

[8] Michel Foucault, "What is an Author?" *Language, Counter-Memory, Practice: Selected Essays and Interviews*, ed. Donald F. Bouchard (Ithaca, New York: Cornell University Press, 1977), 113–38. In addition to Sackville and Norton, the major exception is John Puckering, if Elizabeth's Lord Keeper is the Pickering who wrote *Horestes*, as James E. Phillips suggests in *Images of a Queen* (Berkeley: University of California Press, 1964), 46–49.

nonetheless seem to be men of some defined position—priests, school-masters, crown propagandists, servants of one sort or another within the larger institutional order—whereas the important playwrights of the 1580s (John Lyly to some extent excepted) are all men on the margin: a pamphleteer, a government spy, a gentleman's private secretary with suspect acquaintances. As Alfred Harbage puts it, "A Marlowe or a Greene is a young man uprooted. He is detached from his class but without the means of becoming fully accredited in any higher class. Yet with heightened aspirations, discontent and disillusion stalk him from the moment he steps out into the world."[9]

In the terms developed in the previous chapter, such persons exhibit the effects of rationalization but lack the structurally differentiated setting within which to profit from their special skills. Victims of uneven educational and politico-economic development, they are ideally placed to explore a cluster of issues that center on the notion of authority, real and assumed, fictively ascribed and imperially asserted. Themselves creators of a field of authority within which charismatic actors could strut and preen, yet lacking means to seize that power themselves, the playwrights of the 1580s could hardly help but dramatize the tension between being a writer of signs and being written as a sign within some larger context. Yet as subsequent generations of playwrights found homes within institutions of literary commerce and patronage, as the "office" of playmaking acquired "authority" and some short-lived charisma, writers "naturally" lost interest in the questions which so occupied Kyd and Marlowe. I do not mean to reduce the early playwrights' themes to mere reflections of biography. I do mean to point to an uncannily inverse relation between the situation of the playwright and the situation of the monarchy, so variously figured in the 1580s: the monarchy's greatest moment of charisma coincides with the playwright's most acute marginality. As these "separate" spheres moved away from the eclipsing moment, the theater lost its literariness, at least for readers in the years thereafter, while the crown—after the most destabilized period in its history—attained a new institutional security, in part by substituting a nationalistic and official charisma for one based on religious imagery. We might say that the moment of high drama sets—for a whole people, conscious of themselves as such—charismatic authority as the rewriter of a code from which he/she has sprung, yet which still retains its *own* inscribing powers. This moment cannot persist: charisma inevitably gets absorbed in its own routinization,

⁹ Alfred Harbage, *Shakespeare and the Rival Traditions* (New York: Macmillan, 1952), 98. Cited in Miller, *Professional Writer*, 10.

in the larger recoding which its work enables, in the specialized fragmentation of the language it had once seemed to master.[10]

My second reason for speaking of the actor as either maker of signs or as sign within some larger context is that to do so helps specify why we cannot usefully speak of Shakespeare—or Kyd, Marlowe, Greene, Lyly, and Peele—as caught between the reified incompatibles of medieval and modern, of "feudal community" and "capitalistic individualism." Setting aside the question of whether any sixteenth-century playwright or audience could have felt a conflict first substantively posed by Marx and Weber, and even ignoring the strong evidence that the atomized individual of industrial capitalism had not yet come into being, even linguistically, whereas the social and economic peculiarities of the English had been evident since at least the thirteenth century, there is the question of what counts as the language inscribing us and as the language in which we "authoritatively" inscribe. This question has to do not with distinctions between general modes of production or opposing epistemes, but with differential development within an evolving cultural and world system. Community is never a preexisting fact; it is always created, symbolically propped upon functional relationships themselves modified by the symbolic coding with which they are described. And "feudalism," the hierarchical, patrimonial interdependencies of the *ancien régime*, survives—indeed reappears—throughout the history of the modern world, just as "capitalism"—at least as a local mode of exchange and production—has never been absent even from the ancient or the modern patrimonial (or socialistic) state.[11] But the ever-present interaction between hierarchic interdependency ("feudalism") and analytic self-interest ("capitalism"), with "community" as the stake and field of play, cannot become generally visible unless both the inscribing authority and the language which (re)inscribes him/her/it are themselves public currency, as they were in fifth-century Athens and came again to be in sixteenth-century England.[12]

Again to crudely recapitulate an earlier argument, these are moments in which political, economic, and intellectual developments permit the

[10] The classic discussion of charisma, of course, is Max Weber, *Economy and Society* 2: 1111–57.

[11] See, for example, Arno Mayer, *The Persistence of the Old Regime: Europe to the Great War* (New York: Pantheon Books, 1981), and Georges Duby, *The Three Orders: Feudal Society Imagined*, trans. Arthur Goldhammer (Chicago: University of Chicago Press, 1980), esp. 1–9, 354–56.

[12] On the increased public sensitivity to questions of authority in the late sixteenth century, and the effects of this awareness on and in Shakespeare's plays, see Robert Weimann, "Shakespeare and the Uses of Authority," in *Shakespeare, Man of the Theater*, ed. K. Muir, J. Halio, and D. J. Palmer (Newark, Delaware: University of Delaware Press, 1983), 182–99.

reworking of local communities (tribes, guilds, cities) into ideologically self-conscious and universal groupings, but before ideology itself—its nature as representation, its effects upon the self-awareness of citizens, its origin in education and its role in political science and statecraft—has become an explicit and therefore manipulable concern of the governing classes. In short, as Tracy Strong points out, ages of great drama precede ages of great political theory.[13] For these are moments when allegories of meaning and hierarchy meet ironies of process and deceit; and the moments before ideology itself becomes part of the arsenal of systematic dominance for a given civilization, part of the rational mystification that permits the strategic control of what Durkheim called "organic" societies, societies in which the several parts have self-consciously functional rather than self-consciously ethical relations one to another.[14]

The third reason why I have chosen to speak of actor and context as a matter of making or of being made by signs is that these terms enable a way of accounting for how the new drama of the 1580s engages desire, both in the action and for an audience. Though it will seem an odd trinity, three new matters enter the drama in these years: corpses, the love of women, and the high, astounding terms of theatrical rhetoric. Before Kyd, no corpse motivates an action; before Lyly, no love interest dominates a play; before Marlowe, there is little but jigging veins of rhyming mother wits.[15] And there is love (and rhetoric) in Kyd, fine language (and a resuscitated corpse) in Lyly, some love (and many bodies) in Marlowe, to say nothing of similar but less striking combinations in plays of George Peele and Robert Greene. To show that any necessary relation exists among these matters, and to connect the desire that their interaction generates within the plays to the desire which "we"—both the audience then and the scholar now—have of gazing at them requires some psychoanalytic argument. The essential case can be put in a few sentences, drawing on a tradition as ancient as Plato and as recently exemplified as in the works of Jacques Lacan, but most forcefully present in Christianity.

There, too, a relationship obtains between human desire and the interaction among the Word, a corpse, and the love of women (or of the flesh).

---

[13] Tracy Strong, "Dramaturgical Discourse and Political Enactments: Toward an Artistic Foundation for Political Space," in *Structure, Consciousness, and History*, ed. Richard Harvey Brown and Stanford M. Lyman (Cambridge: Cambridge University Press, 1978), 237–60.

[14] The encounter between allegories of meaning and ironies of process is like those moments which Vytautas Kavolis describes in *History on Art's Side: Social Dynamics in Artistic Efflorescences* (Ithaca, New York: Cornell University Press, 1972): moments when the "metaphoric" and "empiricist" orientations are of approximately equal strength in the mentality of creative elites.

[15] *Horestes* is a partial exception to this claim, but there the Vice, "Revenge," supplies the motive force.

Nowhere does that relation take a strictly dramatic form, though it is exhibited in rather dramatic ways: virgin births, resurrection, glossolalia. But always it has to do with defining (and attempting to heal) the wound caused in nature by the beginning of representation, what Genesis symbolizes in the knowing of good and evil, what Christ (and the Last Judgment) would eliminate in the ultimate union of Word and flesh. Or of the symbolic and the semiotic, our knowing and our doing, our erected wit and our infected will. The plays of the 1580s take place within a kind of wound in the body of the emerging English nation: that wooden O situated on the interactive margin between urban commerce and courtly authority, between a functioning metonymy and an assertive metaphoric power. Elizabeth wanted plays; the city did not: the theaters stood as a site of intrusion and exchange, erotic, distracting, a focus for the play of desire around the problem of authority, around the law of the Father, around the symbolic marking of the flesh, around the always inadequate (somehow female, somehow always already, illicitly, marked) image purporting to be so full as to leave no gap between the body and its sign. And in the plays themselves, language flows almost uncontrollably into that gap, a surplus of signifiers, overdetermining beyond what any mere reading could encompass that law which a critic or moralist (Beard or Battenhouse) would impose.[16] Impelled by such language, the actor would dominate the flesh around him, would himself become pure signifier, the One who marks rather than the many who are marked, but the best he can do—in tragedy, now reinvented—is to make corpses, or become one, at last achieving pure literality, that uncanny subverter of plots. Or in comedy—now separated from mungrel tragicomedy—be resurrected, but somehow spiritually rather than in the flesh: like Edward in *Friar Bacon*, or Endimion in Lyly's play of that name, or the grateful dead man whose burial brings Peele's whirling plot to an end. Representation and the body never quite coincide: plots would paper over that gap, defer its revelation; but the letter—of rhetoric, of unsuspected troping, of an actual dead body—foils the plotter, turns up insistently, shows up the failure of representation. Or else the "natural" order finally asserts itself, but at the price of some separation from the body: a preservation of virginity,

---

[16] I am thinking, of course, of Oliver Cromwell's teacher, the Thomas Beard who wrote *The Theater of God's Judgments* (London, 1597), which instances players in general and Marlowe in particular as mightily punished sinners, and of Roy Battenhouse, whose learned and in some respects quite valuable work on Elizabethan drama seeks to show how playwrights always served orthodox ends. For a recent analysis of the interaction between the marginal and the hegemonic aspects of the Elizabethan theater, see Steven Mullaney, *The Place of the Stage: License, Play, and Power in Renaissance England* (Chicago: University of Chicago Press, 1988).

a life among higher things rather than lower ones, an actual disembodiment.

The Lacanian rhetoric in this last flourish about the drama of the 1580s needs some unpacking. The part of Lacan I draw upon here seems fairly simple: it is the relation he proposes among symbolic representation, the body enfolded in that twisting chain of signifiers, and the phenomenon of desire. In order to keep clear about this relationship, one has to continually remind oneself of Lacan's insistence on the Saussurian insight that no natural connection obtains between the signifier and the signified (S1 . . . Sn / s1 . . . sn, in Lacan's notation). This absence of natural connection requires that all meaning be metaphoric; yet meaning itself (the association of some *S* and *s*) introduces division—what Lacan sometimes calls the "cut"—into the continuum of the Real. But the division introduced by meaning is not the only division there is: life continually displaces itself—through death, reproduction, meiosis, the turning of that great wheel which the Renaissance named Fortune. With only a little—but a crucial—loss of accuracy, we could say that Lacan has Jakobsonian displacement—or Derridean *différance*—operate exclusively within each of the eternally separate chains, S1 . . . Sn (the chain of signifiers), and s1 . . . sn (the chain of the signified), whereas metaphor—Jakobsonian substitution—would operate only across the bar. But this would vulgarize Lacan by suppressing another Saussurean principle, one which puts a stitch that can never be undone, a knot that can be traced but never cut, and consequently never known, into the texture of our language and the fabric of our lives. For the relation between signifier and signified is not that between sign and object: the sign itself is composite, made of the unnatural copula between a signifier and a signified which as we use them are both always already part of language.

In order to say something, indeed, in order to speak (or think) our very selves, we must repress this subversive knowledge, must take the signifier as "literal," a mark attached to something "spiritual," a concept, let us say, pointing with this marked idea—the composite sign—at something in the domain of the Real. Yet in actual fact, the signifier is literal, a mark with no meaning, a mark relating only to other marks; except we cannot see it as it is. "In itself"—the Kantian problem about things uncannily reappearing on the side of the sign—the signifier only marks; it is the Augustinian *res tantum*, untouched by concepts, wholly Other. But to us, this Other always presents itself in the guise of the other, bound up in social—and consequently symbolic—being, part of the structure of meanings with which we find ourselves invested before we have selves to find. In short, the signifier must incarnate itself to be seen, but then we must hide its incarnation in order to make the signifier do its work of naming. It is for this reason, Lacan says, that we veil the penis: to let it function as phallus. And it is also for this reason that God, *res tantum*, the primal signifier, could only be seen through a veil of flesh, and could only be spoken about—through the action of the Holy Spirit—having been (re)veiled at the Crucifixion.[17] Thus we must understand the signifier and the signified as theoretical entities, in the strictest sense. Any attempt to know or to unveil the one necessarily implicates the other, which slides behind or before the sought-for pure thing, like an unwanted shadow; yet in its own theoretical moment, the signifier stands wholly independent of the signified, governs the signified as a variable referred only to another signifier. But though strictly theoretical—as invisible to sight as the Idea of the Good by means of which Plato would have us see (and we remember the paradoxical etymology connecting vision and theory)—the signifier is wholly Real. This is why Lacan insists that the best alternate name for the Other—the domain of signifiers, which corresponds in a startling fashion to the heaven of Platonic Ideas—is that other wholly unknowable: Death. For it is death, the engine of difference, which marks Being but is itself unmarkable; being therefore undifferentiatable, Death is wholly Real, in no way conceptual, social, symbolic. Death never appears itself; it only leaves traces, some of which we call corpses.

But in a larger sense, the flesh—those bodies from which we come and which continually surround us, luring our attention—the flesh is also a trace of death, of the pure signifier. For we encounter the flesh always through the symbolic, yet in that encounter, we sense something lacking, an absence, a fold, at least a potential vacancy, the vacancy that Lacan names as the "gaze," any expectancy or vulnerability in the order of things. This site is the trace of the Other. And it is this empty space—Lacan argues—which we desire to fill, not with ourselves, but with something that signifies us, so that we will stand for the other as signifier, as the One who names, who governs and to whose sovereign absence this other's flesh gives witness in its very empty spaces. And what are these empty spaces? For human beings, they have a double being: at once those permeations in the surface of the flesh which stand as natural signs of parturition and communion, of the labor—etymologically, a "slippage," a "sliding"—that divides us from and joins us to the rest of things; and also those orifices which have become the nonnatural signs of the Other, those foci of others' desire, of our power over others' desire, our specious authority within the order of things. This authority, paradoxically, rests

[17] Jacques Lacan, "Signification of the Phallus," in *Écrits*, trans. Alan Sheridan (New York: W. W. Norton, 1977), 288.

on our capacity to be absent—in the ordinary case, to provoke a yearning in the other; in the extraordinary case—perhaps the essential case—to (re)present death to the other, to be that Reality of which the other's mere body is the trace. Thus Tamburlaine acts out a fundamental imperative of human desire when he chooses to show death—sitting on his soldiers' spear points—to the foolish virgins who have failed to acknowledge him.

The motion of eros, then, connects to the desire of death by a more uncanny chiasmatic circuit than any mere instinct could provide.[18] But eros does not only wish to mark the other's body, to signify the marker's power and absence. It also wishes to resurrect—a word etymologically connected with the "surge" of a wave—all repressed literality, all those subversive markers within the world's body, the body that itself *as* (female?) body is the sign of the world's own power unto death. Eros wishes to unveil those scandalous markers which have been crossed out by the law of the Father, to unveil them from the Virgin's womb, from the tomb which Jewish law demanded and Roman law guarded, in short, from closure of any sort. Simply, as we have always known, eros wishes to free the flesh from the power of the symbolic, from discipline, from representation: from all that is Old Law rather than New Spirit. But what the spirit resurrects—so the Christian story goes, and so Lacan confirms—is spiritual body, body no longer encumbered by law and world, body that is pure signifier, free to be part of the pure play of the Word.[19] In a famous phrase, Lacan says that "man's desire is the desire of the Other."[20] We might also say, man's desire is the desire of language. Activated by the sense of something lacking, language pours into the interstices of the symbolic: through the unstoppable orifice of the ear, through the cuts which both representation and reproduction make in the Real, excess literality eddies, twists, divides again. It pluralizes the never single letter of the law; it sets the other's selfhood at internal odds; it subverts, seduces, wounds, astounds. And though language serves the ends of those who dominate, in the end, they serve that which in language dominates them: the One that cuts through the speaker's being, marking the actor as dif-

[18] See Laplanche, *Life and Death in Psychoanalysis.*

[19] Jacques Lacan, "Direction of Treatment," in *Écrits*, trans. Alan Sheridan (New York: W. W. Norton, 1977), 277. The Hegelian (and Patristic) background of these ideas is clear: the universal genus (image/idea/notion) is always prone to degenerate into a "picture"; the universal individual (Earth, one, the source of negative determinateness) always prone to be mistaken for a dead and evil "thing"; individuality proper (literality, the actor, the momentary intersection of Word/flesh) always likely to be fetishized. See G.W.F. Hegel, *The Phenomenology of Spirit*, trans. A. V. Miller (Oxford: Oxford University Press, 1977), sections 293–94.

[20] E.g., Jacques Lacan, *The Four Fundamental Concepts of Psychoanalysis*, trans. Alan Sheridan (New York: W. W. Norton, 1978), 38, 235–36.

ferent from his context, as a trace of the signifier, rather than the *res* it-self.[21]

Along the plane—or better, along the three-dimensional surface—of the figure formed by the interaction of the symbolic, the body, and de-sire, there is what I shall call "the moving image." This is the image of mimesis, the quintessentially theatrical image: always separate, secretly maimed, like that moving image of eternity which is time. This image is "imaginary," in Lacan's use of that term, though by no means in a sense restricted to the "mirror stage" of infantile development, the "presym-bolic," pregenital stage in which the child forms a body-image, an image of that which is "I." Diegesis—narrative, the circulation of the sym-bolic—always lies secretly behind and before the imaginary: even in being moved about through what Kristeva calls "choric" space, the laughing infant carves an image for itself through the plosive and deictic force, and through the gaze, of the absent signifier.[22] For the activity of that signifier is always masked for the infant in the flesh of the signified, in the inter-pretations and desires of the attending parent, in the symbolically coded toy, in its own always vacant mouth, in the finger which is not itself the pointing, in the already constructed world within which an already marked being must fit its image.

We might think that the child abandons the imaginary (or the mirror stage) as he or she grows up, that the pregenital gives way to the genital in an orderly, linear process of maturation. This is not so. The "pregeni-tal" imaginary, though repressed by genitality, cannot disappear. Geni-tality cannot make the imaginary disappear, not because the imaginary has logical or temporal priority, but because it is necessary, not to the analyst, but to the conscious, functioning human being. This necessity we must understand as a matter of theory: the subject's theory of self, the subject's theory of other; the other's theory of self and other.[23] A blend

[21] On the therefore all-powerful role of speech in psychoanalytic treatment, see, e.g., Lacan, "Direction of Treatment," 275. Cf. Marie Balmary, *Psychoanalyzing Psychoanalysis: Freud and the Hidden Fault of the Father*, trans. Ned Lukacher (Baltimore: Johns Hopkins University Press, 1982). The increasingly Derridean drift of my exposition of Lacan may offend purists.

[22] "Place Names," in Kristeva, *Desire in Language*, 271–94. Kristeva is following Plato, and perhaps Paul Ricoeur, *Freud and Philosophy: An Essay on Interpretation*, trans. Denis Sav-age (New Haven, Connecticut: Yale University Press, 1977), who compares Freud's ac-count of the id to Plato's of the *Khôra*, "which the god shapes into the ordered form of the cosmos" (444).

[23] It is worth noting that this theory has a strong pregenital component: in our deepest sense of self (as mythologized by Jungian depth psychology, or by the Christian notion of soul), "I" has no sex; just as in the high fantasy of intellectual work, the self who theorizes is unmarked by sex. Similarly, even our common-sense theories of the other tend to be "essentialistic"; we know the other as he/she *is*, as given to our (in)sight, not as he/she presents the self in Goffmanian symbolism.

of Husserlian *nous* and *noesis*, the imaginary, then, is what we see reflected
in the mirror of the world: it is the surface of things, *Schein*, the labile
screen dividing one body from another. Common sense forgets that this
screen is constructed—an artifact of the labor that makes, and tries to
maintain, surfaces—perhaps because common sense wants to avoid the
fatal hubris of living as if human beings were the only laboring, bound-
ary-prodding, image-making entities there are. But for all the prudent
skepticism of common sense, the surface of the world—for Lacan as
much as for Plato—is something made, something provisional, and
something given only in theory: in the mind's eye, that probing, testing,
model-making "organ" not different from the working eyes with which
we normally see. Thus we cannot leave the imaginary behind, though we
can forget that it is imaginary, for we can never give up the making of
images, models, and hypotheses that is the interplay of surfaces within
the world. We cannot leave hypotheses behind—not the "first" hypotheses which the child makes of itself in the "mirror," not the hypotheses of science, not the hypotheses (Ingardenian concretizings) we
make of any textuality—because we ourselves are hypothetical, under a
thesis, subject to and rendered subject by the action of the signifier and
its rhythms, steps, and punctuations.

Thesis, theory, hypothesis, theater: the persistence of the etymon
teases common sense to be less deaf. Knowledge—*scientia*, the cognitive
which philosophy has always wanted to free from things imaginary—
knowledge is intimately bound up with theater. As Plato knew. And as
the Greek language knew, its knowledge veiled in the punful senses of the
word *hypothesis*. Liddell and Scott give us these, among others: "supposition," "policy," "an actor's role." A hypothesis, we might say, is a
Machiavellian strategy in our war upon the Real; it is the position from
which we spring into dialogue with the Other—into that *hypokrisis* from
which Greek theater developed; it is the part we choose—as rationally as
we know how—in the social and metaphysical action, the *mythos*, that we
see developing.[24] Push further and a hypothesis turns out to be a moving
image offered by a hypocrite. It is moving because it must move: must
keep up with time's arrow, must move something around, and must
move an appropriate audience, to agreement, to tears, to *jouissance*. It is
an image because that is all that we—or theory—can see. The one who
offers that image, who puts it on—like Paul putting on Christ, like the
comic putting us on for our pleasure in knowing it, like the con man
putting us on to advance his own ends, like the technician putting on a

[24] Martin Hollis develops this idea of the actor rationally choosing a role in the last chapter
of his *Models of Man*, 185–90.

machine to work upon reality—puts on an image, knowing in good faith
or in bad, that neither the one that puts it on nor reality are the same as
the image. Science uses hypothesis because it would be honest. Certifia-
ble, unchanging truth—what Sophia speaks—is not hypothetical, so to
stay honest, science must advance the cause of truth in the guise of hypothesis. But we are not always honest. Some of us lie without knowing
it, a worse thing, says Socrates, than lying deliberately. Freud would say
that we never lie without knowing it, we just repress what we know. In
either case, we take our hypotheses, our images, for truth. Others lie,
knowing that they do so, for advantage, to please themselves, to make us
desire them, to please them. But all this masking, from honest science to
dishonest Autolycus, is hypocritical: in every case we take up a position
(a role, a supposition, a policy) that we know (or "ought" to know) differs from both truth and ego. We go forth as pretenders, and we go
forth—as the etymon again warns us—under judgment, *hypokreinein*.
Krisis, a judgment, a cut: the real will eventually—in time—cut into every
hypothesis, for the real will not be mocked.

Prepared for by the history I have supposed here, working with the
terms I have hypothesized, set as the torus-like surface of struggle (between classes, between modes of social order and domination, between
ways of saying and acting the self), a struggle that could momentarily see
itself in this arena rather than in some other, the English theater of the
1580s still offers us a moving image. Were it not for Shakespeare, whose
authority marked subsequent literary—and imperial—culture in so un-
forgettable a way, we might not return to these plays. Indeed, the only
one of them to make an independent mark on western culture did so not
in its "own" right but as the second in a series of reminiscences that ends
with Mann's *Doktor Faustus*. We who make a profession of reading
Shakespeare return to these earlier plays less for themselves than for a set
of reasons mixed in an inevitable way: for their rawness, their not quite
formed energy, their violent imagery and desire; and for the hints they
give us of what lies beneath Shakespeare's far more elegant, far more
carefully encoded surface. To get to that power in Shakespeare, we must
work upon his texts, must let them work upon us—whence the greater
pleasure and greater truth we find in them. With Kyd, Marlowe, Greene,
Lyly, even Peele, that power asserts itself without our asking—perhaps
without our caring—in a way it sometimes seems fair to call immature,
almost infantile.[25] These days, when we no longer believe in literary evolution, no one would dare speak of the childhood of the Elizabethan

---

[25] For a pertinent and succinct account of the "ferocity, childishness, and lack of self-
control" of sixteenth-century aristocrats, see Stone, *Crisis of the Aristocracy*, 223–34.

theater. Nevertheless, if we look closely at the young, we see in them what we can see in these plays: an explosive, theatrical surface, trammeled in the symbolic, invaded by literality, moved uncontrollably by a desire that does not know its end.

✳

Near the end of *The Spanish Tragedy*, odd things happen to the relationship between words and meanings. The Knight-Marshal Hieronimo stages a masque "in sundry languages" which the printer—as if eager to dispel mysteries—translates into English, "for the easier understanding to every public reader" (IV.iv, SD).[26] In that play within the play, unintelligible language translates into still more unintelligible action, the death in fact rather than in fiction of all its principals. Then after the other actors in the masque have died, Hieronimo explains his means and motive of revenge, not once, but twice, the first time at considerable length; yet the royal fathers of his victims violently profess ignorance:

> *King.* Speak, traitor: damned, bloody murderer, speak!
> For now I have thee I will make thee speak.
> Why hast thou done this undeserving deed?
> *Vice.* Why hast thou murdered my Balthasar?
> *Castille.* Why hast thou butcher'd both my children thus?
>   (IV.iv.163–67)

To which Hieronimo responds, after some taunts and vows to resist torture, by biting out his tongue.

The play's most authoritative editor wants to argue away the strangeness of this ending by positing corruption in the text. In his reading, the extant scene contradicts itself by making Hieronimo vow never to reveal what he has just revealed at length. It lacks "grandeur," moreover, retelling a story the audience already knows. Finally, no entrepreneur as sharp as Henslowe, aiming to please an "unlettered" audience, could have permitted a masque to be spoken in Latin, Greek, Italian, and French. Moved by such considerations, Philip Edwards tells the usual sort of story about pirated scripts, foul papers and uncorrected new editions which transmit error into the middle third of the seventeenth century and beyond.[27]

---

[26] All citations of Thomas Kyd's *The Spanish Tragedy* are from the Revels edition by Philip Edwards (Cambridge, Massachusetts: Harvard University Press, 1959).

[27] Edwards makes his case (and discusses earlier views of the problem) at xxxiii–xl of his edition for the Revels series. Arthur Freeman disagrees with Edwards, citing a contemporary ballad which follows the play in having Hieronimo refuse to tell what he has already shown. From this, Freeman concludes that we should understand Hieronimo by analogy with Iago: he counters "the physical tortures threatened by the King with psychological tortures of his own." *Thomas Kyd: Facts and Problems* (Oxford: Clarendon Press, 1968), 98–101. Most recent critics follow Freeman in this matter. S. F. Johnson further argues that in

Though sane and commonsensical, such a rational tale deflects the real threat of this ending, its dying movement from too many tongues to none at all. An excess of language—the culminating excess in a play whose linguistic self-display set a new fashion in theatrical rhetoric—this superfluity of words gives way to a superfluity of corpses, the last without a tongue in its head. All this signification, revealing nothing but bodies and a missing tongue: prompted by Lacan, we can perhaps recognize here the superfluous, uncontrollable play of the signifier itself; and perhaps see in Hieronimo the finally mad desire to *be* that signifier, deaf to influence, but capable—by cutting off the succession in two kingdoms—of marking the world almost to eternity.

> *Then he makes signs for a knife to mend his pen.*
> *Castille.* Oh, he would have a knife to mend his pen.
> *Vice.* Here, and advise thee that thou write the troth.
> *King.* Look to my brother! save Hieronimo.
> *He with a knife stabs the* Duke *and himself.*
>
> (IV.iv.199–201)

Bodies, tongue, pen, knife, tongue, bodies: if the movement of the signifier finally amounts to the movement of a Real which resists all symbolization, then we can understand Hieronimo as presenting the court with successively more resistant metonyms of that which has cut through his and their illusions.[28] The last and most resistant of all such metonyms is his own corpse, witness to an authority which has reinscribed Spanish history as the Fall of Babylon.[29]

But we cannot tell whether this authority has written "troth." Babylon—named in Hieronimo's fury and clearly figured in his masque—invokes a linguistic profusion beyond the control either of truth or of any plotter.[30] It condenses into one image of confusion the several solipsistic plots which have brought the actors to this juncture. These plots range

---

this scene Hieronimo fulfills an implicit vow of "mutual concealment of purpose" entered into with Bel-imperia at IV.i.43; in so doing, Hieronimo imitates the stoic virtue of Zeno of Elea, who also bit off his tongue rather than "reveal details of a conspiracy." "*The Spanish Tragedy*: or Babylon Revisited," in *Essays on Shakespeare and Elizabethan Drama in Honor of Hardin Craig*, ed. Richard Hosley (Columbia: University of Missouri Press, 1962), 33.

[28] This formulation of the Lacanian Real comes from Fredric Jameson, who quotes *Le Séminaire* 1: 80: "The Real, or what is perceived as such,—is what resists symbolization absolutely." "Imaginary and Symbolic in Lacan: Marxism, Psychoanalytic Criticism, and the Problem of the Subject," in *Literature and Psychoanalysis, The Question of Reading: Otherwise*, ed. Shoshana Felman (Baltimore: Johns Hopkins University Press, 1982), 384.

[29] Johnson, "*The Spanish Tragedy*: or Babylon Revisited," 25–27. See also Ronald Broude, "Time, Truth, and Right in *The Spanish Tragedy*," *Studies in Philology* 68 (1971): 130–45, and John S. Weld, "*The Spanish Tragedy* as the Fall of Babylon," *Mediaevalia* 6 (1980): 335–52.

[30] Hieronimo names Babylon at IV.i.195–96, "Now shall I see the fall of Babylon, / Wrought by the heavens in this confusion."

from Horatio's naive ambition for Bel-imperia to Lorenzo's secret policy
to keep his sister free for greater uses. Between these extremes of openness and cunning stand Balthazar, who fulfills Lorenzo's intentions without understanding more than his own gathering animus toward the Horatio who seems his "destin'd plague" (II.i.118); Bel-imperia, whose
motives for loving Horatio seem part policy, part erotic perversity, and
part unknowable mystery (like those of the Lady Fortune whose favor she
almost represents); and a cast of minor, grasping knaves and normal, self-
interested aristocrats. None have a secure grasp of events, though all have
schemes and opinions.[31]

Hieronimo himself, who finally assumes the mastery of these revels,
stands unknowingly beneath the witnessing Andrea and the slumbering
Revenge, whose plot circumscribes the Knight-Marshal's.[32] Yet even this
framing action of The Spanish Tragedy gives us no place to stand: chorus
to the present tragedy and devisers of the one in Hell that is to follow, the
Ghost of Andrea and his companion come from the wrong place to count
for authorities. Not providential, but hellish, Revenge speaks for repetition, not prophecy, while Andrea—like us—must sit to see a "mystery"
whose outcome he can only desire, not know (I.i.89). Indeed, the Ghost
and Revenge finally speak for nothing more authoritative than a recovered body and an erotic, deadly competition of literatures—"English
Seneca read by candlelight"—and the English nation's erotic competition
with Spanish Seneca's new imperium, as ruled by Philip II and harassed
by Drake's "Revenge."[33] When the chorus leaves, we must still wonder
whether Hieronimo's revenge was as justified as Drake's, whether his
promised future "where Orpheus plays, / Adding sweet pleasure to eternal days" (IV.v.23–24) should be taken for evidence of final damnation or
future bliss.[34] Thomas Nashe, at any rate, knew what Kyd's fate should
be for thrusting Elysium into Hell.

[31] This point is made by several critics, perhaps most forcefully by G. K. Hunter, "Ironies
of Justice in The Spanish Tragedy," Renaissance Drama 8 (1965): 89–104. Frederick Kiefer,
Fortune and Elizabethan Tragedy (San Marino, California: Huntington Library, 1983), 142–
49, characterizes Lorenzo (and Viluppo) as embodiments of Fortune. But these persons pursue Fortune, whose favor—like Bel-imperia's—is willful, fickle, and eventually linked with
the activity of Nemesis. See also Samuel Chew, The Pilgrimage of Life (1962; Port Washington, New York: Kennikat Press, 1973), 55–61.

[32] Barry B. Adams, "The Audiences of The Spanish Tragedy," Journal of English and Germanic Philology 68 (1969): 221–36. See also Barbara J. Baines, "Kyd's Silenus Box and the
Limits of Perception," Journal of Medieval and Renaissance Studies 10 (1979–1980): 41–51, who
claims that the Silenus box emblematically defines the theme of the play, that of "multiple
dramatic perspectives which define the limited perception of characters and audiences" (44).

[33] Thomas Nashe charges Kyd with this derivative ignorance in his preface to Greene's
Menaphon. See the sensible discussion in Freeman, Thomas Kyd, 39–48.

[34] Fredson Bowers, Elizabethan Revenge Tragedy (Princeton: Princeton University Press,
1940), argues that Hieronimo would have been perceived as an unauthorized, private, and

Authority—the question of the author—thus centrally figures in this play. Let me cite three quite different further instances to show the pervasiveness of this question. "O where's the author of this endless woe?" asks Isabella, seeing the hanged corpse of her son. Later, unwittingly the victim of Lorenzo's strategy to suppress all traces of his and Balthazar's authoring that corpse, Pedringano—the name means "errant one"—jests with his own hangman. Next to him stands a boy with a box. Pedringano thinks the box contains a pardon from the king, but it is as empty of authority as his judge's mouth will be at the end of the play.[35] Earlier, at the very beginning of the action, Andrea had recounted his passage through a very literary Hell, the debate between Aeacus and Rhadamanth as to whether he should lodge with lovers or martialists, and the final, secret disposition of his fate by the mysterious illocutionary authority of Proserpine:

> Here finding Pluto with his Proserpine,
> I show'd my passport humbled on my knee:
> Whereat fair Proserpine began to smile,
> And begg'd that only she might give my doom.
> Pluto was pleas'd and seal'd it with a kiss.
> Forthwith, Revenge, she rounded thee in th' ear,
> And bade thee lead me through the gates of horn,
> Where dreams have passage in the silent night.
> No sooner had she spoke but we were here,
> I wot not how, in twinkling of an eye.
>
> (I.i.76–85)

In response to Isabella's outcry, Hieronimo had answered, "To know the author were some ease of grief" (II.v.40). But as these citations show, tracing the "author" leads from emptiness to emptiness, and back "finally" to a mythological figure, whispering into an empty space: that one orifice which the will cannot close.[36] Like Revenge's ear—like Pedringano's box, like Lorenzo's person, like Hieronimo in person and ultimately in mouth—the play is empty of authority, however many deeds, or imi-

---

therefore damnable revenger. Many subsequent studies try to justify the revenge, among them Ernst de Chickera, "Divine Justice and Private Revenge in *The Spanish Tragedy*," *Modern Language Review* 57 (1962): 228–32; E. J. Jensen, "Kyd's *Spanish Tragedy*: The Play Explains Itself," *Journal of English and Germanic Philology* 64 (1965): 7–16; Broude, "Time, Truth, and Right in *The Spanish Tragedy*." But the defenders of Hieronimo have not swept the field: see J. T. Henke, "Politics and Politicians in *The Spanish Tragedy*," *Studies in Philology* 78 (1981): 353–69.

[35] On the origins of the box-trick, see Fredson Bowers, "Kyd's Pedringano: Sources and Parallels," *Harvard Studies and Notes in Philology and Literature* 13 (1937): 241–49; and Frank Ardolino, "The Hangman's Noose and the Empty Box: Kyd's Use of Dramatic and Mythological Sources in *The Spanish Tragedy*," *Renaissance Quarterly* 30 (1977): 334–40. Ardolino asserts that Pedringano's name means "the wandering or morally errant one"(339).

[36] See Lacan, *Four Fundamental Concepts of Psychoanalysis*, 200.

tations, spring from it. Which is to say, *The Spanish Tragedy* is "dramatic."

The "first English dramatist who writes dramatically." Thus G. Gregory Smith, in 1910.[37] Or Arthur Freeman, in 1967, on the best work of this "formidable progenitor": "it contains the first Machiavellian villain; . . . the earliest modern play-within-play; . . . it may also be styled the first modern revenge tragedy. Given a date before 1587 and *Tamburlaine*, one might incontrovertibly call Kyd's play the first extant modern tragedy, without qualification."[38] All this firstness: *The Spanish Tragedy* originates a whole dramatic history, its priority in these several lineages making Kyd the inventor, the forefather, the scrivener whose writing would haunt Ben Jonson's and enigmatically inform Shakespeare's, despite their far greater authority in things theatrical and literary.[39] Yet Kyd's originality—like the motion of his plot—involves, and perhaps crucially depends upon, a certain lack of authority.

One sign of this defectiveness, or possibly another name for it, is the almost complete absence of a sense of "property" in the play. Kyd's name does not appear on the title page, nor in any contemporary record; were it not for a single casual allusion twenty-five years later, *The Spanish Tragedy* would be anonymous.[40] No one company seems to have owned the script; Henslowe's Admiral's Men stage it, but so do at least three other companies. There is a similar uncertainty about the proper boundaries of the text, and not only in its peculiar ending. Elizabethan actors notoriously fiddled with their writers' scripts, yet this play seems to have inspired not silent amendment, but deliberate additions: there were at least two separate courses of revision, one of which—presumably Ben Jonson's—we lack. As Schücking argues, we should understand these revisions as replacements rather than additions.[41] They attempt to keep the

---

[37] G. Gregory Smith, *The Cambridge History of English Literature*, ed. A. W. Ward (Cambridge: Cambridge University Press, 1910) 5: 184. Smith is thinking especially of Kyd's management of the plot, his ability to make episode and situation consequential for the development of character.

[38] Freeman, *Thomas Kyd*, 71, 115.

[39] For the play's popularity and influence, see D. G. Rowan, "The Staging of *The Spanish Tragedy*," *The Elizabethan Theatre, V*, ed. G. R. Hibbard (Hamden, Connecticut: Shoe String Press, 1975), 112–23. Rowan cites Jean Fuzier's conclusion that *The Spanish Tragedy* was the third most popular play during the years 1592–1597, and Claude Dudrap's count of 111 citations to the play during the period 1589–1640 (113). For discussions of Jonson's derisive obsession with Kyd's rhetoric and of the "Ur-Hamlet" in relation to Shakespeare see Freeman, *Thomas Kyd*, 131–32.

[40] Freeman, *Thomas Kyd*, 48. Thomas Heywood names Kyd in his *Apology for Actors*, but solely for a passage referring to the Roman emperors' sponsorship of plays.

[41] Philip Edwards charts the details of these revisions, xi–lxvi. See also the careful discussion in Freeman, *Thomas Kyd*, 124–31. L. L. Schücking, *Die Zusatze zur «Spanish Tragedy»* (Leipzig, 1938), cited in Edwards, lxiii.

play current, substituting new fashion for old indecorum, making up—
in effect—for the play's very originality, for the crudeness, the tone-deaf-
ness, the inelegant blending of "native" and "academic" styles which both
define its originating power and keep it "outside" the tradition that it
spawned.[42] This is lack of authority in the most ironic, Oedipal sense:
establishing a lineage, *The Spanish Tragedy* somehow lacks a place among
its progeny. It stands out, exerting a compulsive force—which ran to at
least nine separate editions and innumerable partial imitations—while simultaneously inspiring scorn and parody.

As perhaps the oddest evidence of what we might call the scandal of
the progenitor, there is the so-called *The First Part of Hieronimo*.[43] Though
its modern editor argues that this play represents a memorial transcript of
Kyd's "own" First Part of a two-part play (the *Spanish Comedy* listed by
Henslowe but otherwise unknown and unattributed), *The First Part of
Hieronimo* probably burlesqued its original. It seems to have been written
for the Children of the Chapel; it both travesties and borrows from *The
Spanish Tragedy* (and from later plays, including *Hamlet*); and—again—it
purports to supply something *missing* from its exemplar: the background
and motivating intrigue for Andrea's revenge. The story told in the *The
First Part of Hieronimo* thinly repeats and embroiders what we "already"
know—that Hieronimo has a meritorious son, that Portugal has refused
tribute to Spain, that Lorenzo hates Andrea for his liaison with Bel-imperia—then it goes on to make clear what Kyd leaves indistinct: that Andrea died in Balthazar's unchivalric rescue by Portuguese troops.[44]

Yet like Kyd's play, the burlesque still insists upon keeping a secret:
Andrea is shown in company with Revenge, rejoicing at his own funeral,
but solely in dumb show, *in signs*. Revenge denies Andrea freedom of
tongue to express love, thanks, or anger: "Secrets in hell are lock'd with
doors of brass: / Use action, if you will but not in voice; / Your friend
conceives in signs how you rejoice" (xii. 9–16). These signs Horatio reads
simply as encouragement, as inspiring further movement in the same fu-
nereal course, not knowing what that funeral will bring in its wake: "See,
see, he points to have us go forward on" (xii. 18). Comic afterthought
that it is, *The First Part* thus supplies antecedent action without in any
way filling the vacancy in *The Spanish Tragedy* itself. Instead, it underscores that vacancy by keeping Andrea silent, making him a theatrical
sign of nothing more readable than forward motion, thereby letting us

[42] Edwards, lxiii–lxiv. For the two traditions, see Freeman, *Thomas Kyd*, 102–7.
[43] See *The First Part of Hieronimo* in the edition of Thomas Kyd's *The Spanish Plays* by
Andrew S. Cairncross in the Regents series (London: Edward Arnold, 1967).
[44] *The First Part*, xi. 106–17.

see something about motivation itself, how it occurs in the empty space between what is said and what can only be seen.

The First Part of Hieronimo is too trivial to bear much weight—no more weight than any other echo of an "original" force. But it helps us realize that there is more in the reception of Kyd's play than successive playwrights' struggle with a "strong" progenitor.[45] Though *The Spanish Tragedy* seems peculiarly susceptible to what Bloom might want to consider "misprision"—betrayals of property, mocking accusations of impropriety, silent warpings of the original toward alien ends—subsequent playwrights do not simply deny Kyd's authority, suborning his work to their own deviant ways. Later Elizabethan and Jacobean writers do not *mis*read an "original." Quite the contrary. The ensuing "tradition" rather fixates upon a problem that we ourselves have recently come to see more clearly about the matter of "origins," a problem that Kyd encapsulates in his astonishing drama. That problem is the one which Freud named *Nachträglichkeit*, implying thereby that every finding of an origin is really a refinding, that every apparent priority is really an afterthought, a repetition, a reinscription of a psychic "present" as a "historical" past. The original trauma, the original Eden, the absent cause of history, all these exist not in themselves, but in retrospective constructions, in the value that culture subsequently secretes around the irritant of "raw" fact.[46] Whether this view of origins forestalls our knowing anything at all is another, deeper question, best avoided here.

Whatever the epistemological status of stories about beginnings, it is clear enough that Kyd understands the dramatic potential of *Nachträglichkeit*, that he sees—like Scribe, but more deeply—how plots depend upon secrets whose only revelation comes, belatedly, through repeated, recollecting error.[47] He may also understand that secrets themselves are nothing more than empty ears. At any rate, as William Empson was the first to notice, Kyd begins *The Spanish Tragedy* with its original "cause"—the dead Andrea—altogether in the dark, not knowing how and "why" he was killed, or what that killing means. Like *The First Part*,

---

[45] I allude, of course, to Harold Bloom's theory of poetic transmission, as developed in *The Anxiety of Influence* (Oxford: Oxford University Press, 1973).

[46] See Jean Laplanche and J.-B. Pontalis, *The Language of Psycho-Analysis*, trans. Donald Nicholson-Smith (New York: W. W. Norton, 1973), entry under "Deferred Action," 111–14. "It is not lived experience in general that undergoes a deferred revision, but, specifically, whatever it has been impossible in the first instance to incorporate fully into a meaningful context" (112). For Jacques Lacan's particular emphasis on *Nachträglichkeit*, see, for example, "The Function and Field of Speech and Language," in *Écrits*, trans. Alan Sheridan (New York: W. W. Norton, 1977), esp. 48–56.

[47] Herbert R. Coursen, Jr., claims that the play entirely concerns secrets, that "all of the actions involve either concealment or discovery." "The Unity of *The Spanish Tragedy*," *Studies in Philology* 65 (1968): 768–82.

Empson would supply this missing information, but understands that omission—not the "facts"—is what matters.

> Andrea has suffered the fate of Uriah; the father and brother of Belimperia, that is, the Duke of Castile and Lorenzo, had arranged to have him killed in battle so that they could marry her to Balthazar the Prince of Portugal. Presumably they informed the enemy Prince, who killed him in the battle, where he was going to be sent and how he could be recognized. There is a reason for not mentioning this (though I agree that one would expect the Ghost to say it at the end) because the Ghost is part of the audience, and it has been arranged by the Queen of Hades that he must discover what happened to him, without being told. The culprits themselves, of course, have no occasion to mention it. If this is assumed, the audience has the interest of keeping half an eye on the Ghost, to see whether he has guessed the point yet, while the Ghost watches the actors and the actors watch the play-within-the-play. I do not think this bold conception has been given its due.
>
> The Ghost opens the play by entering with Revenge, and makes clear at once that he knows of no reason for revenging himself.[48]

In the subtle argument that follows, Empson claims that *The Spanish Tragedy* gives a "more profound treatment of Revenge" than its progeny, not excluding *Hamlet*, whose author was "following a trend" by cutting "out the 'moral' of the old play, in the course of bringing it up to date."[49] This assumes that the "old play"—whether *Ur-Hamlet* or *The Spanish Tragedy*—had a "moral." If it did not—as both critical wrangling about revenge tragedy and the absence of authority within the extant old play would suggest—we might rather conclude that Kyd's work posed for later dramatists a problem like the one Proserpine gave Andrea: "to discover what had happened . . . without being told."

What had happened, I can perhaps now say it more exactly, was something both institutional and literary: the creation of an "image," the attempted imposition of a symbolic order upon the still semiotic body of the world, the invention both in the world and on the stage of a certain genre, of a would-be verbal icon, of the name but not the substance of "Bel-imperia," good rule. I jumble these names and notions together because I do not know how to keep them separate. The brief institution of "revenge tragedy"; the reign initially of a daughter of the English king who first claimed imperial standing in his own realm and later of a foreigner who first fully theorized "divine right"; the invention of a "literary" drama dependent on both courts; the attempt by Kyd's (and the real)

---

[48] William Empson, "*The Spanish Tragedy*," *Nimbus* 3 (Summer, 1956): 16–22; reprint in *Elizabethan Drama: Modern Essays in Criticism*, ed. R. J. Kaufmann (New York: Oxford University Press, 1961), 60–61.

[49] Empson, "*Spanish Tragedy*," 68, 79–80. *Pace* Thomas G. Pavel, Empson does not claim that Andrea remains ignorant of his murderer, rather of his murderer's motive and means. *The Poetics of Plot* (Minneapolis: University of Minnesota Press, 1985), 91.

Spanish king to unify a peninsula (and more) into one empire: all this
thetic behavior, this positioning; perhaps it can count for us as the same,
theatrical, hypothesis. The hypothesis of the "same": the same genre (to
be reckoned with); the same headship (of state, church, and whole body
of the realm); the same "Bel-imperia" (joining kingdoms, yet willing her
"own" choices—including the choice of death—"in secret").

At the beginning of this positioning is the motivating mystery, still (yet
never) to be unfolded in Kyd's play. Andrea's revenge grows out of a plot
that has not yet happened.[50] That plot is to create an identity, to embody—through the person (one might say, the "copula") of Bel-imperia—the union which the Spanish king names in his victory toast:
"Now lordings fall to, Spain is Portugal, / And Portugal is Spain"
(I.iv.132–33). Until the Portuguese defeat, no one could have imagined
this identity or have sought to (re)produce it through a union between
Balthazar and Lorenzo's sister. Empson's story therefore has to be
wrong. But the Spanish plot (as well as the plot Empson attributes to
Castile) nonetheless requires that Andrea be missing. Were he alive, had
he still "In secret . . . possess'd a worthy dame, / Which hight sweet Bel-
imperia by name" (I.i.10–11), the copulative identity of Spain and Portugal would have to proceed by some less visible equation than the one
which Lorenzo proposes. But though "missing," Andrea will not disappear. He keeps turning "up": a corpse that will not stay buried, a presence
from the underworld who watches from above the action; a ghost whose
"secret" function reappears in the friend who then gets hanged up in his
own arbor, his hangmen being later revealed in a letter thrown down by
his lover sequestered above, his body finally reappearing behind the curtain that Hieronimo had knocked up, upstage.[51] This is not strictly persistence of the "letter," perhaps, but it is the persistence of a certain literality which the new order of things cannot successfully keep down. And
this impotence of the moving image, this surprising failure of political
theater to suppress an incongruent textuality that somehow rings within

---

[50] Coursen, defending Empson's thesis, claims that "the motivating force of the play—
the plot in the sense Aristotle uses the term—is the dynastic ambition of the House of Castile" ('Unity of *The Spanish Tragedy*," 770). He is right, but that ambition does not and
cannot motivate the play until after the Portuguese defeat.

[51] Again, Freeman provides the fullest discussion of ways of staging *The Spanish Tragedy*
(*Thomas Kyd*, 110–15). We cannot be sure that Andrea and Revenge sat above the stage,
though it would seem both practically and symbolically the best place for them to be. Freeman posits "a pair of 'houses' facing each other obliquely, with a gallery running above
them—perhaps with wide windows on Castile's side—double doors, an arbour, tree, or
complex of trees on the other, and a section of the gallery or a corner of the main stage
reserved for Andrea and Revenge" (112). Bel-imperia would throw the letter down from
the gallery by "her" house; Hieronimo would "knock up" the curtain in front of the double
door.

and around the image like an aura: this impotence is what makes that image a moving one for us.

Theatrical aura—presence—derives precisely from this partial impotence. An as yet unknown, but somehow apprehended textuality enables presence, yet also threatens it: so when plays grow fully readable, they lose presence, as do actors who altogether become creatures of the script. But this, in turn, suggests that it is *aphanisis*—the lethal "fading" of the subject which Lacan says happens in the presence of the signifier—that constantly threatens and yet also energizes theater. For it is always a question of *which* subject—actor, audience, or "author"—will fade, of who will finally acknowledge that terrible vacancy which drama shows us in its mirror.[52] To put the case now straightforwardly: the inability to keep down literality grows directly—and quite logically—out of the new order's dependency on the letter. The distanced, mediated control which "letters" permit, require, and betray, the control of representation—effected ideologically and practically through classical letters, vulgar literacy, letter-writing bureaucracies, the wily, beguiling letter of the law, of the sermon, of the oration, of the whole theater of the realm—this control enabled the Renaissance state and constructed the Reformed self. Which is to say that identity here is a matter of the letter.

Yet letters, as we now better understand, have a will of their "own"; they speak unintended things, showing up writers for ones unwittingly written. In showing us this work of writing and being written, Kyd has literality assume three importantly different yet ultimately similar forms. First, and perhaps most literally, there are corpses. A corpse signifies power, the apparent power of separating the spirit from the letter in which it moved. Thus the power to make corpses pretends to be the power of the signifier, the power of pure literality itself. I have already explained how the union of Spain and Portugal requires Andrea's corpse. But it also evidently requires the corpses of many common soldiers, both Spanish and Portuguese. In order to bring that union to fruition in a marriage between Balthazar and his sister, Lorenzo has to make more corpses still: Horatio's and Serberine's and Pedringano's. And in order to prevent the discovery of these corpses, he has to seal them up in the only man who knows and cares about their meaning: Hieronimo. Unable simply to kill Hieronimo (unable for the "literary" reason that there would then be no way for Kyd's plot to go on and for the politic reason that a judge's body is harder to hide), Lorenzo must do the next best thing; he encrypts those corpses in Hieronimo's madness, provoking a language too "literal"—or too allegorical, too full of other speech and other letters—to

---

[52] Lacan, *Four Fundamental Concepts*, 216–29.

make sense. Thus the King hears nothing but noise in his knight-marshal's plea for justice.

> Away Lorenzo, hinder me no more,
> For thou hast made me bankrupt of my bliss.
> Give me my son! You shall not ransom him.
> Away! I'll rip the bowels of the earth,
> > *He diggeth with his dagger.*
> And ferry over to th' Elysian plains,
> And bring my son to show his deadly wounds.
> Stand from about me!
> I'll make a pickaxe of my poniard,
> And here surrender up my marshalship:
> For I'll go marshal up the fiends in hell,
> To be avenged on you all for this.
> *King.* What means this outrage?
> Will none of you restrain his fury?
> *Hier.* Nay, soft and fair: you shall not need to strive,
> Needs must he go that the devils drive. *Exit.*
> > (III.xii.68–82)

But the corpses come back, as we have noticed, accompanied by a language run all to "letters."

Second, there is the lone woman of this play, Bel-imperia. The power
to take a woman (to make a woman bear . . . a new paternal name) is like
the power to make a corpse. Again, it is the power (the masquerade of
the power) of the signifier, the power of literality. To further Spanish and
Portuguese designs, the woman must be and remain a punctuation mark,
a conjunction, nothing but syntax and metonymy; thus Lorenzo must
suppress all tendencies (all traces) in her of difference, of a power and will
neither his nor Balthazar's own. He must deprive her of what Grice
would call nonnatural significance, reduce her all to "nature," to material
for his unifying, aggrandizing plot.[53] Only in that way will she serve the
purpose literally—allegorically—figured in her name: Bel-imperia. But
that name—like her being—has it's own erotic depth: *parens*, the power
to nurture, to bring forth; the power, perhaps, to author. Thus Bel-imperia chooses her own lovers, writes her own letters, dies her own death.
Eros, like *thanatos*, will not be owned. No matter how much Lorenzo and
Balthazar may desire.

Finally, there is rhetoric, some of it—literally—dug up: by Hieronimo's poniard, by Kyd's candlelight excavations. The representational
function of corpses and women reappears in the talk about corpses and
women. In this way, there is already play within play before either of

---

[53] H. P. Grice, "Meaning," *The Philosophical Review* 47 (1957): 377–88; "Utterer's Meaning, Sentence Meaning, and Word Meaning," *Foundations of Language* 3 (1968): 225–42.

Hieronimo's masques, even before the main action begins under Andrea's eyes. And it hardly stretches the truth to say that no one in *The Spanish Tragedy* talks about anything other than corpses and women, or the power to make corpses and women, or the power of the letter which subverts corpse- and woman-making Machiavells and masquerades.

Mere rhetoric—like "literariness"—has to do with language cut free of its "original" and referential context.[54] Sophistry and poetry, despite subsequent attempts to effect divorce, exert the same distancing effect on common sense, lure the mind from presence in the same erotic way, and in common draw the world's body into moving figures, not just of speech. The power of rhetoric—obviously—is again the power of the signifier: it makes "reality" fade away, creating and commanding distance. Which is the counterpart of presence, as we know not only from common sense and literary theory but from the difficulty with which Hieronimo brings himself to approach the king. For him, only rhetoric can force presence back, can so distance power as to tame it; and then, within the screen of language, he himself acquires presence—the presence of the madman, of the "presenter" who can celebrate victory with a masque warning against hubris or induce a wedding party to act out tragedy rather than comedy.[55]

"Distance," of course, like "presence," is a figure of speech. Though it may be actual—as in the distance between Portugal and Spain, which permits Villuppo's attempt to do away with the good Alexandro—distance can also grow from epistemological nontransparency. Indeed, distance grows as well as is bridged by figures of speech, for rhetoric—as Jonas Barish puts it—can "turn language into something opaque and deceptive, instead of revelatory and transparent."[56] Distance and presence thus have more to do with knowledge (and the terms of signification) than with geography per se. This is true theologically, as we can see by setting Calvin against St. Thomas; it is also true sociologically, as we can infer from the theoretical (and unstable) difference between face-to-face, or gemeinschaft societies, and gesellschaft societies where relations are functional and mediated.[57] The issue has to do with two sorts of literacy. One liter-

---

[54] Paul Ricoeur, *Interpretation Theory: Discourse and the Surplus of Meaning* (Fort Worth: Texas Christian University Press, 1976); Group M, *A General Rhetoric*, trans. Paul B. Burrell and Edgar M. Slotkin (Baltimore: Johns Hopkins University Press, 1981), esp. 5–21, 228–29.

[55] See III.xii.1–82; V.i.75–198.

[56] Jonas A. Barish, "*The Spanish Tragedy*: or The Pleasures and Perils of Rhetoric," in *Elizabethan Theatre*, ed. J. R. Brown and B. Harris (New York: St. Martin's Press, 1967), 79.

[57] From a philosophical standpoint, this is the distinction that Richard Rorty sees captured in the nominally different practices of epistemology and hermeneutics. *Philosophy and the*

acy works on embodied codes, the other on explicitly articulated textual codes; the presence of the one implies the absence—or the distancing—of the other. Thus mime and script stand in anaclitic relations, one to the other: the actor's presence causes textuality to fade; the excess literality of rhetoric suppresses presence. As Hieronimo's language suppresses the presence (of mind) of Balthazar and Lorenzo; as his knife suppresses their presence as actors; as his unspeakable being finally suppresses the presence of the Spanish king, and the (re)presenting succession of two realms.

Many places in *The Spanish Tragedy* show this interplay between distance and presence at work. One can see it in most of the scenes already cited; and in the rise (and fall) of Villuppo, the seeming restoration of Balthazar's presence (by way of a letter) to his too soon joyful father, and in the interruption (with asides and daggers) that Lorenzo and Balthazar effect in the rhetorically achieved coitus (or "transparency" of love) between Horatio and Bel-imperia. But the most deeply interesting occasion for this interplay is not a single scene, but a recurring pattern, a pattern that lets us understand how Kyd's co-invention of the Machiavellian villain and of the play within the play is a rational coincidence. To grasp this pattern, and this rationality, requires a moment's thought about empire, the second part of Bel-imperia's name, the common thread in Spanish, Portuguese, and Castilian desire. Empire creates nontransparency. It does so by enforcing a union among parties which cannot know one another; if they did—if distance were eroded—the imperial center could no longer feed on the periphery. For if the periphery could speak in the center's terms, and with the center's knowledge, or could force the center to speak peripheral language rather than the language of the center, then it could forestall exploitation. And if the center knew the periphery, acknowledged the other's nonnatural significance (thereby recognizing how center and periphery share one body and should seek one spirit), a real legitimation crisis would ensue. In its own eyes, the center would lose justification: the veil of ideology would drop, or at least be torn.[58] Thus for its physical and moral well-being, empire requires experts of two complementary sorts, experts who can make others (at a "distance") obey the presence at the center and experts who can interpret the present center to itself in a way that seems not too self-justifying, that takes into account the distance between ideology and the Real. Which is to say, empire requires Machiavells and masque-makers. It requires experts who can set

Mirror of Nature, 315–56. For Rorty, the "common ground" on which epistemology relies is as much an illusion as the community of traditional societies.

[58] My analysis here obliquely derives from Jürgen Habermas, *Legitimation Crisis*, trans. Thomas McCarthy (Boston: Beacon Press, 1975).

up a mystifying mask with which the "inside" can trick and dominate the "outside"; it requires experts who can construct a sufficiently chaste(ning) veil with which to keep the "inside" from having a clear view of the "real" effects and motives of its actions.

Yet so far as it knows, empire requires statesmen, not Machiavells, and moral uplift (ideology) rather than (troubling) art. By definition, however, empire is not transparent to itself. Therefore a double encrypting occurs: within the statesman, a Machiavell; within ideology, art. And these disguised and disguising figures seem mirrors one of the other, enantiomorphs who cannot match their other face for face. Enantiomorphism is an apt heuristic for comprehending the duel between Lorenzo and Hieronimo. Or rather, the duel between the part which Lorenzo represents (the part of empire, of what I have been calling the "image") and the part which Hieronimo represents, in masque and finally in person, the part of literality, of an unsilenceable semiotic play that undermines the theater of power. And as the term "enantiomorphism" implies, these two parts are finally *not* two. Each figures (in) the other, as the right hand is a figure in and of the left, for both refigure the "same" authority, the secret authority of this plot, which is—as we have seen—a plot of "history" as well as a plot of "literature." "Both" plots, that is, hypothesize one special kind of author, the one whom we will eventually need to call not just progenitor, but "father."

"Right" and "left," the embodied code by means of which we distinguish hierarchy, privilege, justice, and the *ancien régime* from the sinister, leveling claims of equity, need, and merit. In *The Spanish Tragedy*, Lorenzo—and the Duke of Castile his father, the King of Spain, the Viceroy of Portugal, and Balthazar his son—occupy the position of the "right"; Hieronimo—and the silent dead, the silenced fathers and crazed mother of the silent dead—occupy the "left."[59] Predictably enough, the party of hierarchy divides in two: the royal "fathers" speak for (and know only) the claims of justice; their Machiavellian sons (secretly) perform the deeds necessary for succession. But the party of equity and merit must go in a mask; as Hieronimo first presents, then performs, a masque.

No matter how majestic its vertical claims, hierarchy must reproduce itself—must "multiply"—and must therefore (behind its back) employ the horizontal displacements of the merely literal. Regardless of Horatio's merit—his spirit—Lorenzo and Balthazar want for themselves the prerequisites of rank; "courtesy" requires it.

[59] Henke, "Politics and Politicians," 363, describes the Spanish monarch as "stable, judicious, conscientious, and compassionate," and claims that "from the outset, the Knight-Marshal is predisposed to choose the left-hand path that twists downward into darkness" (369).

King. But tell me, for their holding makes me doubt,
To which of these twain art thou prisoner?
Lor. To me, my liege.
Hor.   To me, my sovereign.
Lor. This hand first took his courser by the reins.
Hor. But first my lance did put him from his horse.
Lor. I seiz'd his weapon and enjoy'd it first.
Hor. But first I forc'd him lay his weapons down.
King. Let go his arm, upon our privilege. *Let him go.*
Say worthy prince, to whether didst thou yield?
Bal. To him in courtesy, to this perforce:
He spake me fair, this other gave me strokes:
He promis'd life, this other threaten'd death:
He won my love, this other conquer'd me:
And truth to say I yield myself to both.
Hier. But that I know your grace for just and wise,
And might seem partial in this difference,
Enforc'd by nature and by law of arms
My tongue should plead for young Horatio's right.
He hunted well that was a lion's death,
Not he that in a garment wore his skin:
So hares may pull dead lions by the beard.
King. Content thee Marshal, thou shalt have no wrong,
And for thy sake thy son shall want no right.
Will both abide the censure of my doom?
Lor. I crave no better than your grace awards.
Hor. Nor I, although I sit beside my right.

(I.ii.152–77)

The "left" comes from nature and force and wants its right; the right depends on courtesy and significance, and insists on grace. Yet the King cannot so easily divide the spoils of love (as he can those of war) between performance and (re)cognition: for Bel-imperia will not divide in two—into tokens and person (however manifold her sexual will). Thus Lorenzo and Balthazar must displace significance—the sugared conceits with which Horatio and Bel-imperia promise union, and the honor, right, and league of amity in name of which Portugal and Spain would join—in order to make imperial union materialize.

Hieronimo, on the other hand, first displays to, then forcibly imposes on these political unions an ironic meaning quite "outside" the royal fathers' ken. He turns raw facts of victory and succession into metaphors of that which lies "beyond" fact and "within" unity: the threat of the Real, of the death and contingency which empire inevitably forgets in its quest for union. At the moment of initial success in the plot of empire, the marshal stages a "pompous jest"—a dumb show—which contents the King's "eye, / Although I sound not well the mystery" (I.iv.138–39). As "old" Hieronimo explains, the successive conquest of three kings refers to two English victories over Portugal and one over Spain. Spanish King and Portuguese ambassador then speak the sense behind these references: Portugal "may deign to bear our yoke / When it by little England hath been yok'd" (I.iv.159–60); "Spain may not insult for her success, / Since English warriors likewise conquer'd Spain, / And made them bow their knees to Albion" (I.iv.169–71). In the beginning, then, Hieronimo puts enough art in ideology to warn his master against pride. And at the end, finally masqued himself, Hieronimo violently allegorizes marriage as tragedy, as that openness to death which sexuality figures in its every deed.

But there is more. If Lorenzo may be said to ironize "fatherhood," separating rank from goodness and power from justice, Hieronimo in his person and perceptions allegorizes fatherhood. He is the spokesman for justice in a kingdom whose rulers have ceased to wield that function themselves. As the play goes on, Hieronimo the judge sees his own wronged fatherhood—his being exiled into mere instrumentality and thus exiled from the paternal metaphor—figured everywhere: in Pedringano's impudence ("This makes me to remember thee, my son" [III.vi.98]); in don Bazulto's supplication for "his murder'd son" (III.xiii.79); in the papers sustaining causes of battery, debt, and lease which he images as the bodies of those that "murdered my son":

Then will I rent and tear them thus and thus,
Shivering their limbs in pieces with my teeth.
                    Tear the papers.
1. O sir, my declaration! *Exit* Hieronimo *and they after.*
2. Save my bond!
            Enter Hieronimo.
        Save my bond!
3. Alas, my lease! it cost me ten pound,
And you, my lord, have torn the same.
Hier. That cannot be, I gave it never a wound,
Shew me one drop of blood fall from the same:
How is it possible I should slay it then?
Tush, no; run after, catch me if you can.
                    (III.xiii.121–32)

Madness—the evidently popular madness which the revisions displace toward earlier and earlier places in the text—this madness plainly results from Hieronimo's being split away from his context. For him, with no son, no true judgeship, no access to the king, and finally no wife, nothing functional remains. All is allegory; and he must be all artist, or nothing at all. To speak (for) "reason," he must lose his—in an absence of authority. So he searches for justice in secret and uncivil places: underground

("Down by the dale that flows with purple gore" [III.xii.7], in "the bow-els of the earth" [III.xii.71]); in old books, Senecan and of his theatrical youth ("*Enter* Hieronomo *with a book in his hand*" [III.xiii, SD]; "See here my lords, *He shows them a book.* / Which long forgot, I found this other day" [IV.i.79–80]). Presence having failed him, he turns to the domain of writing, to hidden literality. In his revenge, therefore, Hieronimo speaks for every displaced, marginalized significance—and especially for writ-ers—against the theater of power. He also speaks for England—little, lit-toral England—against Spain; but in doing so, he also speaks for ex-ploited little Englishmen against reigning big ones. And for that reason, no "name of the Father" can justify his revenge. Hieronimo's justice must come from below.

As this last suggests, *The Spanish Tragedy* will not map onto English ideology.[60] No matter how hard we try, no matter how much weight we place on xenophobic patriotism, or on the providence imaged in any supernatural figure, mismatch is built into the enantiomorphic relation. Take England for left and Spain for right; then Hieronimo usurps the power of another, "Vindicta mihi" notwithstanding. Go by the letter of the law (the left?): Hieronimo cuts out vice, root and branch, leaving only his own king untouched in person, but go by its spirit (the right?): Hieronimo exercises Terror, not justice, punishing not only criminals but all who (metonymically) share in their blood.

Thus analysis (inevitably) circles a möbius band, around an empty space. This emptiness—untouched, unfilled by such circling—makes the play move: move from one episode, one misprision, to another; and in so erring, the plot moves us. Lorenzo and Hieronimo cannot "fit" each other ("Why then, I'll fit you, say no more" [IV.i.70]), for each is blind where the other sees. Outside the other's inside, there is nothing that can rep-resent "fit" to them both; no "mystery" that will match both meanings, no reward that will serve both purposes. So there is always "more" to say: always repetition, a new plot, a new play, a new reading—allegorical or ironical. Each attempt to "fit" left and right leaves something outside and something in, some noise, some sense, both teeming with literality. Each attempt to fit the other into a mastering plot—to make the other all letter—fails to (re)produce the desired effect: Lorenzo wants to further the name of the father, but gets only bodies, as befits his strategy; Hieronimo wants to further the law which that name figures, then to be that One

60 Frank R. Ardolino, "*Corrida* of Blood in *The Spanish Tragedy*: Kyd's Use of Revenge as National Destiny," in *Medieval and Renaissance Drama in England*, vol. 1, ed. J. Leeds Barroll III (New York: AMS Press, 1984), 37–49, argues that the play is straightforwardly nationalistic but takes no account of its contradiction with domestic ideology regarding revenge and insurrection.

himself, but he fails to be literal enough, becoming in the end just spirit—in an aestheticized and endlessly tragic Hell.[61]

Revenge, we should remember, is itself a form of repetition, promising exact reproduction of a criminal's violence on his own person. Eye for eye, tooth for tooth; the *lex talionis* of the old law. It would seem to be no accident, then, that the first truly dramatic play should also be the first revenge tragedy, and perhaps the first tragedy of the classic sort in England, for failed repetition is almost the essence of the tragic. Because there is always body *and* spirit, revenge—like all repetition, all representation—misfires unless it receives some supplement. But supplement, somehow, is always in the other key, never in the right place to supply what reproduction has left out. Though it would repeat a one, by making two it gives us genre, a new and now absent One dividing every repetition from it"self."[62] That genre's "essence" we might name now as the failure of paternity. Which is, in a way, the failure of presence, a failure that springs precisely from the assertion of presence. It is a natural failure, because tragic, because tragedy reproduces for us nature's failure to reproduce itself. As itself. For nature goes on making bodies which exceed their/our signs and kinds, destroying species and empires in order to preserve the whole economy of things. So tragedy is a failure only from the father's point of view, who wants to know and preserve presence as it "is." As *The Spanish Tragedy* shows us—in its action, in its effects, in the obsessive repetition of the afterlife it promises for its characters and achieves for itself—the desire to know and keep a presence leads to a fixation on emptiness.[63] But that emptiness is also a source of fertility, at least of the literary sort. Within the emptiness of empire, there is *parens*. And within the empty space of Revenge's ear, there is a secret. The secret belongs to Proserpine, who lives just a third of her life in Hell.

It should surprise no one to find fertility in the genre(s) which Kyd "invented"—which sprang up, through his scrivening nurturance, from the structured, overlapping vacancies I have described already at such

---

[61] For the argument that Andrea and Revenge reinscribe the aesthetic so that it can "enclose or include" the thematic and existential, see Adams, "The Audiences of *The Spanish Tragedy*."

[62] Jacques Derrida examines the logic of the supplement in *Of Grammatology*, trans. Gayatri Chakravorty Spivack (Baltimore: Johns Hopkins University Press, 1976), 141–64.

[63] Lacan would call this a fixation on the "gaze" (*Four Fundamental Concepts*, 67–119). Finally unable to sustain a similar gaze, Oedipus makes himself sightless, thereby becoming—for us—an emptiness on which to fixate.

length.[64] The rights and wrongs of Cambridge anthropology—of *The Golden Bough* and *Themis* and Gilbert Murray—matter perhaps less to our understanding of tragedy than our sense of the literary fertility of this vacant genre, which is sporadic but much sought for, especially by literary intellectuals. It is as a search to recuperate fertility that we might account for the humanistic obsession with tragedy: the attempt in the Renaissance to lay out its rules and stimulate its revival, the worry in the modern era as to whether mere literature can ever again be tragic, given our moral history, given our unnatural power. (Ur)Spring—in this double and partly ironic sense—has not come often to the theater, probably because the implications of tragedy for paternity and empire threaten the usual sorts of reigning order far too much. Yet Kyd's threat to the order of things seems much subtler, despite the rawness of his play, than that posed by his greater colleague and quondam roommate, Christopher Marlowe.

We would rather read Marlowe. He is a much finer poet, a more tantalizing personality, a better allegorist for modernity. He was also a more productive playwright, with seven works to Kyd's mere two (one of which—that *Soliman and Perseda* which expands Hieronimo's masque into a full script—had no influence at all). It therefore seems odd that Marlowe's achievement inspired so little repetition.[65]

To be sure, Marlowe's mighty line had its impact on theatrical verse. His "Herculean" hero, Tamburlaine, had an unsettling influence upon Elizabethan verities, perhaps so unsettling that even Shakespeare felt obliged to socialize heroism by placing his own rare individuals within an ambiguously providential and historical frame.[66] Moreover, two of Mar-

---

[64] The notion of art springing up from a cleared space I take from Martin Heidegger's "The Origin of the Work of Art," in *Poetry, Language, Thought*, trans. Albert Hofstadter (New York: Harper and Row, 1971), 17–81.

[65] Pierre Spiret, "Antisocial Behavior and the Code of Love in Kyd's *The Spanish Tragedy*," *Cahieres Élisabéthains* 17 (April, 1980): 1–9, argues that the codes of love and honor in *The Spanish Tragedy* have changed so as to make the play incomprehensible. Among many readings of Marlowe which find him emblematic of modernity, see Stephen Greenblatt, "Marlowe, Marx, and Anti-Semitism," *Critical Inquiry* 5 (1978): 291–307, "Marlowe and the Will to Absolute Play," in *Renaissance Self-Fashioning* (Chicago: University of Chicago Press, 1980), 193–221, and Robert B. Heilmann, "The Tragedy of Knowledge: Marlowe's Treatment of Faustus," *Quarterly Review of Literature* 2 (1946): 316–32. It is no doubt true, as Peter Berek suggests, that *Coriolanus* and *Volpone* "could not be the plays they are without the prior fact of Marlowe." "*Tamburlaine's* Weak Sons: Imitation as Interpretation before 1593," *Renaissance Drama* n.s. 13 (Evanston, Illinois: Northwestern University Press, 1982): 81. But the earlier imitations of Tamburlaine's posturing and rhetoric that Berek analyzes emphasize what in Shakespeare and Jonson is an absorbed and transmuted fact: it is the posture and voice, Marlowe's as much as his characters, that has the impact.

[66] Wolfgang H. Clemen, *English Tragedy before Shakespeare: the Development of Dramatic Speech*, trans. T. S. Dorsch (1955; London: Methuen, 1961), 113–62, Eugene M. Waith, *The Herculean Hero in Marlowe, Chapman, Shakespeare and Dryden* (New York: Columbia Uni-

lowe's plays, *Doctor Faustus* and *The Jew of Malta*, seem to have inspired other playwrights to a comic reprise of actions otherwise too stunning to bear repetition; thus we get *Friar Bacon and Friar Bungay* and *The Merchant of Venice*: benign magic and humanized anti-Semiticism. Yet for all this, which all is nearly identical with Marlowe's notoriety—his "high, astounding terms," his "atheist . . . daring God out of heaven," his scandalous, almost bathetic death—the more significant artist turned out to be a lesser progenitor. None of his plays begins a lineage. Marlowe establishes no generic succession, exerts no Laertean compulsion upon subsequent Oedipal playwrights. Of his seven scripts, only *Edward II* achieves determinate dramatic structure, fitting into a class of plays differentiated as a theatrical species, however short-lived: and there the influence may well run from Shakespeare to Marlowe rather than vice versa.[67]

As this case shows, Marlowe might have invented the history play; yet, curiously enough, Edward is the only one of Marlowe's major characters who lacks charisma. It is as if historical structure deprived a hero of potency, made him fade into a victim. So instead of the history play—or imitable tragedy, comedy, romance—Marlowe "discovers" an almost archetypal individualism, an individualism which seems unable to endure or make for itself an adequate dramatic shape of life. Instead, there is the "form of . . . fortune good and bad": the medieval and "natural" rise and fall, *de casibus* without the "new" and self-conscious sense of cause, yet defective in, abstracted from, the "old" sense of significance. Marlowe's heroes therefore seem—like their deeds—gratuitous, as improvisational in their playing as they are lyrical in their speaking.[68] So, too, the plays themselves, oddly defective in their internal plotting, likely to inspire not theatrical but more writerly kinds of repetition: Goethe's long lyric,

versity Press, 1962), David Riggs, *Shakespeare's Heroical Histories: Henry VI and its Literary Tradition* (Cambridge, Massachusetts: Harvard University Press, 1971).

[67] Irving Ribner, "Marlowe and Shakespeare," *Shakespeare Quarterly* 15 (1964): 41–53, A. P. Rossiter, ed. *Woodstock: A Moral History* (London: Chatto and Windus, 1946), 53–71. The best estimate of Marlowe's stature, I believe, is Wilbur Sanders, *The Elizabethan Dramatist and the Received Idea: Studies in the Plays of Marlowe and Shakespeare* (Cambridge: Cambridge University Press, 1968). As M. C. Bradbrook puts the difference, describing Marlowe as the "rival poet" of Sonnets 85 and 86, "Shakespeare's relation to Kyd, and to Lyly, is often of a more detailed kind than his relation to Marlowe, for what they offered were theatrical models of rhetorical speech and dramatic patterning. What Shakespeare learnt from Marlowe, the only figure whose poetic powers approached his own, was shown rather in reaction. . . . Shakespeare reacted to Marlowe in a selective way, and as a person; that is to say, there is an emotional train of associations in his borrowings." "Shakespeare's Recollections of Marlowe," in *Shakespeare's Styles: Essays in Honour of Kenneth Muir*, ed. Philip Edwards, Inga-Stina Ewbank, and G. K. Hunter (Cambridge: Cambridge University Press, 1980), 203.

[68] Cf. Pavel, *Poetics of Plot*, on Marlowe's "tendency to become obsessed with a single artistic mechanism that is overused in a given work and then totally abandoned" (80).

Mann's novel, Brecht's epic theater, Eliot's reflexive criticism. Or opera, or that other theater of power, history itself. For we continue to be haunted by the voluble, compelling demons which Marlowe imagined for us: Barabas, Tamburlaine, Faustus. It is hardly any wonder that Marlowe's dramas inspired so little formal echo. His characters themselves so rupture and are so tormented by form that nothing Marlovian (except a voice) could be absorbed within the developing plot of Elizabethan and Jacobean drama as such.

One way of getting at the difference between Kyd and Marlowe—and maybe also of understanding it—is to notice that Marlowe seems still more acutely sensitive to the question of authority. Kyd, after all, is a translator: in fact, of Garnier and probably of Tasso; in spirit, of "Seneca," of a classical milieu and generic ambience, of the literary and pedagogical heritage of Renaissance humanism. Like Hieronimo, he turns old letters into a theatrical moment, displacing himself—anonymously—as a mere penman, as the copyist whom Nashe accused him of being. Thus it seems apt that his hero, at the moment of greatest hubris and self-assertion, should use a knife to make of himself a pen. But Marlowe's heroes—most especially his first and most compelling hero, Tamburlaine—would be penis, not pen.

To put the case so grossly may violate tact, though it hardly overstates the impulse behind a command like this of Tamburlaine to his lieutenant:

> [Death] now is seated on my horsemen's spears,
> And on their points his fleshless body feeds.
> Techelles, straight go charge a few of them
> To charge these dames, and show my servant Death,
> Sitting in scarlet on their armed spears.
> *Omnes.* Oh, pity us!
> *Tamburlaine.* Away with them, I say and show them Death.
>   *They take them away.*[69]
>
> (1.V.i.114–20)

Like the general pattern of imagery and psychological action which Constance Kuriyama finds throughout the plays—of anal rape, castrating violence, fierce assertions of dominance masking fears of absolute impotence—these words of Tamburlaine's suggest a desire to be not just the signifier, but the signifier as perpetually and uniquely embodied.[70] Though it seems plausible with Kuriyama to refer this desire to Marlowe's homosexuality, we need not go that far. It is enough to see figured

---

[69] All references to Christopher Marlowe's *Tamburlaine the Great* are from the Revels edition of the play, ed. J. S. Cunningham (Baltimore: Johns Hopkins University Press, 1981).

[70] Constance Kuriyama, *Hammer or Anvil: Psychological Patterns in Christopher Marlowe's Plays* (New Brunswick, New Jersey: Rutgers University Press, 1980).

in these heroes the Luciferian desire to supplant the Father, not in order to establish an alternate succession, but to be oneself alone. To be whole, we might say; to be the Word made static, theatrical flesh, never subject to crossing (out).

Marlowe's work thus realizes the latent atheism of theater, its tendency to suppress difference, context, intellect, and all other signs of kindness, of being anaclitically contingent on some absent o/Other. Monopolizing presence through charismatic speech, his greatest heroes come from outside the system—or renounce it—hoping to usurp the center. Yet the center they would usurp—even in Malta—has remarkably little vigor, for the center is effectively *speechless*. Like the theater which Marlowe stormed in 1588.

> From jigging veins of rhyming mother wits,
> And such conceits as clownage keeps in pay,
> We'll lead you to the stately tent of War,
> Where you shall hear the Scythian Tamburlaine
> Threat'ning the world with high astounding terms
> And scourging kingdoms with his conquering sword.
> (Prologue, 1–6)

. . . .

> *Mycetes.* Brother Cosroe, I find myself agrieved
> Yet insufficient to express the same,
> For it requires a great and thund'ring speech.
> (I.i.1–3)

One could track through all the plays how speech triumphs over various forms of writing: Tamburlaine burns books, and takes heaven's silence as a sign that he himself is God('s); Faustus turns from books in his study to Mephistopheles' eloquent stage presence; Barabas, adept in tongues, plays havoc with Maltese law and literality. Yet Marlowe's heroes do not depend solely upon working words. They manifest a working image, as in Menaphon's near-emblematic account of Tamburlaine's person (1.II.i.7–30); they put on a show—as Tamburlaine even to the moment of his death, as Faustus throughout the flawed middle of his play, as Barabas for his own and Ithamore's delectation.

To be sure, it is spectacle that traps these heroes, too. Faustus allows Lucifer's show of the Seven Deadly Sins to distract him from the issue of his soul and lets the image of Helen lure him from repentence. Barabas succumbs not to Christian cunning, but to his own pride in showmanship: needing an audience for his betrayal of the Turks, he lets Ferenze in on the stage-management, to his own great cost. Rather than attend to the politics of maintaining empire, or of raising sons, Tamburlaine chooses to preserve the image of his Zenocrate, "lapped . . . in a sheet of gold" as sterile as the bagged wealth which Barabas prefers to that Abigail whose marriage might have reconciled Malta to his Judaism. So spectacle has limits, even if speech seems not to. Despite the power of voice and spectacle, the actor can hold forth only so long as the (world) stage permits. Barabas finally falls through that stage; Tamburlaine dies on it, on a stage/map that is after all different from the "globe"; Faustus disintegrates into fragmented noise and limbs, cast into and out of the trap.

Thus there is a way in which Marlowe's plays invert medieval drama, as we have sensed and been variously shown for some time.[71] Episodic rather than "dramatic," they too involve the studied, steady repetition of the signifier; they too ignore consequentiality in favor of something insistently thetic. Yet Marlowe takes up just the opposite stance with regard to his audience. Where the Corpus Christi play finally refers an audience back to the letter of their own lives, Marlowe would lure us into a view of the world as all theater, nowhere textually informed. It is not true—though it sometimes seems so—that no agon happens in Marlowe's drama, that his stage is all echo chamber and nowhere dialectical. If we submit to his rhetoric and spectacle, if we agree with its despairing separation from anything Other—from an Other which appears only as a theatrical, fractured body ("See, see, where Christ's blood streams in the firmament")—then there is no dialectic. There are only archetypes, those delusive Selves in which thinghood and concept combine in a pure representational appearance.[72] But we need not submit. No more than we need to submit to the charismatic heroes and villains of modern history, who like Marlowe's characters would assure us that they are at once cunning projectors and creatures of an overmastering destiny, of a promise, of a magic that commands all things. "Bad faith," Sartre would say, for it is impossible to know oneself as a determined thing while simultaneously preserving will, desire, and agency. It is impossible, that is, to be writer and written in the same moment, to be both free and necessary in one's transient union of word and deed. So to break Marlowe's spell, as also to break the spell of those who would (re)enforce his allegories on a compliant world, we need "only" spot the inevitable flaws in that self-replication which even theater cannot forestall or conceal.

With Marlowe, detection is fairly simple. The gaps between episodes, the missing middles in his actions, the reproductive failures of his characters (Tamburlaine has weak sons, Barabas kills Abigail, Faustus abandons his "scholars") all betray the fact that signifier and signified are not

---

[71] E.g., Irving Ribner, "Marlowe's Tragicke Glass," in *Essays on Shakespeare and Elizabethan Drama in Honor of Hardin Craig*, ed. Richard Hosley (Columbia: University of Missouri Press, 1962), 108–14, Hunter, *Shakespeare and the Mystery*, 39–66.

[72] See Hegel, *Phenomenology*, sections 344, 345, 363.

one. Only our complicity, our hidden dialectical return of desire back to the stage, keeps this show on the road. Because we see ourselves in Faustus, and our fears in Tamburlaine and Barabas, because we love to have our ears filled with such charismatic speech, we readily play the game. But Marlowe treads a thin and anxious line between the terrorizing and the ridiculous. Listened to with the wrong ears, looked at with the wrong eyes, his percussive lines and plots seem simply tedious, or self-parodic. One senses that Richard Jones knew his business when he cut "fond and frivolous gestures" from the first edition of *Tamburlaine*: to write out the players' clownage might open the hero himself to some erosion of the image. Because we have grown accustomed to black humor, because we have grown distrustful of Faustian aspirations, we hear the uncertain tonality of *The Jew of Malta* and *Doctor Faustus* as critique of what would otherwise be a grim picture indeed. Yet we cannot be sure how far that critique extends, for like Romantic irony—from which one modern view of Marlowe no doubt derives—it is inherently unstable. Rather than give us a view of the emptiness of power, of the secret, fertile space from which comedy comes and into which tragedy descends, Marlowe's work would make us think that the world itself is empty, that there is no book except the gratuitous and meaningless kind his Machiavells speak. But if there is no book, there is finally no body either: hollow as Faustus's false limbs, as Barabas's soul, as Christian claims to goodness, the repetitive presence of Marlowe's heroes finally just falls apart, unable to embody itself, to inspire (re)inscription in flesh or in literary and historical institutions.

So in the end, what Marlowe gives us—as we try to understand the making of the Elizabethan theater—is neither tragedy, nor comedy, nor history, but voice and spectacle: charisma, that peculiar, momentary union of actual and virtual authority. If history really were the individual project he makes it out to be—if there were nothing to view but one or another "picture in this tragic glass"—then his plays could have established a theatrical lineage. But in that event, with nothing but mirrors and pictures, there would be no "literature." And no Shakespeare.

To the extent that it makes sense to contrast tragedy with comedy, the preceding story about Kyd and Marlowe might imply the following series of imperfect oppositions. If tragedy exhibits a failure of paternity and a fear of repetition, then comedy must deal in fertility and delight in doubling. Or, if tragedy presents a problem about origins, then comedy ought to triumph in its inability to make a proper ending. Or, again, if tragedy demonstrates radical flaws in human identity, then comedy surely shows how life evades, elides, and then somehow restages the Father's law, preserving a certain spirit by resurrecting an uncertainly identified body. Say that tragedy plays out contradiction in the domain of the symbolic, then comedy mimes and embodies dissemination. Suppose that tragedy evokes and mourns the decay of presence, the decline of empire, and the destruction of images, then comedy has to celebrate the virtues of absence, deferral, and imagination. Where tragedy troubles itself and us about authority, comedy should take and give the nearly indistinguishable pleasures of text and sensuality. Where tragedy deals in corpses and rhetoric, comedy—as befits its different understanding of the love of women—needs trade on sex and style.

No doubt this is much too neat. It certainly gets ahead of the argument so far. And in any strict accounting, the history of Tudor and Stuart comedy would fail to sustain such schematism, not least because that history is so profoundly mixed, so entrained in a multiplicity of different traditions and textualities that it hardly counts as a "history" of some determinate thing called "comedy." At best, it is a genealogy—or a congeries of genealogies—that for a moment issues in the "romantic" comedy that Northrop Frye finds paradigmatic of all comedy whatever.[73] Yet this, perhaps, is just the point of comedy—perhaps the double point—that it is on the one hand somehow resistant to history and on the other somehow paradigmatic, though one hastens to add that no comic paradigm is ever quite proper, whether in historical or in moral terms.[74]

One such not quite proper paradigm is the greatest and most influential comedy of the 1580s, Lyly's *Endimion*, which takes as its subject the delicate question of the Queen's two bodies.[75] Her atemporal aspect figured by Cynthia, an earthly body (hers or another's) figured by Tellus (and by

[73] For the most detailed account of what lies in the background of Shakespearean comedy, see Leo J. Salingar, *Shakespeare and the Traditions of Comedy* (Cambridge: Cambridge University Press, 1974). For a recent summary of reactions to Frye's theory of comedy, see Wayne A. Rebhorn, "After Frye: A Review-Article on the Interpretation of Shakespearean Comedy and Romance," *Texas Studies in Literature and Language* 21 (1979): 553–82.

[74] On comedy's evading history, see the somewhat tendentious argument of Shoshana Felman, *Le scandale du corps parlant: Don Juan avec Austin ou la séduction en deux langues* (Paris: Editions du Seuil, 1980), esp. 186–210. Though Aristotle does not quite say, as Felman's citation of a French translation puts it, that comedy *has* no history, her basic point—that a crucial, constitutive element of comedy escapes history—seems sound, and quite compatible with the essentially Freudian depiction of comedy as wish fulfillment which governs part of Frye's account. This view of comedy also seems consonant with Paul de Man's account of the essentially ahistorical character of irony, in "The Rhetoric of Temporality," *Blindness and Insight: Essays in the Rhetoric of Contemporary Criticism*, 2d ed. (Minneapolis: University of Minnesota Press, 1983), 187–228.

[75] Marie Axton, *The Queen's Two Bodies: Drama and The Elizabethan Succession* (London: Royal Historical Society, 1977), Ernst H. Kantorowicz, *The King's Two Bodies: A Study in Mediaeval Political Theology* (Princeton: Princeton University Press, 1957).

her surrogate, Semele), and her vulnerability to time imaged by the aged witch, Dipsas, the virginal first spectator of this play has no single identity within its fictions. Neither the unapproachable and unknowable heavenly idea symbolized by the moon for which Endimion yearns at the beginning of the play nor quite the jealous, capricious, and dangerous dissembler represented by various women in the earthly court, Elizabeth has an unstable, continually redoubled being, the uneasy conjunction of different orders which (like moon and earth) never manage to be fully present to the same viewer at the same time. Correspondingly, the play itself is, as Lyly says in the Prologue, a *"Chymera"* of which there should be neither dispute nor application, *"for there liueth none vnder the Sunne, that knowes what to make of the Man in the Moone. Wee present neither Comedie, nor Tragedie, nor storie, nor anie thing, but that whosoeuer heareth may say this, Why heere is a tale of the Man in the Moone"* (Prologue).[76]

With this coyness, Lyly obviously means both to tease his audience and to evade responsibility for how they take his play. Yet it is equally obvious that *Endimion* occupies—or is permeated by—a margin between different sorts of reality and is therefore chimerical in the fairly strict sense of having no proper, unambiguous being. Because those realities have more than two names, one might more correctly say, "margins." Or gaps. For the action of *Endimion*, curiously static despite its new appropriation of classical formulas for making plots, does not really bridge or join one order to another.[77] Instead, as the carefully articulated hierarchy at the end of the drama suggests, *Endimion* reaffirms distinctions, disparities, and discontinuities. If any connection among orders occurs, it comes about through style, through Lyly's elaborate and often punful verbal play, which constantly provokes and resists interpretation, refusing in its shuttle among realms to be or mean one thing.[78] What margins exist, then, exist in and through textuality, in the discursive space between the neither congruent nor separate domains of being and meaning. Which terms would appear to redesignate the Queen's two bodies, one natural, the other cultural.

For a crucial instance of "connection" through style, consider the mo-

[76] All citations of John Lyly's *Endimion* are from R. W. Bond, ed., *The Complete Works of John Lyly*, vol. 3 (Oxford: Clarendon Press, 1902).

[77] T. W. Baldwin, *Shakespeare's Five-Act Structure* (Urbana: University of Illinois Press, 1947), demonstrates Lyly's adherence to classical models as understood by Renaissance grammarians (493–543).

[78] See Jonas A. Barish, "The Prose Style of John Lyly," *ELH* 23 (1956): 14–35, who analyzes varieties of antithesis in Lyly, noting his delight in unveiling "the contradictions in nature, the infinite inconsistency of the world," and his fascination with "the perpetual ambiguities of human sentiment, and above all, of the most ambiguous of all human sentiments, love" (23–24).

ment of Endimion's rejuvenation. He has been released from sleep by Cynthia's kiss (a *mors osculi* which signifies the passage from one state to another, whether death or life depending upon the earthly or heavenly perspective of the observer).[79] Then under interrogation from his goddess, who has yet to discover the motives and details of the plot which brings them thus together, Endimion describes—and Cynthia renames—his feelings for her. The passage is worth quoting at length.

> *End.* The time was Madam, and is, and euer shall be, that I honoured your highness aboue all the world; but to stretch it so far as to call it loue, I neuer durst. . . . Such a difference hath the Gods sette between our states, that all must be dutie, loyaltie, and reuerence; nothing (without it vouchsafe your highnes) be termed loue. My vnspotted thoughts, my languishing bodie, my discontented life, let them obtaine by princelie fauour that, which to challenge they must not presume, onelie wishing of impossibilities: with imagination of which, I will spende my spirits, and to my selfe that no creature may heare, softlie call it loue. And if any vrge to vtter what I whisper, then will I name it honor. From this sweet contēplation if I be not driuen, I shall liue of al men the most content, taking more pleasure in mine aged thoughts, then euer I did in my youthful actions.
>
> *Cynth.* Endimion, this honorable respect of thine, shalbe christned loue in thee, & my reward for it fauor. Perseuer *Endimion* in louing me, & I account more strength in a true hart, then in a walled Cittie. . . .
>
> *End.* Your Highnesse hath blessed mee, and your wordes haue againe restored my youth: mee thinkes I feele my ioyntes stronge, and these mouldy haires to molt, & all by your vertue *Cynthia*, into whose hands the Ballance that weigheth time & fortune are committed.
>
>   (V.iii. 162–91)

This erotic tangle of syntax almost wholly conceals the reference of the deictic "that" which Endimion will content himself with imagining. Were it a mortal lady's favor, we might think it sexual. Were it a truly heavenly reward, we could consider it that union for which St. Paul yearned, in his "Cupio dissolui et esse cum Christo," which the Dutch emblematist Reusner presents as the explicit meaning of Endimion's desire.[80] Were it more crassly the response which the courtier (whether Lyly himself, or his presumed patron, Oxford) anticipates from or acknowledges by the elaborate gift of this play, we might suppose Sir Thopas correct, and love no more than "some deuise of the Poet to get money"

---

[79] C. C. Gannon, "Lyly's *Endimion*: From Myth to Allegory," *English Literary Renaissance* 6 (1976): 220–43, Robert S. Knapp, "The Monarchy of Love in Lyly's *Endimion*," *Modern Philology* 73 (1976): 353–67.

[80] The emblem is reproduced in Arthur Henkel and Albrecht Schöne, *Emblemata: Handbuch zür Sinnbildkunst des xvi. und xvii. Jahrhunderts* (Stuttgart: J. B. Metzler, 1967), col. 1624. Cf. Knapp, "The Monarchy of Love," 355–56. The Pauline motto comes from the Vulgate version of Phil. 1:23, "I wish to be dissolved and to be with Christ."

(I.iii.12–13).[81] But the play fends off all such indelicate and in one way or another idolatrous specification. Without identifying her "reward," Cynthia names it "favor," and calls Endimion's duty, "love," allowing language—and only language—to join public honor with private, unspeakable desire. The uninterpreted deed of Cynthia's kiss may awaken her servant, but only words can complete Endimion's resurrection and restore his youth.

Language in this play, however, does not always work to such evident good effect. Like *The Spanish Tragedy*, though to a lesser and less obsessive degree, *Endimion* displays a fascination with disruptive tongues. Cynthia banishes Tellus as punishment for her "long tongue" (III.i.45) and later commands that other earthly woman, Semele, to keep silence for a year, or else "thou shalt forfet thy tongue" (IV.iii.73). When at the denouement Semele speaks to refuse Eumenides her love, since he cannot be a faithful lover, having asked for Endimion rather than his mistress, Cynthia threatens to make her "nod heereafter with signes: cut off her tongue, nay, her heade . . ." (V.iii.219–20). But Eumenides offers to sacrifice his tongue for Semele's, drawing this response: "Thy tongue, *Eumenides*? what! shouldst thou liue wanting a tongue to blaze the beautie of *Semele*?" (V.iii.230–31). In an earlier context, however, Tellus promises to distract Endimion from better things by inspiring just such love talk: "All his vertues will I shadow with vices; his person (ah sweet person) shall he decke with such rich Roabes, as he shall forget it is his owne person; his sharp wit (ah wit too sharpe, that hath cut off all my ioyes) shall hee vse, in flattering of my face, and deuising Sonncts in my fauour" (I.ii.54–58).

To be sure, this is mostly banter, though not without point for those courtiers who had praised and suffered from a royal mistress whose tongue, like Semele's, might from this biased male perspective be said to sting "as much as an Adders tooth" (V.iii.204). Recalling that the agent with which Tellus puts Endimion to sleep is Dipsas, Ovid's old bawd whose name also means "adder," we can perhaps hear allusions in these lines both to the wounding power of Elizabeth's tongue, which could banish as well as give favor, and to the demanding rituals of her increasingly Neoplatonic court.[82] But both this negative power of the tongue and its greater power of renewal work to displace and to transform presence into something other than "itself." Whether through discomfiture or

---

[81] The best discussion of topical allegory in the play is Josephine Waters Bennett, "Oxford and *Endimion*," *PMLA* 57 (1942): 354–69.

[82] Knapp, "The Monarchy of Love," 354. For Elizabeth's furies, see especially the discussion in Stone, *Crisis of the Aristocracy*, 605–6; for Elizabeth's imprisoning Oxford for the offense of having seduced Anne Vavasour, see Bennett, "Oxford and *Endimion*," 355.

praise, the rich speech of this play—and the no less complex and punful interaction of the plot—casts doubt upon the very notion of an "owne person" to be remembered, inhabited, and invested with imperial energies. The tongue, and its capacity to inscribe, divide, and dissimulate, breaks up otherwise sterile identity. For textual play, both in the language and in the action, continuously doubles "persons" into quasi-linguistic counters in a higher yet enigmatic narrative, thereby eventually freeing Endimion from an otherwise irresolvable dilemma: "eyther to die, or possesse the Moone herselfe" (I.i.14–15). "Stay there *Endimion*, thou that committest Idolatry, wilt straight blaspheme, if thou be suffered. Sleepe woulde doe thee more good then speech: the Moone heareth thee not, or if shee doe, regardeth thee not" (I.i.66–69).[83] Moreover, the desire to possess Cynthia, though laudable in its yearning for heaven, errs through a grasping concupiscence, and at the same time sets Endimion so at odds with earthly being that he falls prey to Tellus's jealousy and justified complaints. Finally, in his attempt to preserve Cynthia's honor by cloaking his affection with a "pretended" love for Tellus, Endimion earns a response similar to that which Dante receives from Beatrice when he, too, dissembles love for a *schermo* (a screen or defense) in order to excuse a "mangled and disordered minde": "thou art not onlie iealous of my truth, but careles, suspicious, and secure: which strange humor maketh my minde as desperate as thy conceits are doubtfull" (II.i.24–30). Having begun in a kind of epistemological lust, Endimion thus ends in disaffection from the earth and in moral alienation from his heaven. And so he sleeps, his sleep being ambiguously a figure of sinful withdrawal from the good, and of contemplative retreat from the world, this ambiguity implying just the suspension between life and death with which Tellus had threatened him (I.ii.38–40). Only time, grace, and Cynthia's kiss and words can restore him to a place in the normal order of things.

Transforming this religious and ethical description into somewhat more technical and loosely semiotic terms, we could say that Endimion's suspended state derives from a necessarily thwarted impulse to disambiguate experience. By wanting to see Cynthia as all goddess, yet comport himself as one able to possess her, then covering these contradictory desires for purity with the pretense that he loves only Tellus, Endimion strives to simplify what must remain irreducibly double.[84] In each of these gestures of desire, Endimion seeks to eliminate otherness and con-

---

[83] Gannon, "Lyly's *Endimion*," 238, draws out the comparison suggested by Endimion's depiction of Cynthia as "comming out of thy royall robes, wherewith thou dazelist our eyes, down into thy swath clowtes, beguiling our eyes."

[84] This striving for unity is like the implacable "justice" of those irrational laws that Frye identifies as typical obstacles to desire in standard new comedy plots.

tradiction, lured by a vision of union and epistemological control like that which cost Adam and Eve their garden. But Cynthia is not the transcendental signifier, nor is he: like every other sign, she is composite; like every other ego, he is an effect of signification as much as one who wields its power to possess and name. To try to escape into pure meaning—even into the false meaning of one who loves only the earth, as "befits" his station—is truly to dote on "moone shine in the water" (II.ii.2–3). Even the effort to find a univalent way of distinguishing Cynthia from Tellus founders as Endimion works his way through a typically Lylyan series of false antitheses: "O *Endimion, Tellus* was faire, but what auaileth Beautie without wisedome? Nay, *Endimion*, she was wise, but what auaileth wisdome without honour? She was honourable *Endimion*, belie her not, I but howe obscure is honor without fortune? Was she not fortunate whome so many followed? Yes, yes, but base is fortune without Maiestie: thy Maiestie *Cynthia* al the world knoweth and wondereth at, but not one in the world that can immitate it, or comprehend it. No more *Endimion!* sleepe or dye" (II.iii.11–18). Though Lyly leaves the point to his plot, this last claim—that Cynthia has an incomparable majesty—also fails, for no majesty is perfect which depends on another for its condition of possibility. As Tellus sums it up to Floscula, who has similarly insisted on Cynthia's incomparability, "Infinite are my creatures, without which neyther thou, nor *Endimion*, nor any could loue, or liue" (I.ii.25–26).

Among those creatures, and indispensable to the success of Cynthia's determination to cure Endimion, are Eumenides and Geron, themselves each doubles of one aspect of Endimion's character: Geron in his idolatry and consequent age and isolation, Eumenides in his capacity for faithful (but nonetheless divided) love. Without them and the supplemental magic of the message-writing well into which Geron has Eumenides look, Cynthia would not know her own virtue, could not initiate Endimion's release from bondage, might not earn the praise which this play gives her.

Dependence upon another, upon one's own double or another's, is the performative consequence of the cognitive fact that *Endimion* is permeated by margins and gaps. In the most general sense, all drama exhibits this dependency. There must be dialogue and implicit dialectic for drama to occur. The dependency in question here runs deeper (though it may finally not differ in kind), for it is like the processes of dream work. Blocked and suspended in his quest, Endimion can be restored only when his identity in effect splits and rejoins through a narrative of a different order in which his wish can be enacted without stalling upon contradiction. (Which is not to say that contradiction vanishes; it will reappear in

another spot.) Having sought to free himself from the ambiguities of embodiment, Endimion not only comes to a despairing halt in sleep. Like
other sleepers, he relinquishes control; he loses presence, his fortune
given over to a displaced and displacing story in which fortune and contingency play an all important role. Picking up the terms of an earlier
discussion, we can say that Endimion's frozen image must move, must
undergo a certain labor and slippage. Since he cannot possess the moon
through his "own" efforts or in his proper earthly being, his relation to
the heavenly body—itself a paradoxical union of the eternal and the temporal—must occur through some sort of mediation, through the turns
and tropes of narrative, which alone can effect the union that Endimion
seeks.

Doubling narrative, not a plot made up of errors and betrayals, makes
this image move. Given the necessary failure of Endimion's effort to close
the gap between meaning and being, it is suggestive that the story which
frees him from paralysis concerns both the interdependency of knowledge and will and the imperfect match between them. In bare action that
story itself is simple enough. Sent by Cynthia to seek remedy from the
enchanters of Thessaly (with whom Dipsas has a hidden literary connection since she, like Thessalian witches, can make the stars and moon drip
blood), Eumenides chances to encounter Geron, singing by a fountain in
the desert.[85] At this "sacred fountain," Eumenides' pure love for Semele
(his "earth") lets him see beyond Geron's sight to the inscription at the
bottom: "*Aske one for all, and but one thing at all*" (III.iv.81–82). Urged by
the old man, who has learned the commonplace Renaissance distinction
between the fleshly love of women and the "image of eternity" which is
friendship between men, Eumenides chooses to relinquish one for the
other. Yet renunciation has its reward: giving up mistress for friend, asking one for all, he wins both.

Glossing these names both helps us read the action and reveals one of
the many ways in which this saving narrative depends upon textual play.
"Geron" has both typological and moral resonance; "Eumenides" has
providential implications but may also be a double pun, for he is a "well-
wisher" in two senses, being motivated by good feeling and being one
who gazes into a magic well. Though grown wiser through his experience of Dipsas, Geron (like the scriptural old man) cannot use the sacred
fountain committed to his care. Spiritually blinded by his own earlier
idolatry, he has fallen into the heresy that charity, or true love, is nowhere
to be found (III.iv.32–48). Even when Eumenides sees through to the in-

---

[85] Knapp, "The Monarchy of Love," 354. Cf. R. G. Howarth, "Dipsas in Lyly and Mar-
ston," *Notes and Queries* n.s. 175 (1938): 24–25.

scription, Geron's heart remains hardened: "I cannot discerne any such thing. I thinke thou dreamest." To which Eumenides responds: "Ah Father, thou art not a faithfull louer, and therefore canst not behold it" (III.iv.84–87). Yet unlike the Hebrews, Geron is willing to "be satisfied by the euent" (III.iv.88) and finally trusts Eumenides' "evidence of things unseen." He has ears to hear, if not eyes to see. More importantly, it is his knowledge and judgment that make Eumenides ask for Endimion rather than Semele, and it is he who interprets the inscription which he cannot see.

Here Lyly establishes a humorous and significant interdependency between traditional roles: the old man, unable to see the letter of prophecy, can read its meaning better than the faithful lover whose good will makes the writing appear. It is Geron who gives the law to love, who teaches Eumenides the right order of *caritas*, and who directs him to its penultimate object, Cynthia: "who can it bee but *Cynthia*, whose vertues beeing all diuine, must needes bring things to passe that bee myraculous?" (III.iv.180–81). And it is "fortunate" Eumenides, whose name echoes a non-Biblical conversion of hatred into blessing (in his name thus also doubling Endimion's dream of the two ladies, one revengeful, the other merciful), who becomes a vehicle of grace, paving the way for a more general reordering of love. Geron has the antecedently and consequentially necessary knowledge; Eumenides has the right will: together, but enantiomorphically, they reveal and act upon a scripture which can resurrect Endimion.

Eumenides and Geron not only depend on one another, and on their chance encounter, for the revelation of this efficacious word. They also— like the newness and oldness to which their names and actions witness— depend for their effectiveness upon the earth and a fortunate fall. Without Dipsas, who provokes the sleep that seems to bring Cynthia to earth—as if her idolatrous lover had to lose presence, had to "fade," in order for Cynthia to appear as queen rather than unapproachable moon—Endimion would have languished forever in the embrace of "golden thoughts" and "deepe melancholy" (II.iii.5, 22). Agent of the slighted Tellus (and therefore of the body of the sign, the earthly shadow, which Endimion's "Neoplatonism" overlooks), Dipsas brings matters to crisis and so prepares for Lyly's equivalent of the debate among the four daughters of God: "*Three Ladies enter; one with a Knife and a looking glasse, who by the procurement of one of the other two, offers to stab Endimion as hee sleepes, but the third wrings her hands, lamenteth, offering still to preuent it, but dares not. At last, the first Lady looking in the glasse, casts downe the Knife*" (II.iii.61–65).

Again, the action doubles, then doubles again. Like the first Fall, brought about by the snake which Dipsas figures in her name, this one rebukes the greed that would erase the difference between earth and heaven, that would transcend the distinction between being and meaning, signifier and signified. Yet it also inspires the redemptive descent of heaven to earth. Then when heaven descends, it comes doubled, in the form of a woman, and moreover a woman with two natures, cruel and merciful, each figured once in a separate counselor and again in the emblems of knife and mirror. Judge and contemplative Virgin, or assassin and narcissistic Venus: we cannot stabilize the difference. Like Endimion in the second dream, we have neither counsels nor policies, just pictures—given not insignificantly by an old man—that will not quite coincide; on the one hand, a lady casting away a knife, on the other, Cynthia stooping to kiss Endimion.

For Cynthia, too, depends upon and in some sense is Dipsas and Tellus, as the moon depends upon and is an earth and as the queen depends upon and is her aging body. One ironic sign of this dependency is Sir Thopas's dotage upon Dipsas. This fashionable and foolish surrender of Mars to Venus not only parodies erotic artifice but also records the evident biological and historical fact that an old woman with "fine thin hayre. . . . whom none durst vndertake" (III.iii.52,70) has become the not wholly appropriate object of much "drasty ryming."[86] Here history most evidently obtrudes itself. This is a play that thematizes gaps and concludes with a conventional Neoplatonic hierarchy ranging from Endimion's contemplative fervor to Sir Thopas's insistent, "Nay soft, I cannot handsomly goe to bed without *Bagoa*. . . . true loue or false, so shee be a wench I care not" (V.iii.274–80). But Elizabeth's successful and highly political exploitation of that hierarchy played upon the anxieties created by a gap in the order of things that no hierarchy could subdue, not even the spiritual hierarchy implied by the potent myth of the moon-goddess to which Lyly gave canonical literary shape.

One might argue that Elizabeth succeeded so well precisely because the artifice of her reign displaced without really allaying the uneasiness that the fact of her person evoked. The moon, after all, is a specular reality. It is intrinsically double, a mediator between the sun and the earth, its astronomical position played upon by Renaissance emblems depicting the prince, the *vicarius Christi*, as a moon reflecting the Son of glory.[87] To have a woman rather than a man—and now a menopausal, therefore eternally "virginal" woman—occupy that place, brings out the latent unreliability of the lunar metaphor, its destabilizing alternation of light and shadow, of imaginary and Real. Sign of the space between the realm of the Father and the barely governable female earth, this now forever unmasterable Cynthia causes what we might call the "scandal of succession" to come fully into consciousness. Rather than signify the lawful connection between one domain, one name, one body and another, such a ruling moon makes clear how all such connections arise from the interaction of convention and contingency.

There is bite, then, in the compliment to Cynthia, into "whose hands the Ballance that weigheth time & fortune are committed" (V.iii.191). Elizabeth had turned out for sure not to be the Bel-imperia of any man's fantasies. No copula guaranteeing dynastic continuity, but rather the unignorable proof that any dynasty depends on style—on the intervening and uncertain doubleness of women, of language, and of that public custom which honors the "King's style"—Elizabeth had come to embody the dependency of presence upon absence.

The female body always challenges the mastery of a symbolic order, but here the challenge takes place at the highest level of governance as well as at the most intimate level of the psychosexual. This conjunction produces complex effects. On the one hand, it opens a rift in the ideology of governance, forcing an acknowledgment of the way in which earthly rule depends upon facts of embodiment outside its control. In a way analogous to that of the Corpus Christi plays, *Endimion* thus chastens the pretensions of normally paternal authority by asserting the necessity of its submitting to "love," to being ruled by a desire beyond one's knowing. Yet this elevation of the female not only resurrects the body, it also threatens to establish a new, competing ideology—the ideology of pure, unmarked, asexual absence. And perhaps for that reason, as if to preserve balance, the play covertly advances the claims of a very particular male sexuality, resurrecting another sort of literality.

We can now perhaps detect an aggressive import to Eumenides' choice at the well. The codes of this play associate both Cynthia and masculine friendship with the image of eternity, while consigning the love of women to an inferior, fleshly status. The one is pure, the other mixed. But by virtue of her natural female body, Cynthia remains mixed, always bound up with an "impure" shadow. Thus where Endimion stalls, Eu-

32–34, nos. 215–20, 237, 253. In Henkel and Schöne, *Emblemata*, cols. 35–39, there are several emblems of the prince as moon (cf. Peter Saccio, *The Court Comedies of John Lyly* [Princeton: Princeton University Press, 1969], 170–74).

menides seems to work through to that elusive purity, separating male friendship from sexual love. However much the "dread sovereign," Cynthia—unlike Elizabeth's father or her inheriting cousin—is fit neither for male friendship nor for sexual love. Full of power, yet not its possessor (since she depends on others for knowledge of her "vertue"), this moon-goddess ends up in an oddly detached, denatured position. For in her power is the effect not of the signifier but of truth, which can dispel fiction and fraud, but not enter upon or create bonds.

> *Cynth.* Well *Syr Thopas*, it may bee there are more vertues in mee then my selfe knoweth of; for *Endimion* I awaked, and at my words he waxed young; I will trie whether I can turne this tree again to thy true loue.
> *Top.* Turne her to a true loue or false, so shee be a wench I care not.
> *Cynth.* Bagoa, *Cynthia* putteth an end to thy harde fortunes; for being turnd to a tree for reuealing a truth, I will recouer thee againe, if in my power be the effect of truth.
> *Top. Bagoa?* a bots vpon thee!
> (V.iii.275–84)

There is aggression here, too, however much disguised in comedy. Responding "correctly" to Sir Thopas, we should consider him a lusty fool, incapable of seeing beyond the sexuality of those women on whom he "ventureth" (III.iii.69, a Latinate pun on belly that the grammarian's grandson should not have missed). But balancing her favor toward Endimion by arranging a sexual companion for every other native male of her entourage—the syntax of this gift equating her favor with the persons of those women that other men have—Cynthia reveals more truth than Elizabeth may have bargained for.[88] Of all her courtiers, only Endimion has played by the rules of heroic frenzy.[89] All the rest content themselves with notably untranscendent, earthly women. And all these women, the divine but wanton Tellus not excepted, submit themselves to male rule as the price of Cynthia's pardon for their crimes, which are all crimes of dissembling—"that which is most customarie to our sex" (IV.i.27)—or crimes of the tongue. Bagoa, too, had been imprisoned for her tongue (and though Dipsas does not carry out her threat to punish her servant's "whisper that I did this" by turning "thy haires to Adders, and all thy teeth in thy heade to tongues" [II.iii.56–57], she does turn her to an Aspen tree, thus continuing the punning connection between snakes and tongues).

The last male response to this series of sexual gifts that chasten the

---

[88] Here is the line I refer to: "Thou hast my fauour, *Tellus* her friend, *Eumenides* in Paradice with his *Semele*, *Geron* contented with *Dipsas*" (V.iii.272–73).

[89] Gannon suggests that Bruno's *Heroic Frenzies*, which also ends with a compliment to Elizabeth, may be one source for *Endimion* ("Lyly's *Endimion*," 224–31).

female tongue, Sir Thopas's "a bots upon thee," carries an extra, comically disruptive stress. Insulting the woman he has just acquired—with the nasty sexual implications of a curse that wishes small, white worms to erupt from her flesh—Thopas explodes for an instant the whole cult of love that had developed in the late Elizabethan court. As Lawrence Stone has noted, the sexual behavior of Elizabeth's courtiers and maids of honor was often at considerable odds both with Platonizing ideology and with the queen's vehement attempts to establish a general discipline consonant with her own.[90] Cynthia's power of truth had initially healed Endimion of the illusions of his refined concupiscence. Now, in its final effect, this same power exposes dissimulation in the very doctrine that the play itself celebrates.

The best way to appreciate what happens here is to think of *Endimion* as a kind of double game, part flattery, part insolence. Locating Lyly's work in the interactive and admonitory tradition of the Tudor mask, wherein courtiers and prince both "release and reharness" the tensions arising from the everyday practice of social fiction, Marie Axton observes that Endimion and his mistress learn to "live in metaphor."[91] Part of living in metaphor for a fifty-five-year-old queen is acknowledging how much the cult of love is mere fiction and fraud, as much a way of maintaining masculine power and masculine sexual privilege as it is a way of affirming the spiritual superiority of Elizabeth and her court. Endimion is not the only one upon whom this play urges the difference between being and meaning.

Learning to live in metaphor thus also means accepting the concomitant but incongruent force of metonymy, which Kenneth Burke aptly calls "terminological reduction."[92] Such a reductive force might push the queen toward identifying herself as private body rather than as public meaning, to distinguish politic praise from the "facts" of her personal being. Another reductive force arises from the possibility that the first audience of *Endimion* would "apply pastimes" quite unmetaphysically. For they could also understand this play as a cheeky and only partly flattering rehearsal of recent scandal. Josephine Bennett has argued that Lyly's patron, the Earl of Oxford, is the likeliest topical referent for Endimion.[93] Though in one reading (let us call it the metaphoric), the audience might puzzle out Neoplatonic allegory, seeing how every real person dissociates into doubled and redoubled positions in that metaphysic, in

---

[90] Stone, *Family, Sex and Marriage in England*, 504.
[91] Axton, "Tudor Mask," 24, 46.
[92] Kenneth Burke, "Four Master Tropes," in *A Grammar of Motives* and *A Rhetoric of Motives* (Cleveland: World Publishing Company, 1962), 507.
[93] Bennett, "Oxford and *Endimion*."

another reading (let us call it the metonymic), the audience can try the enigma a different way, wondering whether Tellus is Anne Vavasour, with whom Oxford had an affair (for the presumed issue of which Elizabeth had imprisoned him). Left with a little "picture" of her lover (one remembers Tellus's weaving such a picture in the castle where she is imprisoned), Anne—or more probably her friends and family—had tried to implicate Oxford in a papist conspiracy as well, one feature of which was a book "of painted pictures of prophecy" having to do with the succession. Thus affronted both sexually and politically, Elizabeth ordered Oxford himself to prison. Having served as a principal advocate of the match with Alençon in the early 1570s, Oxford did not return to favor until 1586, after much urging of Elizabeth by his father-in-law, Lord Burghley, who had at last also accomplished a reconciliation between his daughter and the profligate Earl. Meanwhile, perhaps during her own stay in prison, Anne had become the mistress of the Queen's master of the armoury, Sir Henry Lee, who therefore makes an apt historical double for Corsites.

Now favored with a handsome pension and reunited with his wife, Oxford can be understood as retelling his own story through this device of the poet to get money. Such a reading carries the suitably self-flattering implication that Oxford had all along been devoted to Cynthia, as a loyal subject, and that he had proved his devotion by exposing an early version of what would become the Throckmorton conspiracy against his monarch. Endimion commits no fault at all, then, being but the victim of malicious tongues. Anne's child is not his, but a picture she wove out of thwarted desire. Those threatening prophecies in the book he had merely record the designs of envious and disloyal ingrates. With his truth and honor vindicated, he expresses thanks to the monarch who has restored him by having her, in a figure, christen that honor "love." Then in an epilogue he rather huffily reminds her that warmth always outperforms mere wind: "A Man walking abroad, the wind and Sunne stroue for soueraignty, the one with his blast, the other with his beames. . . . Dread Soueraigne, the malicious that seeke to ouerthrowe vs with threats, do but stiffen our thoughts, and make them sturdier in stormes: but if your Highnes vouchsafe with your fauorable beames to glaunce vpon vs, we shall not onlie stoope, but with all humilitie, lay both our handes and heartes at your Maiesties feete." If the play celebrates Oxford's rehabilitation, then, it also covertly presumes to advise Elizabeth on the proper conduct of her office: more as the steady sun than as the waxing and waning moon. Further institutionalizing the royal propaganda of Elizabeth as goddess, it covertly rebukes her having either listened to malicious tongues or having played their part as the Dipsas who put Endimion to "sleep." Satirizing Sir Thopas's love for that same Dipsas, it flaunts in Diana's face the less than ideal sexual behavior of her court, and by association almost names her the Ovidian procuress who supplies wenches for men who read dreams in an unrepentantly lustful way.

Neither the metaphoric nor the metonymic reading of *Endimion* is exclusively correct. The play allows for both, but only up to a certain point. Since each reading demands a partially different placement of characters and a different assessment of their function and meaning in the plot, we cannot harmonize the one with the other. Yet we cannot fully separate them, either, for the metaphysical understanding of *Endimion* needs some history in order to make sense, and the historical exegesis needs some metaphysics. Endimion can (though not with a perfect intellectual overlap) be both a fundamentally blameless courtier and a man caught between the aspirations of his soul and the necessities of his body, but in the one case his fall is the effect of malice, in the other a fortunate check to misguided aspiration. Tellus can (though not with equal moral value) be both an errant maid of honor and the teeming, sustaining earth itself, yet in the one identity she suffers undeservedly from the effects of Endimion's deceit while in the other she inflicts on him an undeserved despite. These narrative expansions of *Endimion*'s tropes repeat without in any way resolving the fundamental antinomy which the play records, admits, and celebrates: there is no having one of the queen's bodies without the other, yet they are not the same.

Without being meaningless, then, the chimera that is *Endimion* sets a limit to interpretation. It opens a space in which a fertile indeterminacy comes into play, a place where meaning and being need not pretend to coincide, where identities can dissociate and punfully reassemble. Far from reconciling the demands of spiritualizing knowledge and naturalizing will, it infects each of these domains with the other, alternately affirming and inverting the standard Renaissance hierarchies—which remain our own—of soul over body and male over female. Like the monarch to whom it pays tribute, *Endimion* thwarts the desire of every ideology, its own included, for things to be single, for the representational order to work without style, without the simultaneous distance and excess, gap and supplement that women and writing are, at least from the viewpoint of those self-identified with the signifier.[94]

From that viewpoint, of course, *Endimion* offers a striking vision of a

[94] Here is the appropriate place, perhaps, to record my general indebtedness to Jacques Derrida's *Spurs: Nietzsche's Styles*, trans. Barbara Harlow (Chicago: University of Chicago Press, 1979).

reformed social and erotic order, an Elizabethan New Jerusalem in which all persons have and keep their place. But because of the effects of style, that vision appears as if in a mirror, distanced, doubled, and systematically shadowed with a certain darkness. Like many other comedies, this play seems to set forth the triumph of a new law, an order of the symbolic no longer troubled by the stubborn unwillingness of human material to fit hierarchizing schemes. Pythagoras perhaps most economically marks that triumph: "I had rather in *Cynthia's* Court spende tenne yeeres, then in Greece one houre" (V.iii.290). Only the garment of style, with its interweaving of the imaginary and the Real, saves this vision from being sheer narcissism. Only the fact that Cynthia herself is such an interweaving of contraries gives this vision a force that goes beyond mere propaganda and flattery.

For Cynthia's virtue, both as an occasion of praise and as a figure of the truth that releases and restores, consists in her final unknowability, in her irresolvably enigmatic being. It is fortunate for the history of drama, as we all recognize, that Elizabeth and her state apparatus sponsored plays. But no man could have inspired such a double game as *Endimion*. And thus no king would so "naturally" have provoked the theatrical investigation of that doubleness in human being that derives from our serving, not quite simultaneously, as both sources and effects of signification.

Endimion's virtue, correspondingly, consists in its also not quite simultaneously glorifying authority and extolling style. In this courtly moment of politicized Petrarchanism, authority and style occur as features of literature and features of the high life. Courtly presence, I have argued, depended upon that absence in the order of things which was this Virgin Queen.[95] Whatever anxieties her femaleness excited, she nevertheless held the indispensable place of authority. Yet her presence in that place, much more than her father's and sister's, also depended upon what Wallace MacCaffrey calls "a large body of organized, coherent, and very articulate public opinion . . . which it was impossible either to ignore or effectively to control."[96] The articulating of that opinion counts as authority in the other, lettered sense which Lyly's play both commands and serves. A mere pastime, but without it, no queen. To recognize and enact such

---

[95] G. K. Hunter, *John Lyly: Humanist as Courtier* (London: Routledge and Kegan Paul, 1962), argues at length for the relationship between courtship (in the double sense of wooing women and attending the monarch) and the adroit, witty workings of Lyly's and Shakespeare's comedies. He puts the connection perhaps most elegantly in characterizing that most Lylyean of Shakespeare's plays, *Love's Labour's Lost*: "We see the lords and ladies of an ideal Renaissance court, whose wit is as great as their breeding and their poise greater than either, able to control and turn with dexterity all the weight of Humanist learning and all the force of masculine violence on the pinpoint of mixed conversation" (334).

[96] MacCaffrey, *The Shaping of the Elizabethan Regime*, 474.

an interdependency of positions while refusing to harden them into fixed roles in a clear, contractual structure: that is the essence of this courtly style. In the long run, it may have been a political error—even an important cause of the Civil War—for subjects and monarch to allow style to substitute for a constitution. But in the short term this particular vehicle of style, a new and self-consciously literary comedy, bore great fruit.

Because it is only through style that the symbolic triumphs and yet lives at a necessary distance, I want to call this comedy the triumph of the symbolic through letters. Through letters, through literature, and through play which weaves theatrical hypothesis together with narrative *jouissance*. And if Elizabeth's own success depended in part upon the invention of this sort of literate play, so did Shakespeare's. Just how, is another question. Succession is problematic not only in dynasties, or as signaled by the frank artifice with which most Elizabethan comedies end. Like the Euphuistic speech which swept through and almost as quickly out of courtly speech, Lyly himself became the victim of fashion.[97] It would be impossible to stage his plays today. Shakespeare found a great deal in Lyly—a shared fascination with doubled characters, intricately hierarchical plots, low-life malapropisms, and witty love talk—but he did not find what we would now consider real drama. Or if he did, he so transformed it that we cannot claim Lyly for more than an ancestor whose heir unanxiously expended the legacy.

It is probably their being bound to a ritual occasion and immediate rhetorical purpose (however enigmatic) that keeps Lyly's plays from surviving as theater. They are too literary, and at the same time, too occasional; what body they have belongs too much to the surrounding court and its associated arts. And like those lesser comic playwrights of the 1580s, Greene and Peele, Lyly himself was rather too much the man of letters employing his talent as a way to (or substitute for) better things: preferment, a recognized place in the symbolic order. But without the comic possibilities that Elizabeth provided and Lyly exploited, it seems unlikely that any journeyman Shakescene could have misappropriated these feathers of style.

[97] See Hunter's, *John Lyly*, 267–97.

F I V E

Shakespearean Authority

✳

A crucial part of the creation of literary drama in England involved the differentiation of mungrel tragicomedy into a system of structured and more or less determinate generic shapes.[1] Without such a sorting into coded emphases upon the individual image and its sexual or textual deflection, English drama could not have set its own frame, could not have

---

[1] In addition to the work of Northrop Frye, my discussion of genre derives in part from Jacques Derrida, "The Law of Genre," *Critical Inquiry* 7 (1980): 55–81; Doran, *Endeavors of Art*; David Scott Kastan, *Shakespeare and the Shapes of Time* (Hanover, New Hampshire: University Press of New England, 1982), e.g., "The genres in which he works provide unique angles of vision designed to clarify the possibilities and consequences of human behavior by helping us assay the nature of the world we live in. In the internal logic of these heuristic fictions, in the nature and quality of the represented action, lies the idea of genre that informs the shapes of time" (33); Stephen Orgel, who sees the dichotomy between tragedy and comedy as an interrelationship of assumptions and values, enabling both mixture and distinction, "Shakespeare and the Kinds of Drama," *Critical Inquiry* 6 (1979): 107–33; Ronald Peacock, *The Art of Drama* (London: Routledge and Kegan Paul, 1957), esp. 190–92; and Tzvetan Todorov, *The Fantastic: A Structural Approach to Literary Genre*, trans. Richard Howard (Ithaca, New York: Cornell University Press, 1975), though Todorov would no doubt disapprove of my informal attempt at a logical analysis which he considers unfruitful in principle. The latent Hegelianism of my argument will be evident. Though Frye and such followers of his as Hayden White might not wish to acknowledge the derivation, Hegel's account of the "genres of dramatic poetry and the chief functions it has had in history" (*Aesthetics: Lectures on Fine Art*, trans. T. M. Knox [Oxford: Clarendon Press, 1974] 2: 1192–1234) portrays what Hans Kellner calls Frye's "sacred tropes" ("A Bedrock of Order: Haydn White's Linguistic Humanism," *History and Theory* 19 [1980] Beiheft 19: 14) as logically different articulations of universal and particular, the artistic elaboration of what in the *Phenomenology* Hegel calls "the system of structured shapes assumed by consciousness as a self-systematizing whole of the life of Spirit—the system that we are considering here, and which has its objective existence as world-history" (section 295). Cf. Frye, *Anatomy of Criticism*, 161–62. As Herbert Lindenberger observes, the progression which Frye (like Hegel) discovers on the scale of world historical development can reappear within particular eras, or within the oeuvre of a given artist. *Historical Drama: The Relationship of Literature and Reality* (Chicago: University of Chicago Press, 1975), 65. Cf. Moretti: "In what sense does Shakespeare 'violate' the convention of Elizabethan tragedy? Why not say the opposite: that he was the only writer able to realize them fully, establishing as it were the 'ideal type' of an entire genre?" *Signs Taken for Wonders*, 13; also Stanley Cavell, *Pursuits of Happiness* (Cambridge, Massachusetts: Harvard University Press, 1981), 28: a genre "has no history, only a birth and a logic (or a biology). It has a, let us say, prehistory, a setting up of the conditions it requires for viability . . . and it has a posthistory, the story of its fortunes in the rest of the world."

transcended the determinants of civic ritual and ideological occasion. Yet part of the peculiarity of Elizabethan theater also has to do with its reaching beyond the classically certified set of dramatic genres, thereby complicating the opposition between tragedy and comedy with mutants— history and romance—that neither the playwrights nor we moderns know for sure how to name.[2] And of the many ways in which Shakespeare exercises a peculiar authority in world dramatic history, not least is his unique mastery of the full range of generic shapes, a mastery that both (re)establishes norms for their particular effects and insists upon the covert dependency of such effects upon an absent generic other. Or pair of others, for the histories (mostly) evade tragedy without being comic, except at moments; and the romances keep tragedy at bay only through an artifice so obtrusive and metaphysical that their comic elements seem entrained to other purposes.[3]

Shakespeare's control of tone and generic expectation did not develop all at once, of course. His earliest successes come in comedy; he reaches full stride in history only with the *Henriad*; not until *Julius Caesar* and *Hamlet* does he achieve the full maturity of his tragic vision (which still works within what Susan Snyder calls a "comic matrix").[4] But throughout his career, among the many things that distinguish Shakespeare's plays from those I have just examined is generic impurity: the pressure of death and judgment in *The Comedy of Errors*, the persistence in *Romeo and Juliet* of love and romance (matched in *A Midsummer Night's Dream* by that parodic echo of tragedy, "Pyramus and Thisbe"), the critique of heroism even in such early stuff as the first tetralogy. Where Kyd and Lyly work out the dilemmas of authority with an obsessiveness that unwittingly structures their plays into allegories of representation, Shakespeare—perhaps because he acted in plays as well as wrote them—seems both less anxious and more self-conscious. Not troubled by a direct tie to patronage, nor so bound to the status and profession of letters as to attempt a tendentious distinction between true author and betraying puppets, Shakespeare seems determined from the very start to test the limits of different representational modes, taking the interaction of theatrical positioning and narratival displacement as an infinitely interesting yet almost neutral fact of his life and art. Perhaps for this reason, he largely succeeds in avoiding both the unintentional comedy of *The Spanish Trag-*

---

[2] Kastan, *Shakespeare and the Shapes of Time*, 37–41, notes that until the Folio, no settled nomenclature distinguishes histories from tragedies (or comedies). The Folio itself distributes what we call "romance" between comedy and tragedy.

[3] For the suggestion that the romances are "epic" in character, see Gary Schmidgall, *Shakespeare and the Courtly Aesthetic* (Berkeley: University of California Press, 1981).

[4] Susan Snyder, *The Comic Matrix of Shakespeare's Tragedies* (Princeton: Princeton University Press, 1979).

edy and the ultimately disabling involvement with worldly power and history that makes Lyly's plays unstageable today.

Shakespeare's insistence on impurity thus exemplifies his own unusual authority: in their intricate blending of presence and absence, his plays recapitulate the defining essence of drama itself, its uncertain intersection of word and deed, text and other, literature and excessive act. Yet his apparent awareness of this mirroring interplay, while it prevents him from letting drama succumb to conscious or unconscious code, never leads him to pretend that suspension can persist forever. For another mark of Shakespeare's peculiarly dramatic authority is his insistence on judgment, his forcing events to a crisis which issues in a defining shape, a shape which seems to depend not upon the author's will, but upon a reality whose demands could be refused only by an ideologue or a sentimentalist. It is as if the Shakespearean genres each responded to the claims of finitude, as if each were a way of giving the formula for a particular interaction between some one of the anaclitic pairs I have been exploring in this argument. The claims of finitude, the claims of presence and position; which also rest upon the absent, not quite contrary other, the might-have-been which "Pyramus and Thisbe" signalizes, or that Tate recovered from the old *Leir.*

As the final extension of my analysis, then, I want to claim that Shakespeare's management of the three (or four) Elizabethan and Jacobean genres displays the logically different possibilities of preserving a real—and therefore wounding—indecidability within these variously named but similar antinomies that have governed my discussion: theater and book, symbol and function, cognitive and performative, nonnatural and natural, metaphor and metonym, word and deed.[5] It remains to be seen whether argument can justify this claim, can make it seem more than schematic and fashionable. So I will not attempt proleptic summary. For future reference, however, I want to call attention to four aspects of the case I mean to make. First, it would imply a fairly precise way of specifying one feature of Shakespeare's dramatic authority: his giving form to logically different ways of maintaining balance between the interdepen-

[5] Melville, *Philosophy beside Itself,* 148: "For criticism, 'indecidability' is not a thesis but a fact—the fact that is no longer acknowledged, is no longer even recognized, by 'richness.' " As Melville argues, what matters for criticism is reading, with an almost Arnoldian emphasis on the purchase of criticism on life, and on "responsibility to and contestation of a canon, of literature, of criticism." As Graham Holderness rightly insists, though with a Marxist disavowal of the aesthetic which finally seems undialectical, Shakespeare's authority—and his apparent freedom from orthodoxy's authoritarianism—has historical determinants and limitations: some issues of our lives bear on the plays (even if indecidable in their imagined worlds); others do not. *Shakespeare's History* (New York: St. Martin's Press, 1985), esp. 1–13.

dent and indecidable claims of knowing and doing that structure human experience. Second, it would help confirm that this achievement, while conditioned and uniquely enabled by historical processes, does not reflect them: knowing and doing (like allegory and irony) structure and articulate all our time and space, so that striking their balance—though a balance like, for instance, the one between collective ritual and individual history—cannot reasonably be said to mark an irrecoverable moment between old ways and new. Instead—and this is a third feature of my argument—by not pretending to suppress one of these anaclitic poles in favor of the other, Shakespeare situates his dramatic actions just at that intersection of a structure which is necessarily nostalgic or Utopian and an action which is unavoidably deluded and self-interested, thereby laying out the pattern and archetype for the allegory of temporality itself.[6] Lastly, among the many uncertainties that affect our reading of Shakespeare, not the least significant concerns the number of dramatic genres in which he wrote: the Folio's triad—comedy, history, tragedy—has a dialectical implication which needs exploring, yet the fourth of romance, which now insists in all readings of the last plays, somehow doubles and disrupts the terms of dialectic, forestalling synthesis by calling into question the frame of theatrical order within which tragedy, comedy, and history all occur.

Because so much of my argument has dealt with history, it seems right to start with Shakespeare's historical fictions. And since more than any other of the histories, *Richard II* has come to stand for Shakespeare's meditation on the loss of medieval certainties about the order of things and the nature of representation, this initial play of the *Henriad* best introduces the basic problematic.

The first and certainly most influential critic to identify medievalism in the play seems to have been Tillyard, who described Richard's character-

---

[6] Cf. John Fekete's introduction to *The Structural Allegory: Reconstructive Encounters with the New French Thought* (Minneapolis: University of Minnesota Press, 1984), suggesting that a substantive rationality might be articulated with principles of appropriateness that are context sensitive and decentralized: "it might explore 's is never yet p' in order to translate the dynamic, utopian quality of the Blochian conception into a nonlogocentric form that does not betray its aspirations by implying certitude and that can be read as a complex of romantic, comic, tragic, and ironic modalities" (xviii). See also Burke, "Four Master Tropes," 513, on a truly dialectical history: "History, in this sense, would be a dialectic of characters in which, for instance, we should never expect to see 'feudalism' overthrown by 'capitalism' and 'capitalism' succeeded by some manner of national or international or non-national or neo-national or post-national socialism—but rather should note elements of all such positions (or 'voices') existing always, but attaining greater clarity of expression or imperiousness of proportion of one period than another."

istic actions as "symbolic rather than real," and who saw in the contrasting Bullingbrook one whose world "displays a greater sincerity of personal emotion."[7] Subtracting from Tillyard mainly his claim that the plays educate an audience in Elizabethan ideas of order, Kernan says that *Richard II* embodies "traditional ways of acting and traditional values," which give way to a modern realpolitik both within this play and within the *Henriad* as a whole, as it mimes a sixteenth-century passage from "ceremony and ritual to history."[8] Extending this reading beyond history into epistemology, J. L. Calderwood discovers in *Richard II* the "breakdown of an ontological language. . . . in which words have a kind of divine, inalienable right to their referents," and sees in this "fall of language" Shakespeare's clairvoyant registry of a seventeenth-century "process of linguistic dissolution."[9] Most recently, and put with most feeling, Murray Schwartz imagines Shakespeare in *Richard II* facing "a crisis at once historical and psychological. He saw the presence of ritual meaning and iconic value in the image of human visage, but this presence was on the verge of becoming a memory. He mourned the loss of glory and raged against it."[10]

It testifies to the power of allegory, and to the persistence of modern anxieties about the loss of tradition, that this interpretation of *Richard II* has won such general assent.[11] For we know, of course, that Shakespeare cannot have had in mind what modern authorities would consider real medieval kingship. Even though the historical Richard II somewhat anticipated Tudor monarchs in contemplating a claim to divinely granted absolute authority, standard late medieval doctrines of kingship fell short of the needs of a monarchy intent on demonstrating the virtues of effective and thoroughgoing governance.[12] We know that the state apparatus

---

[7] Tillyard, *Shakespeare's History Plays*, 280, 295.

[8] Alvin B. Kernan, "*The Henriad*: Shakespeare's Major History Plays," in his *Modern Shakespearean Criticism* (New York: Harcourt, Brace, and World, 1970), 246–47. For the governing formula of his argument, Kernan relies on C. L. Barber, *Shakespeare's Festive Comedy: A Study of Dramatic Form and Its Relation to Social Custom* (Princeton: Princeton University Press, 1959), 193.

[9] J. L. Calderwood, *Metadrama in Shakespeare's Henriad* (Berkeley: University of California Press, 1979), 22, 169, 219–20.

[10] Murray M. Schwartz, "Anger, Wounds, and the Forms of Theater in *King Richard II*: Notes for a Psychoanalytic Interpretation," in *Assays: Critical Approaches to Medieval and Renaissance Texts*, ed. Peggy Knapp (Pittsburgh: University of Pittsburgh Press, 1983) 2: 128.

[11] One major, early exception is A. P. Rossiter, *Angel With Horns*, ed. Graham Story (New York: Theatre Arts Books, 1961), 36–39.

[12] Richard H. Jones, *Royal Policy of Richard II: Absolutism in the Later Middle Ages* (Oxford: Oxford University Press, 1968), Gianfranco Poggi, *The Development of the Modern State: A Sociological Introduction* (Stanford: Stanford University Press, 1978), 16–85. Cf. Peter Saccio, *Shakespeare's English Kings: History, Chronicle, and Drama* (New York: Oxford University Press, 1977), 23: "Richard certainly held a theory of the kingly dignity and power more

therefore promulgated the doctrine of divine right through midcentury Tudor homilies, and that the contrary Anglo-Norman theory of the monarch's two bodies—which Kantorowicz proved central to this play— was revived only during the early years of Elizabeth's reign as a lawyerly device to define the "relationship between sovereign and perpetual state," usually in ways that frustrated the queen's efforts to exercise the sort of imperium that her father had hoped to secure.[13]

The issues at stake in *Richard II*, then, were "modern," alive through- out Elizabeth's reign and thereafter. The struggle between Richard's will to be the single, unassailable representative of God and his unruly sub- jects' desire to split the king's being into one natural body capable of death and another immortal body capable of succeeding to a different person, reflects a familiar and immediate controversy as to the powers and identity of the monarch. No doubt the lawyers' theory of two bodies and the Tudor theory of divine right both have medieval and indeed sacra- mental origins. But the tension displayed by means of such historically rooted theories shaped Shakespeare's own era and took a more extreme form in the century thereafter, partly because of new demands upon and resistance to sovereign authority, and partly because of the increasingly sharp ideological contention over these competing claims and theories.[14] As for the obtrusive ceremony and symbolism of the play, that too has medieval origins, but it was Tudor and Stuart monarchs—like their con- tinental brethren—who made spectacles of state into major (and in that way very modern) vehicles of ideological control.[15]

Yet apart from questions of medievalism and modernity, *Richard II* plainly enacts a conflict between two interdependent yet partly incom- patible sorts of authority, and it is this conflict which engages me here. There are several ways of naming the opposing yet related poles. One can say that Richard has the name of kingship, whereas Bullingbrook is the

---

exalted than that of his predecessors. Shakespeare picks this up from Holinshed and has his Richard express a grandiose notion of monarchy, though it is couched of course in language and concepts developed by Elizabethan political theorists rather than in medieval terms." Holderness, *Shakespeare's History*, esp. 42–79, plausibly argues that Shakespeare was well aware of the real character of medieval kingship.

[13] Kantorowicz, *The King's Two Bodies*, esp. 24–41, Axton, *The Queen's Two Bodies*, esp. 17–18, 11–37.

[14] For an account of the medieval origins of both the theory of absolute rule and the theory of limited monarchy, in the context of an argument that the monarchy's seventeenth-cen- tury apologists gave a new, unbalancing emphasis to the sacramental grounds of absolutism, see Eccleshall, *Order and Reason in Politics*. Cf. Sommerville, *Politics and Ideology in England*.

[15] Sydney Anglo, *Spectacle, Pageantry, and Early Tudor Policy* (Oxford: Clarendon Press, 1969); Stephen Orgel, *The Illusion of Power: Political Theater in the English Renaissance* (Berke- ley: University of California Press, 1975).

man who can gather and wield its power.[16] One can take terms from York's perturbed expression of his own dilemma, caught between over-lapping yet incongruent obligations as public subject and as member of a private lineage: "Both are my kinsmen: / T' one is my sovereign, whom both my oath / And duty bids defend; t'other again / Is my kinsman, whom the King hath wrong'd, / Whom conscience and my kinred bids to right."[17] Or one can extend the implications of the somewhat old-fashioned notion that Richard—like Hamlet—is too much the poet to succeed at worldly governance: continually seduced by the conceits of monarchy, Richard plays author to Bullingbrook's actor, writing the script first for his rival's banishment and then even for his own deposition, all the while unable in his own person to join word and deed or to ensure that the active Bullingbrook sticks just to the text of his author's conceiving. On the one side, an authority signified in names, forms, and ceremony; on the other, an authority enacted, empowered, and embodied. Whatever the precise terms of contrast or the characters chosen to personify it, *Richard II* obviously explores antinomies of language and action, symbol and function, public duty and private alliance, cognitive structure and performative force.

But personification, especially that which would set verbal Richard against active Henry, can make us miss the greater difficulty of the play, which is that neither Richard at the beginning nor Henry at the end can bring the words and deeds of monarchy together. Neither can successfully personate an undivided, fully legitimate crown, or make power conform to its ideal image. Richard, of course, is as profligate in expenditures and conduct as he is in speech. Far from maintaining any sort of divinely authenticated match between either the name of kingship and his political practice or between the image of God and his deputized likeness, Richard is altogether too much the "figure of God's majesty," too given to an erotic troping and turning in both language and behavior. His apparent complicity in the murder of Gloucester, his leasing of tax revenues, his perverting the ceremonies of chivalry, like his delight in "lascivious meters" and the "fashions in proud Italy," testify to "unkindness" in the richest metaphysical sense.[18] Though possessed both of the blood and name of proper kingship, he warps that legacy to deviant and improper ends—just as those caterpillars of the commonwealth, Bushy, Bagot, and Green, will be accused of having "disfigured" the "happy gentleman" their sov-

---

[16] Kernan, for instance, calls Bullingbrook a "practical, efficient man" in contrast to Richard, who "mistakes metaphor for science": "*The Henriad*," 248, 260.

[17] *Richard II*, II.ii.111–15. All citations are to the *Riverside Shakespeare*, ed. G. Blakemore Evans et al. (Boston: Houghton Mifflin, 1974).

[18] Quoting II.i.19, 21, 133.

ereign and warped his affections from his proper queen, or as Gaunt disfigures the conventional iconography of the pelican-Christ in order to
torment this wastrel monarch: "O, spare me not, my [brother] Edward's
son, / For that I was his father Edward's son, / That blood already, like
the pelican, / Hast thou tapp'd out and drunkenly carous'd" (II.i.124–27).
In response, of course, Richard repeats the impropriety, seizing the dead
Gaunt's wealth, diverting Harry's legacy to his own uses, razing out another's "sign" (II.iv.25) with mere breath couched in a jingling couplet:
"Think what you will, we seize into our hands / His plate, his goods, his
money, and his lands" (II.i.209–10).

But Bullingbrook, as critics regularly point out, and as Richard insists
all through the play, equally fails to maintain propriety, either as a subject
whose deeds match his obedient speech and symbolic gestures or as a
sovereign with secure and lawful title to the crown that Richard "wills"
him. The riddle in his reiterated insistence that he has "come but for mine
own" will not come clear, since the scope of that property depends not
solely on his name but on the power that informs it. Which is likewise a
power to transform names and alter forms, changing first his "own"
name from Hereford to Lancaster, then crowning that alteration with another, the improper name that Richard scornfully gives him, "King Bullingbrook," and finally assuming the image that makes "high majesty
look like itself"(II.i.295). Yet no more for Bullingbrook than for Richard
does the power to change names and forms confer the power to create a
stable reality. The crown, like any other property or sign, can move from
one head and person to another, but that very capacity for motion and
reassignment prevents possession from being single: the kingdom still has
rebels, the succession is still insecure, Henry still has an "unthrifty son"
whose adolescence promises to be still more riotous than Richard's.

For both the last of Edward's elder line and the first Lancastrian king,
then, a problem exists with respect to identity. Both have trouble keeping
the king's two bodies in harmony, but from different causes and in different ways. The one, though possessed of the proper name of kingship,
cannot keep it free of figures, cannot subdue conceits of language and of
youth so as to inspire continued belief that the "king is himself," that his
body private exhibits the undisfigured image of high majesty. The other,
though his performance at least temporarily inspires confidence in such a
public image, has come to his name only through the "indirect crook'd
ways" to which Shakespeare makes him allude when old and dying.[19]

Such indirection and deviation as afflicts King Bullingbrook, however,
has curiously little to do with his apparent will—except the will to possess

[19] *2 Henry IV*, IV.v.184.

his own. For Bullingbrook's entrance to the throne seems oddly without intention, almost passive. We never see him plan the deposition, except after Richard has seemed to volunteer it. Scene by scene, events move inexorably through Henry's ascent and Richard's decline, but we never hear Bullingbrook express a treasonous or ambitious sentiment. At most, he agrees to Richard's prophecies and York's stage-management of a political theater meant to baffle complaints of illegitimacy, a theater that also baffles us in probing for the right or wrong intentions of the new king. All the turns of fortune, changes of name, and swervings of alliance and affection which lead Bullingbrook to assume the crown are but roads which he traverses, patterns which he follows, conceits in the unraveling of time to which he conforms himself.[20]

Richard's conceits, on the other hand, seem both willful and deliberate. His alertness to the figurative possibilities latent in the grimmest situation—like his penchant for rhyme—dominates the play from beginning to end. Let me quote just two familiar instances, his response to the first exchange between Mowbray and Bullingbrook, and his aria at Flint Castle.

> Wrath-kindled [gentlemen], be rul'd by me,
> Let's purge this choler without letting blood.
> This we prescribe, though no physician;
> Deep malice makes too deep incision.
> Forget, forgive, conclude and be agreed,
> Our doctors say this is no month to bleed.
> Good uncle, let this end where it begun;
> We'll calm the Duke of Norfolk, you your son.
>   (I.i.153–59)

> Down, down I come, like glist'ring Phaëton,
> Wanting the manage of unruly jades.
> In the base court? Base court, where kings grow base,
> To come at traitors' calls and do them grace.
> In the base court, come down? Down court! down king!
> For night-owls shriek where mounting larks should sing.
>   (III.iii.178–83)

The first of these linguistic flights trivializes the sought-for judicial combat, not only by internal and concluding rhymes, alliteration, and the pert diaeresis of the last five lines—all of which impose witty and obtrusive order upon a puzzled complex of injuries in which the unlicensed physician is himself complicit—but also by a reduction of questions of murder, treason, and honor to matters of medicine. Little wonder that these words succeed only in stiffening the challengers' resolve, or that Richard's sub-

---

[20] James Winny, *The Player King: A Theme of Shakespeare's Histories* (London: Chatto and Windus, 1968), 94–100 discusses Bullingbrook's passivity.

sequent conversion of an honorable trial into a banishment of nobles should at best forestall a reckoning for Gloucester's murder. The second elaborate fancy, though Northumberland would dismiss it—"Sorrow and grief of heart / Makes him speak fondly like a frantic man" (III.iii.184–85)—better expresses reality. Going beyond what any other personage will yet acknowledge, Richard's conceit here both captures in an emblem the moral essence of his career and extracts from an apparently neutral architectural term the prophetic shape of what must come, whether his one-time "subjects" will it or not.

This difference between kings—that Bullingbrook follows out tropes within history whereas Richard gives conceit a voice—generates a dilemma that neither characters nor interpreters can resolve. The breath of kings, as Gaunt remarks at the moment of Richard's reduction of his son's years of banishment, can shorten days and "pluck nights from me, but not lend a morrow" (I.iii.227–28); Richard's eloquent conceits can wrong plain language and plain dealing, can trick prophecies of woe and doom out of occasions that might otherwise seem innocent, but cannot charm the world into obedience. Though he can as aptly deck out figures for the defense of sacred kingship as for the Christological implications of its betrayal, he cannot call forth revenging plagues—except after it is too late to do him any good, after he has suffered the crucifixion also invoked in his despairing figures. Conceits that spring from grief—even the as yet nameless grief which his queen shrinkingly possesses "in reversion" (II.ii.33–40)—come true for Richard; the rest do not. Yet history, though it has this tragic dimension, being full of the falls of princes and the defeat of plans, has its successful—or at least surviving—actors too, whose deeds work out designs that go beyond any individual's positive conception, depending on interactive patterns that no single wit can articulate, except, perhaps, by indirection.

The problem for both readers and enactors of history, then, is that the figures of thought and language—those conceits which always outrun and undo pure structure and idea—give only negative knowledge, after the fact. Even the gardener's "model" can show only how infirm England's estate really is; "old Adam's likeness" can divine Richard's downfall, but neither his pruning nor the queen's cursing of the gardener's grafts can improve the state (II.iv). The self, too—that putative origin of all such figures—is equally a vain conceit, as Richard implies in the first despair of his acknowledgment that "nothing can we call our own but death" (III.ii.152). Not the manifestation of an essence, this kingly self is but a name-shrouded nothing which must submit, must be deposed, and can never—so long as the king remains a man—be "pleas'd, till he be

eas'd / With being nothing" (III.iii.143–44; V.v.39–41). Or if not that—if
Bullingbrook rather than Richard—then an impenetrable actor, an image
of authority that outweighs empty names with theatrical power and with
"all the English peers" and commons who have preferred Lancastrian performance over Ricardian conceit (III.iv.85–89). For becoming Richard's
heir does not solve the riddle of Bullingbrook's identity, does not reveal
the essence that Mowbray accuses him of having: "But what thou art,
God, thou, and I do know, / And all too soon, I fear, the King shall rue"
(I.iii.204–5). Yet the curse of being a successful image, ironically, is that
one's words have a performative power that exceeds an ownable origin or
intention. "A god on earth thou art," says the Duchess of York upon
Henry's pardon of her old, errant son. Already risking parody in the
comic context of that scene, this bald affirmation of an ideology for Renaissance princes turns bitter in the very next episode when Sir Pierce of
Exton convinces himself to act on Henry's words and rid him of the "living fear" of Richard. And even this one undoubted coincidence of word
and deed gives no clue to Henry's meaning, either to his real will or to
the sense his actions ought to have in the book of life or in the hell where
Exton's deed "is chronicled" (V.v.116).

    One could say with some justice that such a balance of imperfections—
of hollow or at best negative conceits against successful but impenetrable
performances—seems like a suspension of judgment between tragedy and
comedy. Certainly the juxtaposition of Aumerle's pardon and Richard's
murder, which encapsulates the larger juxtaposition of the rise of one
prince and the fall of another, suggests as much. So, too, does the still
larger suspension within the *Henriad* as a whole between the tragedy with
which the quarto titles *Richard II* and the recurrent comedy of the two
parts of *Henry IV*, a suspension resolved only by a further impenetrable,
theatrical image, *Henry V*, flanked by two textual disclaimers of the
power of the image: the prologue, which unfavorably compares the resources of the stage to the lost reality of history, and the epilogue, which
takes note of the fleeting and unstable character of the momentary model,
the "brief garden" that Henry made of England.[21] Nor is an uncertain
balance between a failed symbolic order and a redemptive but unauthorized performer unique to the *Henriad*: part of the unsettling tone of *King
John* arises from the tension between the inept designs of its titular hero
and the ridicule of all heroic language and conceits by that nonetheless
successful patriot, the Bastard Faulconbridge. The first tetralogy, too,

---

[21] For an especially useful account of the interplay between comedy and other generic
implications in the histories, see Moody Prior, "Comic Theory and the Rejection of Falstaff," *Shakespeare Studies* 9 (1976): 159–71.

sets up an unresolved interaction between fruitless or unsustainable he-
roics and a recurrent strain of comedy, whether in Joan la Pucell's unintended parody of the heroic image, or the burlesque of the Jack Cade
scenes, or the Ricardian mock-heroics which run through the two last
plays of the series.[22]

But this formulation, though it names one way in which these plays
depend upon implicit generic alternatives, does not obviously pick out
any special logic that the histories exemplify. To begin to get at that, I
want to work out more of an issue that troubles *Richard II* from the start.
I have argued that the play engages the difficulty of legitimate persona-
tion, a difficulty which arises from the impossibility of keeping present
words and deeds in harmony with the absent symbolic order that should
confer identity and meaning. At the root of this difficulty lies a now familiar paradox of repetition. For there to be any person positioned within
and measurable against symbolic order, repetition—as of shifter pro-
nouns, proper names, qualities and attributes—must seem to return the
same, fixed meaning and being. Yet in any return is an alteration, a displacement, that belies the sought-for sameness: from the tidy couplets of
Richard's speech to the structural parallels which invest Henry with the
terms that failed Richard or which seem to make him as culpable of murder as the king that he deposed, repetition differentiates and exceeds even
while enabling position and comparison. On the one hand there is what
we might—with Owen Barfield—call legal fiction, the repeated terms of
which constitute the persons and entities of any governable order.[23] On
the other hand, there is an uncanny and illicit doubling that divides both
royal and ordinary persons from origins, intentions, and authority. And
each of these effects of repetition seems as necessary, and as irreducible,
as the other. The structural doubling that prevents our establishing a stable moral opposition between Richard and Henry serves at the same time
to construct positions that each actor fills in turn, despite intentions, even
while simultaneously preventing anyone from being more than an im-
personator, one who lacks authority of his own.

York's impassioned question—addressed to Richard in hopes of dis-
suading him from seizing Gaunt's estates—thus cuts deeper than he understands: "how art thou a king / But by fair sequence and succession?"
(II.i.198–99). For nowhere in the background or the action of this play
does *fair* sequence and succession occur; no repetition, no doubling from
father to son, king to governor, God to king, or one king to another,

---

[22] This description, and most of its specific terms, comes from Riggs, *Shakespeare's Heroical Histories*, esp. 93–139.
[23] Owen Barfleid, "Legal Fiction and Poetic Diction," in *The Importance of Language*, ed.
Max Black (Englewood Cliffs, New Jersey: Prentice-Hall, 1962), 51–71.

takes place in a way that preserves justice.[24] Richard does not adequately embody "Edward's sacred blood"; York—though "he is just and always loved us well"—cannot effectively serve as deputy of the anointed king; however much "God's substitute," Richard has only an uncreating word; and Henry, despite his party's fictions, succeeds in name only but not in blood (except the blood of violence) to his cousin's crown.

Henry's unthrifty son, of course, fails also—until the miraculous fulfillment of his most self-interested and self-fulfilling prophecy—to successfully repeat his father's politic ascent to the throne. Only by repeating, but in a fictive and self-knowing way, that father's excess—that part of his inheritance which is illegitimate, transgressive, and "merely" mimetic—can Hal truly, but still only in an *image*, become a perfect repetition, the mirror of all Christian kings. And in that very perfection, Henry V seems excessive in another way: too good to be true, too calculating to be good, too fully merged with the demands of office to show a self, too much the successful mime to be quite trusted or believed. He becomes so perfect a repetition, in fact, that actors and stage cannot but parody him in their gross attempt at homage.

This "perfect" repetition—this mirror of perfection, of a perfect and paradoxical unity of spirit and flesh, God and man, sovereignty and humility—achieves his stature by means of a double gesture of negation, in effect canceling both of the possible ways to mistake the nature of repetition insofar as the self participates in its perpetual activity of alienation and reconstitution. It is easy to specify these ways of misapprehension: one can take oneself as primary rather than secondary—as Lacanian signifier rather than as effect of signification; or, one can suppose oneself a free, perpetually ironic *dédoublement*, a repetition pure and simple and therefore unconditioned, unmixed with effects of significance. These are not just theoretical errors. *The Henriad* embodies them in its characters, arranging these in a dialectical progression which prepares Hal's succession to seeming legitimacy. Richard willfully errs in both ways, taking himself as primary, as the source of meaning, yet denying connection, consequence, and significance in his own "giddy" play at being king. Bullingbrook—compelled by necessities of state and driven by the will to possess his own—commits both errors despite himself: improper and illegitimate from the start of his rise to power, he never becomes for his kingdom more than a "counterfeit" king, fixed forever in the role of usurper, of the one (like Lucifer, but without an obviously Luciferian

---

[24] For an extended account of the problem of succession in the second tetralogy, see Burckhardt, *Shakespearean Meanings*, 144–205.

will) who mistook himself for primary and can therefore never be more than a temporarily ascendant lie.

But it is Hotspur and Falstaff, of course, who exemplify these errors in their most striking and opposed forms. And as everyone knows, Hal's successive overcoming these two threats to his future enables his impossibly fair succession.[25] Here the *Henriad* becomes as overtly dialectical as a play can be. On one side, the sincere egoist of honor, who hates the vile politician's hypocrisy, who scoffs at Glendower's fantasies, who yet behaves like an automaton of chivalry, so spirited, so filled with "great imagination, / Proper to madmen" (*2 Henry IV*, I.iii.31–32), that he lives an allegory of his own devising, in which he only "apprehends a world of figures here, / But not the form of what he should attend" (*1 Henry IV*, I.iii.209–10). On the other side, that reverend vice, the perfect nominalist for whom honor is air and life a continuous improvisation and jest, the actor who ironizes everything but his own flesh, that perfectly insignificant literality which only death can counterfeit: "Counterfeit? I lie, for I am no counterfeit. To die is to be a counterfeit, for he is but the counterfeit of a man who hath not the life of a man; but to counterfeit dying, when a man thereby liveth, is to be no counterfeit, but the true and perfect image of life indeed" (V.iv.114–19).

Between these, as double negation, is Hal, who only imitates the simulacrum of his father's thievery, who lets Percy serve as factor and simulacrum of the honor he will attain (and of the purified father he would succeed), who allows the credit for slaying that representative to go to the one for whom all (or nothing) is counterfeit, who in the process imitates an archetypal incarnation and ascension into and out of this world, and then, like "Alexander the Pig," does away with his (counterfeiting, fleshly) friend: "I speak but in the figures and comparisons of it: as Alexander kill'd his friend Clytus, being in his ales and his cups; so also Harry Monmouth, being in his right wits and his good judgments, turn'd away the fat knight with the great belly doublet. He was full of jests, and gipes, and knaveries, and mocks—I have forgot his name" (*Henry V*, IV.vii.43–50). On the one side, position that mistakes itself; on the other, displacement that fails to avoid significance: between them, shuttling back and forth between the spirit of a failed representative and the flesh of an impure mimic, is the soon-to-be king who knows and mocks and negates both, who can himself be known only through impossible comparisons, lame figures and bad actors: "Yet sit and see, / Minding true things by what their mock'ries be" (IV.Pro.52–53).

---

[25] Arthur Quiller-Couch, for instance, found in the plays "a Contention for the Soul of a Prince," *Notes on Shakespeare's Workmanship* (New York: H. Holt, 1917), 125–27.

Still the necessity of a negative gesture: we must cancel out mockery to get at truth; we must see through theatrical counterfeits to an inexpressible logos. And what is the true thing that Harry has become? Having negated both Hotspur's unactable allegories and Falstaff's unmeaning ironies does not make Hal the ideal synthesis of word and deed, however much his success at seeming to recuperate and preserve what he cancels out. Not the ideal king (whether Shakespeare's or his audience's) nor even the kingly idealist (living his own allegory); not the perfect Machiavell (enacting a politic lie) nor yet the agent of others' interests and fancies (whether conniving churchmen or desiring audience): Henry V is neither architectonic idea nor mere actor. To be one or the other of these would simply repeat—on a grander scale—what he has already known, mocked, and negated in Hotspur and Falstaff. But to be *neither* of these—or to thereby conjoin such contraries—is to be a charismatic something that cannot be known as such, to be the political equivalent of repetition "itself," a surface that seems to hide and reveal at the same time, a surface whose specular interior is always just another such surface, just another public meaning.

It is also—like it or not—to be the embodiment of power, the King of all, given in a theatrical image. Which is to be something that *we* can experience only as allegory—with its necessary distance from functional circumstance—or as a lie; in either case, as *mere* image. If we read that image as ideal, it must provoke a certain mourning, for as mere image (which even the best of kings can only be, on or off the stage), it reminds us of the unavailability, the loss, even the failure and decay, of the paradoxical union that it figures. If on the other hand, we take that image as a knowing construct (which even the best of kings must knowingly construct), it becomes something that we can view only with apprehension, something that through self-interested artifice separates us from the desired union of spirit and flesh. Either an irrecoverable Eden or an alienating, modern imitation: in either case, this image forces us to feel the power behind and within repetition, the power of that nameless authority which repetition cannot control, which we experience in and as history, and which keeps us from finding in history anything more than an unrent veil or a succession of unacknowledgeable masks.[26]

For that power to work upon us, it must both promise to reveal itself

---

[26] Cf. Goldberg, *James I and the Politics of Literature*: "it is precisely in ambiguity that power resides, making it as capable of direct as of indirect action. . . . A kind of infinite regress is established in which the affirmation of power is cloaked in denials, and the assumption of power is effected by erecting one's truth as absolution and submitting to the invention" (12). Cf. Rabkin, *Shakespeare and the Problem of Meaning*, 62: "The inscrutability of Henry V is the inscrutability of history."

and resist our efforts to know and name it. Hal understands this better than any other character in Shakespeare, obscuring his contemplation under the veil of wildness even to the point of gracing Falstaff with the honor of having defeated Hotspur. Where his father had been a prisoner to other men's opinions and desires, never able to go beyond acting out those meandering but necessary forms that led him to the throne yet kept him from enjoying civil peace, Hal preserves his power—and the liberty of action which power enables—by falsifying men's hopes, Falstaff's included. While heir apparent, Hal can deploy this power (over us, over his father, over his companions) with an easy wit and gracious cruelty. Assured of his inheritance—provided only he can make it good against Percy's championship of Mortimer—he can resist behaving as the heir should, and by resisting that decorum, prevent himself from being assimilated to a merely coded social and political identity. That resistance not only keeps him unknown and seductive, it lets him seem incarnate: by associating with publicans and sinners, by mocking the claims and pretensions of the law, Hal manages to speak for and lure the whole of the kingdom, not just that honorable and ceremonial part which will be his by right of name, but that low and earthly part with which he joins himself by "participation." In so doing, he develops what Richard never could: a fully realized body private, distinct from and critical of the illusions and delusions of personifying the body politic. The tavern (and Falstaff) thus creates for him—for his several audiences—strong metonymic connections with the rest of mere humanity, connections which veil, oppose, and covertly buttress the substitutive, metaphoric claims of kingship, which are as yet only promised (and not by Hal, who after all could not reasonably *promise* to be king, that effect being warranted instead by his mother's word and his father's villainous trick of the eye).

The greater difficulty comes into play when Hal redeems the time and ascends the throne. Many critics, especially those of antimonarchical persuasion (and few are not), think that neither Harry nor Shakespeare meet it successfully. Imaging true kingship, especially a conquering kingship, risks becoming as mechanical as Francis the drawer and Hotspur the rebel, as tedious, repetitive, and predictable as the Tamburlaine whom Harry indeed imitates at least once, threatening destruction and hot violation should the citizens of Harflew not yield to his mercy. How to present power in its "proper" embodiment and on the open stage, without its going flat; how to show power in its public form while holding something back, something which can elicit and yet frustrate all our desires to know and thus usurp that power—this is the task that Shakespeare and his mirror of all Christian kings confront in *Henry V*.

Creature and creator employ many devices toward accomplishing this end, most of which serve to position Henry as one not yet come into his "own." For instance, having surprised the clergy not only with his reformation but with at least indifference toward a bill that would strip the church of temporal holdings, Henry submits to their interested interpretation of his right to the French crown. Putting on "my gracious Lord of Canterbury" all the burden for establishing the justice of his cause, while more than hinting (I.ii. 13–32) what we already know, that the Archbishop has reason to "fashion, wrest, or bow" his reading of the law, Henry thus keeps his motives and ultimate identity secret. His cause is God's—as God's interpreters read it and as God will grant him victory. With another legacy and crown in view, Henry can then once again become the heir apparent, can put off having a history or even a name until he has broken through another set of clouds:

> Or there we'll sit,
> Ruling in large and ample empery
> O'er France and all her almost kingly dukedoms,
> Or lay these bones in an unworthy urn,
> Tombless, with no remembrance over them.
> Either our history shall with full mouth
> Speak freely of our acts, or else our grave,
> Like Turkish mute, shall have a tongueless mouth,
> Not worshipp'd with a waxen epitaph.
>
> (I.ii.225–33)

Then threatening to defy the Dauphin's expectations and successfully cutting off the hopes of the treasonous Cambridge, Scroop, and Grey, Henry further establishes himself as one more knowing than known. Whereupon Shakespeare places these several moments into a complex figural relationship: God's discovery of the conspirators' purposes becomes an omen of his as yet unacknowledged vicar's success abroad, and the now legitimated heir can exit with the cry, "No king of England, if not king of France" (I.ii. 193).

Such figurative patterns pervade the histories. It is essential to their logic and to their characteristic temporal suspension, their open-endedness and sense of futurity, that Henry V receive definition from those sacred and profane figures in all things which neither Fluellen's theology nor Shakespeare's stagecraft nor the constant reminders of the transience in glory quite let us triumph in this royal actor's fulfilling.[27] Henry's refusal to give ransom to the representative of the effete French recapitulates Hotspur's rebuff to the perfumed milliner who brought the elder Henry's

----

[27] Cf. Kastan, *Shakespeare and the Shapes of Time*, on the open-endedness of the histories, esp. 37–55.

request to him at Holmedom, just as his speech before the battle at Agin-court fulfills what in Percy at Shrewsbury was mere bravado. Harry's wooing of his Kate displays far more wit and erotic vitality than Hotspur's his, yet equally subsumes the personal in the public; and he copes with his bride's foreign tongue far better than Mortimer can, just as he also far more securely wins the affection of the unfashionable Welch.

But the power evoked within these patterns still keeps its seductive secrets, largely by keeping the Henry we see from perfecting any such figures. In part, this erotic frustration occurs through Shakespeare's stringing us along with hopes that Harry can break free of the very meanings that such patterns create and sustain. In another part (perhaps simply the converse of the first), it develops from Shakespeare's insisting on the suspect theatricality which is Harry's only being—on the stage and in his kingship. Whatever the origin, this frustration of fulfillment reminds us that Henry is not the idea of kingship, but a trope of that idea, a veiled or veiling excess.

There are many ways in which Shakespeare leads us to expect an interior excess of Henry. Like the reported scene of Falstaff's death, the pathetic and frustrated clowning of Bardolph and Pistol keeps alive our desire for the old Hal, for evidence of a body private to ironize these triumphs, to speak for what escapes the order of Henry's new imperium. When Shakespeare gives us a touch of Harry in the night, we may anticipate some of the old fun, just when we and the army need it most. And some of that fun we do get. Henry cloaks his glory, sets up a joke on Michael Williams (that incidentally assures us that the coming battle can't be *that* serious), and elegantly recapitulates Richard's insights (without Richard's self-pity) into the hollowness of ceremony. But as in the final scene of the play, when in his wooing Henry ranges from Hotspur's professions of plain speech to Falstaff's parody of Euphuism, the king cannot or will not reveal to anyone anything that the idea of kingship does not effectively recuperate. He cannot woo Kate in a way that will "conjure up the spirit of love in her, that he will appear in his true likeness" (V.ii.288–90), cannot make himself beloved apart from his majesty. He cannot—except by deputy—make good on his promise to duel with Williams. The private being of the King remains out of our reach; he tells us it is there, but he does not show it to us, does not let us *know* he has a soul that in any respect differs from what his public identity requires. It is as if he has become all ceremony, despite his protestations; all theater, despite his distrust of shows. The promised revelation remains a promise, up until the moment when the epilogue tells us it is irrecoverably past, like Eden.

Yet it is just this theatricality that gives Henry power, that keeps his power imperfectly revealed, that thus empowers this history. For by continually reminding us how poor the stage is by comparison with its great exemplar while at the same time presuming upon that greatness with the antics of harlotry players, Shakespeare gives Henry the private reserve he might otherwise lack. There are, I think, three effects to be noticed here. First, Shakespeare's references to his "unworthy scaffold" keep us imagining that the original of this history has a being that exceeds what the stage can hold: "may we cram / Within this wooden O the very casques / That did affright the air at Agincourt?" (Pro. 12–14). Second, the constant references to theatricality both lead us to attribute to the actor's "crooked figure" rather than to Henry himself any actual incapacity to reveal the person behind the office, and cause us to see that problem as an effect of theatricality in history itself. And third, by reminding us that we watch theater rather than these events themselves, Shakespeare forces an indecorous and therefore also excessive fleshly body upon the warlike Harry, who would otherwise, "like himself, / Assume the port of Mars" (Pro. 5–6). Insisting on the materiality of his medium, Shakespeare thus reasserts the metonymic contrary to the equally theatrical metaphors of kingship.

This last effect seems most important, both for defining the generic logic of Shakespearean history and for situating that history within some story about representational space in England. Throughout this account of the *Henriad*, I have suggested that Shakespeare's kings live in the dangerous middle ground between mimesis and figuration, between being the player king and being the specular consequence of some figural pressure or procedure. The danger here is not keeping to the middle, losing power and place by slipping toward one pole or the other: so Henry IV (were it not for his son) would finally be exposed for one poor counterfeit player among the many who wear the king's armour; so Richard, led by his own disfiguring conceits, finally becomes a fallen allegory of that betrayal and death which waited on the only God who ever came to earth. Henry V keeps his balance—or Shakespeare keeps it for him—not just by never allowing us to know him, but by constantly reminding us that this king is both a theatrical body and a figure in a play of signs. Because he has a body, because his is the sort of kingship that can be played, he remains one of us—and the history he enacts thus remains "ours," believably associated with our motives, our mortality, and our Falstaffian awareness that some part of life escapes the play of signs. Yet because this Henry also participates in several partly overlapping figurative patterns, he is more than a "mere" player: not just a "self" like us, he is also a significance, an effect of signifying processes. Since we cannot know and master that significance, however, it retains its own kind of hold upon us.

More than just a performative force, yet not (yet) a present cognitive transparency; flesh like us, but bound to and partially revealing patterns of meaning to which we, too, are bound (as members of the nation and as members of the Body of Christ), Henry exerts a fascination not unlike the fascination which his creator's works exert. The temporal open-endedness which characterizes the histories in general becomes for this one king also an interpretive open-endedness in which he preserves "his" power. Here is where the phenomenon of "modernization" genuinely affects the possibility of history plays. In a later era—not much later—the English political nation would consolidate its power in the person of a monarch much more the representative of a system than a power in his own right. But at this Shakespearean moment, the idea of kingship has become an idea that theater can encompass. For it is still conceivable that a person like us can wield and be accountable for such power, accountable in the same ways that we are held accountable. The monarch still goes on progresses, still washes paupers' feet on Maundy Thursday, still sponsors the same plays that anyone else can see, and is still threatenable by a clever usurper. And yet that same person has acquired a mythic and ideological structure—and source of potency—unprecedented in English history. Much of this new source of potency consists in the audience's—and commonwealth's—will to have itself personated by such an actor, and in this way (as Lyly so well understood) desire has become central to the structure of monarchical authority. Monarchy—and governance—has thus become conceivable as an art that seems impossibly to join body private and body politic in one royal person. The construction of such a person is the subject and structure of Shakespearean history, as it was the (failed) project of Tudor "absolutism." Part of the power—and most of the nostalgia—of Shakespeare's histories consists in their acknowledging what the state could not: that such erotic unions are always just out of reach.

One of the ways in which Shakespeare's comedies differ from his histories is that in the comedies, nothing seems out of place. Just as the charismatic Henry V exercises power over us by seeming to keep something out of sight—even if that something is a theatrical body in plain view—so the history plays as a whole resist the schematizing they inspire by devoting time to persons and incidents (usually low-life or at some linguistic distance from power, like the ostler's interchange in 1 *Henry IV*, or Falstaff's scene with Davy and Justice Shallow in 2 *Henry IV*, or Fluel-

len's discourse upon figures in *Henry V*) which no ingenuity can make
fully meaningful. Not so with the comedies. There everything promised
is fulfilled, with all present persons finally conformed to one another and
to a code of mutual intelligibility. Even the *idiotes*, whether Jacques or
Malvolio or bastard Don John, still occupies a spot in the symbolic order,
a place that helps define harmony through judgmental or vicious opposition to reformed society.[28] For all its evocation of Saturnalian disorder,
Shakespearean comedy finally leaves no place on stage for unincorporated
excess: even Bottom and Parolles make sense, take parts in a hierarchy,
become tokens in an exchange, moments in an ordering rhyme. Revelers
and clowns, Sir Toby, Touchstone, Dogberry, the Dromios, the mechanicals, antagonists all of everyday reason, play necessary roles within a festive economy that steadily measures and incorporates their anarchy into
its own new law. In that law, there is no middle ground, no irrelevancy
not captured at last by such extremes as those which Rosalind defines for
As You Like It: "the full stream of the world," or "a nook merely monastic"; the "mad humor of love" or the "living humor of madness"
(III.ii.418–21).

To say this is no more than to say that Shakespearean comedy, like all
comedy whatever, deals with decorum. The action may begin in rigidity
and folly, it may insist on a passage through disorder and madness, but
by the end, everything goes according to rule: there are no unpaired lovers, no unassimilated Jews, no one unmarked or unmeaningful. This exclusion of the unmarked extends, as everyone knows, to Shakespeare's
unusual exploitation of the conventional prohibition of women from the
Elizabethan and Jacobean stage. Of course Elizabeth herself, in this as in
so many other things the great exception, had been at least twice seated
on the stage—like any important male patron—a possibility that both
Lyly and Peele rely upon for crucial effects, comparing a choir boy's imitation with the queen's far more theatrical reality.[29] But Shakespeare's
comedies were neither written with that ambiguous presence in primary
view, nor do they imply her, not as a figure within the action nor in the
patriotic prophecy of the only notable non-Lylyan comedy of the 1580s,

---

[28] Northrop Frye, *A Natural Perspective: The Development of Shakespearean Comedy and
Romance* (New York: Harcourt, Brace, and World, 1965), 93–104. The histories act in ex-
clusionary ways, exiling and executing rebellion and disorder, but always falling short of
satisfying either our desires for unity or our sense of justice; whereas the comedies work in
incorporative ways. The only exiles are those who choose isolation, who will to be separate,
and whose initial functions, whether as blocking characters or downright villains, come
arbitrarily rather than from any sense of wrong.

[29] Women took part in the amateur, occasional drama of the medieval civic theater. Only
with the suppression of that drama and the development of regulated adult companies (and
companies of schoolboys) did women disappear from the sixteenth-century stage. See
Wickham, *Early English Stages*, esp. 1: 271–72; 2.1: 10, 111, 179.

Greene's *Friar Bacon and Friar Bungay*. Freed from explicit historical allusion, yet acting in a context established by Elizabeth's disorienting actuality, the women in most of his comedies play a far greater, more active, and determining role than in any earlier (or later) comedy.[30] As if by way of compensation, or as emphasizing what is for other playwrights a given, a natural fact of their theater, Shakespeare seldom neglects to make his audience notice that these crucial roles are themselves played by boys, boys disguised as women, often in turn disguised as men.

Self-consciously ruling women out of bounds, representing their unruly being only through costume, language, and explicit theatrical convention, Shakespearean comedy thereby rules out the customary representative of nature. By implication, nature (and associated notions of "kindness") becomes entirely a matter of constitutive rules. So far as we can be shown it, the most basic generic distinctions of all become merely a matter of artifice, of everyone's agreement to a particular configuration of signs, thereby fulfilling a collective word. Like the difference between female and male, the differences between nature and culture, country and city, nonhuman and human, flesh and spirit—each such contrast being a potential metonym of the other—grow similarly unstable. And as these distinctions blur, others tremble also: *The Merchant of Venice* puts the difference between cupidity and charity into aporia; *As You Like It* blurs the opposition between Touchstone's self-interested fraud and Rosalind's enabling, poetic hypothesis; *The Taming of the Shrew* weakens our grasp on the distinction between animal cruelty and human kindness. These assimilations of difference into a ruling artifice, which seem finally to confirm Touchstone's cynical syllogism that good manners and salvation are one and the same, work to displace (but not wholly dispel) the tension between natural being and social meaning. In place of that tension is style in its several senses, style become a doublet of this suppressed difference, there being nothing not assimilable to its civilizing equivocations, to the delight which all but the most self-serious characters take in style's capacity to dissolve identity, to work apparent contradictions into mediating puns, reconciling figures, and ordinary laughter at a theatrical world self-consciously pretending to be as readable (and writerly) as a book.[31]

---

[30] The tradition of the dominant female in comedy does persist in the Roaring Girl plays, but in ways that rather flat-footedly preserve norms. These plays are discussed in Simon Shepherd, *Amazons and Warrior Women: Varieties of Feminism in Seventeenth-Century Drama* (New York: St. Martin's Press, 1981), 67–92.

[31] Keir Elam, *Shakespeare's Universe of Discourse* (Cambridge: Cambridge University Press, 1984): "An impressively dense and intense concern with meaning and its production, with the status of the linguistic sign, and with the relationship of language to the world, marks the entire comic canon." What the comedies "offer, in effect, is language placed (structurally, thematically, theatrically) 'en abyme' " (21).

This capacity for stylistic delight—which in Shakespeare develops into a joyfulness that the very greatness (and convention-transcending power) of his subject forbade Lyly—sets these comedies apart from most others in the western dramatic tradition. Hegel may have been the first to make this familiar point. Associating Shakespeare with Aristophanes for "frank joviality," he suggests that these two playwrights (and perhaps only these) succeeded in writing "a type of comedy which is truly comical and truly poetic." Other comedy descends to prose, on Hegel's view because the characters in ordinary modern comedy—Hegel cites Plautus, Terence, Moliere, and the "Spanish" (those practitioners of the new comedy upon whom Northrop Frye bases what has become the dominant modern theory of comedy) but might well have added the Ben Jonson who objected to Shakespeare's "affrighting nature"—are so "deadly serious in their aims" that their own "folly and one-sidedness" can appear laughable only to the audience, the characters themselves being incapable of laughter at themselves, unable to acknowledge either their own inflexibility or the fiction that gives them being.[32] By contrast, Shakespearean characters, performing the conceits that give them being, live within the orbit of conventions that they (and we) laugh at even while jointly delighting in the satisfaction of desires that convention so thoroughly enables.

Laughter at convention, at and by the selves convention decorously distributes into positions that match (interior) nature and (exterior) status—restoring Titania to Oberon and Duke Senior to his court, while reserving Phoebe for Silvius, Viola for Orsino, and Malvolio for bitter isolation—in no way satirizes such unions or our satisfaction at them. Such laughter instead celebrates the momentary safety that conventions offer, these collective promissory notes that prevent problems of knowledge—or of history, of having to act in time with inadequate knowledge—from seriously arising. Rather than present such intractable problems as only an incarnate miracle like Henry V can pretend to master, the plots of Shakespearean comedy operate like riddles. And like riddles, which in order to be riddles must deliver on their generic promise to come clear, the stylistic conventions of these comic plots assure us that solutions will always exist, that there is no conundrum which a conversion, a quibbling reinterpretation, or explicit recourse to the device of the double will not

---

[32] Hegel, *Aesthetics* 2: 1233–36. Cf. Robert Weimann's discussion of Shakespeare's "laughter of solidarity" in *Shakespeare and the Popular Tradition*, 253–60, and his critical remarks on Hegel's theory (255). One way to describe (and also begin to explain) Shakespeare's difference in this regard is to notice another aspect of the ruling artifice in his comedies: there is always some concluding figure of authority, who until *Measure for Measure* is always represented as or by a double, most frequently by a woman (often revealed as formerly disguised), who is in turn often part of an authoritative couple who set the play's standard for style and manners.

unravel. In Shakespeare's comic universe, only those with an ill will or a stubborn literality need fail of consensual participation in these solutions.

The device of the double, conversion, and reinterpretation: an odd list, perhaps. It combines one standard trick of the classical comic repertoire (which Shakespeare employs from his first comedy to his last, from the natural double of the twin Antipholi to the Machiavellian one of the Duke/Friar and his bed trick on that false representational double, Angelo); a motion of the soul (whether a sort of voluntary miracle or healing metamorphosis, like Proteus's or Demetrius's or Oliver's, or one that circumstances force, like Kate's, Shylock's and Bertram's) that Shakespearean comedy shares with mysteries, moralities, and hardly any other comedy in the European tradition; and a kind of comic casuistry (usually perpetrated by a woman, a Rosalind, Portia, or Helena) that transforms old law and recalcitrant persons into a new state of agreement and grace.[33] But there is an evident affinity among these means through which all the comedies save *Troilus and Cressida* undo their tangles (and even in that anomalous comedy, conversion, reinterpretation, and doubleness centrally inhere, as occasions of satire rather than joy). Like resurrection— that magic through which Lyly defeats literality, exploiting the anaclisis of embodiment and the uncertain margin between being and meaning— Shakespearean conversion and reinterpretation alike rely for their purchase upon a latent or overt doubleness in human nature and in the signs that provide public and private identities. Those who try to control contexts so as to forestall this doubleness—those fathers, egoists, hypocrites, and comic villains who would eliminate the possibility of conversion or reinterpretation, who would prevent those supplements of identity called children, words, and self-images from making new connections and having new meanings—become the victims of their own rigor, condemned to singleness like Malvolio, or forced like Phoebe, Angelo, Bertram, and Shylock to recognize a pluralizing potency in things they had thought foundational.[34]

Conditions of happiness: John Austin's term for what allows a performative utterance to go through; the conditions of happiness can always go awry. One's priest can be an Oliver Martext, disabled either in ability

[33] The terms of this list draw from the two traditions—medieval and classical—that Shakespeare draws upon for his comedies. See especially John Russell Brown, *Shakespeare and his Comedies* (1957; London: Methuen, 1962), Larry S. Champion, *The Evolution of Shakespeare's Comedies: A Study in Dramatic Perspective* (Cambridge, Massachusetts: Harvard University Press, 1970), Ruth Nevo, *Comic Transformations in Shakespeare* (London: Methuen, 1980), 1–17, and Salingar, *Shakespeare and the Traditions of Comedy*.

[34] Cf. Marjorie Garber, *Coming of Age in Shakespeare* (London: Methuen, 1981), who remarks on those outsiders who fail to undergo a rite of passage, which rites of course acknowledge a kind of doubleness, individual and social (21–22).

or ascriptive standing from properly certifying one's bond; or a Venetian moneylender or Bolognese doctor can turn one's conventional oath into deadly or erotic earnest, taking as mere token of exchange something (whether flesh, or ring, or that ring of flesh which marriage promises for only one Endimion's little finger) that has a priceless use in some other (embodied) context. Or the Sebastian to whom one lent one's purse can return as a disguised Viola, ignorant of promises and obligations to repay. Or the letter upon which one founds a love-conceit can turn out to be a forgery, or the identity one had sworn to maintain forever can yield to a recalculation of initial assumptions: "When I said I would die a bachelor, I did not think I should live till I were married" (*Much Ado about Nothing* II.iii.242–44). Or the woman (or the man) one had sworn to love turns out to be the other, and wrong, sex. Crossed in the conditions of happiness, quick, bright things come to confusion—unless some hidden force controls the context as no single human ego can, some powerful double which not only rereads the text of a bond but also brings home ships to the trusting merchant (figure of all us narcissists) who has behaved as if the ocean itself were part of a community bound by promises of friendship.[35]

> But, my good lord, I wot not by what power
> (But by some power it is), my love to Hermia
> (Melted as the snow) seems to me now
> As the remembrance of an idle gaud,
> Which in my childhood I did dote upon;
> And all the faith, the virtue of my heart,
> The object and the pleasure of mine eye,
> Is only Helena.
>   (*A Midsummer Night's Dream* IV.i.164–71).

We, of course, have seen the power that effects this change, described here in terms that resonate of the transformation from allegories of the old law to the grace of the new; we have witnessed the manipulation that makes Hermia say of her past, "Methinks I see these things with parted eye, / When every thing seems double" (IV.i.188–89). But we have nothing that can count as knowledge of the forces that transfigure minds and stabilize the happiness conditions in *A Midsummer Night's Dream*. The fairies, though implying that the natural world functions according to ideas of agency and purpose consonant with ours, give us no access either to fundamental nature or to transcendental providence. Instead, like the me-

---

[35] On Antonio's narcissism, and on narcissism as a continuing topic of Shakespearean comedy, see MacCary, esp. 168–70, and Joseph Westlund, *Shakespeare's Reparative Comedies: A Psychoanalytic View of the Middle Plays* (Chicago: University of Chicago Press, 1984), esp. 17–34; on Portia as a witch, see Leslie Fiedler, *The Stranger in Shakespeare* (New York: Stein and Day, 1972), 118–27.

chanicals but in a different register of that which remains outside the boundaries of fully civilized society, the fairies are representational doubles of the world we know: Oberon for Theseus, Titania for Hyppolita, their "unnatural" quarrel and its dissolution through the species-mixing "marriage" of Bottom and his queen of dreams serving as a figure for the good will and good fortune which have forced a somehow fitting conjunction between the philandering Athenian duke and an Amazonian warrior who has never yet known man, a conjunction further mirrored in the agreement among four formerly warring Athenian youths and maidens.[36] Yet the fairies, their forest, and the mechanicals also mediate and embody erotic powers that both escape and govern the knowable world; thereby they also figure what good will and good fortune uncontrollably depend upon.

In *As You Like It*, the power which conjures rude will into the proprieties of performative happiness is more obviously social but no less resistant to control. Rosalind-as-Ganymede, the knowing double of Orlando's all too conventional love, keeps his (and her own) erotic will at one mediated remove, beginning the love action as a sport (her arbitrary object of affection soon found in a newcomer to the unlikely but not inappropriate sport of wrestling), then teaching her inept lover how to enact his earnest passion through submitting himself to the discipline of a fiction in which all promises must be kept. Framing that fiction, the forest, too, keeps its promises, there being nothing in it not conformed to an audience's desires to see nature as imbued with and fulfilling humane (or at least human) intents and purposes. The good Duke's elaborate discovery of books in brooks, Jacques's moralizing on the deer, the would-be simple and Edenic Corin who nonetheless gets his living "by the copulation of cattle," the painted serpent and romantic lion which appear at just the right juncture to convert Oliver from unnatural tyranny to repentant brotherhood: in all its aspects, the forest remains a social fiction that keeps unaffected, uninflected "nature" one unreachable remove away. From its introductory discussion of the relationship between a father's will and a brother's breeding to the concluding moment when Rosalind finally calls in everyone's promises, with Hymen suddenly appearing as heavenly officiator at rites which bring "earthly things made even / Atone together" (V.iv.109–10), *As You Like It* reminds its audience (as Theseus had re-

[36] David P. Young, *Something of Great Constancy: The Art of "A Midsummer Night's Dream"* (New Haven, Connecticut: Yale University Press, 1966), Paul A. Olson, "*A Midsummer Night's Dream* and the Meaning of Court Marriage," *ELH* 24 (1957): 45–119, Ronald F. Miller, "*A Midsummer Night's Dream*: The Fairies, Bottom, and the Mystery of Things," *Shakespeare Quarterly* 26 (1975): 254–68, Jan Kott, "The Bottom Translation," *Assays: Critical Approaches to Medieval and Renaissance Texts*, ed. Peggy A. Knapp (Pittsburgh: University of Pittsburgh Press, 1981) 1: 117–49.

minded the revelers watching *Pyramus and Thisbe*) that our consensual playing by the rules is the only guarantor there is of that virtue in "If" which enables community, that "noble respect" which manages to ascribe kindness and good intentions even to their most flawed enactors.[37] Yet for all this distancing, all this insistence on the play's enactment of *our* will, *our* desires, and *our* conventions, there is a necessity that transcends convention and desire in these characters' letting all hinge on the fulfillment (and the reading) of a promise, in their becoming convertites dependent on the interpreted signs of another's will. What Oliver refuses at the beginning of the play, the players themselves (represented by the double player, Rosalind) perform at the end: they submit themselves to others' liking, as founded ultimately on the interpretation of signs ("good beards, or good faces, or good breaths," ambiguously natural and non-natural) that stand in relation to erotic delight as a bush to good wine.

Even when the converting power seems to lack all transcendence whatsoever, as in the game-playing Petruchio who tames Kate, Shakespeare still suggests that the kindness and atonement finally arrived at go undefinably beyond mere convention. Neither we nor the witnesses on stage can tell whether the reformed Kate—who has learned to name things however Petruchio will have them named, despite the evidence of her eyes—is a mocker and an actress when she delivers a homily on the rules that should govern a wife's behavior. Yet she has indisputably grown kind. All that keeps us from fully believing her (a reservation not available to Lucentio, his wife, and their friends and relatives) is our knowledge that Kate's reform is an act, a decision (however prudent) to play a social game supposed to embody a good (female) nature, a willed assumption of a civilized identity from which she (unlike Christopher Sly) may never awaken because according to these rules a good nature should not. In a world of supposes, of identities subject to others' construal, the best are those that quick wits devise in order to make "jarring notes agree."[38]

In *The Comedy of Errors*, as in *Twelfth Night*, the metamorphosing power which produces agreement lies explicitly in the overt device of the double. Yet again Shakespeare suggests that any other solution to these riddles would violate more than a conventional sense of what is right and natural. Egeon, whose "end / Was wrought by nature, not by vile of-

[37] David P. Young, *The Heart's Forest: A Study of Shakespeare's Pastoral Plays* (New Haven, Connecticut: Yale University Press, 1972), 38–72, Maura Slattery Kuhn, "Much Virtue in If," *Shakespeare Quarterly* 28 (1977): 40–50.

[38] Cf. John C. Bean, "Comic Structure and the Humanizing of Kate in *The Taming of the Shrew*," in *The Woman's Part: Feminist Criticism of Shakespeare*, ed. Carolyn Ruth Swift Lenz, Gayle Greene, and Carol Thomas Neeley (Urbana: University of Illinois Press, 1980), 65–78, and Zvi Jagendorf, *The Happy End of Comedy: Jonson, Moliere, and Shakespeare* (Newark, Delaware: University of Delaware Press, 1984), 28–43.

fense," escapes his fate because an unnatural law has finally to yield to a force (is it Nature's or an Ephesian Circe's?) which has rendered civil identity undecipherable:

> *Duke.* One of these men is genius to the other:
> And so of these, which is the natural man,
> And which the spirit? Who deciphers them?
> *S. Dro.* I, sir, am Dromio, command him away.
> *E. Dro.* I, sir, am Dromio, pray let me stay.
> *S. Ant.* Egeon art thou not? or else his ghost?
>   (V.i.333–38)

When the Abbess/Amelia (in her Fortune-inspired disguise as in her conventionally signified womanhood another doubled representative for doubling nature) solves the riddle by identifying the twins that she bore Egeon "at a burthen," the artificial distinction between Ephesus and Syracuse—and the law inscribing that distinction—has to fall, though its fall is procured by obviously artificial means. Notions of naturalness similarly lie behind the solutions in *Twelfth Night*. Olivia (though with a better motive than Isabella) must not keep to a melancholy, pleasureless isolation which even a hypocritical "Puritan" casually abandons; Orsino cannot be allowed to persist in his obstinate pursuit of a woman who "cannot love him." So the play sets up a mediator between these unnatural poles, an interface who doubles again, providing an acceptable mate for each, thus guaranteeing against the success of any determinedly single will.

Though Malvolio deludes himself with the egoistical belief that God has written the script he determines to follow—"Well, Jove, not I, is the doer of this, and he is to be thanked" (III.iv.83)—the mediators of union often do seem to act for a force that transcends convention in a supernatural direction. Behind the events of *Much Ado about Nothing*, one can make out the pattern of the Neoplatonic ascent from flesh to divinity which Beatrice's name evokes; both *Measure for Measure* and *The Merchant of Venice* woo us with indications that something metaphysical is at stake in the movement from law to love; *All's Well That Ends Well* excuses Helena's presumption both as healer and as lover by associating her success with a providential (and then with a royal) will.[39] But a certain illegiti-

[39] Janice Hays, "Those 'soft and delicate desires': *Much Ado* and the Distrust of Women," in *The Woman's Part: Feminist Criticism of Shakespeare*, ed. Carolyn Ruth Swift Lenz, Gayle Greene, and Carol Thomas Neely (Urbana: University of Illinois Press, 1980), 79–99, Barbara Kiefer Lewalski, "Love, Appearance, and Reality: Much Ado about Something," *Studies in English Literature* 8 (1968): 235–51, Lawrence M. Danson, *The Harmonies of "The Merchant of Venice"* (New Haven, Connecticut: Yale University Press, 1978), Darryl J. Gless, *"Measure for Measure," the Law and the Convent* (Princeton: Princeton University Press, 1979).

macy in the mediating figures of these comedies holds us back from knowing their success for anything more than an effect of our collective interest in (re)union. These scripts may have affinities to patterns laid down in heaven—or at least in sacred books—but the agents who wring conversion out of an unpromising set of circumstances work through deceit, sharp practice, and slippage of linguistic meaning. A false friar (whom Lucio aptly describes as a bawd), a lady disguised as a quibbling lawyer, an Arragonese Don unable to distinguish between the fiction by which he unites Benedick and Beatrice and the fraud that his brother uses to separate Claudio from Hero, a low-born woman who "doubly" wins in marriage her high-born beloved, a constable whose command of the law is so tenuous that he has no need to regret not having been "set down an ass": all these act at best outside the law; at worst they perpetrate lies and deform normal discourse in order to bring about a happy ending. "Craft against vice I must apply" may be good strategy; disguise against the disguised may be necessary when dealing with those whose jests-turned-earnest threaten the community; an inability to keep straight the hearing of the eye and the seeing of the ear may feelingly figure an encounter with transcendence, but these are doubtful ways of behaving for anyone we might suppose a proper representative of divinity.

Whether through an anaclisis that leans toward nature or one that leans toward the divine, the mediating force which brings about the conversion of selves and senses necessary for a culminating harmony thus displays an obtrusive impropriety. Though the final cause of comedy be decorum, a fit between signs and intentions, outsides and insides, public meanings and private desires so perfect that nothing (except laughter) escapes a proper meaning, the double and the proper remain inevitably at odds. Atonement, the perfection of propriety, occurs within a space both created by and bounded by an improper, marginal figure, often at the last converted into one (like Rosalind-as-boy-actor, or Puck or the King-as-Epilogue) that acknowledges the impropriety of theater itself, its both-ways juncture of body and soul, presence and absence, word and deed. With the plot fully unriddled, constitutive rules run through and through these worlds; everyone and everything is in its proper place or willfully outside the site of happiness. But in all these comedies the question still arises as to whether we can in any way control, or even adequately name the theatrical force that has procured everyone's and everything's agreement to fulfill the conditions of happiness.

That the comic double embodies a connective (and therefore also disruptive) force beyond cognitive management, shows most clearly in the circumstances of Shylock's conversion. Rebuking the presumption of all those males (and especially of real and surrogate fathers) who imagine that they can control signs and tokens (including the sign and token of their own or of a woman's physical self), Portia forces all letters into conformity with erotic desire. Inspiring (and perhaps coaching) Bassanio's reading of her father's casket test (a test whose "right answer" depends on recognizing the incongruence of outward sign with inward meaning), she then welcomes the man who has enticed Shylock's money, ring, and daughter to betray and go between the Jew and Christendom, next (in illegitimate disguise) strains the words of Shylock's bond away from his declared intentions (though when he entered on that bond, he had allowed those intentions to be read as in jest rather than earnest), then helps force his reluctant conversion, and (with Nerissa) finally demonstrates to Bassanio and Gratiano that no token, no ring, no flesh can be prevented from adhering to unintended, foreign contexts, thereby acquiring new meaning. Destabilizing bonds, reconfiguring signs, subjecting all performatives to the violence of new contexts, the double that is Portia thereby also deranges the boundaries that mark off Jew from Christian, interest from charity, nonhuman from human.[40]

The result of this derangement privileges neither Christian nor Jew; it does not allow us to believe that we should follow Antonio's melancholy example and hazard all (much less imitate Shylock's dour attempt to restrict all within the bounds of his own kind). With a double interest in Portia, both erotic and financial, and with the aid of her music, this second Jason of a Bassanio enters a partially rigged game, the only penalty for loss (other than the unlikely loss of Portia) being an oath to stay single—like Antonio. And though *The Merchant of Venice* does promote the virtue of mercy, it does so in a way that enforces rather than suppresses the more than etymological connection among mercy (that which overrides the strict boundaries of a necessarily representational justice), merchandise (as engaging in the transfer of vendibles between more or less bounded entities), and interest (as an additional *merx* or reward taken in acknowledgment of the difference, the betweenness, the *interesse* that use makes in the representational value of money).

One locus of this connection among mercy, merchandise, and interest, and the most disorienting of the many ironies in this play, is Shylock and Antonio's coming to be bound by more than the words that Portia reinterprets: for in imitation of Antonio's universalizing Christian charity, Shylock abandons his usual practice with respect to the stability of tokens. Having abandoned "usance," in a real or feigned indication of his

[40] Cf. Marc Shell, *Money, Language, and Thought: Literary and Philosophical Economies from the Medieval to the Modern Era* (Berkeley: University of California Press, 1982), 47–83.

wish to be the Christian's friend, to abolish one mark of the boundaries between them, Shylock also abandons any sense of calculable use or interest in the token he determines to extract for Antonio's failure to perform his bond. Then meeting Antonio's scorn for interest with an equivalent disdain for mercy, he joins him in another odd chiasmus with respect to what exceeds the letter of the law and the nominal value of money. Finally, Shylock accords to a cultural, interpretive context a confidence equivalent to that which Antonio (with an equivalent misplacement) gives to the natural context from which he expects his ships to return as readily as a loan to a trusted friend. Of course the disruptive force which Shylock encounters—as befits his erring in a nonnatural context rather than a natural one—is Portia, whereas for Antonio, that force is the sea itself. But as several critics have observed, Portia seems to extend her rule over the sea itself, returning Antonio's pledged wealth only after he has entered yet again into an incautious bond where he undertakes to guarantee the stability of Bassanio's "double self": "I once did lend my body for his wealth, / Which but for him that had your husband's ring / Had quite miscarried. I dare be bound again, / My soul upon the forfeit, that your lord / Will never more break faith advisedly" (V.i.249–53).

Having just heard Portia notice the importance of context—"Nothing is good, I see, without respect"—and before the music that she praises having listened to Jessica and Lorenzo tease each other with famous betrayals and miscarriages of love, an audience may find it odd that Antonio still presumes so much while knowing so little, and may take some pleasure in his response to Portia's ultimate disclosure: "I am dumb." Gratiano, at any rate, who with Bassanio had earlier offered to sacrifice their wives' lives in exchange for Antonio's, acknowledges (in one of those breathtakingly obscene jokes that joins culture and nature by unveiling a metaphor) that there is no exchange free of interest, no way of separating tokens from their embodied vehicle and context, that at the boundary between nature and nonnature, use and value, it takes a special force to ensure the performance of promises: "Well, while I live I'll fear no other thing / So sore, as keeping safe Nerissa's ring" (V.i.306–7).

The problem of suitably naming these performative forces arises most acutely in *All's Well That Ends Well*, a play which also makes it especially clear that the conversions—and the mediating figures—of Shakespearean comedy occur at, occupy, and are traversed by the very boundary between nature and culture which comic solutions, subsuming everything to the performative, would utterly efface. From start to finish, this play addresses two questions, each a figure for the other: whether young

Count Bertram's blood and virtue, his inherited physical nature and his "moral parts," will prove congruent; whether he will bestow the ring betokening his "six preceding ancestors" upon a common woman, one who would "bring me down" (V.iii.196; II.iii.112). Helena, both the occasion of Bertram's testing and the trickster who forces moral metamorphosis upon him, herself embodies another version of the same question: whether her "low" breeding can be made to match her "high" virtue (which comes not from the natural but from the cultural heritage of her physician father, himself a mediator between body and mind). For their elders—who see themselves "Where adoption strives with nature," as supplying a dead parent's place—both Bertram and Helena are riven by yet another aspect of the "same" division: between adolescent passion— "It is the show and seal of nature's truth, / Where love's strong passion is impress'd in youth" (I.iii.132–33)—and "reason's force,"which the "oil and fire" of "natural rebellion" "o'erbears . . . and burns on" (V.iii.7–8).

Of course in another respect, Helena and Bertram make a kind of chiasmic figure of these oppositions: lower than he in breeding, she is his superior—and tutor—in virtue. Where he follows the lead of Parolles—a distant scion of the vice and braggart warrior, a conceptual figure for the natural lusts and amoral giddiness of a prodigal Juventus—she manifests "a heavenly effect in an earthly actor." Yet the nominal displacement of her arbitrary erotic will toward God's purposes, as backed up by a king who feels honor bound to coerce Bertram to fulfill his own sovereign promise (undertaken in exchange for Helena's fulfillment of *her* father's will and promise), does not adequately distinguish one lover from the other. Both rely on the "both-sides rogue" of an eloquence separated from deeds, Bertram for his go-between in the earthly seduction of Diana, Helena for the union of her earth with the sun that she adores. Encouraged in her natural will to lose virginity by the quibbling Parolles, presented to the skeptical king by Lafew as by a self-styled pandar, she works with an eloquence described as the "powerful sound" of a "blessed spirit" "within an organ weak" to persuade him (as he characterizes it) to "prostitute [his] past-cure malady / To empirics" (II.i.175–76; 121–22). Her actual healing of the monarch we never see, though we hear it celebrated in extravagant language, first in prospect by Lafew, then in accomplishment by a ballad for the proper glozing of which Lafew and Parolles compete.

Between the first of these descriptions and the second there reappears the same distinction between the natural and the nonnatural that every other conversion in this action turns upon. For Lafew-as-pandar, Helena is grapes for a royal fox in need of a raising: "I have seen a medicine /

That's able to breathe life into a stone, / Quicken a rock, and make you dance canary / With spritely fire and motion, whose simple touch / Is powerful to araise King Pippen, nay, / To give great Charlemain a pen in's hand / And write to her a love-line" (II.i.72–78). With the raising accomplished (that Bertram will later argue should not logically or morally entail his bringing down), Lafew and Parolles vie in other terms to explain the effect on this fisher-king than whom "your dolphin is not lustier":

> *Par.* Nay, 'tis strange, 'tis very strange, that is the brief and the tedious of it, and he's of a most facinerious spirit that will not acknowledge it to be the—
> *Laf.* Very hand of heaven.
> *Par.* Ay, so I say.
> *Laf.* In a most weak—
> *Par.* And debile minister, great power, great transcendence, which should indeed give us a further use to be made than alone the recov'ry of the King, as to be—
> *Laf.* Generally thankful.
>   (II.iii.27–38)

If anything privileges the nonnatural reading over the natural, it is only that good deeds (though not her "own") follow Helena's words. Referred to and enforced by the performative will of two fathers, the power behind her promise is out of normative control: "supernatural and causeless" rather than "modern and familiar," the proper occasion of "an unknown fear" rather than of "seeming knowledge" (II.iii.2–6). Even in the ensuing action, despite the addition of a third father's will, Helena would remain without Bertram's assent "but the shadow of a wife . . . , / The name, and not the thing" (V.iii.307–08). And that assent Bertram gives only when it is proved to him that his own high blood has failed to discriminate between one woman and another, that as the king had urged—though not with the intention that Bertram should discover it among the maids in France—"Strange is it that our bloods, / Of color, weight, and heat, pour'd all together, / Would quite confound distinction, yet stands off / In differences so mighty" (II.iii.118–21).

Like the Platonic *pharmakon*, aptly enough for one who is the king's medicine and her enforced husband's bane, ambiguously the agent of sensual and of intellective power, Helena is an "equivocal companion" who goes between the hierarchized poles of nature and nonnature in such a way as to resist identification.[41] What preserves her for the purposes of comedy, what gives her a continuing, if also disconcerting, moral supe-

---

[41] "Equivocal companion": the king's phrase for Parolles at V.iii.250. Cf. Jacques Derrida, "Plato's Pharmacy," in *Disseminations*, trans. Alan Bass (Chicago: University of Chicago Press, 1981), 61–172, and William C. Carroll, *The Metamorphosis of Shakespearean Comedy* (Princeton: Princeton University Press, 1985), 14–25.

riority over Bertram—which is also what distinguishes her bivalent being from that of a hero of history—is not a difference in essence, but in attitude, in her understanding of the relationship between self and the authority of signs. Where Bertram makes an idol of his name (though all too willing to exchange its tokens in order to have his sexual way), Helena is willing to hazard all her reputation on the event of her words in order to realize her erotic will, offering to raise a body (the king's, her own, and by extension, her father's) at the risk of being called what in one dimension she is, a go-between who profits from the exchange between realms of which her physical being is both vehicle and token.[42] In her first interview with the king she ventures loss of these, both of name and of life: "Tax of impudence, / A strumpet's boldness, a divulged shame, / Traduc'd by odious ballads; my maiden's name / Sear'd otherwise; ne worse of worst—extended / With vildest torture, let my life be ended" (II.i.170–73).

Though Helena finally wins her wager, she pays something very like this price: she is shamed for her "ambitious love," she undergoes emotional torture, undertakes exile, submits herself to seeming to play the part of a strumpet, and has herself reported to be as dead in fact as she is in Bertram's affections. In all this—as in her initial encounter with the king—she acknowledges herself as dependent on others' fulfillment of her words and of the words her several fathers give her. While treating herself as the sign and effect of a will greater than anything convention, reason, or her beloved's intentions can manage, she lets her life be governed by that same will's guidance of others' reading. Whether that will is above or beneath civilization remains unresolvable. Yet in the renewed rejoicing of the courtly Lafew and his good Tom Drum, Parolles, captain no longer but "simply the thing I am," Shakespeare once more suggests that the force of comedy has little to do with the modern and familiar.

Only in the last play that a modern sense of genre considers comic does Shakespeare have a man explicitly assume the power of the double.[43] Whether or not *Measure for Measure* in any way allegorizes King James, or responds to and expresses a heightened anxiety about representation that could be said to accompany the reign of the Stuarts, a troublingly different tone and set of problems appears in the one Shakespearean comedy that self-consciously situates itself as post-Elizabethan.[44] The blatant ar-

[42] Of course Hal, too, risks his reputation. The difference between Helena and Hal is that Hal knows the plot of his own play and enacts power in his own person.

[43] Petruchio is the one partial exception, playing a part in order to tame Kate.

[44] Josephine Waters Bennett, *"Measure for Measure" as Royal Entertainment* (New York: Columbia University Press, 1966), Goldberg, *James I and the Politics of Literature*, 28–33, 230–39.

tifice and coercive manipulation of the last act, in which the Duke plays on Isabella's affections and awe to win (albeit publicly and "honestly") what Angelo could not obtain from her in secret; the absence of even a hint of an alternate world to that of corrupt Vienna; the similarity of this plot to some of Jonson's in its relentless unmasking of vice; the most unjovial disgust with sexuality manifested by a play in which only bawds unashamedly advocate love: in all these ways, *Measure for Measure* deviates from Shakespeare's earlier comic practice.[45] Only Lucio's accusation that the Duke is himself a bawd—though it unknowingly captures an essential quality of the Duke's service as sexual mediator between Marianna and Angelo—directly points to any impropriety in the force that resolves the plot. Where in other plays the double's ambiguity provides joyful (if also disconcerting) solutions to riddles, here there are only defensive justifications and embarrassed confessions of guilt: the Duke's tetrameter jingle rationalizing his own practice—"Craft against vice I must apply"—and Angelo's despair at his unmasking: "O my dread lord, / I should be guiltier than my guiltiness, / To think I can be undiscernible, / When I perceive your Grace, like pow'r divine, / Hath look'd upon my passes" (V.i.366–70). As if in corollary response to this unease about impropriety in the mediator, *Measure for Measure* contains little—if any—laughter at the expense of self and convention, unless one finds it in Lucio's slander first of the Duke and then of the friar his double, neither of which Vincentio finds in any way amusing.[46]

One might begin to account for all these differences by noticing that only in *Measure for Measure* does Shakespeare put the boundary between nature and nonnature where Lyly puts it in *Endimion*: at the juncture of the sovereign's two bodies. In fact, he distributes this margin in three "places": in the representational relationship (that is to be tested by the plot) between the Duke and Angelo; in Vincentio's double role as duke and friar, governor of an earthly realm and minister of heaven; and in the prenzie Angelo, divided between his heavenly pattern and his earthly lusts. All these junctures occur at a known margin of an inescapable power, at a place where a private person wields an officially delegated

---

[45] Of course *Troilus and Cressida*—if a comedy, and not a tragedy or history, as the placement and title pages of quarto and folio (and the absence of the play from the folio's table of contents) imply—manifests a similar disgust with sexuality. It could have been written as late as 1603.

[46] Even *Troilus and Cressida* has characters laugh at doubleness, as Ulysses does, sneering at Cressida for the "language in her eye, her cheek, her lip" (IV.v.55), or as Pandarus finally laughs at himself and his trade. When Petruchio plays at being mad, a tamer of a beast, his acting remains at least partly within the realm of a witty game, part of his combat with Kate. But there is no room for game in the Duke's play with Angelo: he acts as a double of *his own person.*

public authority over other private persons. Except for the Duke's Erastian assumption of spiritual authority—which by providing a dead Ragosian at a critical moment, Providence keeps him from abusing—all these delegations of authority unquestionably follow accepted performative rules. Though the Duke behaves idiosyncratically, no one doubts that he has the right to transfer power to a representative or to go among his people like God's spy, and though many doubt that Angelo should make an example of Claudio, no one—not even the disguised Duke—questions his right to do so. Indeed, were Angelo capable of maintaining the great figure which his previous public character has supposedly led the Duke to think worthy this commission, the Duke's own expressed intentions might well compel Claudio's execution.

Given an ostensibly legitimate, mirroring relationship between aspects of these doubles, figurative play itself—with its capacity for displacing boundaries—becomes a matter almost exclusively of sin. Since the Duke and Angelo have a "natural" right to exercise a power which (unlike Lyly's Cynthia) they know to be their own, the least suggestion of impurity—of their power's being situated at a chiasmus joining the inferior with the superior margins of civilization—has to be fended off, expressible only by a "light" companion whom the sovereign can no more silence than Callidore can muzzle the Blatant Beast. Where the female sovereign—or any woman wielding the double's power—must face both ways, being an object both of (natural) desire and (nonnatural) awe, the male who "rightfully" possesses the signifier can only fall toward the body he should not let taint his deeds or rise toward the Father whom he should adequately mirror.[47] Either a tyrannical Angelo, then, or a Duke "like pow'r divine": a stark alternative that makes the doubles of this play into truthful or hypocritical representatives rather than mysterious performative forces.

This would seem to suggest a partial explanation why the Duke's motivation in this play remains so puzzling, so troubling, so unfunny. He knows himself and his own power; Angelo does not. Where in other comedies the source and nature of the double's power resists proper identification, here the only mystery is the motive for hiding that power—and the knowledge of himself and Angelo which is its basis. Like a *deus absconditus* willfully testing his creation, Vincentio has a fully privileged position that keeps him free of any taint of sin or ignorance, which in this play amount to much the same thing, so he seems to act entirely out of a

---

[47] Cf. Richard P. Wheeler, *Shakespeare's Development and the Problem Comedies: Turn and Counter-Turn* (Berkeley: University of California Press, 1980), for the tension between Vincentio's idealization and the latent connections "that link him to deep conflict" (130).

dispassionate desire to know whether an ostensibly pure severity can stay self-consistent when given the authority of a public mediator between heaven and earth. As we subsequently learn, he has reason to think not: where Vincentio has kept his own severity hidden, Angelo (as the Duke knows) has kept hidden his own most interested refusal to complete his marriage contract with Marianna. With this superior knowledge—revealed to us late in the plot—the Duke is shown to control interpretation from the very start. Where other comic doubles depend on an invisible and uncontrollable otherness in letters and in things, Vincentio occupies the position of the Master: only his sudden proposal to Isabella—and the claim that he finds "an apt remission" in himself—at all suggests that his mercy is anything other than a freely willed, fully comprehended gift.

But this positioning of the governor, which transforms comic performatives into the cognitive matters normally the province of tragedy, implies the traditional conundrums of theodicy. Not inappropriate in the first Shakespearean play (and only Shakespearean comedy) performed at the court of the self-professed expert in theology who so forcefully advocated divine-right monarchy, such conundrums have none but ideological solutions. As the earthly source of meaning, responsible for transmitting authority along a patriline, no male sovereign could play Cynthia's part—much less endure being teased about impurity in his twin natures (especially when for the Duke's Stuart counterpart, impurity was a widely suspected fault). So Isabella, who has expressed no desire to marry anyone, must be forced out of her convent: for her to prefer an absent God to this present perfection might suggest that Lucio had rightly found some reproachable distance between the two bodies he unwittingly reveals to be one.

Elizabeth I died on March 24, 1603. According to the accepted chronology, Shakespeare's last two comedies—*All's Well that Ends Well*, and *Measure for Measure*—were written within little more than a year on either side of this long-feared event. By comparison with the rest of the comic canon, both plays evince exceptional anxiety about the double's role, and in both plays that anxiety has much to do with the unusually overt way in which these mediators manifest heavenly effects in an earthly actor. But Helena, as her several fathers' daughter, procures the comic solution in a way that still preserves some freedom of interpretation, though much less for a Bertram forced to reread his own life than for us (or for Parolles and Lafew), making the performative effect of her words dependent on others' response to the force of her mysterious being. Of course the Duke, too, has a certain mystery, but his is far more like Henry V's (absent all but the slightest hint of a Falstaffian past), the power of a player-sovereign who writes his own apocalyptic script. That script, for those fortunate enough to be recipients of an arbitrary grace, has a comic shape. But given its potential for *méconnaissance*, for a tyrannical mistaking of a convention for a simple fact of nature, this comic pattern can occur once only, and still be comic: after an unveiling, at the end of a finite time.[48]

✳

According to the pattern of argument thus far, the generic logic of Shakespearean tragedy must turn on problems of knowledge. Performative happiness, cognitive catastrophe; a world forced into consensual transparency, a world in which opacity and deceit entail the hero's fall: if there is merit to the case I have been trying to make, this should be a plausible way to begin describing the relationship (and difference) between Shakespeare's comedies and Shakespeare's tragedies. It should follow that whereas in the comedies, doubleness enables slippage and harmony, in the tragedies it prompts usurpation and failure, often accompanied by disgust with women—with Otherness in general—and a latently religious fear of all that induces self-division within the image of authority.[49]

But these are commonplace observations. From Aristotle to Stanley Cavell and Stephen Booth, everyone agrees that tragedy turns in large part upon epistemological dilemmas that generate a cluster of familiar issues. Aristotle's causal analysis of plot, and within that analysis his reliance on a metaphor from archery (*hamartia*) that a Judeo-Christian critical tradition found especially resistant to dispassionate understanding, explicitly attributes the peculiar and best effects of tragedy to intellectual error and its fatal recognition. Though addressing only a few plays, ones especially suited to his larger philosophical concern with skepticism, Cavell makes intellectual error doubly the concern of tragedy: not only in substantive mistakes of judgment (especially Lear's and Othello's) but also and most fundamentally in a formal misapprehension about the scope of understanding, a misapprehension derivable from fantasies of mastery and independence whereby the tragic hero would avoid acknowledging his need for others.[50] Booth, elaborating an analytic tradition

---

[48] Cf. the extensive argument about *Measure for Measure* and the restoration of patriarchy in Leonard Tennenhouse, "Representing Power: *Measure for Measure* in its Time," in *The Power of Forms in the English Renaissance*, ed. Stephen Greenblatt (Norman: Pilgrim Books, 1982), 139–56.

[49] Among others, see Linda Bamber, *Comic Women, Tragic Men: A Study of Gender and Genre in Shakespeare* (Stanford: Stanford University Press, 1982), and Catherine Belsey, *The Subject of Tragedy: Identity and Difference in Renaissance Drama* (London: Methuen, 1985).

[50] Stanley Cavell, "The Avoidance of Love in *King Lear*," in *Must We Mean What We Say?*

rooted in the Romantic association of tragedy with the sublime rather
than with Christian conceptions of moral error, locates the pleasures and
anxieties of tragedy in a tension between infinitude and art, between an
indefinition of event and meaning and a determinate structure that solicits
(even while defeating) an audience's attempts at comprehending what
that structure presents.[51] Even theories of tragedy current in the early
modern period, though differing from standard modern accounts (as well
as from the Aristotelian one) by seeing in the hero's failure both an effect
of sin and a vindication of Providential order, associate tragedy with the
original Fall in a way that makes epistemological pride—as ultimately an
attempt to comprehend and control the unknowable things of an infinite
deity—the central motive of the genre.[52]

Moreover, at least one discussion—Cavell's analysis of *Coriolanus*—implies that tragic epistemological failure in Shakespeare occurs at a juncture
of complementarity such as Norman Rabkin first identified, between two
directions of circulation, one from a surrounding context toward the
bounded self, the other from that self toward an indeterminable commonalty.[53] If the tragic hero can be said to fantasize himself as either mastering this circulation so it flows toward ego only or as eschewing circulation altogether, maintaining the self as a separate, sovereign entity, it is
no leap to suggest that tragedy demonstrates the impossibility of sustaining a representational, substitutive identity free of entrainment with a
surrounding, unknowable continuity. Whence the mischief of tragic
irony: metonymic connectedness undoes the conceits of a metaphoric
self.

This way of putting things begins to specify a logical relation peculiar
to tragedy. It says nothing about the specificity of Shakespearean tragedy,
nothing that might find its place in an argument about the particular history leading to and from *King Lear*, or *Othello*, *Macbeth*, and *Antony and*

A Book of Essays (1969; Cambridge: Cambridge University Press, 1976), 267–353, *The
Claim of Reason: Wittgenstein, Skepticism, Morality, and Tragedy* (Oxford: Oxford University
Press, 1979), esp. 483–96, "*Coriolanus* and Interpretations of Politics," in *Themes Out of
School: Effects and Causes* (San Francisco: North Point Press, 1984), 60–96.

[51] Stephen Booth, "*King Lear*," "*Macbeth*," *Indefinition, and Tragedy* (New Haven, Connecticut: Yale University Press, 1983), W. P. Albrecht, *The Sublime Pleasures of Tragedy: A
Study of Critical Theory from Dennis to Keats* (Lawrence: University of Kansas Press, 1975),
Normand Berlin, *The Secret Cause: A Discussion of Tragedy* (Amherst: University of Massachusetts Press, 1981).

[52] E.g., Battenhouse, *Shakespearean Tragedy*.

[53] Cavell, "*Coriolanus* and Interpretations of Politics," 89. Cavell makes claims only for
the late Roman plays, but his line of analysis easily extends to the others. Though he at first
suggests that *Coriolanus* does not fit his standard concerns with problems of knowledge,
Cavell's understanding Coriolanus's "fault" as narcissism makes narcissism a form of skepticism and the play itself one that falls just short (or wide) of tragedy by the measure of
narcissism's difference from skepticism.

Cleopatra. Yet the terms here in play have affinities with Nietzsche's story about the way in which Greek tragedy came to embody and express an irresolvable conflict between an Apollonian *principium individuationis* and a Dionysiac encounter with a unity beyond utterance.[54] Though never much in favor with historians of Greek theater, Nietzsche's account of the development of a tragic poet (and tragic hero), products of an Apollonian civilization who yet can see past lies of culture to the truths of nature suffered by an individuated dream-image of Dionysus, has a quasi-historical denouement quite reminiscent of the standard way of placing Shakespearean tragedy between an era of collective mystery and a delusory moment of enlightenment in which "to be beautiful everything must be intelligible."[55] The post-Shakespearean development of a rigorous philosophical (and political-philosophical) discourse, the contemporaneous attempt to reduce drama— particularly tragic drama—to rational regulation, the Restoration's revisions of Shakespearean complexity into conceptually clear exempla of tragic pathos or poetic justice: such developments seem to imply that the birth and death of tragedy, as well as the most central effects of the best tragedies, depend upon the maintenance within collective understanding, as well as within a particular artist's work, of a certain balance—even a certain indecidability—between complementary dimensions of life and language.

For one recent student of Greek tragedy, the elements in the Athenian version of that balance are myth and civil law, counterpoised in the fifth century as equally plausible yet competing systems of order and sense. Corresponding to this balance in the world at large is another in his reading of the plays: whether to see daimon as character, given by forces beyond individual control, or character as daimon, as an inward force that shapes individual lives by its capacity to will and choose.[56] Casting this difference between pathos and ethos in terms of the present argument, the hermeneutic uncertainty of tragedy would lie between character as a token in some larger and fatal script, and character as self-originating— in Coriolanus's phrase—"As if a man were author of himself / And knew

[54] Friedrich Nietzsche, *The Birth of Tragedy*, trans. Walter Kaufmann (New York: Random House, 1967), esp. § 1. See the analysis in M. S. Silk and J. P. Stern, *Nietzsche on Tragedy* (Cambridge: Cambridge University Press, 1981).

[55] Nietzsche, *Birth of Tragedy*, § 12. Cf. Jean-Pierre Vernant, "The Historical Moment of Tragedy in Greece: Some of the Social and Psychological Conditions," in *Tragedy and Myth in Ancient Greece*, ed. Jean-Pierre Vernant and Pierre Vidal-Naquet, trans. Janet Lloyd (Atlantic Highlands, New Jersey: Humanities Press, 1981), 1–5, and Timothy Reiss, *Tragedy and Truth: Studies in the Development of a Renaissance and Neoclassical Discourse* (New Haven, Connecticut: Yale University Press, 1980).

[56] Jean-Pierre Vernant, "Tensions and Ambiguities in Greek Tragedy," in *Tragedy and Myth in Ancient Greece*, ed. Jean-Pierre Vernant and Pierre Vidal-Naquet, trans. Janet Lloyd (Atlantic Highlands, New Jersey: Humanities Press, 1981), 6–27.

no other kin" (V.ii.36–37). A tragic outcome would thus occasion pathos or manifest justice, depending on the view one took of the originating force—of the authority—within the sequence of events.

   Some Shakespearean tragedies lend themselves especially well to disagreements staged in this way. *King Lear*, for instance, regularly invites argument between those who see Lear as the death-bound victim of ungovernable nature, of a cosmic context at last revealed for its absurd, unruly self and those who see Lear as courting and deserving misfortune through his willful violation of established roles and limits.[57] Without pretending to reduce their complexities to these simple schemas, it seems useful to see even Booth and Cavell as occupying positions so opposed. For Booth there is no escaping tragedy, except within the delusory but magnificent comforts of art: no determinate self or reading can avoid being overwhelmed by death and indeterminacy. For Cavell, tragedy springs precisely from the avoidance of a comparable fact, from an unwillingness (natural enough, but not incurable) to face the limits to knowledge and control that logically derive from our embodiment in and as particular persons. Where one reading emphasizes suffering, the other insists upon final responsibility in the narcissistic self that chooses not to abandon itself to the imponderables of love.

   In their original, full-fleshed form, these readings are powerful and instructive. As one imagines them taken together, they not only capture complementary aspects of *King Lear*, they also suggest a way of naming the balance that Shakespeare's tragic heroes fail to attain: a balance between the self as capable of a certain knowledge—at least of the limits to knowledge—and the self as given by and meaningful in a mysterious context that always outruns knowledge, even, perhaps, the knowledge of one's limits. Since the margin between these views of the self cannot itself be fixed—the self that is to know its limits being in part the product of that which lies beyond those limits—critical uncertainty as to where to put the blame for the hero's fall becomes inevitable. But there is one dimension to Shakespearean tragedy that these epistemological readings—even as provisionally conjoined—seem to miss: a certain dignity, the dignity appropriate to a heroism which consists in more than stubbornly adhering to a commonplace mistake (even one as inescapable as narcissism) or in enduring to the point of madness what Booth calls the common human "folly" of attempting to perceive pattern where none ex-

---

[57] See the judicious assessment of the argument in Joseph Wittreich, *"Image of that Horror": History, Prophecy, and Apocalypse in "King Lear"* (San Marino, California: Huntington Library, 1984).

ists.[58] Though one cannot casually assume that tragic heroes have the dignity which a long critical tradition has thought fit to assign them, especially when we live in an era incapable of tragedy except on a scale so general as to be the unimaginable effect of massive stupidity, it seems wrong to disregard both that tradition and the way in which the stage survivors of tragedy regularly honor their great dead.[59]

Tragic heroes, everyone acknowledges, acquire a peculiar literary stature, the stature of originals, of being archetypes who shed their influence not only within a literary lineage but through the culture at large, becoming universalized particulars, touchstones of the quintessentially human such as no merely historical (or psychological, or philosophical) figure can ever be. What one wants to call dignity, I think, is the consequence and confirmation of this peculiarity that somehow obviates normal categories of judgment, making the hero primary (even primitive) rather than secondary, an exemplar immune to our assessments of good and evil. In part, this special stature—like literariness itself—is a resistance to being known, but not the resistance of something's being kept hidden. Quite the reverse; unlike the figures of history, Shakespeare's tragic heroes keep nothing back. Their mystery lies rather in capaciousness of presence, in a power (both for action and for suffering) that has no transcendental reference, that doubles for nothing.

One might derive part of this mystery from our hesitation as to how we should construe the hero's fall. Whether in the relatively simple manner of *Romeo and Juliet*, where the play provides its own terms of indecision—between a star-crossed fatality and a culpable, erotic haste—or in the sterner dialectic of *Coriolanus*, where we encounter an almost Hegelian opposition between irreconcilable principles each seeking self-universalization, Shakespearean tragedy thwarts our efforts to apportion blame between a fatal context and an errant self. More sinned against than sinning: taken literally, the formula will not fit Macbeth; even for Lear, it may err on the side of self-service, but one can read it nonetheless in a generalizably true sense, as implying Bradley's insight that the hero's failure proceeds from who he is, from a *virtù* turned fatal through its own success, through so fully realizing what a context has provided that one's acts become passions, as much suffered as authorized. Where one cannot distinguish cause from effect one cannot satisfactorily locate an error or actor to blame in the way one blames subjects of the civil law. Even that most certifiably evil of Shakespeare's heroes, the butcher Macbeth, acts

[58] Cf. Nietzsche, *Birth of Tragedy*, § 9, on the *dignity* of sacrilege; Booth, "*King Lear*," uses the term *folly* at p. 22.
[59] Macbeth is the major exception to this practice.

in a world so graceless and yet so fixed in the succession of event upon prophecy that he seems as much the prisoner as the author of his fall, fated to take illusions for realities, to mistake the boundary between inner and outer mysteries, and yet passionate in his choice to be the man he believes himself determined to be.

But there is more to one's response to tragedy than indeterminacy, than an irresolvable hesitation between two models of humanity. One does not leave a performance of *Othello* or *Antony and Cleopatra* feeling indecisive. Stephen Booth seems right to say of *King Lear* what one might extend to all the late tragedies: that it makes us want to interpret "oracular truths we feel but cannot see."[60] Where Booth, however, argues that this sensation of truth is illusory, a consequence of "the omnipresent, never-quite-circumscribable patterns" which wheel and circle throughout our experience of the play, I want to risk the further claim that these tragedies do indeed manifest a genuine truth. The ordered flurry of incongruent readings which Booth thinks motivates our perception of an illusion does, as he suggests, inspire our search for something interpretable; it also testifies to that truth's perfect resistance to interpretation. But to be uninterpretable need not mean to be nonsense, to be (as modern philosophy and modern aesthetics have regularly said of art) altogether outside the realm of the cognizable. To be uninterpretable can also mean to be true, true in the way that tautologies are: once you acknowledge them, there is nothing more to speak of. The rest is silence.

To be an original: that might mean, so thoroughly to choose and enact the givens of a life that you seem to have invented yourself. A dark, self-generating singularity, dangerous, vulnerable to error, fatal to itself and others, yet expressing some truth about human being that ordinary mortals—too lucky, too banal in their goodness or evil—fail to embody. A truth, if you will, about being a singular embodiment: that unique and uniquely fatal conjunction of body and soul, being and meaning, nature and nonnature that each of us just is, whether or not we can—or can will to—visibly enact it. These sorts of things seem right to say about tragic heroes, especially Shakespearean ones, for whom the givens of a life are never the sorts of heavenly scripts that come by way of oracles—or even as familiar patterns of Christian prodigality and Christian kingship—but which rather attend upon the hero as signs (always earthly and often infernal presences) of the very singularity that is to be acknowledged and expressed, thereby conjoining two systems of meaning, one an embodied code of which the actor is a sign, the other an elaborated code which the actor seeks to control.

[60] Booth, "*King Lear*," 22.

Yet the most striking thing about the tragic hero's singularity is its impossibility: an impossibility unarguably proven by the tragic hero's death.[61] For the tragic hero's nature—the necessary condition of his heroism—is, in the phrase with which Aufidius describes Coriolanus, "not to be other than one thing" (IV.vii.42). And that, as the action of all the late tragedies demonstrates, is impossible. One way in which they demonstrate this truth is by taking forbidden unions as their subject. I am not thinking only of incest, though one cannot help being struck by the frequency with which Shakespearean tragedy sets up perilous conjunctions between fathers and daughters or sons and mothers. None go so far as Oedipus, of course, but it is not only in *Hamlet* that the Oedipal boundary between nature and culture loses its powers of separation. What Pericles and Prospero avoid, Lear succumbs to: so insisting on a merging of wills between himself and his favorite daughter that he twice brings on destruction, once when she refuses the ceremony he desires, again when he prefers a heaven of "we two alone" rather than "see these daughters and these sisters."[62] From Titus Andronicus's bloody alliance with Lavinia (perhaps foreshadowed by his willingness to kill a son in the attempt to determine this daughter's choice in husbands) to Coriolanus's subjection to his most potent mother, Shakespearean tragic heroes are compelled by unions with interdicted others: Othello with Desdemona (a "mangled matter" not just in Iago's bestial imaginings); Macbeth with the designs of the weird sisters (who, as Booth observes, uninterpretably unite male beards and female shapes); Antony with the sword-stealing "serpent of old Nile" (who unites herself with snakes in order to join herself to Antony).

I have previously argued that the play generally agreed to stand first in the line of English Renaissance tragedy similarly demonstrates the impossibility of various sorts of union: the coercive union of empire, the king's attempt to give both nature and grace their rights in the spoils of war, the incongruence between ascription and merit in Bel-imperia's suitors, the revenger Hieronimo's forced coincidence of blood and justice. But working within the violent schematism of *The Spanish Tragedy*, and in a fictional world where raw ambition (political and sexual) seems to drive all unions, the ostensible hero of the Elizabethan Ur-tragedy falls

[61] Cf. Julia Kristeva on Oedipus, in *Powers of Horror: An Essay on Abjection*, trans. Leon S. Roudiez (New York: Columbia University Press, 1982), 84–86.

[62] Not that I want to claim that Lear sends himself to prison, just that he avidly assents to Edmund's will, and that we could easily imagine a scene in which Lear helped Cordelia insist on being brought into some public place. Here, as elsewhere, Lear's will becomes one with the forces leading him to death. Walter C. Foreman, Jr., *The Music of the Close: The Final Scenes of Shakespeare's Tragedies* (Berea: University Press of Kentucky, 1978), has especially perceptive remarks on the way in which the desire to die becomes an assertion of self.

short of anything we might call dignity. "Hieronimo's mad again": the subtitle advertises the mechanical, repetitive essence of this hero, whose pathos, though genuine, threatens to erode into the demonic or the merely jocular, thereby depriving him of real dignity (even as his play lacks real authority).

The impossible unions of Shakespearean tragedy, however, seem more suffered than willed. Forces beyond these heroes' management position them to choose unions that present themselves as destiny. Antony's playing Osiris to Cleopatra's Isis seems the working out of a mythical structure deeper than anything that mere hedonism or ambition could devise.[63] Coriolanus's insistence on being one thing from casque to cushion, however much it makes him susceptible to charges of arrogance, also seems to express an uncontrollable sincerity: like a male Cordelia, he cannot lie, cannot flatter the plebs into believing that by entering into public office he has in any way metamorphosed from old soldier to new politician, especially when the tribunes provoke him into reaffirming that one, unified self. Having been shocked out of complacent ceremony by his variously "natural" daughters, Lear unites with wild nature in a way that still casts this king, though not "ague-proof," as the "every thing" he had been from the beginning. Hamlet, unlike Hieronimo in both station and stature, takes up the union of injured son and appointed justicer as an unwelcome burden, urged upon him by insistent ministers and signs. Having like Hamlet done nothing to invoke such powers, Macbeth finds himself solicited by beings mysteriously in touch with his own contingent truths, then succumbs to the lure of joining their illusions and purposes with his. Othello, accused of witchcraft in bringing on the treason of the blood that joined him and Desdemona as the beast with two backs, excuses himself by appealing to her passion for his story: "She wish'd she had not heard it, yet she wish'd / That heaven had made her such a man. She thank'd me, / And bade me, if I had a friend that lov'd her, / I should but teach him how to tell my story, / And that would woo her" (I.iii.162–66).

But these occasions for one or another sort of countermanded union that come to Shakespeare's tragic heroes serve as outward manifestations of a deeper unity that they discover and embrace in a passion of self-disclosure. "I am not what I am," says Iago to Roderigo in the opening scene of *Othello*. Prompted by encounters not of their own making—often among them encounters with disguisers like Iago (or riddlers like the witches, flatterers like Goneril and Regan)—Shakespeare's tragic heroes

[63] Janet Adelman, *The Common Liar: An Essay on "Antony and Cleopatra"* (New Haven, Connecticut: Yale University Press, 1973).

choose rather to be what they are, by their wholehearted actions acknowledging and bringing into theatrical view a being that would otherwise remain latent and obscure. In many of the plays, that being lies outside the boundaries of civility; in this sense, at least, Shakespeare's heroes do partake of something Dionysiac. The "bloodier villain than terms can give . . . out" which Macbeth makes of himself, the "ruin'd piece of nature" that Lear presents, the titleless "thing / Made by some other deity than Nature" which Coriolanus becomes, the dotage beyond all measure from which Antony and Cleopatra take their fame: in various ways, all these tragic heroes manifest things to which civilized, sane humanity defines itself by opposition and taboo.[64]

Nowhere is the decision to embody—and therefore knowingly to unite with—something exterior to civilization clearer or more ironic than in *Othello*.[65] For the being which Othello enacts is one whose name and interpretation comes from the Venetian context to which he remains forever alien. Critics have often remarked upon the way in which Othello comes to accept Iago's characterization of him, how his imagination grows infected with the terms of his lieutenant's prejudice, how in his fits (indistinguishably the effect of an epileptic body or a jealous soul) he adopts the bestial, primitive character that finally merits Emilia's naming him a "blacker devil," "ignorant as dirt." But it is not Iago alone who understands Othello as intrinsically other. Iago's calumny of Desdemona takes its plausibility from the very circumstances of Othello's initial winning of his bride. "Nature erring from itself," lured by the fact and story of Othello's otherness, might be twice capable of deceit: if when she loved him most Desdemona could yet "seem to shake and fear" the Moor, she might in her "rank will" be ready to make her name "begrim'd and black / As mine own face." In Venetian terms and fantasies, Othello's union with Desdemona figures his own chimerical being: a beast imperfectly united with a sophisticated civility. So it seems apt, in the way that only tragic ironies can be, that in murdering his bride (thereby punishing both his "blackness" and his presumption as well as her), the Moor apes

---

[64] Cf. Menenius at V.iv.16–29 of *Coriolanus*: "he no more remembers his mother now than an eight-year-old-horse. The tartness of his face sours ripe grapes. When he walks, he moves like an engine, and the ground shrinks before his treading. . . . He wants nothing of a god but eternity and a heaven to throne in. . . . There is no more mercy in him than there is milk in a male tiger, that shall our poor city find." Though his conclusions have a certain moralizing air, J. Leeds Barroll's historically based argument about the tragic ethic in Shakespeare seems exactly right: that tragedy shows persons violating the "ordered principles" of the cosmos and consequently coming to grief, and yet that in the end there is a certain triumph, found not "in their disintegration but in their mighty efforts to stay whole." *Shakespearean Tragedy* (Washington: Folger Shakespeare Library, 1984), esp. 279–88.

[65] Michael Long, *The Unnatural Scene: A Study in Shakespearean Tragedy* (London: Methuen, 1976), esp. 52–58, Greenblatt, *Renaissance Self-Fashioning*, 222–54.

the attitudes and procedures of civil law, as if badly imitating a humanity he had acquired only in name. Yet he claims that cultural identity in earnest truth—while still remaining outside the boundaries of the law—when he executes himself, continuing to insist upon his ability to do some service to the state even in the extreme moment of consuming the being he had chosen to become. (Scape)goat and monkey both, sacrificed through his passionate enactment of a being nameable only in terms that define it by exclusion, Othello perfectly becomes himself only in the moment when his two natures extinguish each other, when his knowing soul destroys a being brought by his actions fully into (theatrical and theoretic) view.

No other Shakespearean tragedy works out so exact a coincidence between a moment of recognition and the extinction of the hero's revealed being. *Coriolanus* and *Macbeth* similarly have their heroes enact a process of self-construction and fulfillment that ends in a conjunction between a knowing consciousness and its entrained embodiment. But they are actors of their singleness, not its judges. So Coriolanus stays his single self, no less Roman then ever in refusing the name of "boy" with which Aufidius taunts him, though in yielding to his mother he had anticipated the mortal danger attendant on acknowledging himself her son. Like Coriolanus, Macbeth runs out his chosen fate to the edge of another's blade; seeing the sense that has finally come of the union between exterior and interior promptings, he still enacts it to the last. Not recognition, but constancy—Cleopatra's willed acknowledgment of the famous and therefore eternal union they have made—is the issue in *Antony and Cleopatra*, an issue not decided until confirmed by her reenactment of that union in choosing death over Octavius. And though Lear recognizes his erring judgment of Cordelia, by the end, judgment itself—not only Lear's but the final horror—has become a question.

But from the beginning of *King Lear*, judgment had been the issue, the study of "deserving" which Edmund undertakes at the moment of his introduction to Kent, the trial of his daughters' love that brings disaster on the king who had "ever but slenderly known himself." And from the opening scene of *Antony and Cleopatra*, the overriding question had been whether and how to acknowledge a union that is the "nobleness of life": "to do thus—when such a mutual pair / And such a twain can do't, in which I bind / [On] pain of punishment, the world to weet / We stand up peerless" (I.i.36–39). In each of these quite different plays, moreover, what is at stake is a willful refusal to distinguish private realms from public. Gloucester's self-satisfied acknowledgment of his bastard son erodes the difference between the order of law and the order (if any) of nature;

Lear's obstinate insistence that his dearest child find a ceremonial voice for her love, heaving the "ponderous" things of the body (and its connectedness) into the light arena of the mouth, not only denies the difference between his will and hers, it also seeks an impossible coincidence between nature and merit.[66] Urged by Octavius and his own Roman honor to separate himself from Cleopatra, Antony chooses rather to follow his pleasure, to "be himself. But stirr'd by Cleopatra" (I.i.43–44). Giving "his empire / Up to a whore," in Octavius's phrase, he joins himself with her "in the public eye," abandoning a name in one arena (but a name which, as the soothsayer rightly tells him, can only wither in Caesar's company) for a place in a more compelling story, not as an Osiris become emperor of Rome, but as the "crown o' th' earth" (V.i.63). Though doomed in his attempt to triumph as the champion of this alternate order to Rome's, to rule still as the captain of this great fairy, "day o' th' world," Antony nonetheless succeeds in uniting his Roman honor with one whom others wish to think of as the object of a private lust, but only, of course, in death, when she is "bravest at the last."

These unions *in extremis*—Lear at the moment of his death still looking on the lips of the Cordelia who had refused to make her private nature public; Antony and Cleopatra, dying upon and for a kiss (and the image of a kiss, in the asp's suckling)—achieve (or figure the achievement of) a coincidence between orders that none but the heroes of tragedy can effect. Were Lear and Cordelia to survive Edmund's plot (as they do in both Shakespeare's source and Tate's adaptation), the old question of a difference between the love that a daughter owes her father and the love she owes her husband would reinsinuate itself.[67] (For this reason, if no other, it seems fitting that France had to return before the climactic battle.) But were Lear to acquiesce in Cordelia's death, though he might seem less mad, would also mean for him to acquiesce in a difference he had been unwilling to abide from the beginning. Similarly, were Cleopatra to follow Antony's advice, making peace with Caesar, she would acquiesce to another sort of difference, to the prospect of seeing herself and her husband extemporally staged by "the quick comedians." This allusion to the conditions of Elizabethan performance has the mind-stopping effect of other Shakespearean self-references: spoken by the very "squeaking Cleopatra" who now "boys" her "greatness / I' the posture of a whore," these

[66] E.g.: "my love's more ponderous than my tongue." "I cannot heave my heart into my mouth." "Which of you shall we say doth love us most, / That we our largest bounty may extend / Where nature doth with merit challenge."

[67] This is why the child of the main plot has to be female, for with a male child there would always be the prospect of a difference in will and authority, no prospect of perfect union (since to homosexual union there is no complementarity in the domain of "natural" symbols).

lines reinforce Cleopatra's stature as a mythic original, somehow in charge of both the meaning and the bearing of her life. In a similar but more indirect fashion, Lear's "Look on her! Look, her lips, / Look there, look there!" gives him control over the very facts of the scene we witness. Only the pressure of this insistence keeps us from the comic (or romantic) realization that Cordelia's lips may well be moving, that the boy-actor's breath has to "mist or stain the stone" were it really so positioned; and the suspension of that given reality sustains an alternate illusion, that in some vision (whether mad or immortal hardly matters) Lear does see those speechless lips move.

So even in Shakespeare's most expansive tragedies, the ones least suited to analysis in schoolroom terms of their heroes' having learned or matured, there is still a self-accomplishment whereby the hero successfully wills an impossible effacement of difference, becoming knowingly and visibly one with what would normally remain private, unseen, and unvoiced (unless in a competing, incongruent discourse).[68] Of course the tragedies are full of such competing discourses, though the hero (and the flow of the audience's sympathies) refuses to accept their force. Banquo's mild remonstrances (and Malcolm and Macduff's self-serving piety), "the tongues o' th' common mouth" (III.i.22) which speak against Coriolanus's "tyranny," Octavius's (and Octavia's) Roman thoughts, the several construals of the nature with which Lear would join himself, with or without ceremony: these alternatives, each more narrowly fitted to particular interests within an ordinary time, maintain a certain rational distance from things which the tragic hero eschews. Where Gloucester, Edmund, Edgar, Albany all devote themselves to different theories of the world, ranging from desperate fatalism to a Hobbesianism *avant la lettre*, which help them make sense of themselves as actors or authors of a plot, Lear simply embodies his knowledge. From his first misapprehension of Cordelia's truth (itself stated in the differential terms of a plainness that resonates with those "modern" discourses that deny the virtues of ceremony) through the full passion of the storm to the last vision that he sees, Lear allows no gap to intervene between intellect and being, no room for a plurality of discourses or for a difference between what is known and what is done. The king who banishes Kent for attempting to "come betwixt our sentence and our power" still lives in the "natural fool of fortune" who proclaims that "none does offend, none, I say none, I'll able 'em"; he converts what he knows into imperatives, even in ordering the

---

[68] Cf. Jacques Derrida in "White Mythology: Metaphor in the Text of Philosophy," in *Margins of Philosophy*, trans. Alan Bass (Chicago: University of Chicago Press, 1982), on Aristotle's account of the tragic hero, claiming that tragedy depends on the difference between thought and speech: "He exists and acts within tragedy only on the condition that he speaks" (233).

stage audience to howl "so / That heaven's vault should crack." This unwillingness to brook difference, to acknowledge the disjunction of embodiment and soul which enables both other minds and their occasional
agreements, looks like a kind of pride, and is fatally vulnerable to the
doubleness in other beings.[69] Like other tragic heroes, Lear suffers from
a certain naiveté, from an unwillingness to take the world as it is, self-
divided. Yet in his fatal integrity, in the rashness with which he embodies
his knowledge, he becomes the cultural equivalent of a natural fact: fully
present, and in that presence, inexplicable. Viewed from a normal perspective, the tragic hero's denial of difference constitutes either sin or
folly; yet that denial, making him into the enacted idea of his own unique
being, is just what gives him an unmistakable authority.

   In this account of things, tragedy still has to do with problems of
knowledge and still occurs at a peculiar moment in relation to the process
of rationalization. But the unity which tragic heroes impossibly attain is
neither old nor new; the vision of a homology between a contextual
otherness and a knowing self is not a lost Eden or a missed Utopia. Instead it is a momentary coherence between public and private realms,
willed by a kind of hero unimaginable in an earlier or later era. For the
multiplication of different discourses which is one of the primary dimensions of rationalization is both a principal cause and one of the main reasons for the disappearance of tragedy. Here one has to agree with
Nietzsche, and with a recent follower of his (and of Foucault): without
the ambition for a certain sort of representational sufficiency, tragedy
could never have arisen.[70] But to stop short with an unanalyzed notion
like "representation" will not explain enough. For behind what Foucault
calls the order of representation there is the cultural aspiration to articulate nature in what Basil Bernstein calls elaborated as opposed to restricted discourse. And this cultural aspiration is in turn the effect of various sorts of specialization: without the impact of Euphuism, for
instance, a specialist discourse which audibly lurks behind Goneril's and
Regan's flattery, there could be no *King Lear*; there would be no terms in
which to insist upon the ceremonial voicing of a daughter's love. And
without the similarly specialist discourse of Protestantism (and also of the
newly revived plain, Senecan style), there would not have been a repertoire of terms and ideas upon which Cordelia could draw for her refusal
to engage in empty ceremonialism. Yet just this proliferation of different
discourses prevents the hero from uniting being and meaning in anything
other than death.

   [69] For an especially penetrating discussion of Lear's quest for immediacy, his desire to
abolish the "inherent 'between-ness' of all discourse," see Burckhardt, *Shakespearean Meanings*, 237–59.
   [70] Reiss, *Tragedy and Truth*.

Before the rise of competing specialist discourses (among them that of
the professional theater), a displacing civic drama could in the restricted
codes of myth take all actions and all selves as figures of imitating or
opposing the Christ who in his own self-evacuation bound word with
flesh: himself the great original of the world theater, both image and likeness, mind and act. As the various specialist discourses separated one institutional context from another—court from country, shows from literature, and the king no longer going on a progress—the tragic hero's
ambition to incorporate all his being into unified words and deeds ceases
to make sense.[71] With a self distributed among the different contexts—
and necessarily different discourses—of an increasingly differentiated institutional setting, the attempt to unify private morality and public deeds
becomes a vastly more impossible project. As the king—even in the Jacobean era—becomes more the spokesman for a party, openly surrounded
with friends and agents known to be as much the shapers of policy as he,
and as the gap between private self and public meaning becomes a matter
of general acknowledgment (as it could not be in the era of a virgin queen
whose public power depended at least mythically upon her private divinity), the materials for tragedy—for the making of a heroically united
self—cease to exist. One cannot make the court into the hero of a tragedy;
that is a subject only for satire. But in that moment before we reconcile
ourselves to fragmentation among different languages and contexts, yet
after the ambition to put nature into coherent language had arisen (an
ambition that no doubt reveals only a fragmentation always already
there), there occurs the possibility of tragedy, which gives us an enduring
image of our fatal human capacity for chimerical self union, which is also
a figure for the otherwise unrepresentable but nonetheless commonplace
fact not just of biological uniqueness, but of that inalienable individuality
in which we are each specifically situated by the interplay between mutually irreducible discourses: one for our private bodies of desire, another
for our public structures of exchange.[72]

Where the tragedies portray a hero who seeks to deny distinctions, to
unify otherwise separate discourses in his single enacted being, the ro-

---

[71] As Lee Bliss puts it, "In the early seventeenth-century drama, tragic protagonists are
forced to act in increasingly confusing and corrupt worlds—arenas that distort or inhibit
heroic action and trivialize the transcendent aspiration they cannot understand. A diminished sphere of actions reveals, or produces, a diminished race of heroes." *The World's Perspective: John Webster and the Jacobean Drama* (New Brunswick, New Jersey: Rutgers University Press, 1983), 198.
[72] See Green, *Tragic Effect*, esp. 186–244.

mances seem to emphasize difference itself: between art and nature, between experience and innocence, between belatedness and the imaginary unity which it always posits, between diegetic mediation and mimetic sheerness of display.[73] Symptomatic of all these differences, and treated with an obsessive recurrence, as if so difficult to overlook as to be in danger of continual repression, is the difference between fathers and daughters. One way to understand this would be to work from the explicit theme of *Pericles* to its implicit counterpart in *The Tempest*, arguing that the romances engage and then eschew the threat of incest, that they begin with a father's effort to control a daughter's will, then end, happily, with a father's acknowledgment of his daughter's (different) sexuality.[74] But in two of the romances, there is more at stake than a daughter's sexuality: wives come under a suspicion that daughters escape. So the more general way to put this issue is to say that Shakespeare's romances successively explore the means whereby patriarchal power (at least in its earthly versions) can be made to acknowledge and faithfully endure the gap between its current knowledge and the significance of one who does not just mediate realms but has an independent and in some sense uncontrollable being. And in the tragicomic romances, with their severer threats to happiness, more realms come explicitly into play than in the comedies. Where the comedies bring things to harmony through the agency of an evident (and finally uninterpretable) double, mediating an authority not its own and never named, in the romances authority somewhere speaks in its "own" voice, figured as Gower, or Apollo, or Jupiter, or the Prospero whose book enables him to write the script for others' edification and his own redemption. In each of these plays, Shakespeare thus not only makes thematic matter out of the way in which human beings enact meanings beyond their present understanding, he insists that such enactment requires the intervention of an epistemological and ontological other, as if the dilemmas of the present world could not be solved out of its own resources, but rather needed overt help from a normally absent structure of governance.

Rather than survey the last plays for this trait, I want to look in some detail at one romance which strikingly exhibits a tension between the modes I have been calling theater and book. An obvious choice would be *The Tempest*, whose opening alternation between a brutally immediate

[73] For the argument that romance has essentially to do with deviation and belatedness, to such a degree that Derridean *différance* can be conceived as the philosophical formulation of the genre's essential trope, see Patricia Parker, *Inescapable Romance: Studies in the Poetics of a Mode* (Princeton: Princeton University Press, 1979), esp. 221.

[74] See Stanley Cavell's argument about Hollywood comedies of remarriage, which he would derive in part from Shakespearean romance. *Pursuits of Happiness*, esp. 57.

storm and Prospero's dry narration of its causes establishes an explicit interdependence between a visible scene and its as yet to be revealed narrative foundation. That interdependence remains centrally important throughout the play, whether one thinks about the way in which the island (and its master) reconstructs the motives and the lived realities of most of the shipwrecked Neapolitans, or the way in which Miranda discovers "mankind," or the way in which Prospero finally cedes his own authority to a still higher power. Despite the ideological suggestions of the ending, even there the interdependency—and separation—of theater and book keep the play from slipping into mere doctrinalism. Casting the audience ambiguously in the position of suppliant souls and a forgiving deity, Prospero's epilogue still leaves some margin for uncertainty as to where the authority of this cloud-capped spectacle really comes from: how one sees the ending depends upon narrative hypothesis to the very last, even as to how one should understand the sense of those "crimes" from which the audience would be freed. But *The Tempest* is almost too well suited to my purposes. For that arbitrary reason, if no other, I want to concentrate on *The Winter's Tale*.

More insistently than any other late play, *The Winter's Tale* invites our venturing on well-worn conundrums: pastoral (and academic) puzzles about the relationship between nature and nurture, nature and art, original and imitation. The bear, the baby, and the statue—Rosalie Colie's list—to which we might add other marvels, almost at will; Leontes's artificial jealousy, Perdita's "natural" virtue, Autolycus's doing good despite his nature and intentions: all these confront us with what G. Wilson Knight calls "the sphinx-like boundary between art and life."[75] When Antigonus disappears in obedience to that notorious stage direction ("Exit Antigonus, pursued by a Beare") or when we discover that—like Leontes—we have been tricked (by Shakespeare as well as by Paulina) into believing that a woman is a statue, we find our generic expectations thrown into momentary aporia. Not that we ever forget that we are in the presence of art—for Shakespeare both outrageously insists upon the artificiality of his play and challenges us to be knowing gulls; rather that the "proper" relations between art and life keep being reversed.

What the conventions of romance would have us accept as "natural"—the bear—turns out to be both more full of meaning (as a figure at once of Leontes' tyranny and the vengeance of heaven) and rawer in nature ("how the bear tore out his shoulder-bone") than we had been led to ex-

[75] G. Wilson Knight, " 'Great Creating Nature': An Essay on *The Winter's Tale*," in *Shakespeare: Modern Essays in Criticism*, ed. Leonard F. Dean (New York: Oxford University Press, 1957), 403.

pect.[76] Later on, what the play itself encourages us to take for art—the statue—turns out to be "natural" ("O, she's warm," says Leontes) and yet in her forgiveness far more civil, far more the product of art than Leontes, whose life both before and after his repentance has obeyed the dictates of illusion rather than those of reality. [77] At such junctures, such shifts of frame and tone, something we had taken to be securely on one side of the "sphinx-like boundary" turns out instead to have had that boundary running *through* it. In a manner that contemporary deconstructive criticism has made almost tediously familiar, the provisionally stable binarisms of pastoral turn out—not on closer examination, but through the all-too-obvious workings of the plot—to be composed of terms themselves infected by the very confusion they purport to forestall.

Nor, as I have repeatedly claimed, is this phenomenon peculiar to *The Winter's Tale*. Theater itself has—as the phrase goes—always already been afflicted with a certain doubleness. At least in nonimprovisational theater, there has always been a structure of absence (the script, at least), a supplement of writing somehow inside and yet unbounded by the ostensible presence which this peculiarly bastard art pretends to have. Normally, we accede to theatrical presence, though with a secret and therefore ineffectual skepticism, perhaps because theater, by letting us all know that its being is infected with writing, helps us repress the fact that our own presence to ourselves and to other people suffers from precisely the same radical flaw.

Be that as it may, in *The Winter's Tale*, Shakespeare refuses to let us forget what we all know. Nonetheless, it is easier to acknowledge his stubbornness and gaiety on this point than to say just what it is that *The Winter's Tale* forces us to keep in mind and in view. Even to say—as so many critics do—that the play affirms "the interchange of art with nature" secretly supposes (in clear defiance of the play itself) that we can know and say what art and nature independently are.[78] Beyond that pitfall stand those of ideology, the temptation to privilege one term or the other, either "great creating nature"—with its implied transcendence of things merely human or merely natural—or the art that nature makes, which "offers human nature a chance to civilize its brutalities."[79] Both propositions, like the one that they depend upon, that art and nature exist in mutual interchange, seem—at a certain level—true enough, but tame;

[76] See Dennis Biggins, " 'Exit pursued by a Beare': A Problem in *The Winter's Tale*," *Shakespeare Quarterly* 13 (1962): 3–13.

[77] Rosalie Colie makes this point at pages 279–83 of *Shakespeare's Living Art* (Princeton: Princeton University Press, 1974).

[78] Colie, *Shakespeare's Living Art*, 283.

[79] For the first of these positions, see Knight, "Great Creating Nature" 407–8; for the second, Colie, *Shakespeare's Living Art*, 283.

more what we ought to say than what we feel in the face of this odd play. If my hunch is right, that *The Winter's Tale* keeps making us stumble over a fact of theater (and of our lives) that we ordinarily repress, there should be something about that fact more threatening to human identity, something resistant in principle to domestication, something we must rather acknowledge than pretend to know and say.[80]

Having by this last move both blocked and excused myself from having to say outright just what the *skandalon* of *The Winter's Tale* consists of, I must still try to say something about how the play makes us stumble. In very schematic terms, I think it works like this. Time and again—and more than once while calling our attention to the wide gap of time (and therefore to the absence) that every sign (and play) implies—*The Winter's Tale* sets up a dissonance between showing and telling.[81] There are obvious instances: the Clown's comic and yet ineptly cruel report of the ship's sinking and the bear's dining as set against the newborn baby that the old shepherd shows his son and us; the gentlemen's account of the old kings' meeting, "a sight which was to be seen, cannot be spoken of"; Paulina on the implausibility of what she has just proved, "That she is living, / Were it but told you, should be hooted at / Like an old tale; but it appears she lives, / Though yet she speak not" (V.iii.115–18). Beyond these evident cases is the action of the whole first part of the play, wherein the story that Leontes tells himself and his court stands plainly at odds with what we and all the other characters take to be Hermione's trustworthy appearance. Leontes will be disabused of his own story only through another (the oracle) as backed up by the reported (but "real") death of Mamillius and the shown (but "illusory") death of Hermione. Yet this "same" death has just the opposite effect on Antigonus. When Hermione appears to him in a dream, he concludes that she has died, and from that inference takes another: that her child is a bastard which "should here be laid, / Either for life or death, upon the earth / Of its right father" (III.iii.44–46).

This dissonance between telling and showing repeats and foregrounds a dissonance that we more obscurely sense in the genre itself—the non-coincidence, for example, between what the characters tell one another and what we are able to "see" through their words and gestures—and also the dissonance between the two parts of this particular play, the first so

---

[80] Stanley Cavell, "Knowing and Acknowledging," in *Must We Mean What We Say? A Book of Essays* (1969; Cambridge: Cambridge University Press, 1976), 238–66.

[81] As Barbara Mowat puts it more generally for the last plays, the "potency" of the romances "comes as much from the power of story as from the very different power of drama." *The Dramaturgy of Shakespeare's Romances* (Athens: University of Georgia Press, 1976), 69.

intent on working out the narrative and apparently consequential logic of
jealousy, the second so blatant in its theatrical and discontinuous display
of images and transformations that no story can adequately account for.
But there is more to this dissonance than generic self-reference. As showing and telling repeatedly fail to coincide, yet manifestly ground one another, I think that we may begin to notice that the real issue of *The Winter's Tale* is less the connection between nature and art and more the
deeper relation between being and meaning, precisely as entailed by the
modal interaction of theater and book. And that interaction has its peculiar formula: being and meaning cannot coincide just because the one is
always "hidden" in the other as its condition of possibility.[82]

Now *The Winter's Tale*, of course, does not say any such thing; it
talks—or rather its characters talk—of nature and nurture, nature and art,
original and imitation. But it does, so to speak, display this mutually anaclitic relationship, wherein what the Christian tradition calls flesh and
Word lean one on the other in the effect named "incarnation." Allegoriz-
ers of Shakespeare have been especially fond of *The Winter's Tale* just on
account of this display; it evokes religious thoughts, more precisely,
thoughts of that resurrection which consists in restoring flesh to Word
and Word to flesh after their temporary encryptment as and through the
dead letter of the law (of representation). When Hermione steps out of
her sixteen years' silence, giving a new life to the perpetually mortified
Leontes, we and he have to confront what it is always much more convenient to forget—though of course we all know about it—the scandal of
incarnation. The final miracle, however, does not stand alone in forcing
us to reckon both with the fact of and our forgetting of incarnation, both
with the fact of and our forgetting of the mutual implication and yet non-
coincidence of being and meaning. For the whole play forces this reckoning upon us.

I say "two principal ways" of forgetting how meaning and being stand
as each other's condition of possibility. One is to take everything as
meaning—roughly the idealist's error; the other is to take everything as
being—roughly the materialist's error. Though it would be tedious to
show in detail how these twin mistakes chase each other in the course of
our viewing, I think that I can claim, with a fair show of plausibility, that
Leontes commits them both, one after the other. In the first part of the

[82] For the Lacanian origin of this formula, see Lacan, *Four Fundamental Concepts*, 203–15.
For the early Derridean formulation of this noncoincidence as difference, see Jacques Der-
rida, *The Origin of Geometry: An Introduction*, trans. John P. Leavey, Jr. (Stony Brook, New
York: Nicolas Hays, 1978), 153. See also the discussion in Vincent Descombes, *Modern
French Philosophy*, trans. L. Scott-Fox and J. M. Harding (Cambridge: Cambridge Univer-
sity Press, 1980), 142–45.

play, he moves from idealized friendship—that image of a pastoral youth with Polixenes, to be repeated now in a continued twinning in Sicily with his brother king—to the dark but no less idealizing conceits of paranoia. In both cases—though perhaps not quite in the same way—Leontes denies the need of mediation, positing an imaginary identity first between subject and object (himself and his brother king), and then between his own imaginings and the world. With no blind spot of being in meaning or of meaning in being, the world seems transparent: all either as it appears or all as we know it to be, despite appearances. But Leontes' obsession with meaning yields, finally, to the fact which reminds us all that after all we are incarnate beings, too: the fact of death. Then in the second part of the play, Leontes' guilt—and Paulina's insistent reproaches—keep him locked up in that literal, material fact. Childless, bound to his past, blocked from a future by a reported oracle that he cannot fully understand, Leontes pays for his prior obsession with meaning by a correlative obsession with sheer being. Indeed, Paulina (behaving here like a particularly grim version of the standard comic double) makes him confess a faith in literal being that goes beyond all reason: first by holding him fast to the memory of the dead, then by fixing his gaze on what appears to be a mere object. Then when she makes that object move, she taunts him with the superstition— the credulity about meanings and motives—which had ruined him in the first place: "Start not; her actions shall be holy, as / You hear my spell is lawful. Do not shun her / Until you see her die again, for then / You kill her double" (V.iii.104–7).

"You kill her double." The words have an ambiguous sense: to kill her twice, to kill her twin. But of course that is what Leontes had in effect already done; he killed her once in making her nothing but a signifier in his own fantasy, and then he killed her again, in being, by killing her and then her child; and yet in both instances, he only—but crucially—killed her "double." In the terms I have been developing, to forget incarnation is just to kill the other's double: in effect, to commit soul-murder with one's unbridled will to know. One way of saying what it is that Shakespeare's play makes us remember, then, is the necessity—and again the mutual implication—of both faith and skepticism: faith that there is being beyond what we know; skepticism that what we see bears meaning on its face.

These obviously Cavellian terms strike me as finally apter for the analysis of romance than of tragedy. Perhaps this is because the romances, with their insistence on redemption through a willed (and yet usually prompted) self-abnegation on the part of paternal authority, so directly take a question of epistemological limitation for their subject, and be-

cause they make it unmistakably plain that their errant fathers and husbands are (with the exception of Prospero) simply, even ignobly, wrong.
Where the tragedies inspire a blend of woe and wonder at a heroic excess
which figures our own ensoulment, the romances keep us distanced.
Every sphere of action in the romances has its insistent frame; nothing
suggests the unlimited, oceanic economy in which most of the tragic heroes try to stake their bearings.[83] For all their fancifulness and artifice the
romances therefore acquire from these explicit framing gestures an air of
the genuinely real. Making thematic capital out of their own fictional
foundations, the romances refuse to tidy things up; demanding that we
notice how every resolution comes from some arbitrary imposition of
narratival control, they do not pretend that any authority can work its
will without gaps and slippage. Where the comedies may have an *idiotes*,
the romances have unresurrected corpses like Antigonus and unlamented
ones like Cloten, or representatives of nature who will never grow civil,
agencies of the spirit who must finally be freed. With comic harmony an
increasingly fragile possibility, purchased often at the price of some ideological power's ruling some sorts of persons out of civil bounds, and
with tragic error so easily exposed as folly by a mere shift of frame, romance reasserts its eternal, inescapable allure, an irrecoverable "medieval"
form that expresses a "modern" condition, the condition of the necessarily unintegrated self.[84] The genre par excellence of frames—though only
in the most knowledgeable hands acknowledged as such—romance
breaks up the dyad of tragedy and comedy by insinuating a third which
is no synthesis, but as history's doublet, a necessary fourth. For like history—especially like history absent a Henry V—romance displaces authority toward an absent other, known only through prophecy, appari-
tion, or specular allusion.

But the difference of Shakespearean romance from Shakespearean history tells us more about its equally short-lived generic history; and therefore more, too, about Shakespeare's peculiarly literary theater. The authority veiled in Shakespearean history—especially in the guise of a hero
who if unveiled would have to come as close to tragedy as a historical
personage could—has the apparent self-sufficiency and wholeness that
goes with governing the real world rather than its double. However fab-

[83] *Coriolanus* may be an exception to this claim—the only oceanic thing in him is the part
that is like Tamburlaine. See also Frank Kermode, *The Sense of an Ending: Studies in the
Theory of Fiction* (New York: Oxford University Press, 1967), 82, for the observation that
tragedy takes place in the *aevum*.

[84] Howard Felperin, "Romance and Romanticism: Some Reflections on *The Tempest* and
Heart of Darkness, Or When is Romance No Longer Romance," in *Shakespeare's Romances
Reconsidered*, ed. Carol McGinnis Kay and E. H. Jacobs (Lincoln: University of Nebraska
Press, 1978), 60–76.

ulous, Henry's famous victories are no mouldy tale. History—even Shakespearean history—is not quite fiction and, despite mythic exaggerations, cannot allow us to misunderstand its tropes as referring merely to one possible world out of many. In order to supply either patriotic thrills or the distress occasioned by successful Machiavellianism, in order to make an audience yield to its threat and promise of the unified private and public body, the history plays have to be known as dealing in actualities, as engaging an apparently impersonal or transpersonal narrative force that issues in the events of a world by common consent our own. Moreover, the histories are constructive, not restorative; their heroic mimesis effects what it cannot quite unveil, leaving it up to viewers to infer a truer but analogous form from their inadequate mirror.

By contrast, the romances operate with a corrective movement, displacing moral error with aesthetic deviation, relying on a particularized intervention from some higher plane to undo subjective fancies. Thereby they also emphasize the fictional, alternative character of the world which intervening authority makes possible. Like the green world of the earlier comedy, this alternative seems to figure the triumph of life over death; in it, healing metamorphoses occur.[85] But where the two worlds of Shakespearean comedy work in dialectical sequence, with liminality serving both as refuge from civil wrongs and as an independent power for disruption and conversion, there is in the late romances finally just one world— first a world gone wrong, then a world miraculously righted—alternative to ours only in achieving resolution. Belarius's mountain cave (a "cell of ignorance" to Cymbeline's sons); Perdita's sheepfold (wherein the transformations come more from Florizel's behest than from any intrinsic power); even Prospero's (or is it Caliban's?) island: these inset worlds do not stand as doubles to the everyday; one cannot go there for a refreshed vision or moral chiropractic. Infected already by the politics and powers of the real world, their "natural" artifice will not suffice. Instead, they further contribute to a tangle of illusions and half-mistaken motives that cannot be resolved except by a superior art that shows up this web as the otherwise graceless result of egotism, error, and deceit.

In the histories, the hope of creating some perfect guess at a future's plot always promotes the possibility of heroism; in the comedies a performative happiness seems always in reach, given only good will, some patience with convention, and an ear for style; in the tragedies, the error to which the hero succumbs has about it that universality and inevitability which counts as a kind of victory, not for the individual, but for what

[85] Northrop Frye, "The Argument of Comedy," in *Shakespeare: Modern Essays in Criticism,* ed. Leonard F. Dean (New York: Oxford University Press, 1957), 79–89.

Hegel called the "eternal substance of things."[86] But in the romances, neither heroism nor conversion will suffice, for the gap between sign and
significance is too great except for forced reading—not even Autolycus,
versed in both theft and ballads, can tell what's what—yet the errors to
which a Posthumus, a Leontes, an Alonzo yield themselves, or the villainy perpetrated by a Dionyza or a Jachimo, are all too petty to command either admiration or fear. What *they* misread and misdo, no one
should, with a good will or their wits about them; and yet the accumulation of these sins and errors, compounded by the vagaries of weather,
bears, and other less-or-more than human forces, makes up a puzzle that
no wholly immanent plot can work through, no remorse undo, no suffering at all redeem. Whence the recourse to superior narrative agency: to
Gower's book, or Prospero's, or the one that Jupiter leaves on Posthumus's lap, or the old tale whose last marvel Paulina makes manifest.

But in taking recourse to books—to oracles, tales, and repositories of
magic—these plots personate an authority in no way whole or self-sufficient, but rather obviously frail and fictional, and never to be encountered
in the world of history as here imaged. Gower is an ancient man, whose
rhyme goes on "lame feet" (*Pericles* IV. Pro. 48); without his book, Prospero's a "sot"; Jupiter and Apollo, though they may figure authentic
powers of heaven, are no more than figures, figures from a familiar, pa-
gan, literary past. What such figures provide may at first seem unintelligible— like Jupiter's book, "Or senseless speaking, or a speaking such /
As sense cannot untie" (*Cymbeline* V.iv.147–48)—or like Gower's tale (or
Mamillius's) something that to "latter times, / When wit's more ripe"
(*Pericles* I.Pro.11–12) needs faith and forebearance—or like Prospero's,
simply boring. Yet as Posthumus says, "The action of my life is like it"
(*Cymbeline* V.iv.149); and that likeness, that subsequent theatrical
embodiment, is what proves the story's "truth." So even as theatrical
presence depends upon an intrusive, bookish authority for its resolution,
so that authority depends upon the action—and on an audience's credit-
ing that action—for its credibility.

Even so, the stage world needs this authority, and by demanding that
we recognize its need for a magical artifice that we will credit as authoritative—not just the artifice of civil society, or of partly masterable history,
or even of the art of dying well—Shakespeare undermines the defining
pretense of theater to be self-sufficient presence, to being *theater*, seen,
heard, enacted, but not told, not mediated through some figurable intentionality. Falling short of immediacy, shown up as dependent upon some
authority other than the partial ones immanent in the stage world, Shake-

---

[86] Hegel, *Aesthetics* 2: 1199.

speare's romances thus exhibit a certain failure that we have lately learned to associate with modernity, a failure to be pure, to escape the mixed conditions of the art itself. But the failure these plays acknowledge is not quite the one that Paul de Man describes, arguing that the specificity of literature, of the literary consciousness, has to do with the unattainable desire for a modernity defined as unmediated spontaneity, the free being of a pure act.[87] For it is not quite "anteriority" which the romances fail to suppress, however belated and dilated their representational mode, and not quite "freshness" of presence which they fail to attain, and certainly not the burden of history, whether actual or literary, that they fail to escape. Indeed, to the extent that the romances revive an older literary and theatrical form, they do so not with an Oedipal grudge or an anxiety either of originality or influence, but with what feels like an affectionate, relaxed delight.

In fact, there is something quite joyful about the romances' very modern failure to evade the logic of their origins, a joyfulness that I would associate with release from the bonds of pretense. For in a way that is paradoxical only at first sight, the authority to which the romances appeal, however frail and fictive, is at the same time entirely real. In order to justify this assertion, I need to redefine the pretense from which the romances escape as the pretense not only of theatrical presence, but also as that of secularity. Antitheatricality from Plato onwards counts in large part as the moral objection to this mimetic pretense that there is no world elsewhere, nothing sacred or ideal to which "this" world must respond and from which it must acquire its real intelligibility. It may well be true, as John Guillory has claimed, that literary history (at least the history of narrative and lyric forms) is a prolonged effort to deny our secularity, that "literature emerges in an effort to distinguish itself from the sacred text . . . without giving up a *scriptural* authority," without giving up its claim to be derived from a sacred, inspirational origin. And as Guillory further implies, such a specifically literary resistance to the nonscriptural may embody an inescapably Oedipal reluctance to acknowledge one's merely human debts.[88] But Shakespeare makes no claim to be inspired—the closest he comes is in the Chorus's apologetic wish for a "Muse of fire" at the start of *Henry V*—and he exhibits no desire for laureate standing, no reluctance to incorporate other texts, and no uncertainty about beginning. For the problem which the various sorts of "scriptural" authority solve in the romances is neither the theological problem of origins nor the secular

[87] Paul de Man, "Literary History and Literary Modernity," in *Blindness and Insight: Essays in the Rhetoric of Contemporary Criticism*, 2d ed. (Minneapolis: University of Minnesota Press, 1983), 142–65.
[88] Guillory, *Poetic Authority*, esp. 62, xii.

one of beginnings: it is the problem of bringing things to an intelligible end.[89] This is not a problem for the muse, but for the *deus ex machina*, a solution not available to the writer of diegetic narrative, who is always already somewhere figured in the mediator's position, and so once started, lacking further unmediated access to any other epistemological or ontological register, is either doomed to "endlesse worke" or challenged to construct a plot entailing an ending that will come like revelation, the unveiling of a latent and prophesiable order.[90]

As if reflecting on the history of his own accomplishment with a Euripidean skepticism about such conventions of plot, and debarred by the very temporality of his art from even the illusion of an endless deferral, Shakespeare in these romances flaunts a nonmimetic authority, a capacity—intruded upon the playworld in some surrogate form—to redefine that world's premises in such a way as to produce an internal recognition. And this is what makes that authority seem, and in a certain sense, be *real*: it forces an acknowledgment of a reality about recognition itself, that it is in no way necessary, being a mere possibility whose actualization depends on some other ungovernable power that must intervene, like accident or grace.[91]

It is in this way that I would understand Shakespeare's habit in the romances of keeping secrets from the audience, of blocking inferences, of supplying potions, magic arts, and unprepared surprises wherever needed to enable closure. Of course these are the stock devices of the Greek narrative romances that lie behind these plots, though in the metamorphosis into drama they take on a different valency.[92] And to be sure, in Hermione's unveiling, or the reappearance of the bosun and his crew, or the masque of Jupiter, or the lucky encounter between Pericles' dead queen and the good physician Cerimon, an obtrusive theatricality calls attention to itself, and therefore to the medium in which Shakespeare works, to its capacity for winning consent with a good show. But the unpredictability—the apparent implausibility, the lack of motivation—of these intrusions also works to defeat the pretensions of secular order, indeed, of any order on which prophecy might bear. And so the eruption

[89] For origins versus beginnings, see not only Guillory but also Said, *Beginnings*, esp. 372–73.

[90] See, of course, Kermode, *Sense of an Ending*, and Jonathan Goldberg's poststructuralist (but also Beckettian) view of Spenser in *Endlesse Worke: Spenser and the Structures of Discourse* (Baltimore: Johns Hopkins University Press, 1981).

[91] I take this as a way of putting a familiar Derridean point, that the condition of possibility of a letter's reaching its destination is that it must be capable of going astray. See Jacques Derrida, "Le facteur de la vérité," in *La carte postale: de Socrate à Freud et au-delà* (Paris: Flammarion, 1980), 472.

[92] See Carol Gesner, *Shakespeare and the Greek Romance: A Study of Origins* (Lexington: University of Kentucky, 1970).

of "authority" in these plays has an impact much like that of Shakespeare's own within that other secular order which we call cultural history: that of a kind of absolute encounter, limited and to some extent promoted by that order, yet ultimately outside the control of any masterable code.

The "modernity" I have been trying to describe in these last pages consists, then, not in Shakespeare's *text* failing to attain the status of pure being, but in his *theater's* subjection to an authority which has the disruptive effect of forcing recognitions where none could have been predicted. At the level of the playworld of the romances, this is clear enough: though the marks are always there to be set in a decodable relation, it takes the intervening will of the story to move them into meaningful positions. Relative to the secular order of the playworld, that intervention is absolute and uncontrollable; here in the fourth of the dramatic genres, which intensifies and thematizes what the others suppress, or at most allude to, recognitions are gratuitous, set up not by the action inside the theatrical frame, but rather enabled by the parergonic imperfection of the mimetic frame itself.[93]

For subsequent theatrical history, which turned away both from Shakespeare's romantic comedy and from these later and more blatant explorations of the limits to convention, recognition took the form of avoidance. In place of these disruptions by an extramimetic authority, Jonson and his heirs in English new comedy substitute the internalized difference between Truewit and false, thereby denying that there need be a radical flaw in the present world, asserting instead that moral correction is a matter of good sense.[94] However inescapable romance may have been in the narrative and lyric traditions, in the mimetic ones it skips first to opera, then to film, as if dependent for its purchase on a certain novelty in the medium, whose practitioners thereafter would find themselves incapable of such infantile delights.[95] One could explain this denial of the marvelous by appealing to a decline in providentialist assumptions, or to a greater sense of the niceties of theatrical decorum, or to a more emphatically illusionistic protocol of representation, or perhaps more plausibly, to the appropriation by the court of all such masquing devices for its own political program, thus effectively depriving it of sympathetic interest for

---

[93] On the parergon, and framing in general, see Jacques Derrida, *The Truth in Painting*, trans. Geoff Bennington and Ian McLeod (Chicago: University of Chicago Press, 1987), 15–147.

[94] For the ideological implications of these comedies, see especially Laura Brown, *English Dramatic Form, 1600–1760* (New Haven, Connecticut: Yale University Press, 1981).

[95] For this hopping from one medium to another, and for the sense that the genre's lifetime in film was as brief as its stage life, see Cavell, *Pursuits of Happiness*, 51–52 and 19–34.

dramatists aiming at a wider public.[96] Suppressing the marvelous would then be a way of suppressing reference to a worldly authority progressively less available for purposes of moral correction or of liberation from the confines of the everyday. But one might also see in this suppression of a fact about mimesis the effect of a repression of Shakespeare's own authority. Because Shakespeare himself had no strong predecessor, his romances can allow themselves to be invaded by an authority that seems indecidably "his" and a simulacrum for whatever power there might be that could recall the world to intelligibility. Subsequent drama, however, cannot avail itself of that device without being "Shakespearean," without registering a dependent literariness. Yet in giving up what one might quite properly call the "primitive" dimension in Shakespearean theater—primitive because foundational both for its logic and its delight—this later drama loses its modernity, its capacity to keep on criticizing the present by showing how the present can neither be, nor recognize, itself.

And how can we understand for ourselves, in our own secular history, the will to force these recognitions, to provide a historical content for what would otherwise be merely arbitrary marks? I want to take it as just as a will to criticism, criticism both of the premises of theater and of those persons represented in this theater—by whom we ourselves are represented, the more obviously by being equally denied access to the playwright's secrets—persons who behave as if there were never any authority that could force them beyond the order that they know. But whose will is this? It is our will, of course, our W/will, to whom and which we concede that power, needing it, because we know that it is needful for life that something force such recognitions, that some more than personal authority compel our reassessment both of the lives we lead and of the stories that we tell.

"Because he is *not* the word of God," so Morton Bloomfield puts it, "Shakespeare is more satisfactory as a canonical and monumental text."[97] One function of his literary authority, one of the purposes to which we put that authority, a purpose for which the dramatic logic of his work especially suits it, consists in confronting us with our own inability to be modern—with the inability of any actor just to be—and at the same time with the irreducible difference between all actors and the texts that inhabit and determine them. The contingency of Shakespeare is an essential fact in the labor of this confrontation. Things that neither he nor his text could have determined—like the success of British imperialism, which

---

[96] For the political implications of the masque, see especially Orgel, *Illusion of Power*.

[97] Morton Bloomfield, "Quoting and Alluding: Shakespeare in the English Language," in *Shakespeare: Aspects of Influence*, ed. G. B. Evans (Cambridge, Massachusetts: Harvard University Press, 1976), 7.

gave to a provincial European tongue the world utility which Alexander's conquests procured for Greek—contribute as necessary conditions to his becoming and remaining literary. Yet even in this there seems to be more than accident at work, the sort of veiled necessity that prompts one to give a certain credence to Hegelian stories about the interaction between human self-awareness and the logic of history. That Shakespeare and Sophocles survive to affect us in ways that Racine and Seneca do not, cannot be the result of *mere* contingency, though their continuing survival undoubtedly depends on factors beyond our control, however much energy we devote to trying to ensure that future generations will wish to number themselves among the friends who read him, and again, and again.

Index

absence: authority and, 40–41, 137–38, 146, 149, 157–59; comedy and, 166; presence and, 57, 154, 175; theater and, 38, 184, 210, 235–36. *See also* presence

actor: freedom of, 39–51; moving image and, 140–41; presence of, 38–39, 52–53, 73, 151, 154

actors, persons as: in drama generally, 34–35, 38–43; in Elizabethan drama, 10, 18–19; in Kyd, 154–59; Lacanian symbolic and, 130–42; in Lyly, 170–74, 177–79; in Marlowe, 163–65; in Reformation theology, 44, 107–11; in Shakespearean comedy, 203–4, 210–11, 216–17; in Shakespearean history, 24–26, 189–201; in Shakespearean romance, 235–39; in Shakespearean tragedy, 27–33, 220–22, 224, 228. *See also* signs, persons as

Adams, Barry B., 144n, 159n

Adelman, Janet, 226n

aesthetic, 15, 55, 77, 79, 84, 129

Albrecht, W. P., 220n

allegory: in *Endimion*, 166–70, 172–74, 177–79, 183; history and, 19, 22–26; irony and, 15, 17, 23, 27, 35, 125, 129, 134, 155–58, 185; meaning and, 134; medieval narrative and, 16–17; medieval vs. early modern, 12–13, 20, 123–24; mimesis/diegesis and, 34–44; modernity and, ix–x, 12–13, 83–84, 89, 186; poets', 34; representation and, 9–15, 89–92, 128–30, 183; in Shakespearean comedy, 206, 215; in Shakespearean history, 21–24, 26–27, 185, 195–96, 200; in Shakespearean romance, 237; in *The Spanish Tragedy*, 151–52, 157–58, 183; structural differentiation and, 124–25; temporality and, 185; as threat to the dramatic, 42; Tudor interludes and, 89–93

Altman, Joel B., 11n

ambiguity, *See* indecidability

anaclisis, 14, 128–29, 210, 237

Andrewes, Lancelot, 86n, 109

Anglicanism, 81–82, 109–111

Anglo, Sydney, 95n, 187n

aphanisis, 151–54

aporia, 35, 94, 203

Ardolino, Frank, 145n, 158n

Aristotle, 6–7, 36, 38, 41, 52, 129, 166n, 219

Arnold, Matthew, 4, 81, 184n

Artaud, Antonin, 37n

Ascham, Roger, 82

Augé, Marc, 6n, 80n

Augustine, Saint, 22, 40, 49n, 51, 56, 58n, 136

Austin, John, 128, 205

authority: absence and, 40–41, 137–38, 146, 149, 157–59; centralizing, 84, 117–18, 130–32; desire and, 137–38; divine, 22, 36, 40–41, 49–55, 73–74, 104–11; drama and, 40–42, 241–43; Elizabethan playwrights and, 130–33; Elizabethan theater and, 135; *Endimion* and, 180–81, 183–84; imperial, 154–58; juridical, 61–64, 96–97, 109–10; literary drama and, 40–42, 130–31; Marlowe and, 162–65; modernization and, 123–25; political, 39, 66, 82–83, 132–34, 149–51; in *Richard II*, 187–88; Shakespearean, x, 3–4, 9, 141, 146, 183–85, 186–244 *passim*, 245–46; *The Spanish Tragedy* and, 143–48, 154–58, 183–84; symbolic/semiotic and, 41n, 130–33; as target of displacement, 66–68. *See also* governance

Axton, Marie, 166n, 174n, 177, 187n

Axton, Richard, 94

Bacon, Francis, 20n, 86n, 116, 123, 125

Baines, Barbara J., 144n

Baldwin, T. W., 167n

Bate, John, 90–91, 93

Balmary, Marie, 139n

Bamber, Linda, 219n

Bangs, Carl, 109
Barber, C. L., 186
Barfield, Owen, 193n
Barish, Jonas A., 40n, 153, 167n
Barker, Francis, 9n, 12n
Barney, Stephen, 13n
Barroll, J. Leeds, 227n
Barthes, Roland, 45n
Barton, Anne, 4n. *See also* Anne Righter
Baskerville, C. R., 95n
Battenhouse, Roy, 9n, 135, 220n
Battestin, Martin, 84n
Beadle, Richard, 49n
Bean, John C., 208n
Beard, Thomas, 135
Beckett, Samuel, 41, 48, 243n
Belsey, Catherine, 10n, 219n
Bendix, Reinhard, 121n
Benjamin, Walter, 79
Bennett, Josephine Waters, 169n, 177, 215n
Berek, Peter, 160n
Berger, Harry Jr., 37n
Berlin, Normand, 220n
Bernard of Clairvaux, Saint, 51, 65
Bernstein, Basil, 76n, 119n, 231
Bevington, David, 8n, 90n, 93, 98n, 100n
Bible: medieval drama and, 53–55, 72–73;
    problem of enacting, 53–55, 72–73, 92;
    rationalizing method and, 119; Shake-
    speare and, 3, 245; Tudor interludes and,
    95
Blanchot, Maurice, 26n
Bliss, Lee, 232n
Block, K. S., 57n
Bloom, Harold, 7n, 148
Bloomfield, Morton, 245n
Bloor, David, 20n
body of the sign: deconstruction and, 68;
    defined, 55–59; excess and, 59, 64, 108–
    9; glorified by medieval drama, 68; rela-
    tion to idea of the play, 129
Bonaventure, Saint, 56n, 65, 69, 99
Bond, R. W., 167n
book. *See* theater, book and
Booth, Stephen, 219–20, 222–23
Bossy, John, 82n, 101n
boundaries: between signifier and signified,
    20, 50, 85–86, 105–8, 115, 136–37; be-
    tween theater and book, ix, 19–20, 87;
    between two bodies of monarch, 32,
    167, 179, 187, 216; dissolution and dis-
    placement of, 68, 73; festival, modern
    reader and, 51, 54, 76–77; figuration and,
    58; permeability or rigidity of, 51, 86,
    107, 115–16, 124; rationalization and,
    85–87, 92–93, 97, 114–16, 133–34
Bourdieu, Pierre, 93
Bowers, Fredson, 144n, 145n

Boyle, Robert, 20n
Bradbrook, M. C., 161n
Bradford, John, 102, 108n
Bradley, A. C., 223
Breward, Ian, 106n
Bristol, Michael D., 46n
Broude, Ronald, 143n, 145n
Brown, John Russell, 205n
Brown, Laura, 244n
Brownlee, Marina Scordilis, 16n
Bunyan, John, 13
Burbage, James, 84
Burckhardt, Sigurd, 25n, 194n, 231n
Burke, Kenneth, 177n, 185n

Cairncross, Andrew S., 147n
Calderwood, J. L., 186
Calvin, John, 86, 107–8
Calvinism, 82, 130
Campbell, L. B., 101n
canon, 3–5, 37–38, 80–81; Shakespeare and,
    ix, 3–4, 245–46
capitalism, ix, 111, 133
Capp, Bernard, 23n
Carroll, William C., 214n
Caspari, Fritz, 92n
Catholicism, 18, 76, 81–82, 101–11, 130
Cavell, Stanley, 9n, 129n, 182n, 219–20,
    222–23, 233n, 236n, 238, 244n
Chambers, E. K., 59n, 63n
Champion, Larry S., 205n
charisma: Henry v and, 196; Marlowe's he-
    roes and, 163–65; routinization of, 132–
    33
Chaucer, Geoffrey, 7, 16–17, 95–96, 124
Chew, Samuel, 144n
Christianity: excess and, 57–59, 104–5,
    108–9, Lacanian psychoanalysis and,
    134–36; literary theory and, 55–59, 67–
    68; medieval drama and, 43–78; moder-
    nity and, 12–13, 83; Shakespeare and,
    12–13, 36, 237; textuality and, 15–17, 75;
    tropic structure of, early modern, 86,
    101–11; tropic structure of, medieval,
    48–59, 64–68, 79
Chydenius, Johan, 56n
civic consciousness, early modern, 82, 112,
    117
civic festival; medieval, 53, 59–64
Clark, Peter, 122n
Clarkson, L. A., 118n
Clemen, Wolfgang H., 160n
Clopper, Lawrence M., 63n
closure: myths of, 79–81; illusionistic, 113–
    14
code: content and, 116; doctrine and, 45–
    46; drama and, 4; elaborated vs. re-
    stricted, 76n, 119n, 125, 130, 153–56,

224, 231–32; medieval drama and, 48; noncode and, 11, 41, 57; overcoding and, 55; recoding and 132–33; revival of, 43; social tension and, 61–62
cognitive: anxiety concerning, 109–10, 111–12; diegesis and, 36; performative and, 14, 53–54, 94, 104, 128, 156, 184; reading and, 38; Shakespearean indecidability and, 25; status of in Reformation theology, 106; theater and, 27–28, 39, 140; tragedy and, 165–66, 219–32. *See also* performative
Cohen, Walter, 45n
Coleman, Christopher, 117n
Coleridge, Samuel Taylor, 55, 79, 129
Colie, Rosalie, 235n
Collinson, Patrick, 120n
comedy: doubleness and, 165–66, 172, 205; gender and, 165–81 *passim*, 203–19 *passim*; history and, 166, 201–2; impropriety and, 166, 210; performative convention and, 171–72, 203–19; Shakespearean, 201–19; style/textuality and, 165–67, 179, 181, 203–4
community: boundaries of redrawn by modernization, 111–13, 121, 133–34; *communitas* and, 46, 62, 66; early modern England and, 116–26; empire and, 154–55; gemeinschaft/gesellschaft and, 76, 80–81, 153–54; medieval towns and, 60–64; myths of, 79–83, 111, 121–22, 133, 154n; individual and, 123, 126; relation to symbolized by penance, 101–11
complementarity, 25–26, 128–30, 220–22. *See also* indecidability
conceptual disembodiment, 119–26; irony and, 124
Condell, Henry, 3–4
Cook, Ann Jennalie, 118n
Counter-Reformation, 81, 115
Coursen, Herbert R., Jr., 148n, 150n
Coventry, 60–63
Craik, T. W., 11n
Cranmer, Thomas, 82
Creeth, Edmund, 9n
Creizenach, W., 36n
Cressey, David, 83n, 118n
Crewe, Jonathan V., 7n
Crupi, Charles W., 50n, 87n
Cunningham, J. S., 162n
Curtius, Ernst Robert, 88n

D'Amico, Robert, 6n
Danson, Lawrence M., 209n
Dante, Alighieri, 16, 170
Davenant, William, 110
Davidson, Clifford, 62n, 67n
Davie, Donald, 5n

Davies, Horton, 8n, 82n, 125n
Davies, John, 110–11
Davis, Norman, 72n
Dawson, Giles E., 97n
de Chickera, Ernst, 145n
deconstruction, 14, 35, 41, 44, 68, 129
de Lille, Alain, 44
de Lubac, Henri, 73n
de Man, Paul, 4n, 13n, 42, 79, 128, 166n, 242
de Meun, Jean, 17
Derrida, Jacques, 6n, 7n, 39n, 75n, 80n, 130n, 136, 139n, 159n, 179n, 182n, 214n, 230n, 237n, 243n, 244n
Descartes, René, 86
Descombes, Vincent, 237n
Dessen, Alan C., 9n, 98n
Dickens, A. G., 82n
didacticism, 11–12, 41–42, 45–46, 63, 87–92
diegesis, ix, 12, 38, 44, 139–41, 200. *See also* narrative; theater, book and
differentiation: as assertion of symbolic over semiotic, 130; death and, 137; interpretation and, 45–46; medieval drama and, 57, 59; social and moral, 88–89; tradition and, 78; Tudor interludes and, 100, 112. *See also* structural differentiation
displacement: charity as, 59, 64; civic festival and, 61; low comedy and, 66; medieval drama and, 52, 59, 64–73; narrativity and, 129, 183; recognition and, 65; repetition and, 193, 195; reproduction and, 155; resurrection as, 64–65; reunification and, 68; self-effacement and, 70; substitution and, 136–39
Dollimore, Jonathan, 10n
Donne, John, 5n, 13
Doran, Madeleine, 8n, 18
Dorrell, Margaret, 47n
Douglas, Mary, 19n, 76, 125n
Dowey, Edward A., Jr., 109n
Drakakis, John, 9n
drama: constituting pretense of, 39, 241; history of, 9–13, 42–43, 146–48, 161, 204, 232, 239–40, 244–45; literary drama, 3–6, 11, 14, 35, 37–44, 128, 149, 182–83; literary history and, 4–6; mimesis and diegesis in, ix, 12, 19–20, 34–44, 184, 235–37; narrative drama, 17–19, 73–74; nationalism and, 5, 132–33; negative capability and, 41–42; origins and development of (in general), 5–8, 11–12; (Elizabethan), 89, 101–2, 141–42; relation to narrative, 19–44, 111–12, 127; ritual and, 6–7, 16, 46–47; special generic features of, 4–6, 18, 38–43, 150
Duby, Georges, 133n

Dumont, Louis, 80n
Duncan, Joseph E., 5n
Durkheim, Emile, 60n, 85, 134

Eccles, Marc, 51n, 52n
Eccleshall, Robert, 19n, 187n
Eco, Umberto, 55n
economy and society: of early modern
    England, 63–64, 77–78, 82–86, 88, 111–
    12, 116–25, 130–34; of English medieval
    towns, 60–64, 121–22
Edwards, Philip, 8n, 142n, 146n, 147n
Edwards, Robert, 68n
Eisenstadt, Shmuel Noah, 80n
Elam, Keir, 38n, 203n
Eliot, T. S., 5n
Elizabeth I, 13, 22, 82, 85, 93, 135, 169,
    174–81; Shakespearean comedy and,
    202–3, 218–19
Elizabethan drama: desire and, 134–36,
    141–42; representation and, 84–87; revo-
    lutionary, 7, 84, 128–33, 141–42, 146–47
Elizabethan settlement, 81–83
Elliott, John R., Jr., 72n
Ellis, John M., 4n
Else, Gerald, 7n, 36
Elton, Geoffrey R., 82n, 117n
Empson, William, 148–49
enantiomorphism, 155–58, 184
Endimion, 166–81
England, George, 48n
Esler, Anthony, 121n
Evans, G. Blakemore, 21n
excess: charity and, 57–59; Christianity
    and, 57–59, 104–5, 108–9; civic pag-
    eantry and, 62; feasting and, 60; literality
    and, 150–54; repetition and, 159

Fekete, John, 185n
Felman, Shoshana, 128, 166n
Felperin, Howard, 8n, 12n, 13, 239n
Fergusson, Arthur B., 118n
Ferry, Anne, 10n
feudalism, 130, 133
Fiedler, Leslie, 206n
Fielding, Henry, 7
figura, 48–59, 73, 89
Fineman, Joel, 10n, 50n
Finlay, Robert, 122n
First Part of Hieronimo, The, 147–48
Foreman, Walter C., Jr., 225n
formalism, 8–10
Foucault, Michel, 6n, 9, 75n, 131
Fox, George, 126
Foxe, John, 22, 90–91, 119
Frank, Grace, 115n
Fraser, Russell, 116n
Freehafer, John, 4n

Freeman, Arthur, 142n, 144n, 146, 150n
Freer, Coburn, 6n
Freud, Sigmund, 79, 141, 148
Fried, Michael, 80n
Frye, Northrop, 6n, 79, 166, 170n, 182n,
    202n, 240n
Furnivall, F. J., 51

Gadamer, Hans-Georg, 4n
Gannon, C. C., 168n, 170n, 176n
Garber, Marjorie, 205n
Gardiner, Harold C., 19, 115n, 116n, 127
Gasché, Rodolphe, 9n
gemeinschaft/gesellschaft, 76, 80–81, 153–
    54
Genette, Gérard, 38n
genre, dramatic. *See* comedy, history, ro-
    mance, tragedy
Gerrish, B. A., 109n
Gesner, Carol, 243n
Gilbert, Neal Ward, 119n
Gillette, William Hooker, 40n
Glacken, Clarence J., 13n
Gless, Darryl J., 209n
Glossa ordinaria, 25n, 57n, 65
Goffman, Erving, 139n
Goldberg, Jonathan, 9n, 196n, 215n, 243n
Goldman, Michael, 39n
governance, 94, 109–11. *See also* authority
Gower, John, 17
grace. *See* law, grace and
Green, André, 130n, 232n
Greenblatt, Stephen, 9n, 160n, 227n
Greene, Robert, 7n, 85, 131–35, 141
Gregory the Great, Saint, 59–60
Grice, H. P., 152
Gründler, Otto, 107n
guilds, medieval, 62–63, 83
Guillén, Claudio, 6n
Guillory, John, 6n, 7n, 242

Habermas, Jürgen, 80n, 154n
Haidu, Peter, 17n
Hanson, Donald W., 8n, 82n, 117n
Harbage, Alfred, 4n, 87n, 112, 132
Hardison, O. B., Jr., 46n
Harris, William O., 93n
Hartman, Geoffrey H., 80n, 128
Hatfield, Glenn W., 83n
Hawkins, Harriett, 9n
Hays, Janice, 209n
Hegel, G.W.F., 85, 138n, 164n, 204, 241n,
    246
Heidegger, Martin, 75n, 160n
Heilmann, Robert B., 160n
Helmholz, R. H., 70n
Heminge, John, 3–4
Henke, J. T., 145n, 155n

Henkel, Arthur, 168n, 175n
Henry VIII (King of England), 81, 85, 91, 93, 123
Henry IV (King of England), Part 1, 20–27
Henryson, Robert, 16
Henslowe, Philip, 84, 142, 146–47
Hernandi, Paul, 4n
heroism: lack of, in medieval drama, 70–73, 77; Marlowe and, 160–65; Shakespearean tragedy and, 222–31
Heywood, Thomas, 27n, 146n
Heywood, John, 97, 100
Hieatt, A. Kent, 7n
historicism, 8–9, 54
history: English, 8, 13, 18–19, 111–23, 149–50; ideas and, 29–30; literary history and, 4–5, 8, 18–20; Shakespeare's place in, 3–4, 7, 11, 245–46
history (dramatic): comedy and, 192, 201–2; generic logic of, 200–201; romance and, 240–41; Shakespearean, 20–27, 185–201; tragedy and, 183, 192
Hobbes, Thomas, 86n
Holderness, Graham, 184n, 187n
Hollis, Martin, 130n, 140n
Honigmann, E.A.J., 4n
Hooker, Richard, 33n, 104, 106
Horestes, 8, 99, 134n
Howarth, Herbert, 11n
Howell, A. C., 86n
Hugedé, Norbert, 56n
humanism, 8–10, 44, 106, 130; literariness and, 37; tragedy and, 160
humanists, Tudor, 87, 106, 119
Humphreys, Sarah C., 80n, 121n
Hunter, G. K., 144n, 180n
Hunter, Robert G., 102n, 164n
Hyde, Lewis, 60n

iconoclasm and iconophilia, dialectics of, 56, 124–26
idea of the play: defined, 113–14; rationalization and, 114–16, 126–27; relation to body of sign, 129
ideology: drama and, 6, 92–101; Elizabethan, 82; empire and, 154–55; Endimion and, 175–79; governing classes and, 134; ideas and, 91–95; modern, 51; representation and, 92, 234; The Spanish Tragedy and, 158
image and likeness, theology of, 48–55, 73–74, 108n
indecidability: anaclitic antinomies and, 184–85; Endimion and, 179; literariness and, 16–17; Shakespeare and, 3, 8, 10–11, 25–26, 128–29, 184, 224; The Spanish Tragedy and, 158
indeterminacy. See indecidability

individualism: capitalistic, x, 83, 133–34; early modern, 111–12; Marlowe and, 161–65; medieval, 122; Shakespeare and, 10, 160
Ingarden, Roman, 38, 140
intentionality: iron and, 33; signs and, 26–27; texts and, 13, 16, 53–54
interpretation: instinct of, 11; labor or, 51, 59; literariness and, 11, 45–48; need for, 47; schools of, 8–9
irony: actor and, 38; allegory and, 15, 17, 23, 27, 35, 125, 129, 134, 155–58, 185; conceptual disembodiment and, 124–25; deconstruction and, 37; Elizabethan drama and, 18; drama and, 40–41; ideas and, 33–34; medieval drama and, 55, 63, 66, 68; medieval narrative and, 17; modernity and, 19; narrative and, 39; penance and, 44; plot and, 33; process and, 134; ritual and, 76; Shakespeare and, 9, 10, 15; in Shakespearean history, 23, 27, 194–96, 199; in Shakespearean comedy, 211; in Shakespearean tragedy, 31–32, 220, 227; vision and, 33, 35; Tudor interludes and, 88

Jacquot, Jean, 20n
Jagendorf, Zvi, 208n
Jakobson, Roman, 55, 128–29, 136
James I, 85, 215–18
James, Mervyn, 60–61n, 82n, 117n
Jameson, Fredric, 10n, 143n
Javelet, Robert, 48n, 73n
Jeffrey, David L., 56n
Jensen, E. J., 145n
Johnson, S. F., 142n, 143n
Johnson, Samuel, 38, 79
Johnston, Alexandra F., 47n, 63n
Jones, Emrys, 74n
Jones, Inigo, 114
Jones, Richard H., 186n
Jonson, Ben, 3–4, 114, 146, 244
Jungman, J. A., 62n

Kahrl, Stanley J., 70n
Kant, Immanuel, 55, 136
Kantorowicz, Ernst H., 166n, 187
Kaske, R. E., 48n
Kastan, David Scott, 182n, 183n, 198n
Kavanagh, James, 4n
Kavolis, Vytautas, 134n
Kelley, Donald R., 92n
Kellner, Hans, 182n
Kermode, Frank, 30n, 239n, 243n
Kernan, Alvin B., 4n, 186, 188n
Kerridge, Eric, 118n
Kevan, Ernest F., 101n
Keifer, Frederick, 144n

King, John N., 95n
kingship: divine right and, 149, 187; Hamlet and, 32; Henry v as image of, 26–27, 197–200; in medieval drama, 66; medieval vs. sixteenth-century ideas of, 186–87; women and, 174–75
Knapp, Robert S., 44n, 168n, 169n
Knight, G. Wilson, 10n, 234n, 235n
Kolve, V. A., 47n, 66n
Kott, Jan, 9n, 207n
Kristeva, Julia, 128–30, 139, 225n
Kuhn, Maura Slattery, 208n
Kuriyama, Contance, 162–63
Kyd, Thomas, 17, 85, 132–34, 141–59, 183; *The Spanish Tragedy*, 142–59, 225–26

Lacan, Jacques, 41n, 92, 134–43, 145, 148n, 151n, 159n, 237n
Lamb, Charles, 38
Landor, Walter Savage, 5n
Langland, William, 13, 16, 124
Laplanche, Jean, 61n, 138n, 148n
Laslett, Peter, 80n, 122n
Latimer, Hugh, 82
law: grace and, 57, 66–68, 101–11; nature and, 87–89
Lever, J. W., 12n
Levin, Harry, 4n, 33n
Levin, Richard, 41n
Levy, Marion J., 80n
Lewalski, Barbara K., 124n, 209n
liminality, 61
Lindenberger, Herbert, 182n
Lipking, Lawrence, 80n
literacy, 85; types of, 153–54
literariness: defined, 3–5, 11, 13–15, 37–38; interpretation and, 11, 16–17, 45–48; literature and, as interested category, 80–81; medieval drama and, 43–44; negative definition of, 16; overcoding and, 55; reference and, 14–15; relation to rhetoric, 153; Shakespearean, 3–44, 182–85, 241–46; unreadability and, 27
literary drama, 3–6, 11, 14, 35, 37–44, 128, 149, 182–83; conditions for development of, 44, 77, 84–87, 127, 141–42, 180–81, 231–32, 245–46
literary history: binary oppositions and, 9–10, 12–13, 89; cycles of, 42–44; discontinuity of, 4–5; distinguished from theatrical history, 4, 5–7; evolution and, 6, 89, 141–42; linguistics and, 129; non-dramatic, 5–6; Shakespeare's place in, 7, 242–46; special place of drama in, 4–6; theory of modernization and, 120
Little, David, 114n
Locke, John, 86

Lodge, Thomas, 131
Long, Michael, 227n
Lorrain, Jorge, 92n
Lotman, Juri, 76
Luhmann, Niklas, 92n, 119n
Lumiansky, R. M., 49n
Luther, Martin, 69, 107, 123
Luxton, Imogen, 102n
Lyly, John, 17, 93, 110, 131n, 132–35, 141, 166–81, 183; *Endimion*, 166–81

MacAdoo, Henry R., 82n
MacCaffrey, Wallace T., 82n, 92n, 180n
MacCanles, Michael, 10n
MacCary, W. Thomas, 12n, 206n
Macfarlane, Alan, 8n, 80n, 122n
McGinn, Bernard, 22n
McLelland, Joseph C., 99n, 102n, 119n
MacPherson, C. B., 83n
Mallarmé, Stéphane, 81
Malory, Thomas, 16
Mankind, 5, 3, 53, 66–67
Manley, Lawrence, 86n
Mann, Thomas, 141
Manning, Roger G., 82n
margins. *See* boundaries
Markus, R. A., 49n, 56
Marlowe, Christopher, 85, 101, 131–34, 141, 159–65; *Doctor Faustus*, 101; *Tamburlaine the Great*, 138, 160–65
Marshall, Gordon, 114n
Marshall, Robert D., 56n
Marx, Karl, 116
Mayer, Arno, 133n
medieval drama, 11–12, 15–19, 43–78; Abraham and Isaac plays, 70–73; audience of, 15, 44, 46–47, 50–51, 55n, 59, 62–64, 73; causality and, 73–74; contrasted with medieval narrative, 16–18; cycle plays, 45–51, 57–58, 60–73; doctrine and, 45–54; doubleness in, 57–59; exemplarist theology in, 52–59; lack of intrigue in, 45, 52; *Mankind*, 5, 3, 53, 66–67, 87; Marlowe and, 164; Marxist criticism and, 45; modern tastes and, 11, 43–45, 74–75; moralities, 74; paratactic structure of, 73; part of larger social process, 63–64; penance and, 44, 46, 50, 53–54, 76; realism in, 90, 114; ritual and, 46–47; self-referentiality and, 56–57; sexuality in, 70; Shakespeare and, 74–78; sixteenth century aesthetics and, 114–15; spectacle in, 52–53; typology in, 69–72; *Wisdom, Who Is Christ*, 51–59, 87
Medwall, Henry, 87–88, 90
Mehlman, Jeffrey, 81n
Melville, Stephen W., 41n, 50n, 184n
Merquior, J. Q., 92n

metaphor: history and, 10; meaning and,
136; metanoia and, 49, 107; metonymy
and, 14, 37, 75, 105, 109, 128–29, 135,
177–79, 184, 197, 200, 220; textuality
and, 41; normal discourse and, 13–14,
17, 21; structural differentiation and,
125; paternal, 157
method, 84, 118–19
Miller, Edwin H., 131n
Miller, Ronald F., 207n
Mills, David, 49n
Milton, John, 6n, 7
mimesis, ix, 12, 35, 38, 44, 139–41, 200,
240. See also drama; theater, book and
Miner, Earl, 6n
mirror, trope of, 27–34, 93, 106–7, 174–75,
180, 194
modernity, 3, 8, 11; freedom and, 42, 242;
Marlowe and, 160–65; romance and, 239;
Shakespeare and, 3–13, 83–84, 128, 133,
185, 241–46; transition to, 3–4, 7–13, 18–
20, 79–87, 111–12, 121–22, 128, 133–34
modernization, 78, 80n, 81, 119–34; as
heuristic, 121; history of English drama
and, 129–30; religious controversy and,
97–99; Shakespeare's histories and, 201;
theory of, 80n, 120–21
Moeslin, M. E., 87n, 88n
Mondin, Battista, 75n, 99n
Moretti, Franco, 12n, 25n, 32n, 182n
moving image: absence and, 158; definition
of, 139–42, 149–50; narrative and, 172;
textuality and, 150–51
Mowat, Barbara, 236n
Muir, Kenneth, 4n
Mullaney, Steven, 135n
Murrin, Michael, 13n

Nachträglichkeit, 148
narrative, 17, 18–19, 27, 40; medieval, 16–
17, 95–96; relation to dramatic, 19–44,
111–12, 127; textual play and, 172–73.
See also diegesis; theater, book and
narrative drama, 18–19, 37–44, 73–74
Nashe, Thomas, 144
nationalism: drama and, 5, 132–33; sixteenth-century English, 81–83, 112–13
nature: as figurative, 46–59, 87; as non-fig-
urative, 87–89, 104, 108
Nef, John U., 118n, 122n
Nelson, William, 116n
Nevo, Ruth, 205n
New, John H., 82n
new comedy, 43, 170n, 244
new historicism, 9
Nicoll, Allardyce, 113n
Nietzche, Friedrich, 9, 221
Nuttall, A. D., 9n

Oberman, Heiko A., 69n, 73n
Olson, Paul A., 207n
Orgel, Stephen, 182n, 187n, 245n
origins, problem of, 5–8, 11–12
Oxford, Earl of, 177–79

Pantin, W. A., 55n
Parker, Patricia, 233n
Partrides, C. A., 23n
Paul, Saint, 103, 105, 140, 168
Pavel, Thomas G., 149n, 161n
Peacock, James L., 97n
Peacock, Ronald, 182n
Peele, George, 101, 133–34, 141
penance: medieval drama and, 44, 46, 50,
53–54; reading and, 44, 75–76; theology
of, 101–11
performative: comedy and, 171–72; 203–
19; diegesis and, 36; in theater, 39. See
also cognitive
Perkins, William, 82, 105–6, 110–11
Peterson, Joyce E., 89n
Peterson, Richard S., 4n
Phillip, John, 96n
Phillips, James E., 131n
Phythian-Adams, Charles, 60–62
Picinelli, Filippo, 174n
Pickering, John, 8, 131n
Pinsky, Robert, 5n
Pinter, Harold, 48
Plato, 12, 14, 35–36, 41, 134, 137–39; Ref-
ormation and, 35
Platonism, 35, 40–41, 54
Plautus, 36
plot, 10, 36, 74, 143–44; creation of iden-
tity and, 150–52; deceit and, 35, 57; Lyly
and, 167; modern drama and, 42–43;
ideas and, 30; in relation to error, 29–33,
148–49, 158–59; Shakespearean comedy
and, 204–5
Pocock, J.G.A., 18
Poggi, Gianfranco, 186n
political nation, English. See civic con-
sciousness
Polyani, Karl, 80n
Porter, H. C., 106n, 109n
possessive individualism, theory of, 83
poststructuralism, 9, 12n, 51
Potter, Robert, 46n
Pound, Ezra, 5n
Pound, John, 118n
presence: actor's, 38–39; distance and, 153–
55; tragedy and, 166. See also absence
Preus, James Samuel, 73n, 123n
Price, H. T., 36n
Prior, Moody, 192n
Prosser, Eleanor, 46n
Protestantism, 13, 81–84, 88, 101–130; Pla-

Protestantism (*cont.*)
    tonism and, 35; theater and, 35, 94–95,
    104–11
prudence, virtue of, 83
Prudentius, 67, 97
Pseudo-Augustine, 72n
Pseudo-Bonaventure, 46n, 51n, 65n
psychoanalysis: Elizabethan theater and,
    134–42; Christianity and, 76, 134–36. *See
    also* Lacan
Puritanism, 82, 109–11

Quiller-Couch, Arthur, 195n

Rabkin, Norman, 25n, 42n, 196n, 220
Ramus, Peter, 105
rationalization, 68, 81, 114–26, 132–33; as
    redrawing of boundaries, 85–87, 92–93,
    114–16, 133–34, Counter-Reformation
    and, 81; early modern England and, 114–
    27; medieval drama and, 114–16; method
    and, 84, 118–19; neoclassicism and, 114–
    15; Reformation and, 81; theology of
    penance and, 101–11; theory of, 114,
    116–20
readability, 11, 13–14, 20, 26, 39–44, 45–
    51, 53, 203
reality: Lacanian *Real*, 136–37, 143, 154,
    156; models of, 128–29, 139–41; tropes
    and, 13
Rebhorn, Wayne A., 166n
reference, 13–15, 23; medieval theology
    and, 52–53; non-figurative, 56, 86
Reiss, Timothy, 221n, 231n
repetition, paradox of, 193–94
representation: art as, 15; ideology and, 92,
    134; indirection and, 29–32; logic of, 86;
    modes of, 10–12, 15, 127; early modern
    rearrangement of, 81–87; new order's at-
    tempt to control, 150; religion as mode
    of, 18; religious controversy and, 82; role
    of women in Elizabethan drama and,
    134–35, 152; Shakespeare and, x, 10–14,
    20–34, 183, 185–246; tropes and, 13–15
Ribner, Irving, 161n, 164n
Ricoeur, Paul, 139n, 153n
Riggs, David, 161n, 193n
Righter, Anne, 113–14. *See also* Anne Bar-
    ton
ritual: drama and, 6–7, 16, 46–47; ritual
    process, 46, 61–63
Robertson, D. W., Jr., 52n, 79
Robinson, Forrest, 116n
romance, being and meaning in, 238–39;
    comedy and, 238–40; framing and, 185,
    239, 244; generic logic of, 233–34, 240;
    history and, 239–41; modernity and,

239, 242–44; Shakespearean, 232–44;
    tragedy and, 233–34, 239
Rorty, Richard, 8n, 153n
Rossiter, A. P., 161n, 186n
Rowan, D. G., 146n
Rozett, Martha Tuck, 102n
Ruiz, Juan, 16
Russell, Patricia, 90n
Rymer, Thomas, 11

Saccio, Peter, 175n, 186n
Sacks, David Harris, 60n, 63n, 122n
Said, Edward W., 6n, 243n
Salingar, Leo J., 166n, 205n
Schalk, Ellery, 122n
Scharlemann, Robert P., 74n
Schmidgall, Gary, 183n
Schoenbaum, Samuel, 87n, 131n
Schücking, L. L., 146
Schwartz, Murray M., 186
Scribe, Eugene, 42, 148
Searle, John, 38n
self: changing ideas of, 10, 126; literal vs.
    figurative, 56–57, 107–8; others as sign
    of, 29, 137
self-understanding: European, 3–4, 10, 15;
    modern, 43, 45, 54
semiotic vs. symbolic, 128–42, 149–50,
    174–75
Shakespeare: Christianity and, 12–13, 36,
    237; comedies, 201–19; contingency of,
    245–46; difference of from other canoni-
    cal dramatists, 7, 183, 246; European
    self-understanding and, 4–5, 13; generic
    range in, x, 183; histories, 20–27, 185–
    201; indecidability and, 3, 8, 10–11, 25–
    26, 128–29, 184, 224; interpretive dis-
    putes and, 8–9, 10–12; judgment and,
    184; literary theory and, 7; medieval
    drama and, 74–78; modernity and, 3–13,
    83–84, 128, 133, 185, 241–46; relation of
    to other Elizabethan playwrights, 7, 131,
    160–61; representation and, x, 10–14,
    20–34, 183, 185–246; romances, 232–44;
    tragedies, 27–34, 219–32; Tudor myth
    in, 22–26; uses of, 8
Shakespeare's plays: *All's Well That Ends
    Well*, 209–10, 212–15; *Antony and Cleopa-
    tra*, 228–30; *As You Like It*, 207–8; *Com-
    edy of Errors*, 208–9; *Coriolanus*, 220, 223,
    228; *Hamlet*, 27–34, 147. 149; *1 Henry
    IV*, 24–25; *2 Henry IV*, 20–27; *Henry V*,
    195–201; *King Lear*, 222, 224, 226–31;
    Macbeth, 228; *Measure for Measure*, 209–
    10, 215–18; *Merchant of Venice*, 209–12;
    Midsummer Night's Dream, 206–7;
    Othello, 226–28; *Richard II*, 23, 185–94;

Tempest, 233–34; *Twelfth Night*, 209;
Winter's Tale, 234–39
Shakespearean authority, x, 3–4, 9, 141,
146, 183–85, 186–244 *passim*, 245–46
Sharrat, Peter, 105n
Shearer, Beatrice, 122n
Shell, Marc, 211n
Shepherd, Simon, 203n
Sidney, Philip, 32n, 112, 114–16
Siemon, James, 10n, 119n
signifier: boundary with signified, 20, 50,
85, 105–8, 115, 136–37; naturalization of,
88; power of, 136–39, 151–53; self-effacement and, 70
signs: audience as, 50; materiality of, 52,
136–38, 150–53; natural vs. nonnatural,
26, 107–8, 152, 184; Reformation view
of, 104–9
signs, persons as: Kristevan semiotic and,
130–42; medieval drama and, 43, 52–55,
64–73; Reformation theology and, 104–
9; in medieval and Tudor drama, 10, 18–
19; in Shakespeare's tragedies, 31–32,
220–22, 224, 228, 230–31; in Shakespeare's comedies, 203–4, 210–11, 216–
17, in Shakespeare's histories, 24–27,
189–201; in Shakespeare's romances,
235–39; theatrical illusion and, 38–44.
See also actors, persons as
Silk, M. S., 221n
Simon, Joan, 118n
Simonson, Lee, 114n
Skelton, John, 89, 93
Slights, Camille Wells, 106n
Smith, Anthony D., 80n
Smith, G. Gregory, 146
Smith, Lucy Toulmin, 49n
Smith, Macklin, 67n
Smith, Wilfred Cantwell, 94n
Snyder, Susan, 183
social structure. *See* economy and society
Sommerville, J. P., 83n, 119n, 187n
Sophocles, 41, 246
Spanish Tragedy, The, 142–59, 225–26
Spenser, Edmund, 7, 110, 124
Spiret, Pierre, 160n
Spivack, Bernard, 8n, 89n, 90n, 97n, 98n
Spufford, Margaret, 119n
Starkey, David, 117n
States, Bert O., 20n, 129n
Stevens, Martin, 47n, 60n
Stone, Lawrence, 13n, 83n, 121n, 126n,
141n, 169n, 177n
Stowe, John, 64
Strong, Tracy, 134
structural differentiation, 79, 119–26, 132–
33. *See also* differentiation
style, comedy and, 166–81, 204

Tarlton, Richard, 90
Taylor, Jerome, 45n
Taylor, John, 27
Tennenhouse, Leonard, 219n
Tentler, Thomas N., 102n
Terence, 36
textuality: actor's presence and, 37–39;
150–54; Christianity and, 15–17, 51, 57,
75–78; medieval narrative and, 16–18;
Shakespearean, 20; tradition and, 79–80;
truth and, 17
theater: amateur, 73; history of, as distinguished from literary history, 4–6; impropriety of, 37–39, 184, 210; hypothesis
and, 140–41; professional, 84, 127, 130,
135
theater, book and: boundary between, 19–
20, 87; indecidability and, 128–29, 189;
interaction defined, ix, 34–44, 128–30,
139–41, 241–46; interaction illustrated,
20–34, 233–38
theatricality: aphanisis and, 151; causes of,
151; defined, 27–28; freedom and, 38–41,
241–43; governance and, 109–11; medieval theology and, 51–59; modernity
and, 244; power and, 200
Thomas Aquinas, Saint, 56n, 99
Thomas, Keith, 47n
Tillyard, E.M.W., 11n, 22n, 185–86
Todorov, Tzvetan, 26n, 37n, 182n
Tönnies, Ferdinand, 81
Torrance, T. F., 104n, 105n, 107n
Tourneur, Cyril, 13
tradition: constitution of, 78, 101, 148;
Elizabethan gentry and, 101; medieval
drama and, 75; modernity and, 121;
Shakespeare and, 1–5, 9, 133; traditional
society, 79–81, 121–22
tragedy: causality and, 36; comedy and, 36,
165–66, 218–19; "fatherhood" and, 155–
59; generic logic of, 219–27; imperialism
and, 149–51, 154–58; invention of, 146,
149–50; Shakespearean, 27–34, 219–32
trope: reality and, 13–14; truth and, 29, 49,
53, 72–73, 78, 106, 125. *See also* metaphor, irony
trope, persons as. *See* signs, persons as
Trousdale, Marion, 119n
truth: Tarskian, 14; theatricality and, 28;
ideology and, 93. *See also* trope
Tudor interludes, 11–12, 15–16, 18, 78, 87–
101, 113; audience of, 95, 100–101, 127;
historical allusion in 93–94; history of,
89–91; historicized reality in, 88–89; ideology in, 91–101; medieval drama and,
92, 94–100, 112; medieval narrative and,
95–96; modern tastes and, 78, 92–93; nationalism and, 112–13; realism in, 90–92;

Tudor interludes (*cont.*)
  religious controversy in, 94–95; taxon-
  omy of, 112; Vice in, 90, 92, 97–100
Turner, Edith, 61n
Turner, James, 10n
Turner, Victor W., 46n, 61
typology: medieval drama and, 69–72; representation and, 124

undecidability. *See* indecidability
unreadability. *See* readability
Unwin, George, 63n

Vacant, Alfred, 102n
Vann, Richard T., 122n
Vernant, Jean-Pierre, 221n
Viner, Jacob, 13n
von Hallberg, Robert, 4n

Wager, Lewis, 95
Waith, Wugene M., 160n
Wallace, Ronald S., 102n
Weber, Max, 114n, 119n, 133n
Webster, John, 13
Weimann, Robert, 20n, 45n, 90, 133n,
  204n
Weinberg, Bernard, 114n, 115n
Weiner, Andrew D., 115n
Weld, John S., 101n, 143n
Wellek, René, 81n
Wentworth, Peter, 82
Westlund, Joseph, 206n

Wheeler, Richard P., 217n
Whitaker, William, 82, 124
White, Hayden, 42n, 182n
White, Stephen D., 122n
Wickham, Glynne, 8n, 95n, 127, 202n
Wightman, Carolyn L., 63n
Wilde, Oscar, 12
Wilden, Anthony, 129n
Willet, Andrew, 108n
Williams, Raymond, 63n
Wilson, Robert, 90
Wingren, Gustaf, 107n
Winkler, John J., 7n
Winny, James, 190n
Winters, Yvor, 5n
Wisdom, Who Is Christ, 51–59, 87
Wittreich, Joseph, 23n, 222n
Woolf, Rosemary, 46n, 69n, 71n
world as book/text: medieval Christianity
  and, 18–20, 51–78; in Shakespeare, 20–
  27. *See also* theater, book and; signs, per-
  sons as
world as theater, 18–20, 27–34, 107–11,
  113; Protestantism and, 20, 105–11; in
  Marlowe, 164; in Shakespeare, 27–34.
  See also theater, book and; actors, per-
  sons as
Wright, L. B., 13n
Wrightson, Keith, 80n, 121n, 123n
Wrigley, E. A., 121n

Yates, Frances A., 97n
Young, David P., 207n, 208n